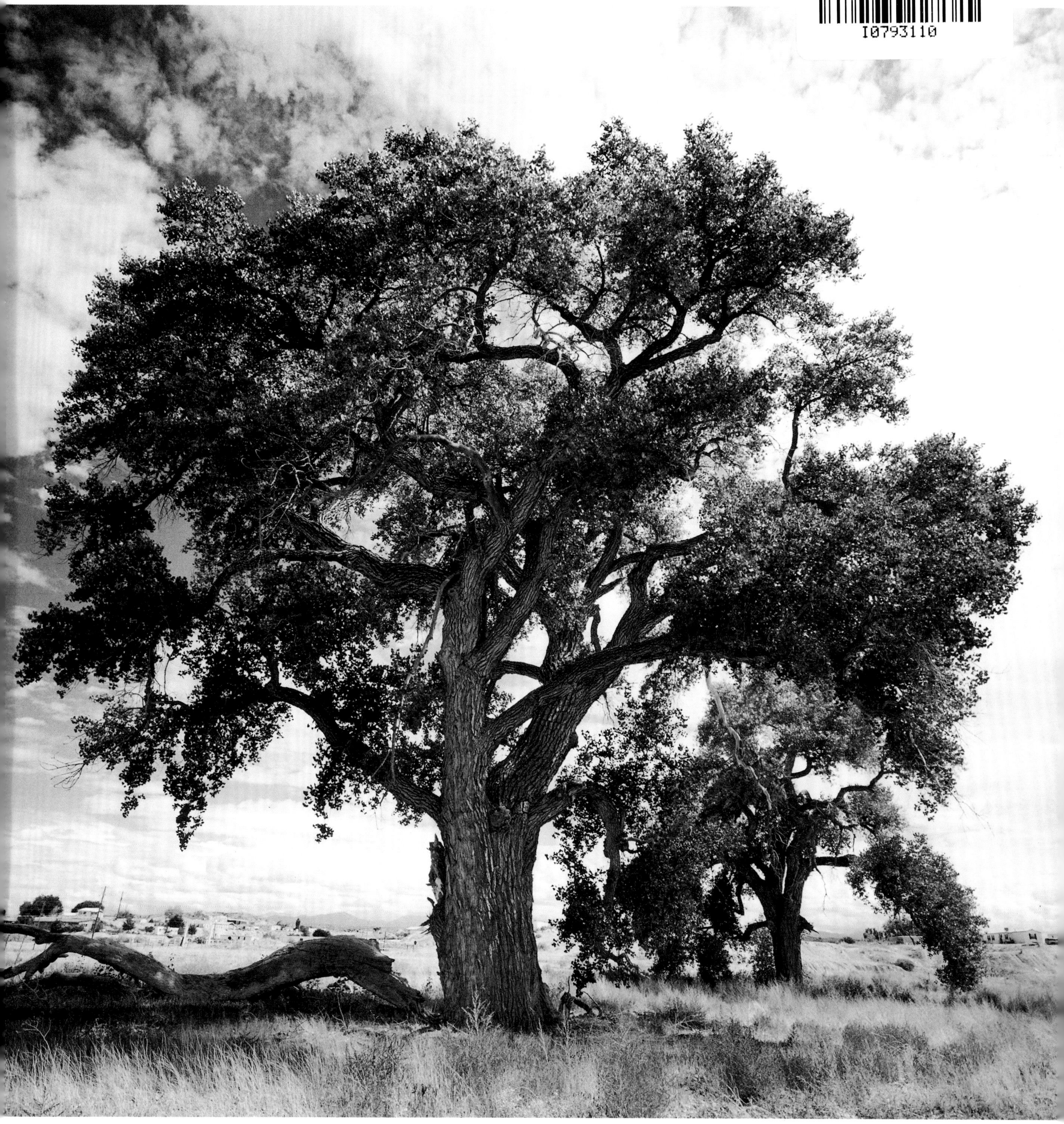

CLASSIC HOPI AND ZUNI KACHINA FIGURES

PHOTOGRAPHS BY ANDREA PORTAGO   TEXT BY BARTON WRIGHT

MUSEUM OF NEW MEXICO PRESS   SANTA FE

 Barton Wright's essay was originally published in an altered form in *Iconography of Religions*, Section X: North America, Fascicle Four, ed. by Th. P. van Baaren et al., Institute of Religious Iconography, State University Groningen, published by E. J. Brill, Leiden, 1986.

Museum of New Mexico Press is a division of the New Mexico Department of Cultural Affairs.

Project editor: Mary Wachs
Art director: David Skolkin
Composition: Set in Minion
Map drawn by Deborah Reade
Manufactured by Tien Wah Press, Malaysia
10 9 8 7 6 5 4 3 2 1

978-0-89013-596-9

Library of Congress Cataloging-in-Publication Data
Portago, Andrea.
Classic Hopi and Zuni kachina figures / photographs by Andrea Portago ; text by Barton Wright.
p. cm.
ISBN: 978-0-89013-483-2 (clothbound : alk. paper)
ISBN: 978-0-89013-596-9 (paperbound : alk. paper)
1. Kachina dolls. 2. Hopi dolls. 3. Zuni dolls. 4. Hopi mythology. 5. Zuni mythology. I. Wright, Barton. II. Title.
E99.H7P67 2006
745.592'2108997458—dc22

2005034286

IN MEMORY OF MY BROTHER TONY

The first time I came to the Southwest was in 1976 to visit my brother Tony, who had bought a ranch, where he lived, in Española, New Mexico. Even though Tony was the younger one, he led the way, as always; he loved this land first. When asked, Tony used to say that he liked to live in New Mexico because with the mesas being so high they made the heavens nearer and he felt closer to God.

CONTENTS

PREFACE

Pablo Picasso collected kachinas. Georgia O'Keeffe made paintings of her kachinas. Andy Warhol painted kachinas and included images of them in his 1986 silkprint series *Cowboys and Indians.*

The German surrealist artist Max Ernst lived in Sedona, Arizona, for many years beginning before World War II. His collection of kachinas was later well known among other European artists. André Breton, Marcel Duchamp, Emil Nolde, and Cuban artist Jorge Camacho also collected kachinas, as did writer André Malraux and the poet Paul Éluard. The famous German contemporary artist Horst Antes later bought many of the surrealist artists' kachinas.

I started taking photographs with a Minox B camera when I was nine years old. As I grew older my relationship with cameras grew to encompass working at both ends of the lens. From my late teens to late twenties I worked as a model in various capitals of Europe and America, much of it editorial work for *Vogue, Town and Country, Harpers Bazaar,* and as one of the original cover girls for *Tatler* and Andy Warhol's *Interview.* Then I won an exclusive contract to be the face of a new perfume called "Farouche" made by the Parisian house of Nina Ricci.

During time spent in their studios, I was privileged to have some of the most famous fashion photographers of the day take the time to teach me what made a good photo and what didn't, or why a detail could ruin a picture. This surreptitious on-the-job training laid the foundation for the way I learned to "see" photography. The way I think about photography in my mind's eye, what I know and understand, is based on a very specific concept of glamour in photography that existed in the late sixties and seventies, which had everything to do with lighting and using a pure range of medium gray in black-and-white photography. Among some of the photographers I was lucky enough to work with and learn from who epitomized this style of photography were Francesco Scavullo, Deborah Turbeville, David Bailey, Clive Arrowsmith, and Chris Von Wangenheim.

In the early seventies, Andy Warhol introduced me to a private art dealer named George Terasaki, from whom he was buying Native American art. The first time I saw a kachina was with Andy at George's studio.

Despite keeping an eye out, over the next twenty-five years I never saw another old kachina nearly as beautiful as the one in George's studio until 1997 when Santa Fe artist and gallery owner

Alan Kessler's collection was put on exhibition for sale at Sotheby's auction house in New York City. Kessler's extraordinary kachinas served as the impetus that launched me on a quest to learn as much as I could about these beautiful old carvings.

I photographed the kachinas as people because that is the way I saw them. In photographing them, not one ever seemed to me to be without movement and drama, passion and personality. They all seemed to say "...here I am in all my finery. . . . I am so proud of my nature. . . . I will stand here and pose for you to photograph me in all my beauty."

I photographed the kachinas using available light throughout so as not to distort their true colors. Photographing in a museum, such as the American Museum of Natural History, using available light meant shooting at the end of a hallway by a large northern window, and in winter, after the time it took to set up, there might be only a few hours of light left over to shoot in. I would have had to abandon all hope of photographing the kachinas at the Museum of Northern Arizona, a charming old stone building with very small windows and insufficient light, were it not for Roger Clark, formerly Vice President for Public Programs, who rose to the occasion, trusting me and assuming responsibility. Understanding how imperative natural daylight was to my photography and allowing for some creativity in finding enough daylight for me to work, Roger literally saved the day for this project. Shooting time in Flagstaff was often curtailed by the midday thunderstorms of the summer monsoon season.

Three different backgrounds were used, made to specification from metal, deliberately rusted. One backdrop was weathered as dark as possible to look as though it had been standing out in the elements for years; another was hammered to give it texture and made nearly black, similar to the black lava earth at Sunset Crater north of Flagstaff; and the last one was left a light golden copper color only slightly distressed—all three different to suit individual kachinas.

From among the museum collections, art dealer George Terasaki was instrumental in helping select which kachinas to photograph. All the other kachinas were my personal choice based on my own visual aesthetics, and this book makes no attempt to represent the entire pantheon of approximately 250 to 300 kachinas in Hopi and Zuni cosmology. Once the kachinas were photographed, Barton Wright organized them in their correct order and categories, also matching them up with the appropriate landscapes for the layout of the book. Besides aesthetics, another criterion was that the kachinas be made prior to 1940 because after that time the carving style changed dramatically.

The old-style carvers imparted not only beauty to their handiwork, but also through their artistry spoke of their culture and illustrated a sense of the inherent pride, dignity, humor, and distinct individual character of each kachina. The old-style carvings have the power to draw a person in. They make one want to look closer and learn more. The old kachinas possess qualities that make them seem vibrant and alive. They transmit a depth, something from within, that transcends their status as carved objects, possessing what some art historians have called "the spiritual in art."

To underscore the cottonwood tree's importance to the area, its contribution to man's survival, and its primary role in the making of kachinas, the first and last images in this book are of cottonwoods. The photograph of the cottonwood tree in the front of the book represents the summer solstice, a time when the kachinas come to the villages on the mesas bringing life-giving rain needed to grow crops. The bare-leafed tree at the end of the book represents the winter solstice when the kachinas once again leave the Hopi. Besides being a source of shade in summer, the cottonwood always grows near water, thereby indicating availability of one of life's most elemental, yet scarcest of resources in the high desert region. The Hopi, who live high up on the northern desert mesas, mostly carve their kachinas from the root of the cottonwood tree, while the Zuni, who live down from the Hopi mesas on top of the Mogollon Rim, usually fashion their kachinas from pine.

Interspersed throughout this book are black-and-white landscape photographs. As much as possible I shot these landscapes to feel contemporary. I wanted to convey a sense of immediacy, hoping to give the viewer the feeling that they could walk right into this place, one corner of the earth where man is not dominant and cannot harness nature. These landscapes are meant to give a sense of the smallness, the insignificance of any living person standing anywhere within this land, surrounded by the vastness of sky and horizon.

The landscapes are in the book to give context to the kachinas. As Barton Wright has pointed out, it is the land that created the need for kachinas in the first place. The kachinas and the land cannot be separated one from the other. This is the land where they live, where they come from, you can go there and this is what it looks like today.

Andrea Portago
Los Angeles, California

ACKNOWLEDGMENTS

Malcolm Kirk's 1981 photographic essay on the tribesmen of New Guinea, *Man As Art,* served as both inspiration and blueprint for this book. Thank you to Malcolm for initial technical advice and encouragement.

Thank you to my friend Jerome Albertini, who very kindly initially accompanied me on photo shoots and on location, generously helping me with on-the-job technical tutorials and who later contributed to helping edit my work, supervising printing, and whose technical expertise I relied on throughout.

Thank you to George Terasaki for his help and much-appreciated constructive criticism, holding me to a higher standard. Thank you also to Ellen Naipura Taubman, formerly head of Sotheby's Native American and Tribal Arts Department, for originally suggesting and encouraging me to make this book as well as for providing introductions to people in the field.

Thank you to Sean Byrnes, whose editorial eye I would trust with any work and who oversaw, edited, and coordinated lab printing and layout work. Thank you to Carole Fondé, outstanding master printer, as color printer for all the kachinas, and Rick Hemmings at Pointlight, who printed the black-and-white landscapes, both of their individual work on this project making all the critical difference.

Thank you to Barton Wright, whose lifetime dedication to the scholarly study of kachinas makes him a national treasure of information, much of it otherwise lost. All of the landscapes in this book were photographed at Barton's directive. Thank you also to Margaret Wright for her help, support, and knowledge.

Thank you to Dr. Patrick Houlihan, former director of the Heard Museum, and his wife Betsy, whose moral support, scholarship, editorial help, introductions and advice opened critical doors for me. This book could not have been made without their active help and friendship.

Thank you to Bill Breed in Flagstaff, Arizona, who kept me informed of good photography weather conditions in Hopi and around the Peaks in Flagstaff; who so generously and always with great good humor made himself available over several years, and on usually little notice, to accompany me on photography expeditions in the field.

Thank you to Michael J. Fox, former director of the Museum of Northern Arizona and Dr. Edwin Wade, former senior vice president of the Museum of Northern Arizona for giving me permission to photograph the kachinas at the Museum of Northern Arizona. Thank you also to Tracy Murphy, former associate collections manager at the Museum of Northern Arizona.

Thank you to Christy Sturm, former collections manager, and Lee Goodwin, former Indian Arts Research Center coordinator, at the School of American Research in Santa Fe for permission and for helping arrange the right light conditions for me to be able to photograph the kachinas at SAR.

Thank you to Dr. Laila Williamson at the American Museum of Natural History in New York, who stands out as an example of the very best kind of scholar and museum curator that exists.

Thank you to everyone who allowed me access to their collections both public and private, including those who wish to remain anonymous. At Morning Star Gallery in Santa Fe, thank you especially to Henry Monahan. Thank you also to Catherine Whitney at the Gerald Peters Gallery in Santa Fe for help in my research.

Thank you to Heléne Alexopoulos, Betty Catroux, Chris Haynes, and also to Shelley Wanger for going out of their way in helping with introductions to publishers. To Robert Tracy, not only for introductions to publishers but for the inspiration I gained from his books and for editorial help with this project. Thank you to Patrick New for help and advice. Thank you also to Reid Callanan, director of the Santa Fe Workshops, for keeping his door open to all students, past and present, with encouragement, help, and advice.

Thank you to Richard W. Bulliet, Professor of History at the Middle East Institute at Columbia University, who was my advisor and whose influence on me and encouragement permeates my endeavors.

Thank you to Burt Boyar, for his much needed and appreciated professional editorial help and guidance without which I might not have made it through the final last gasp of this project.

A. P.

CLASSIC HOPI AND ZUNI KACHINA FIGURES

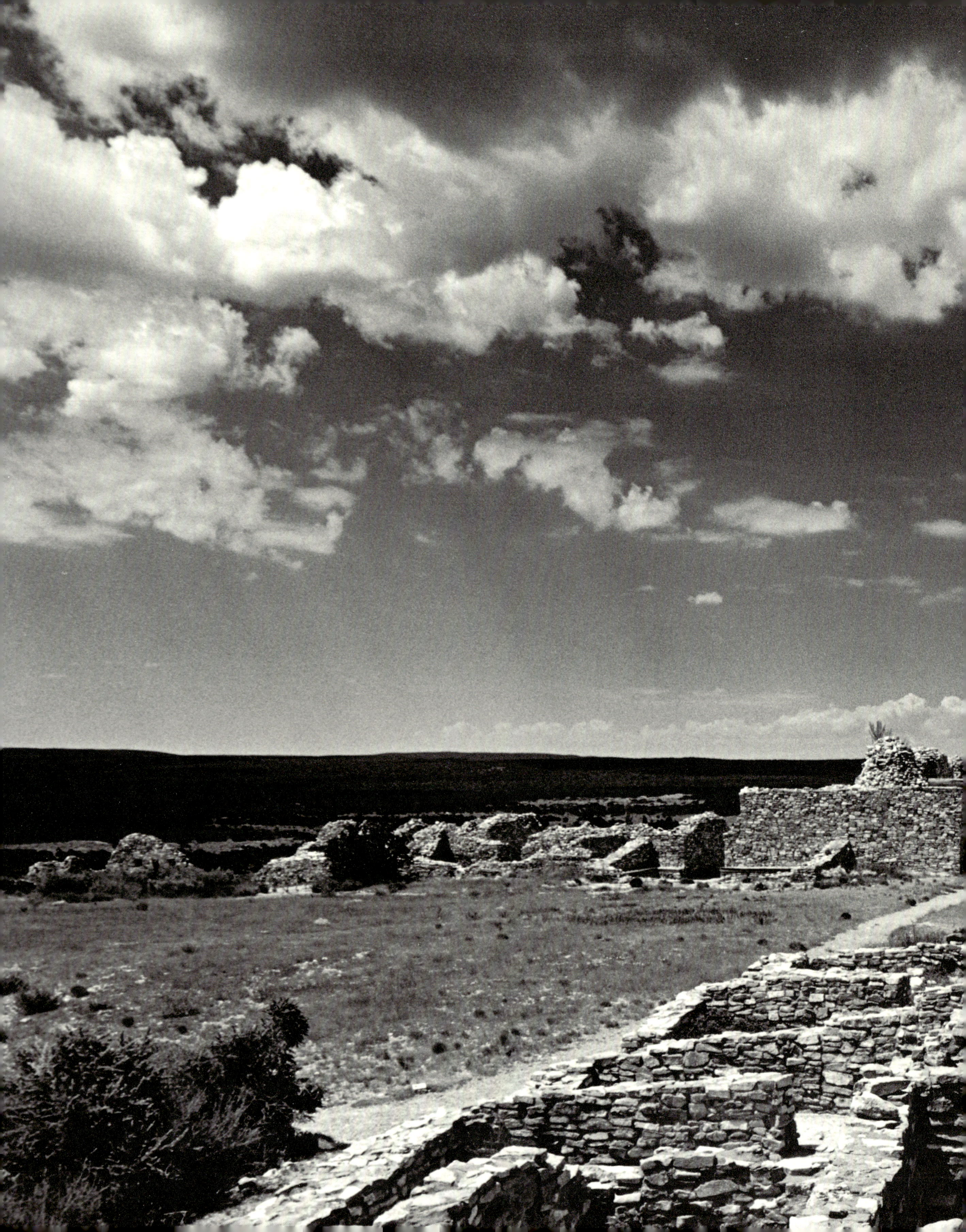

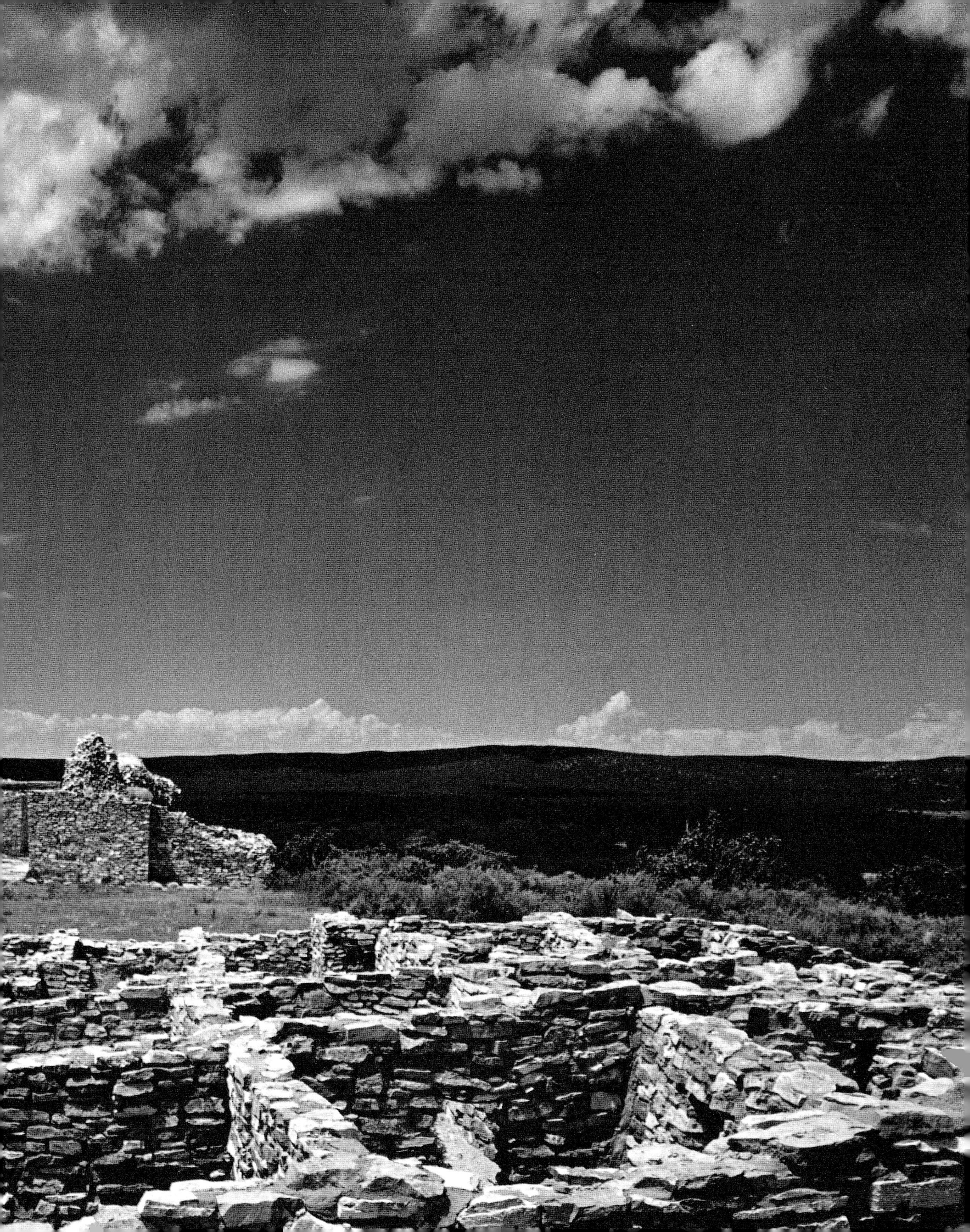

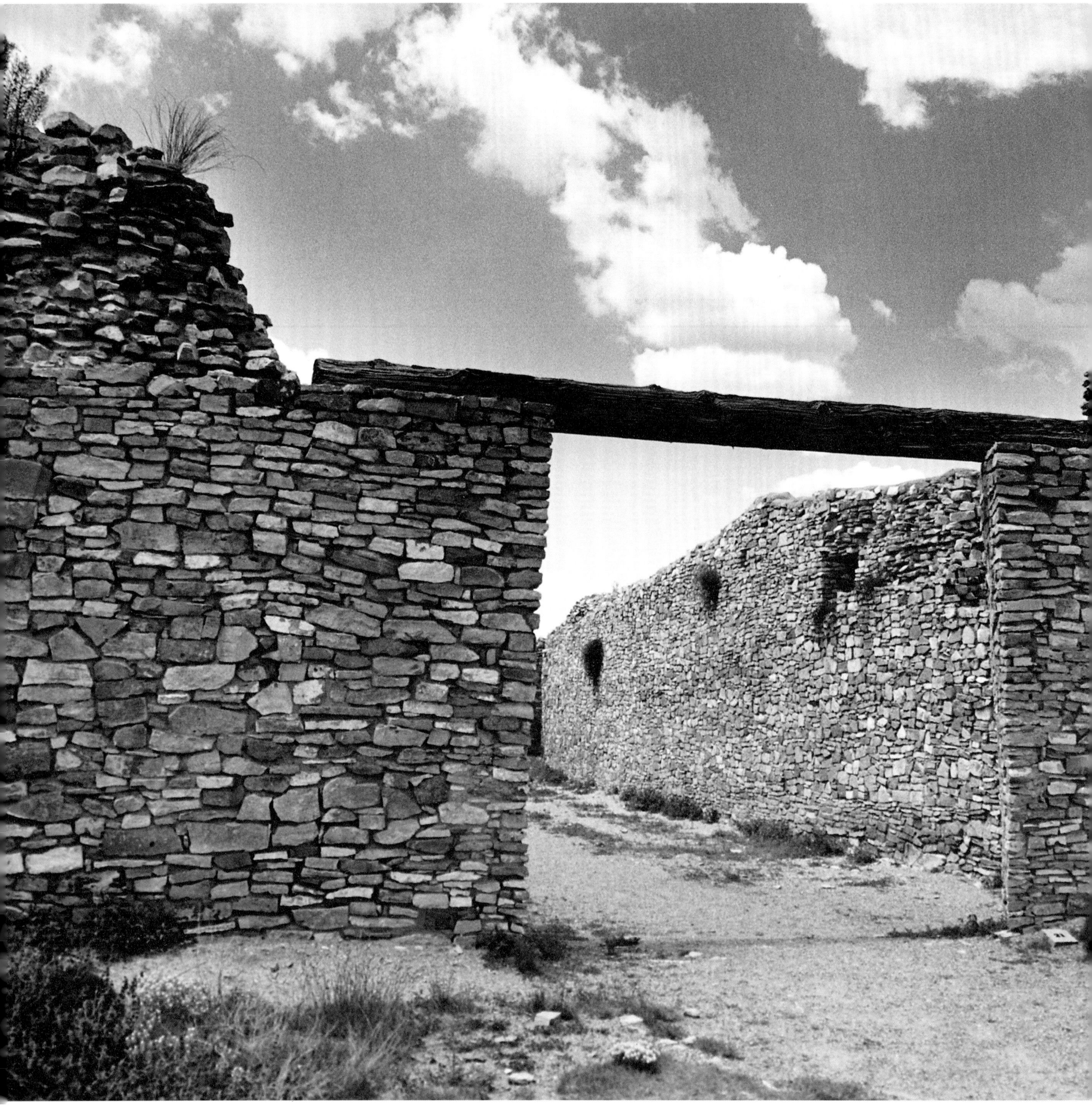

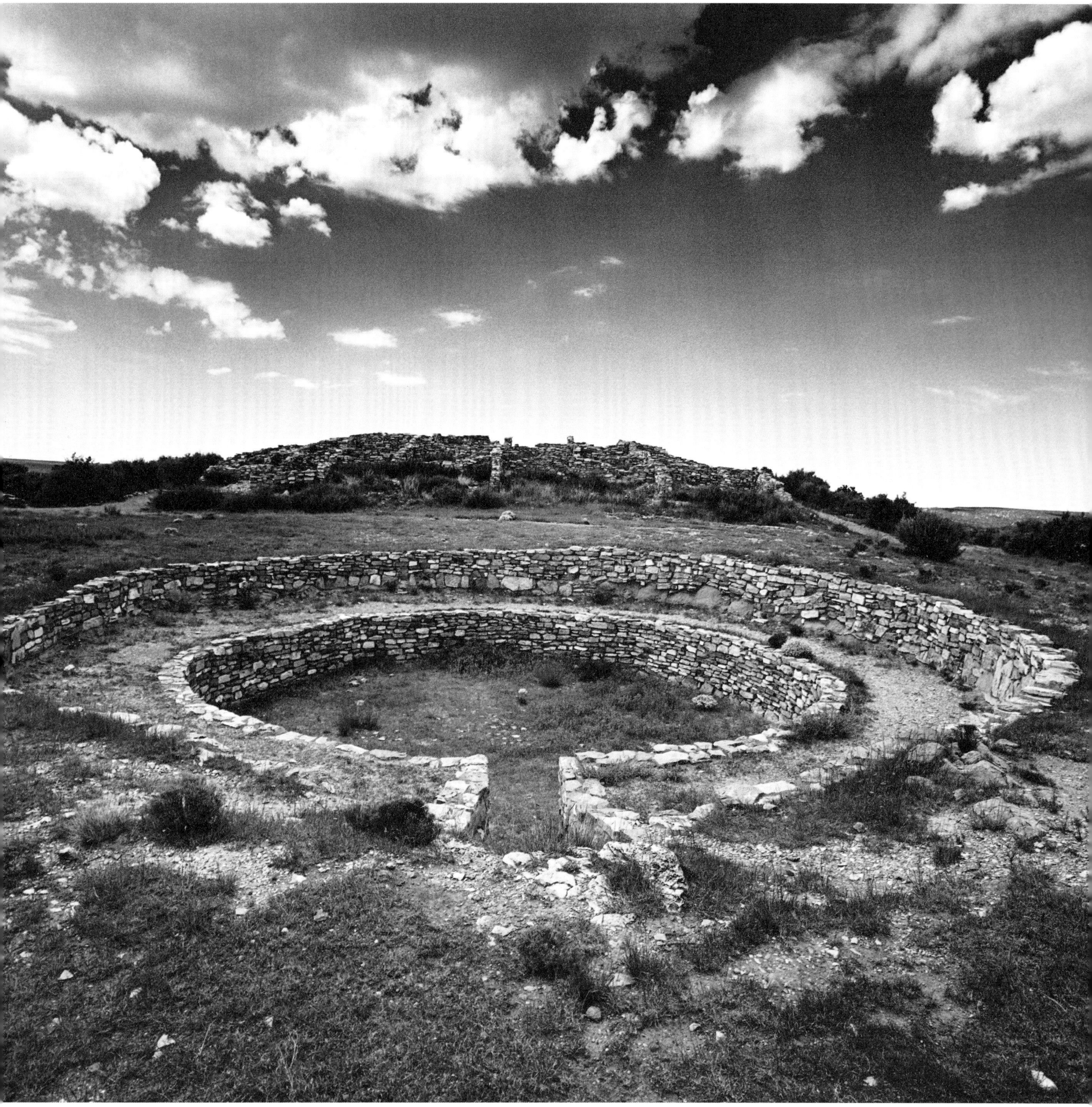

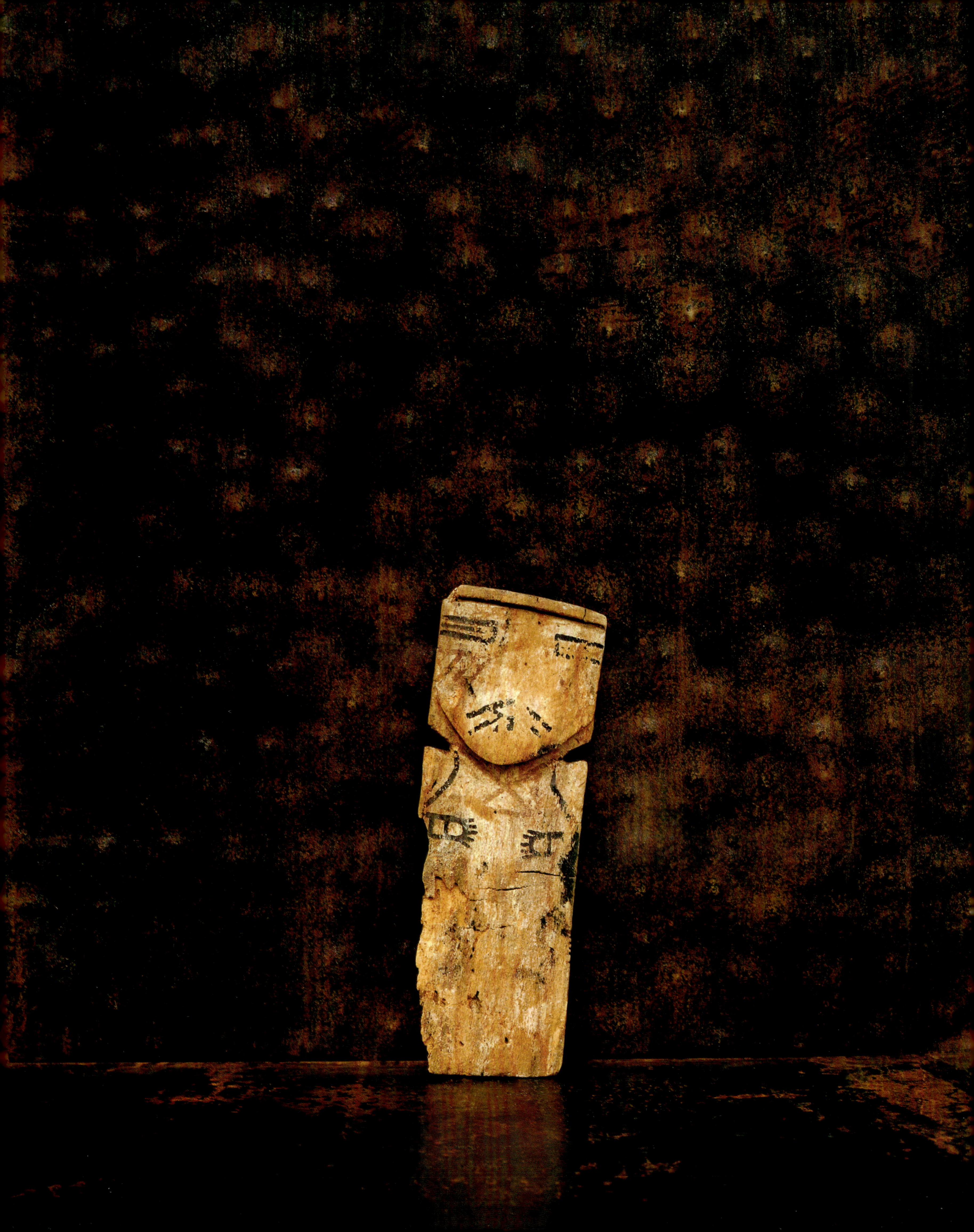

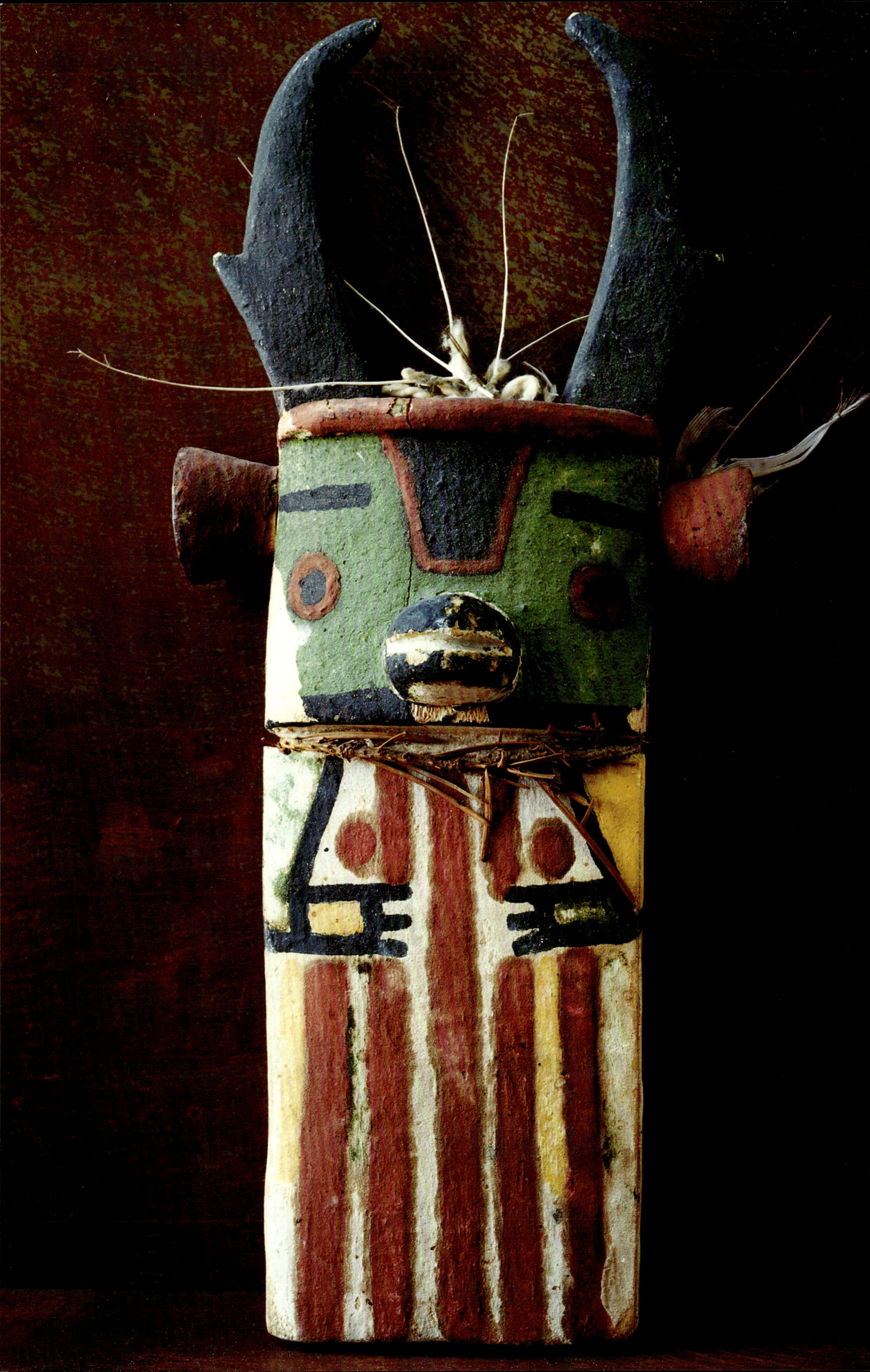

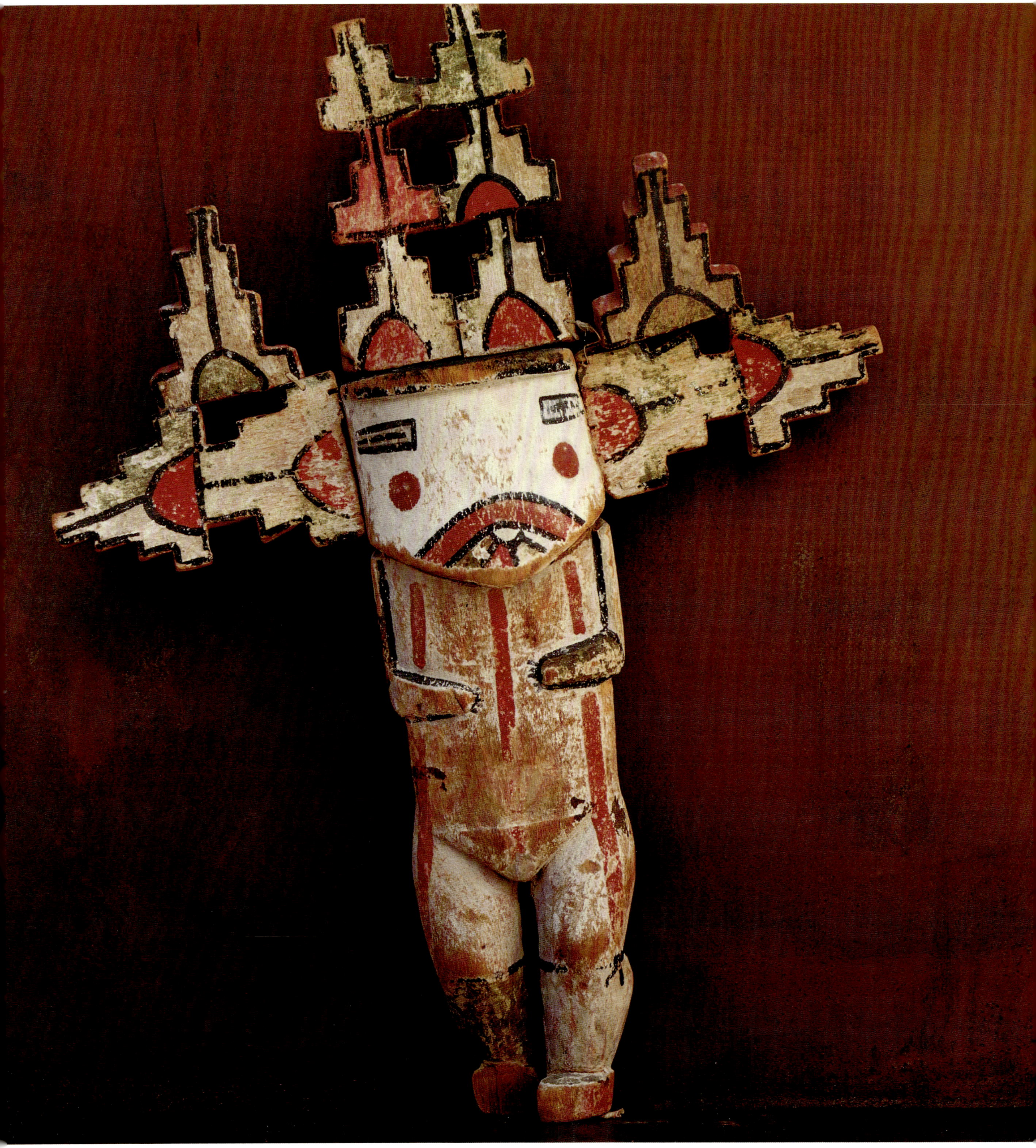

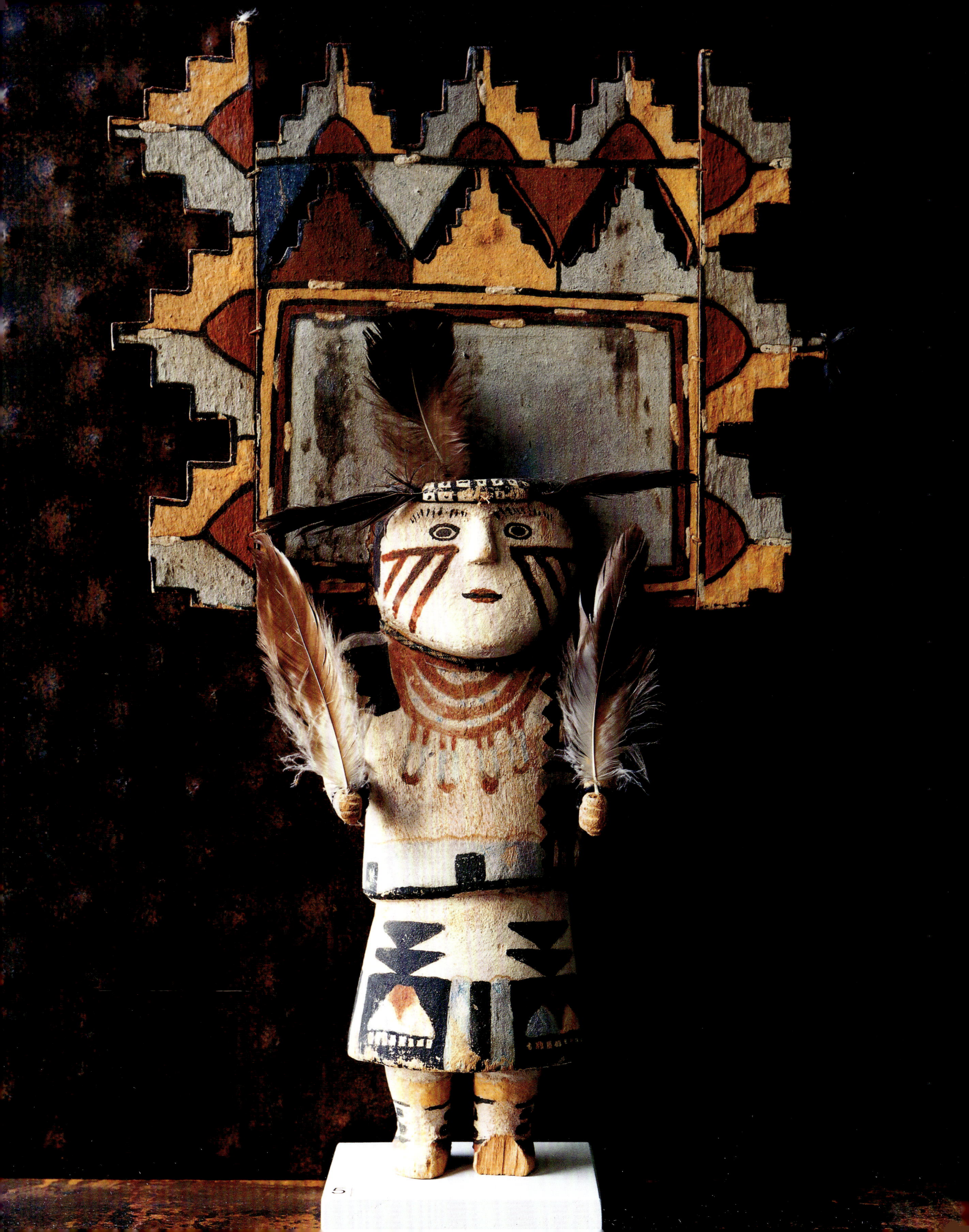

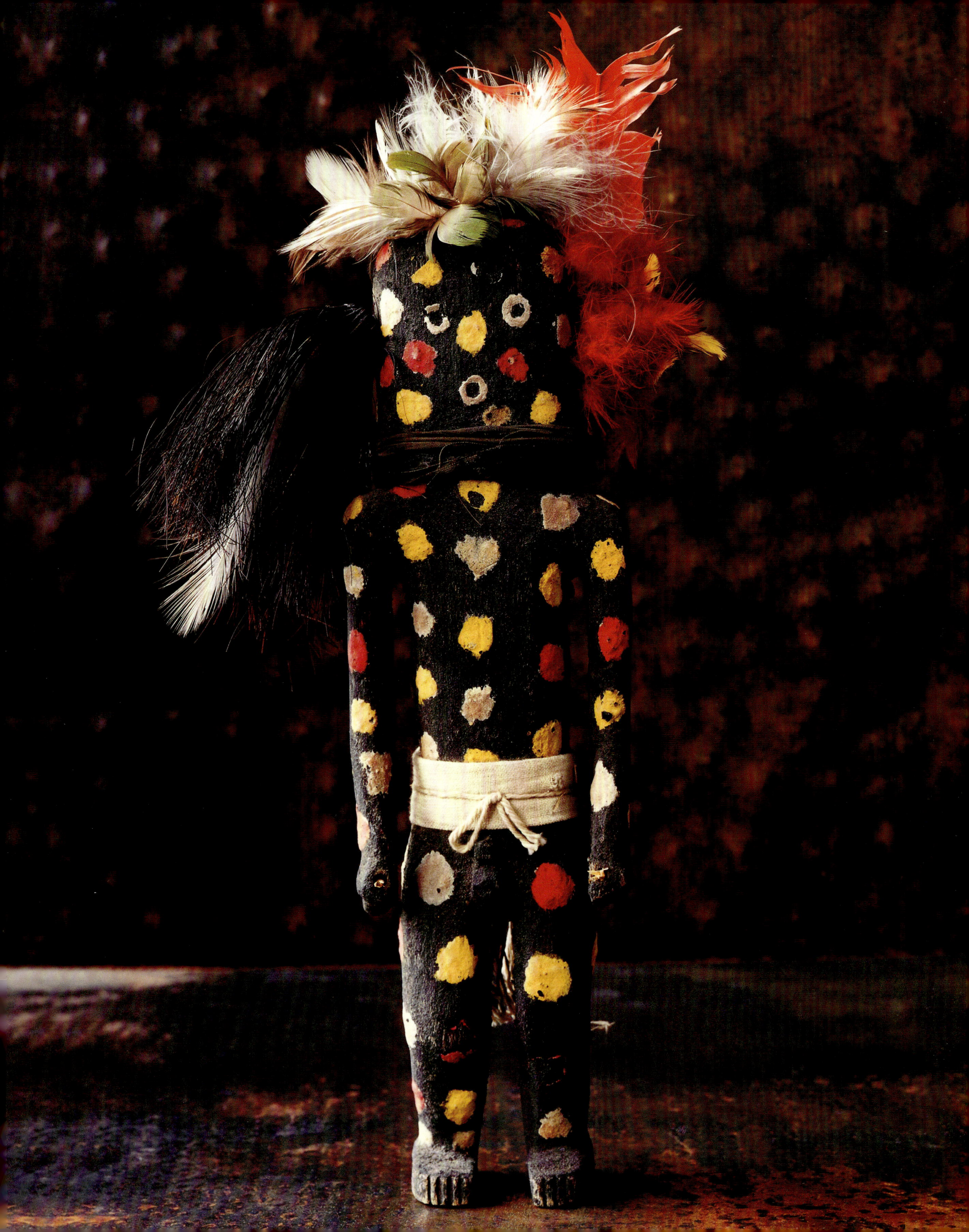

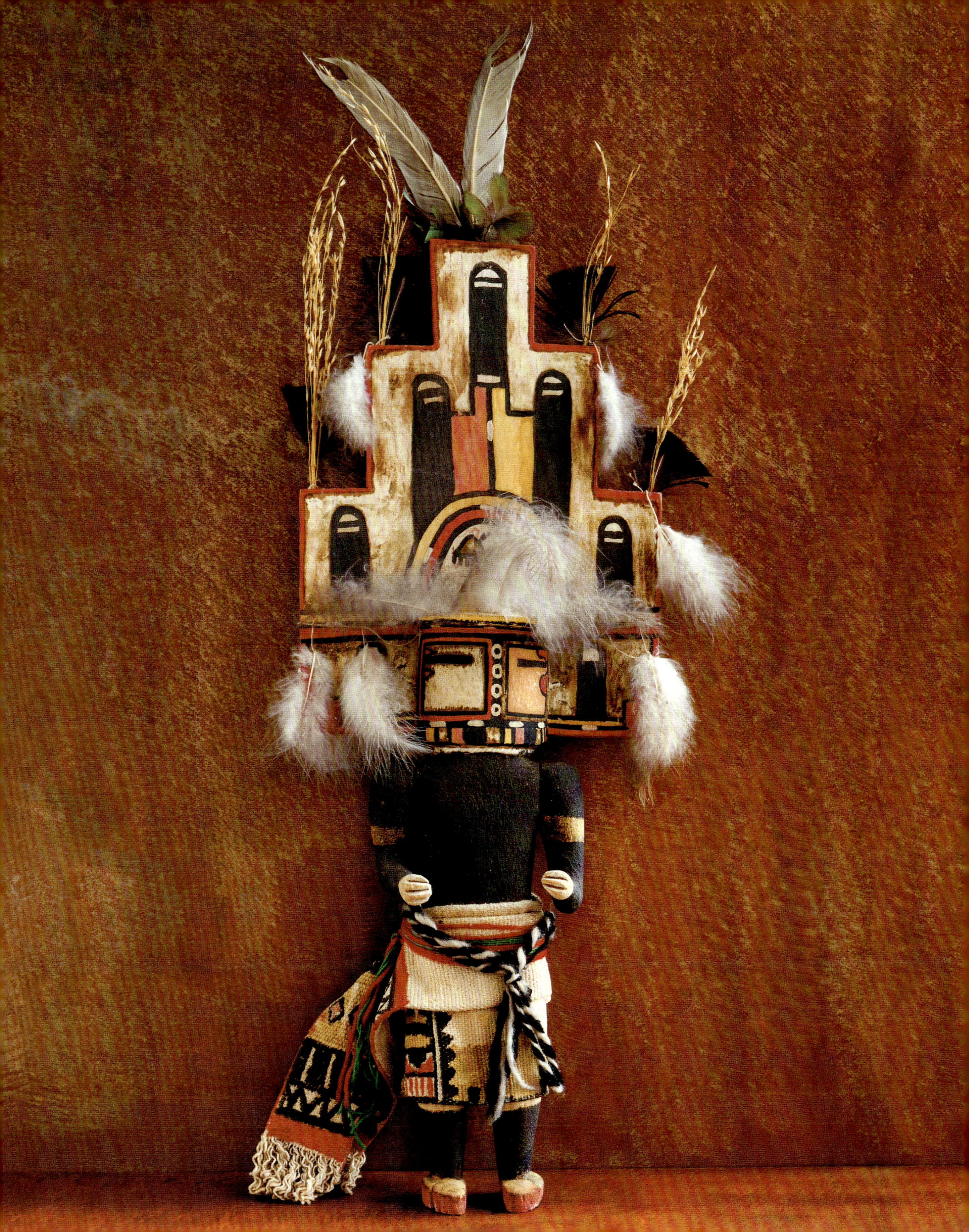

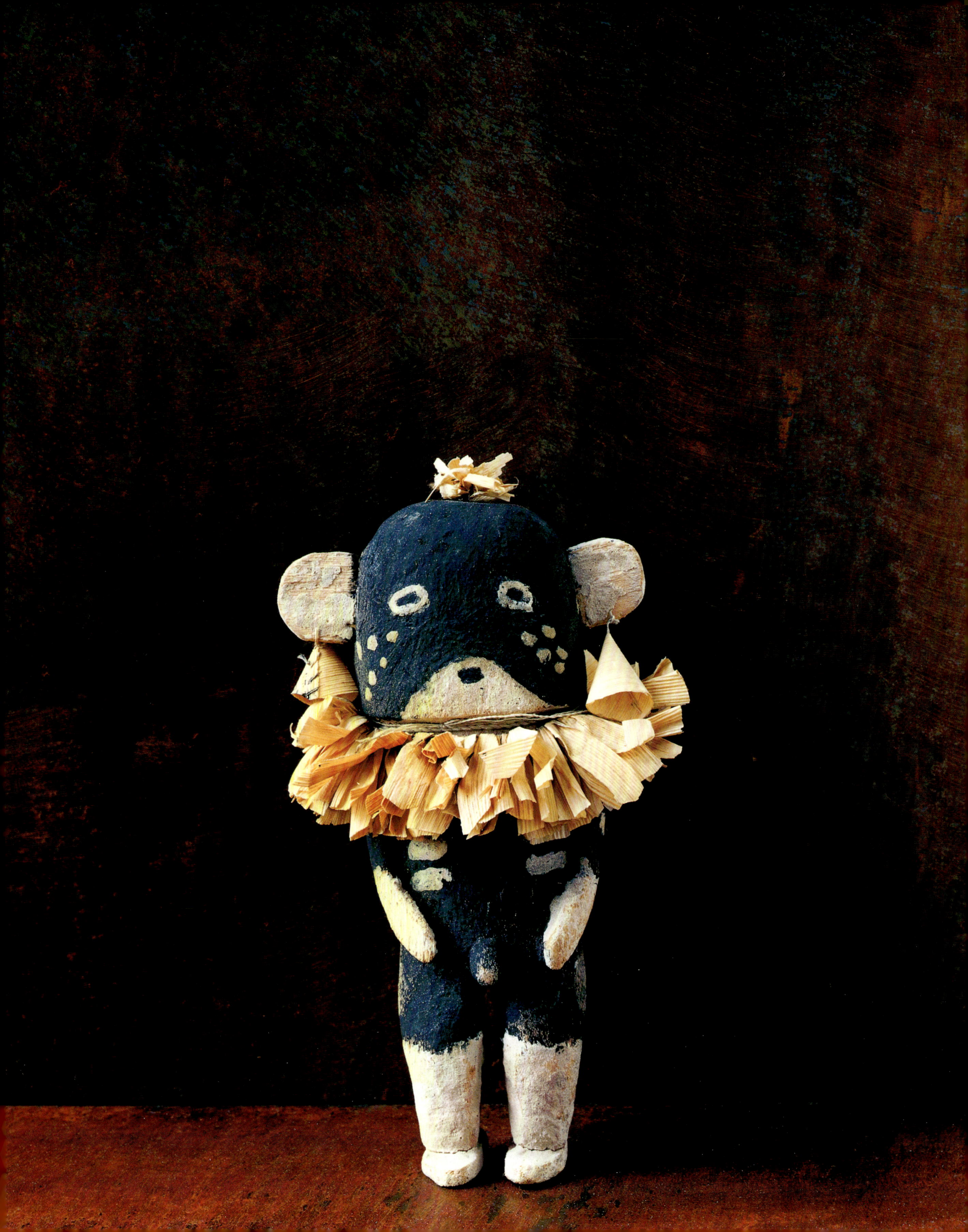

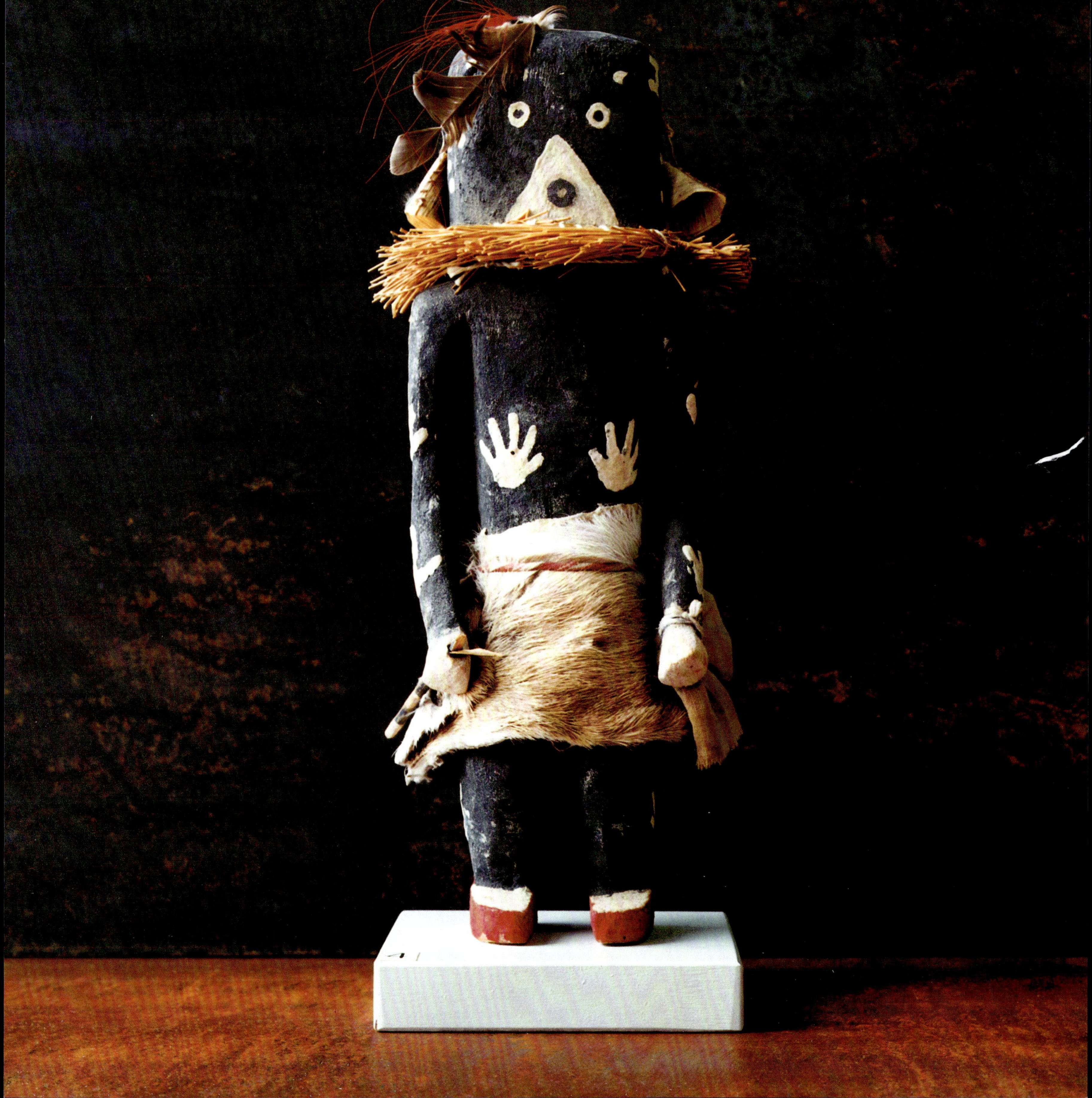

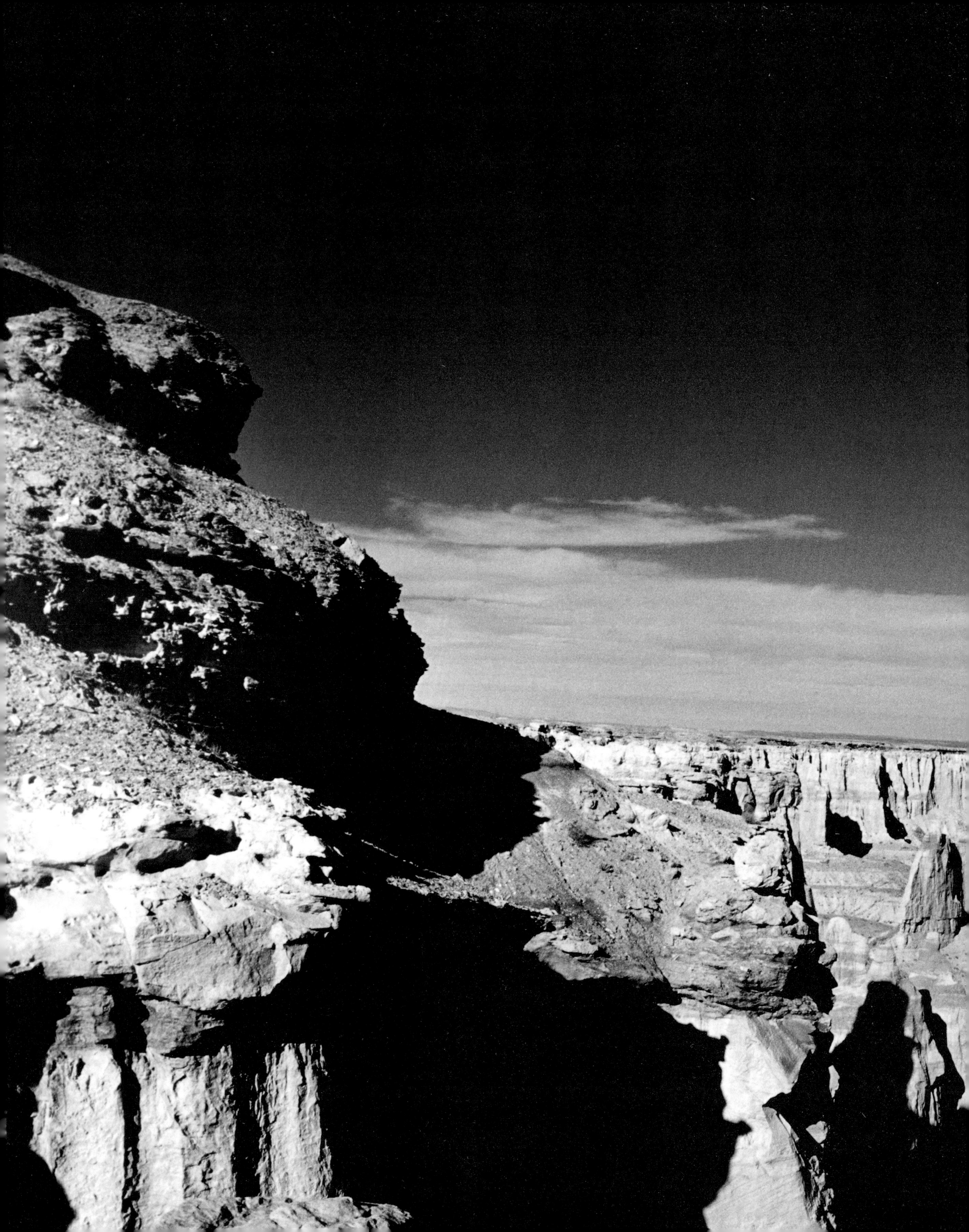

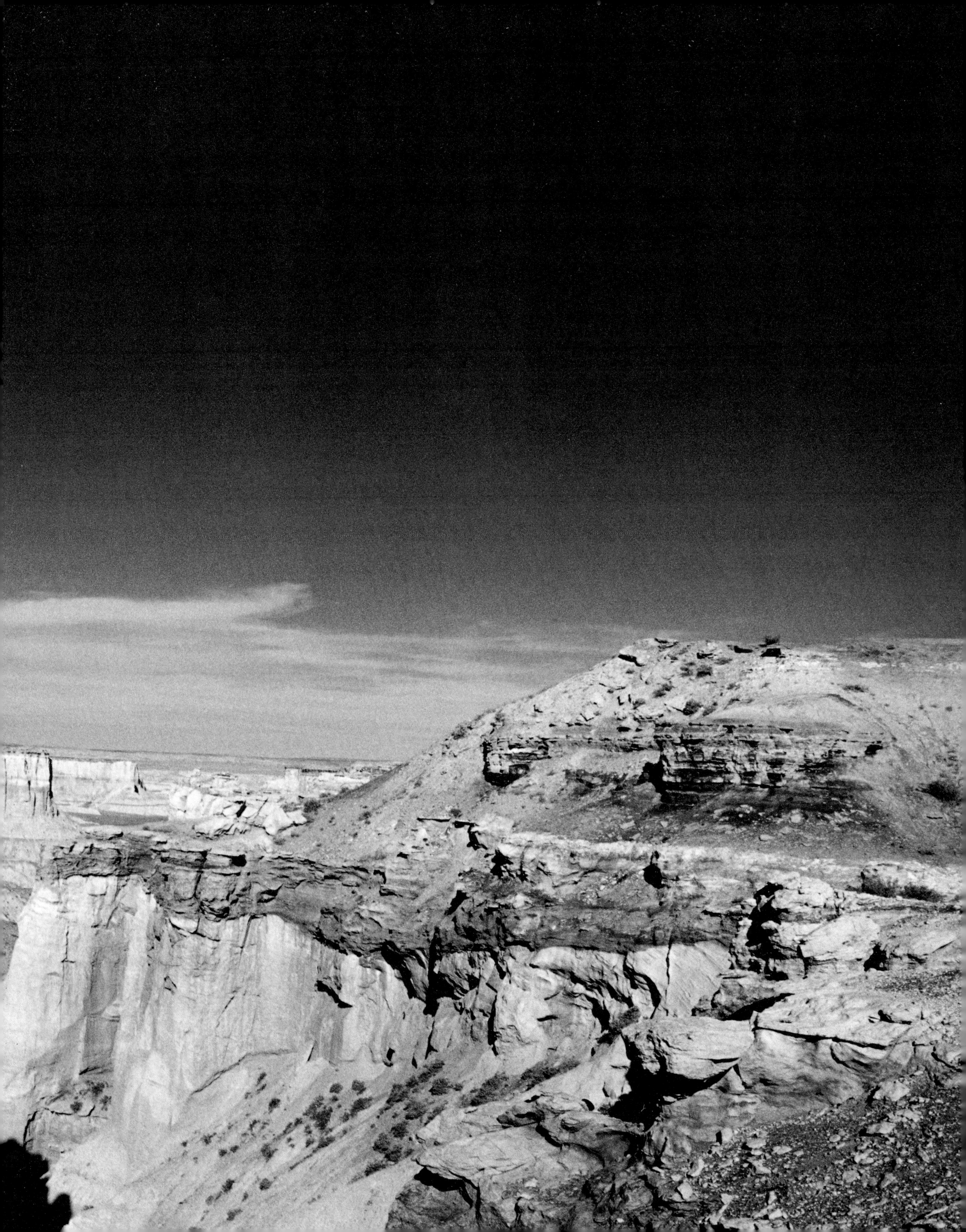

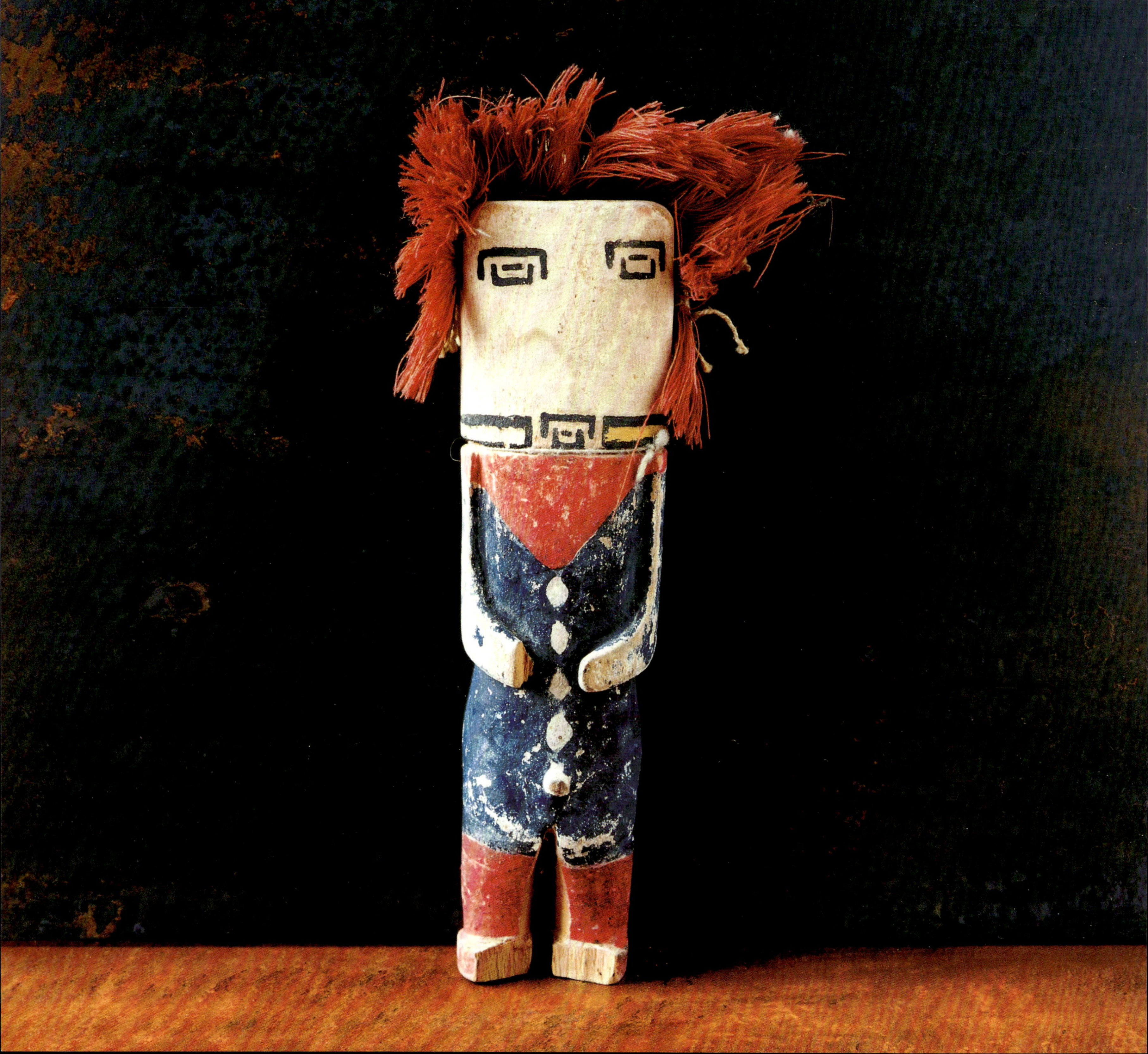

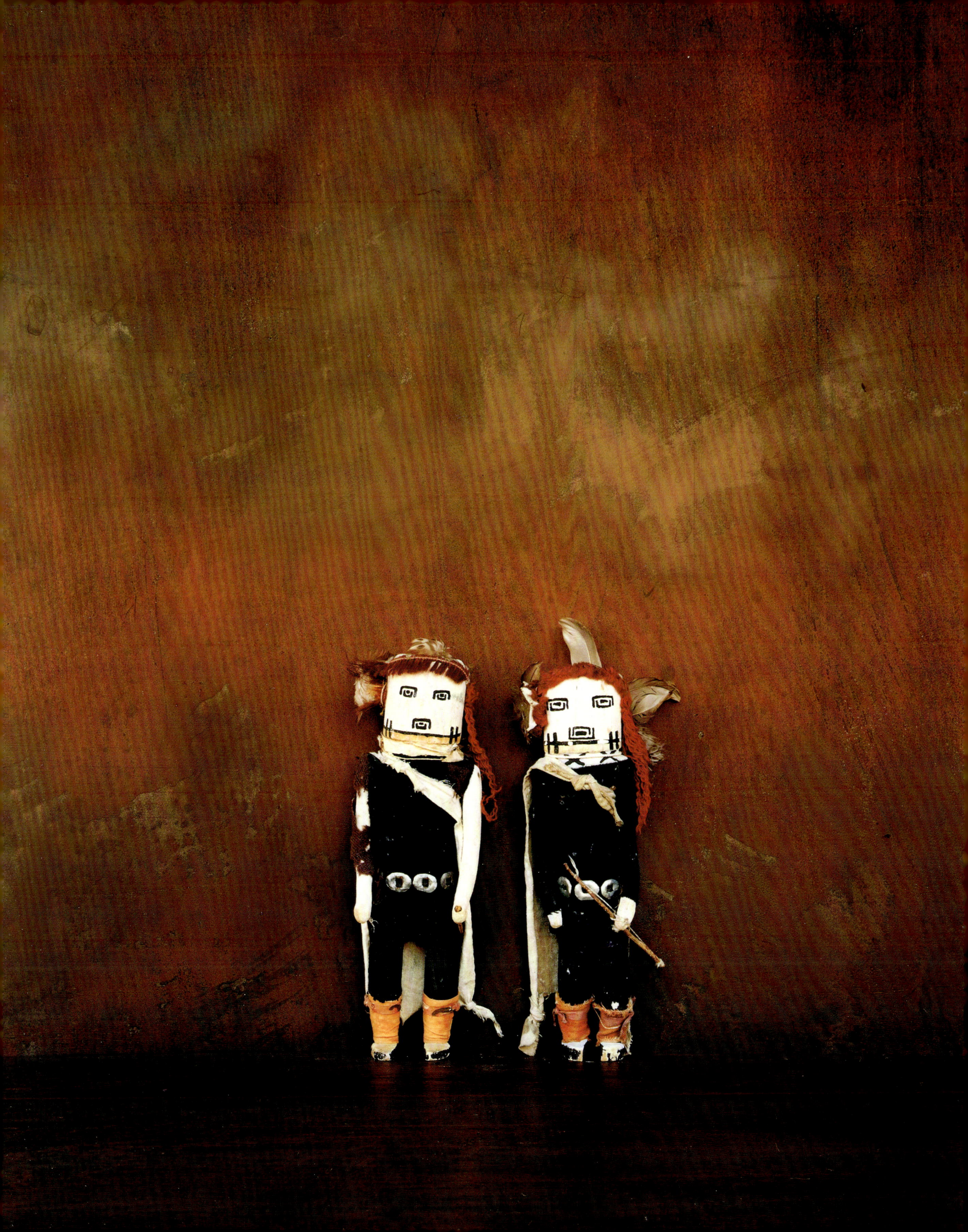

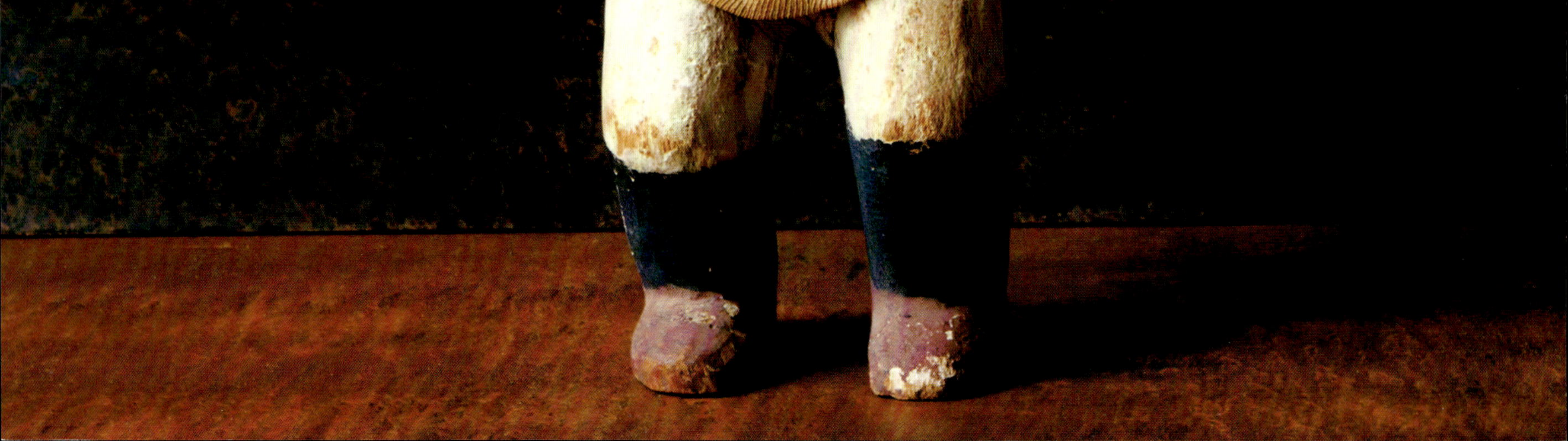

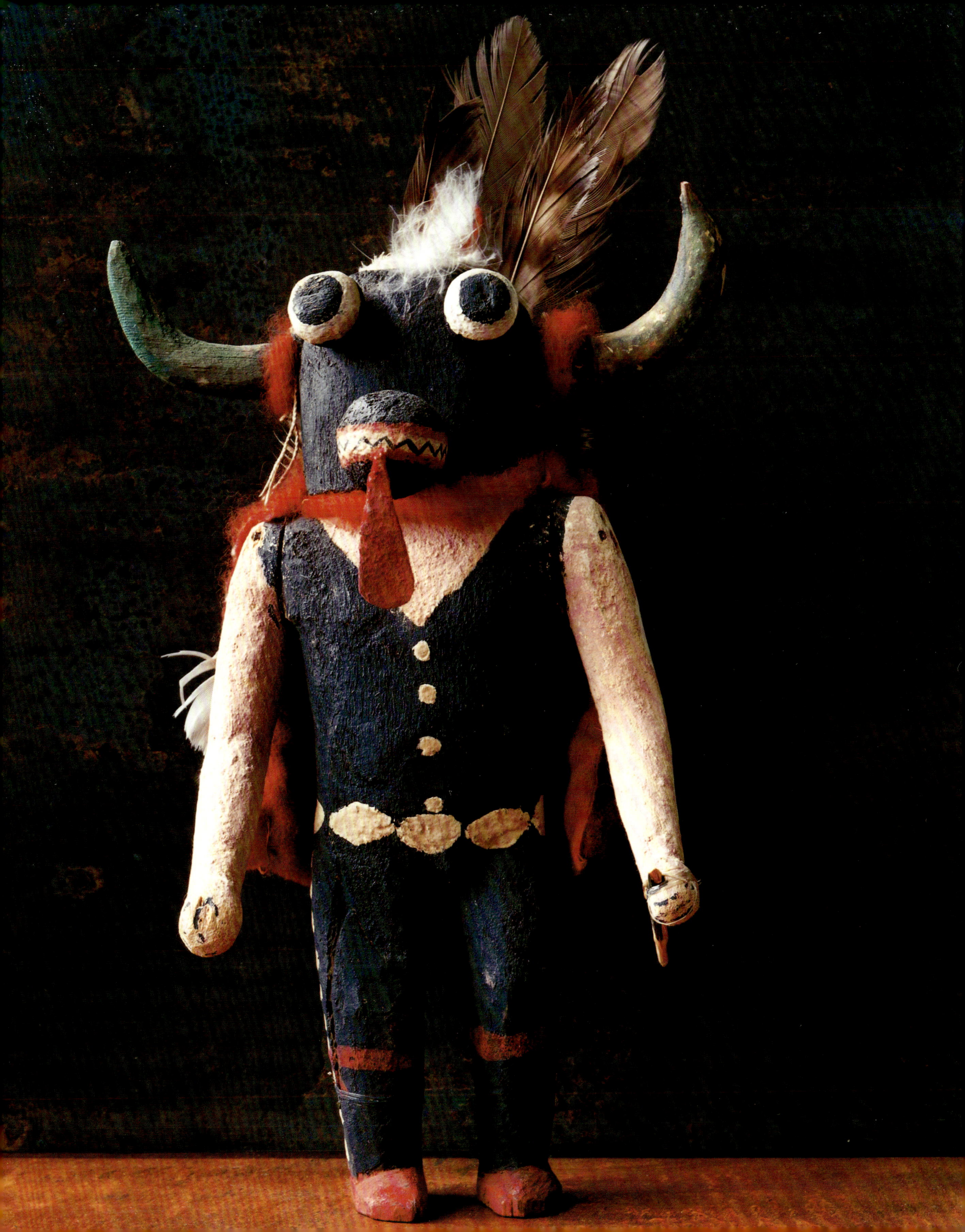

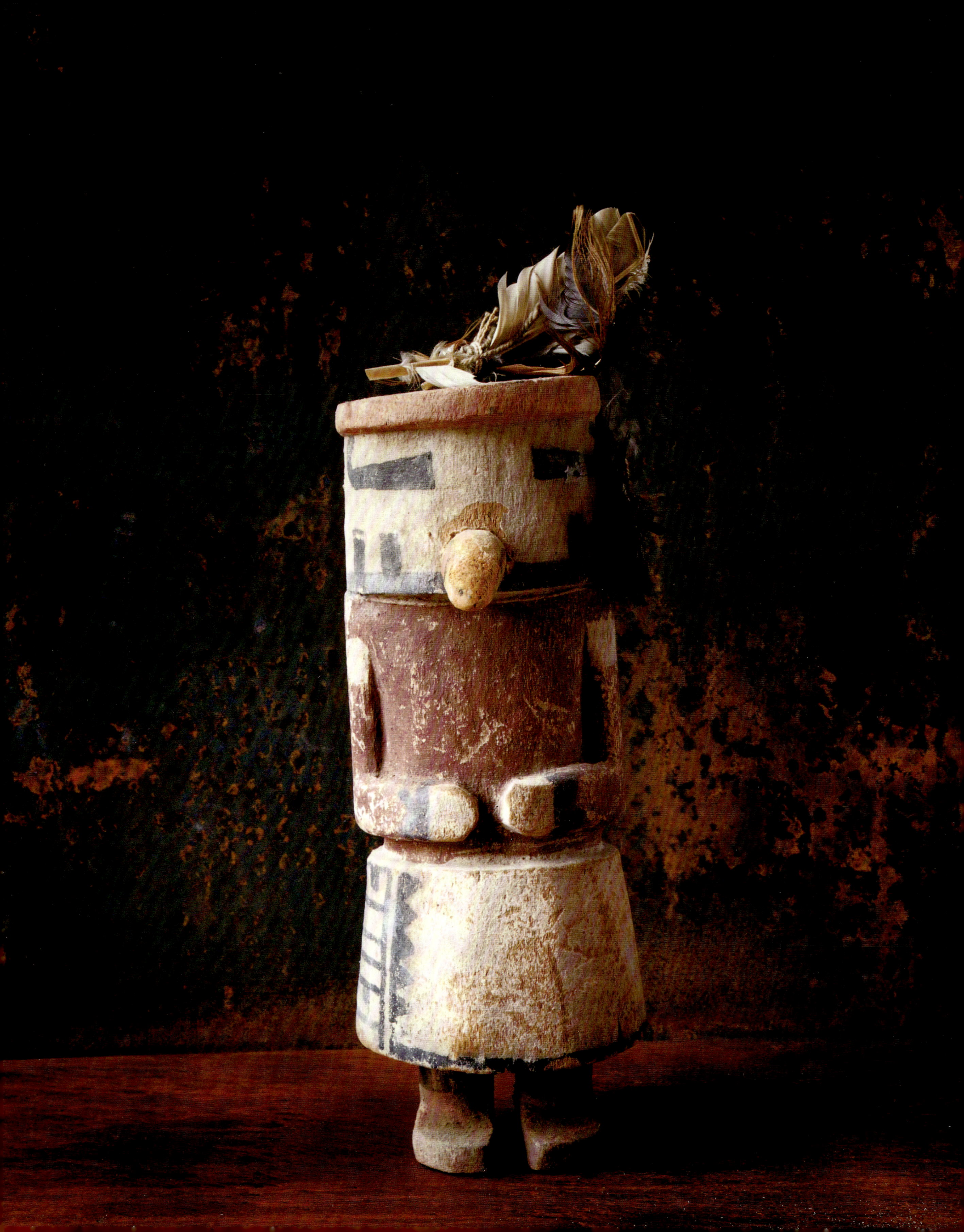

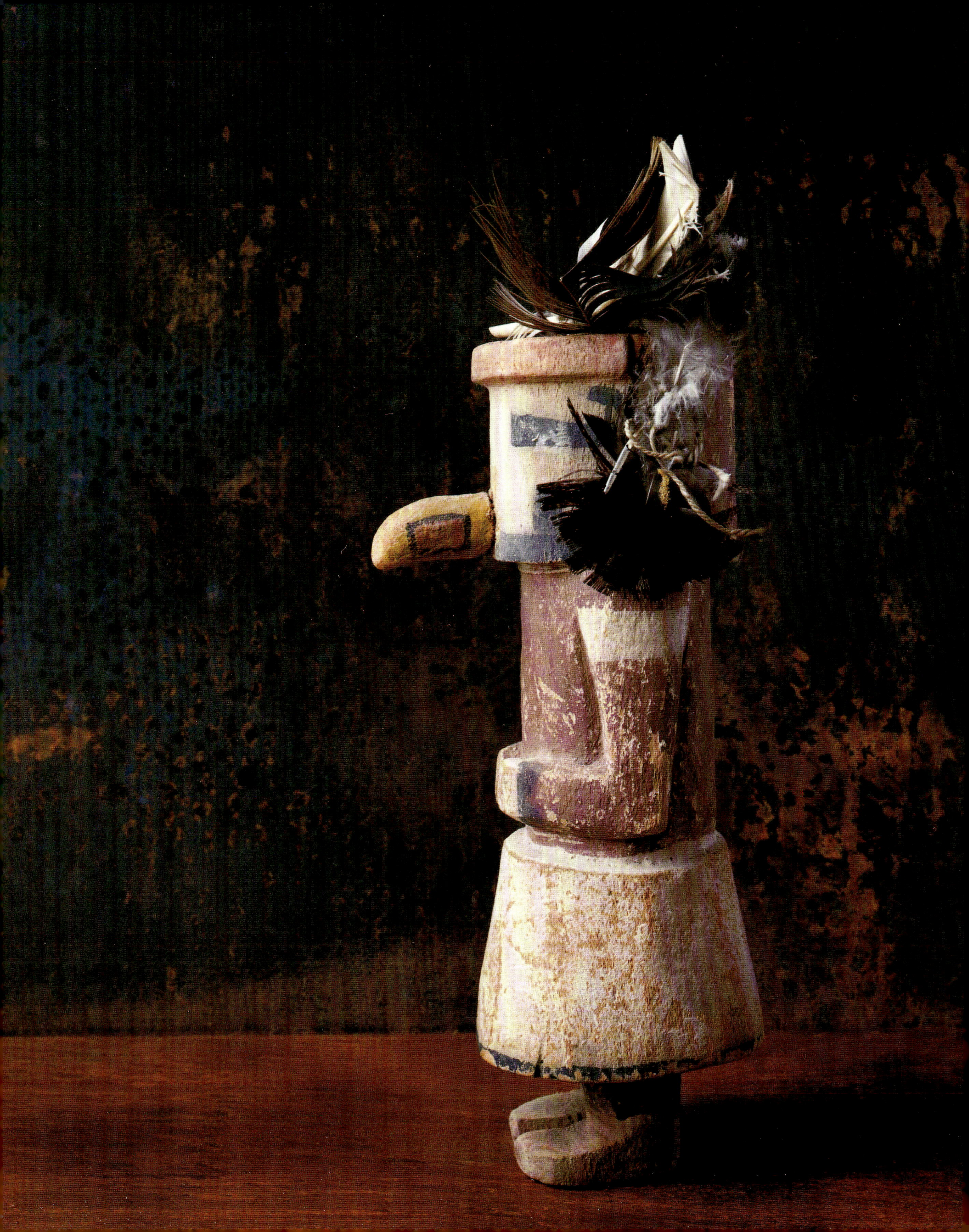

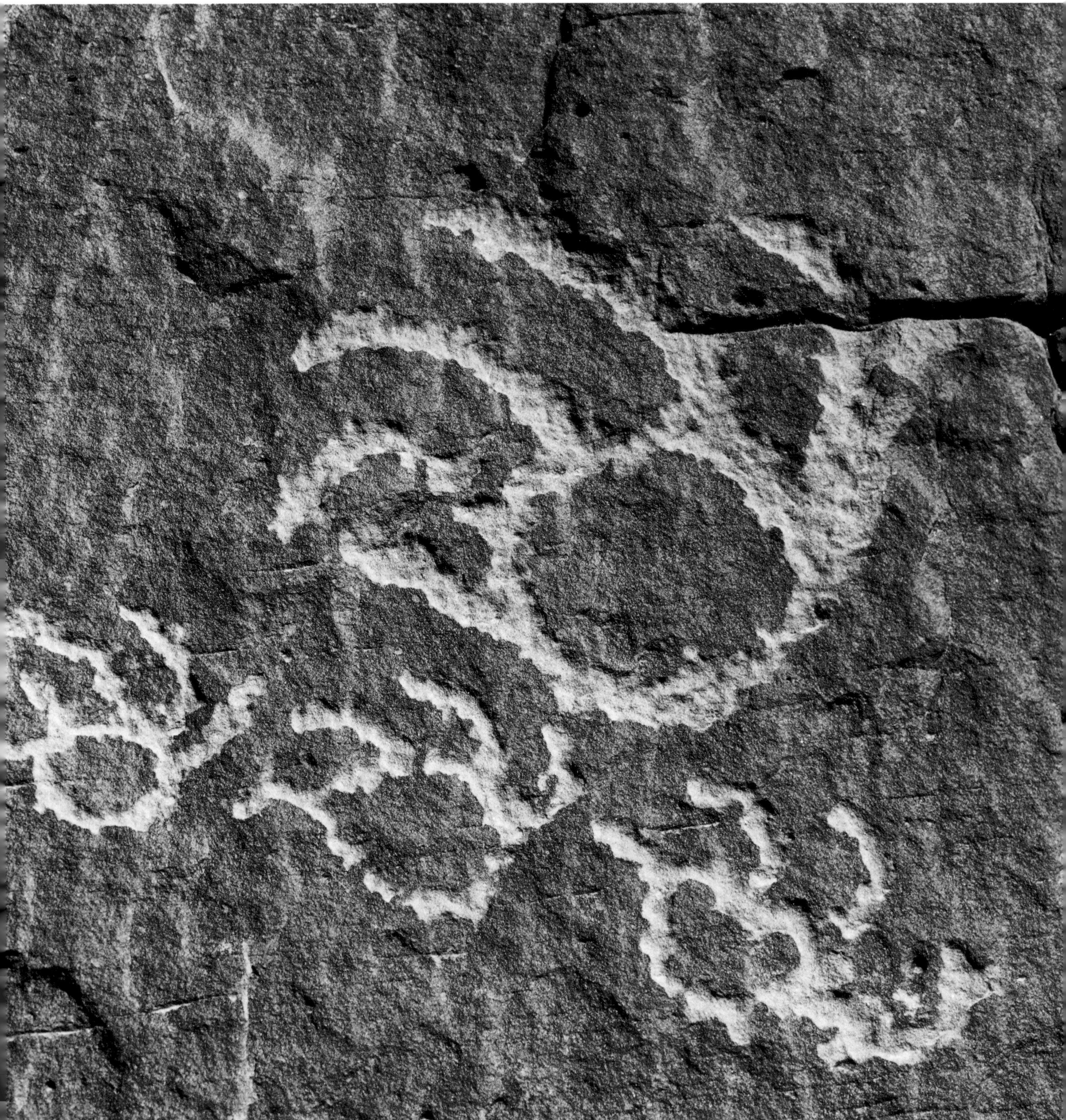

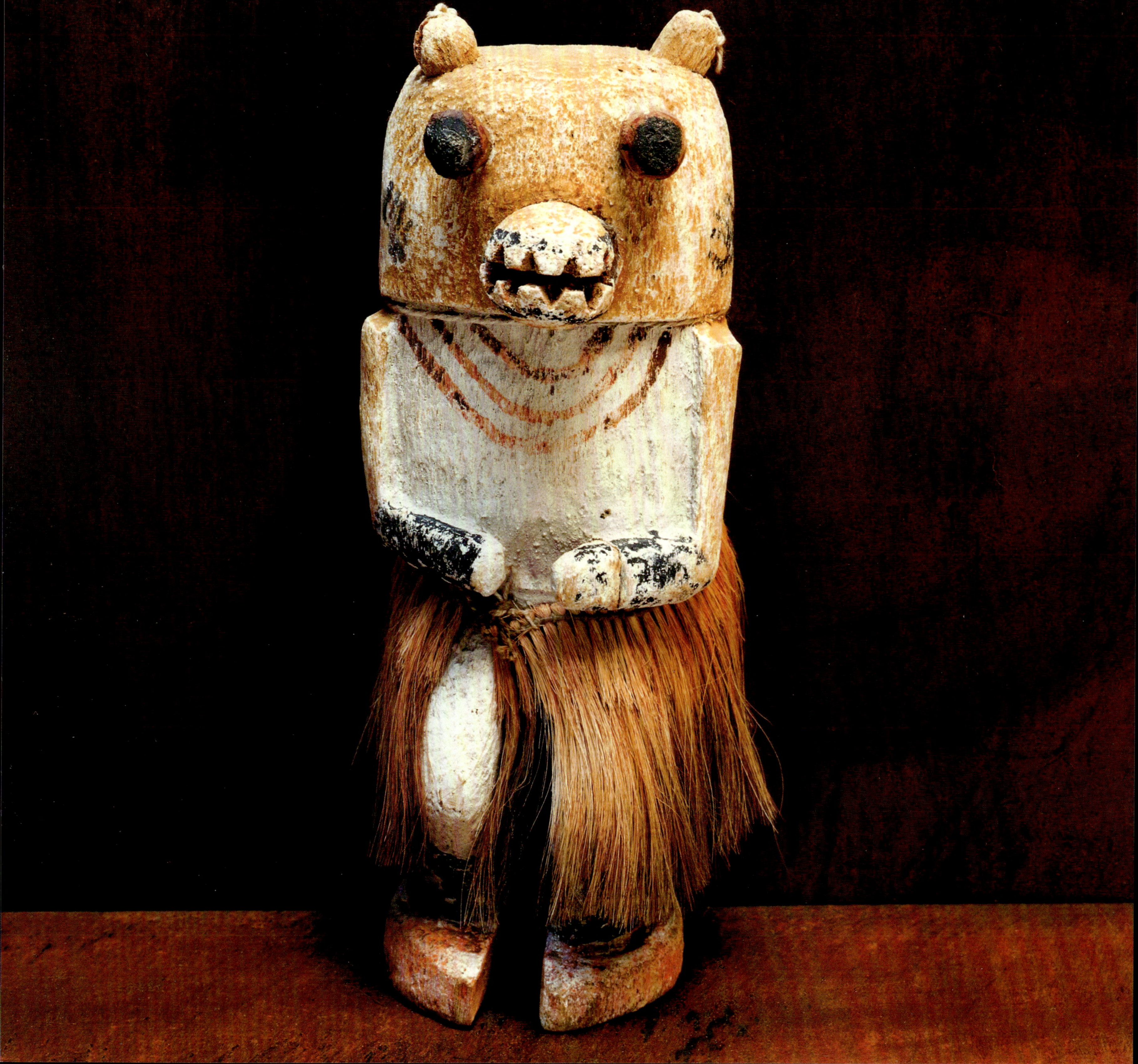

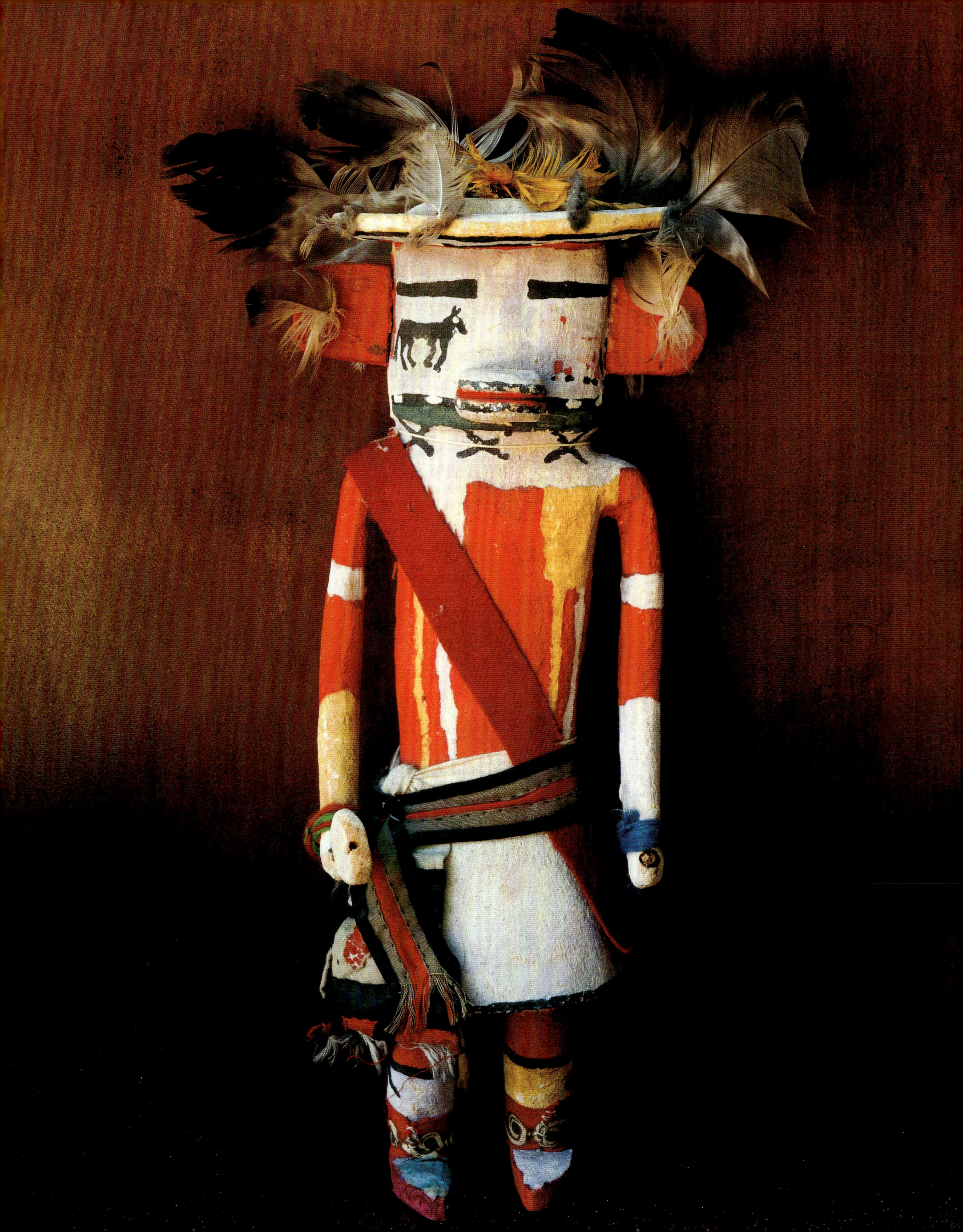

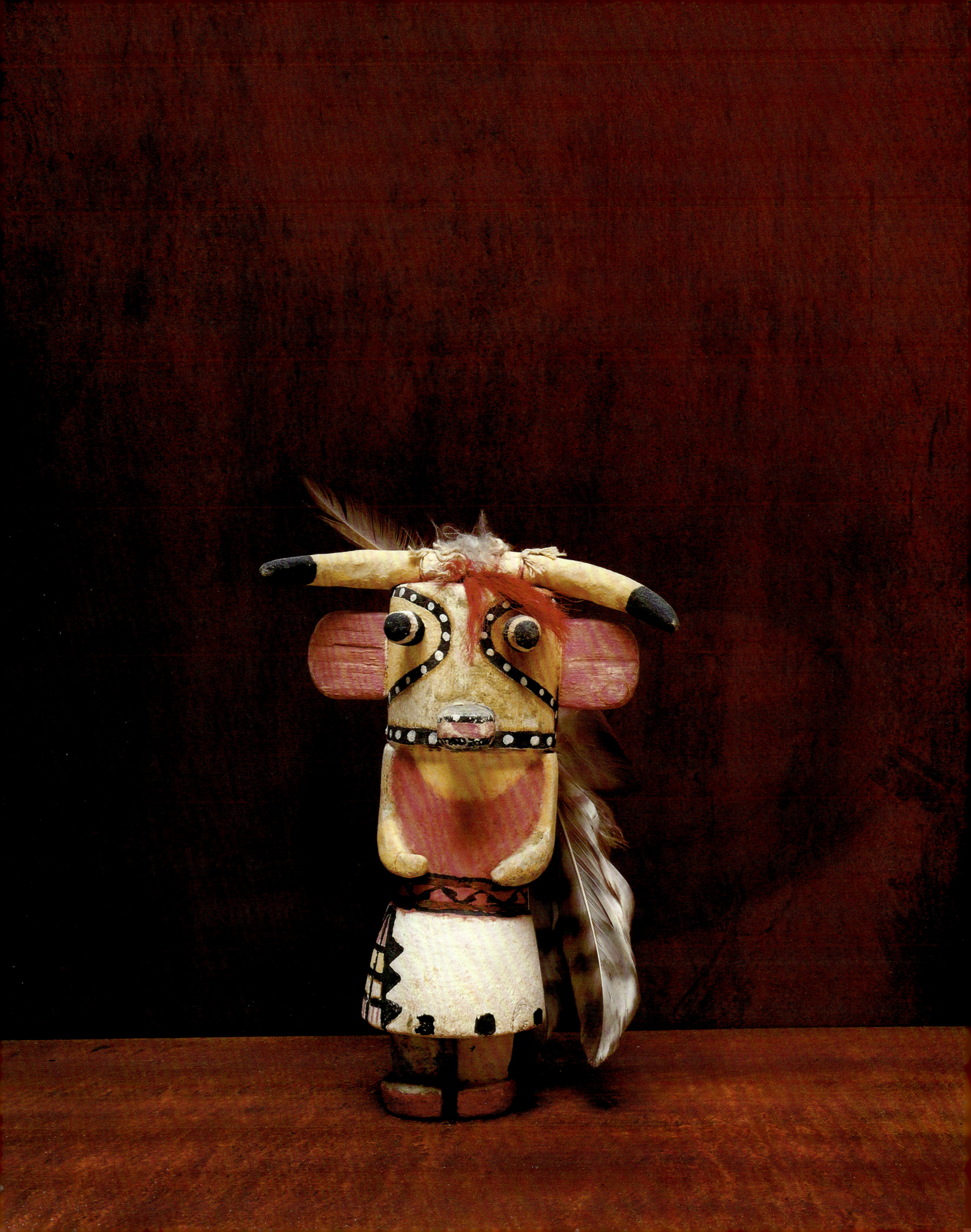

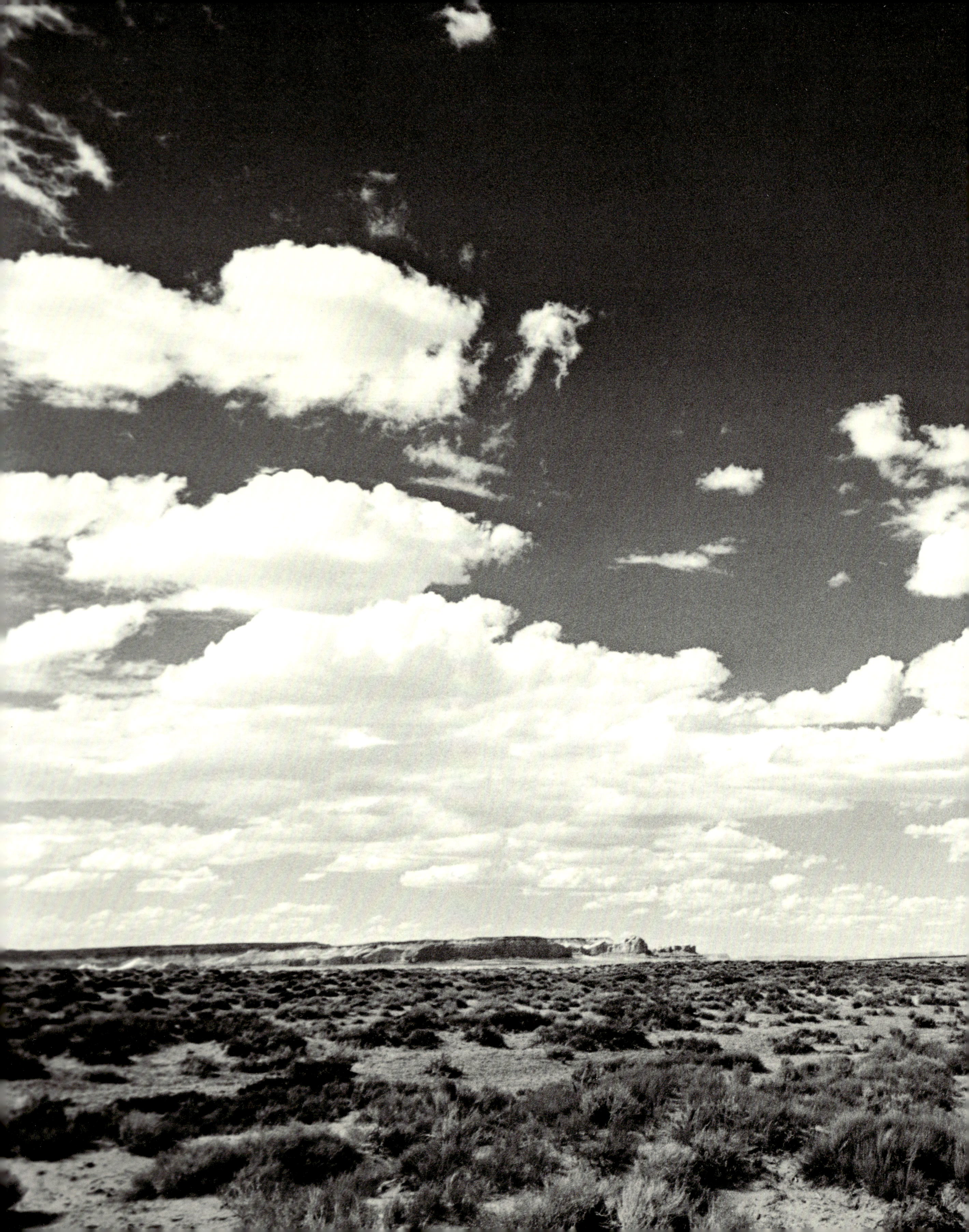

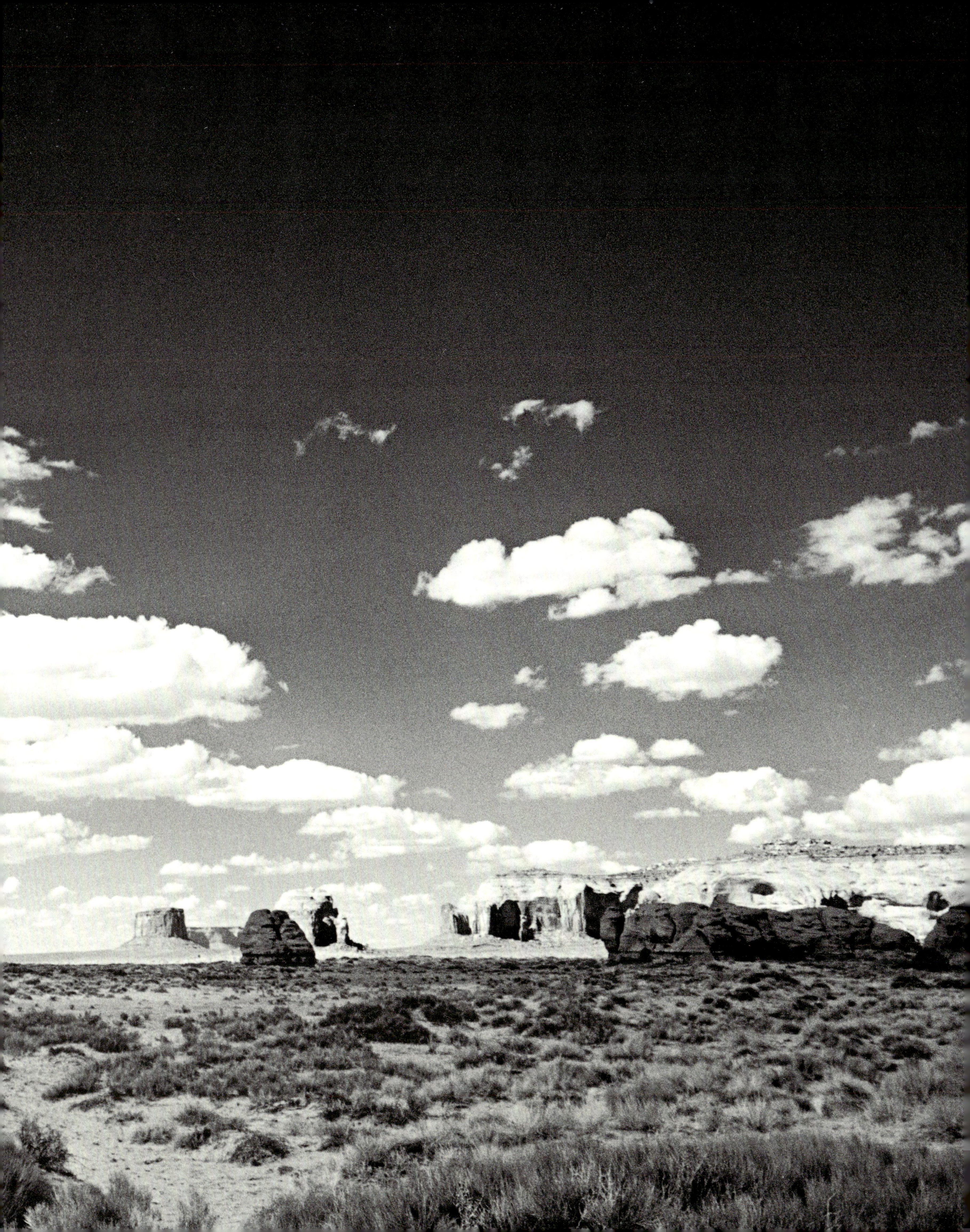

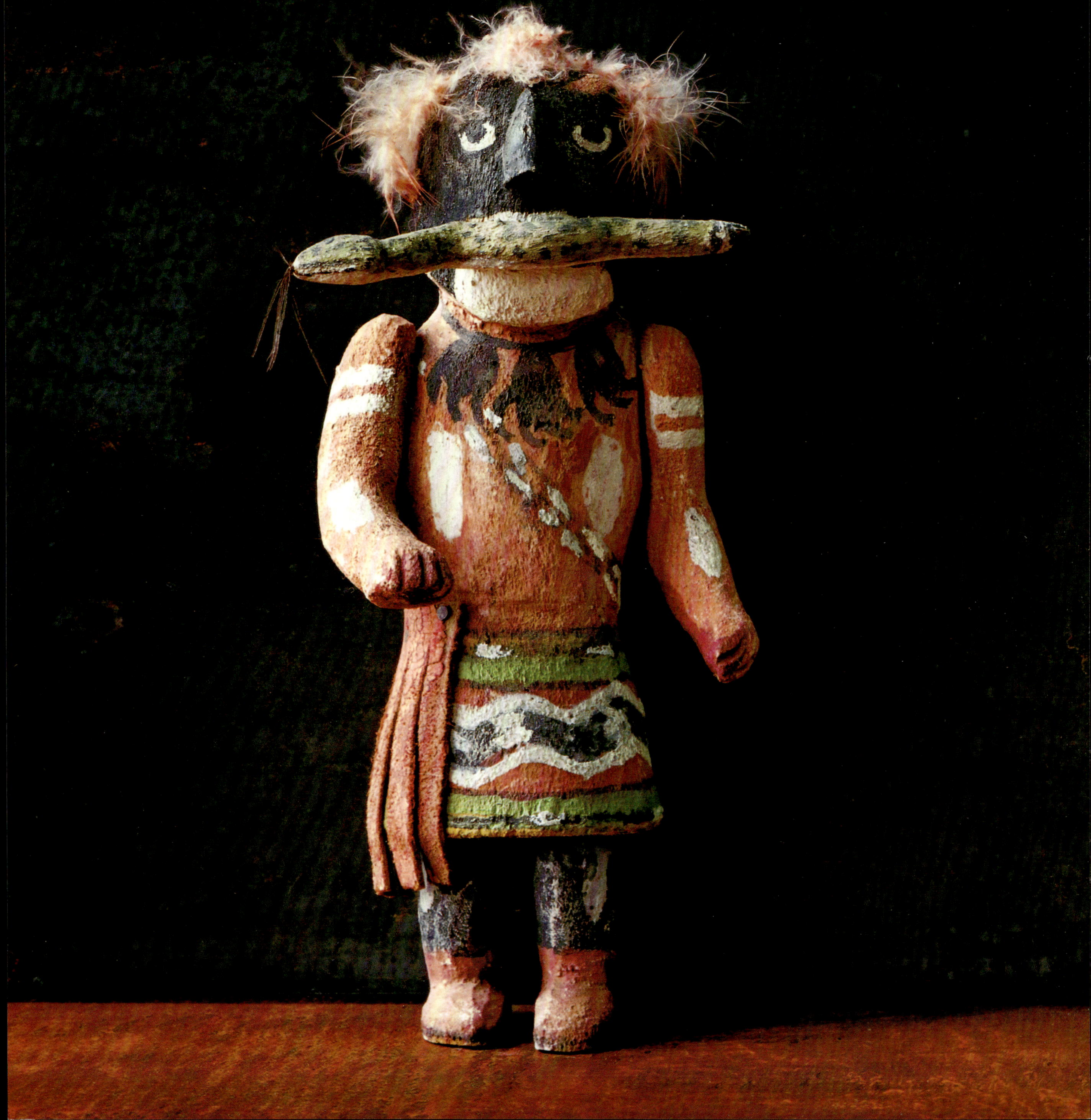

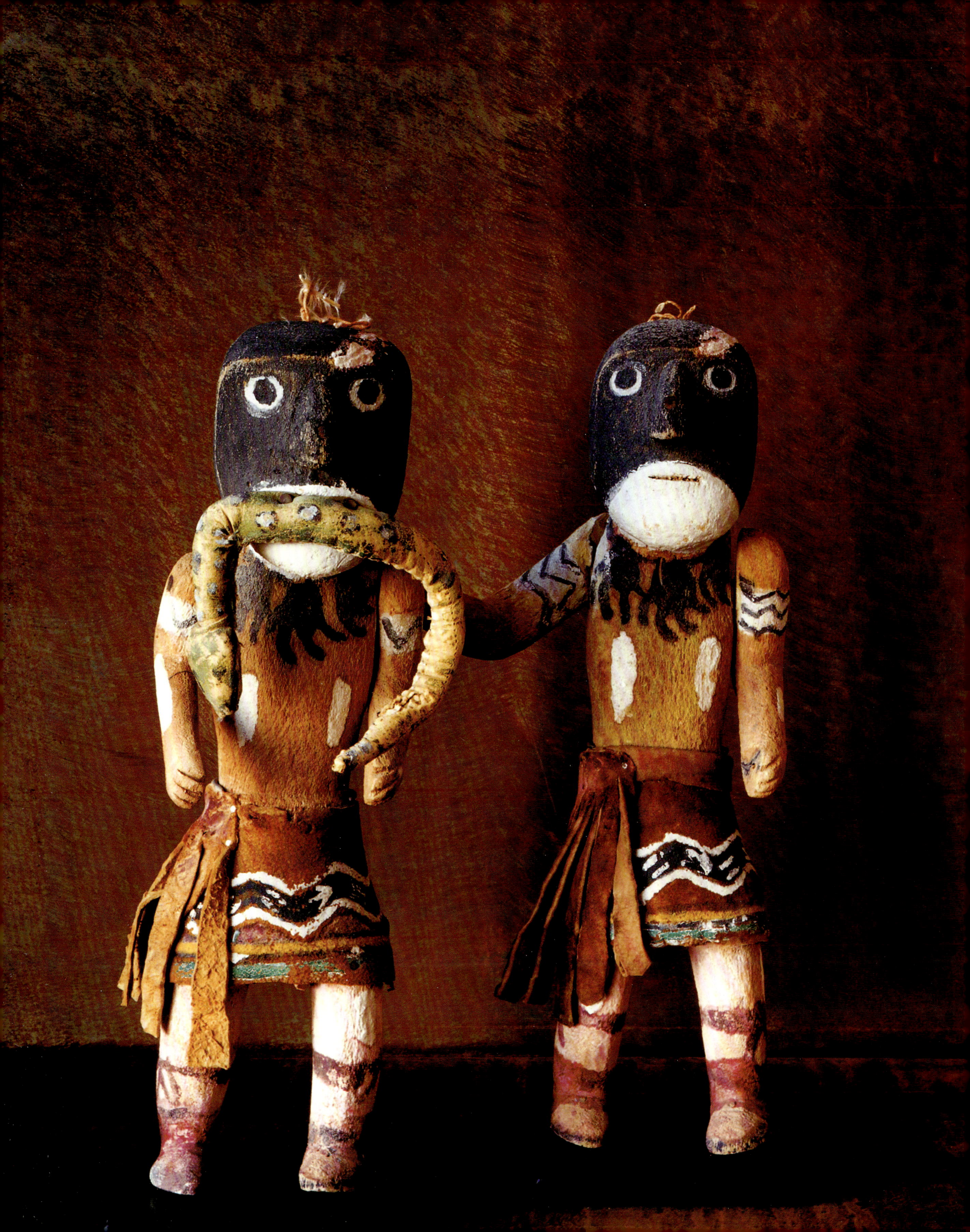

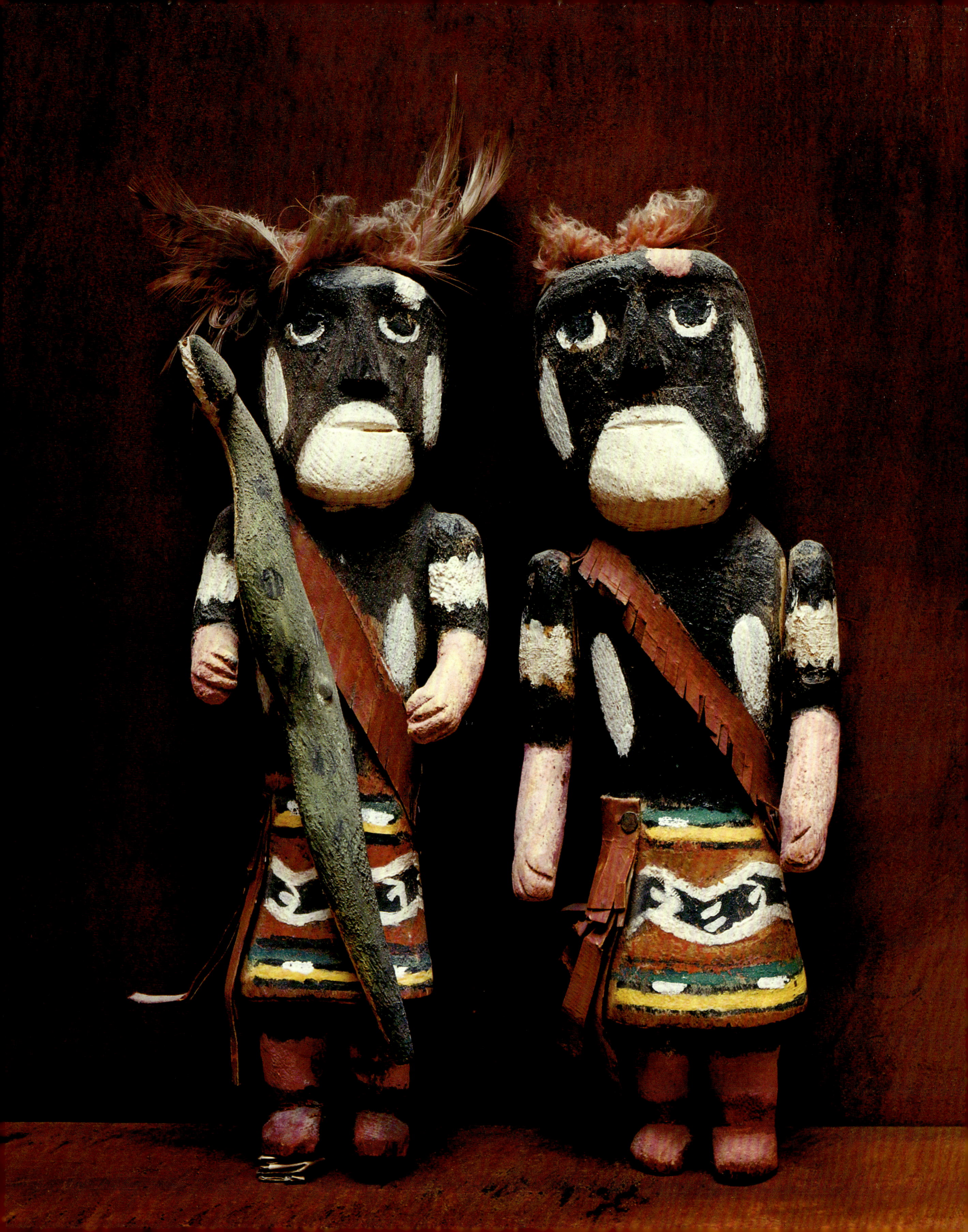

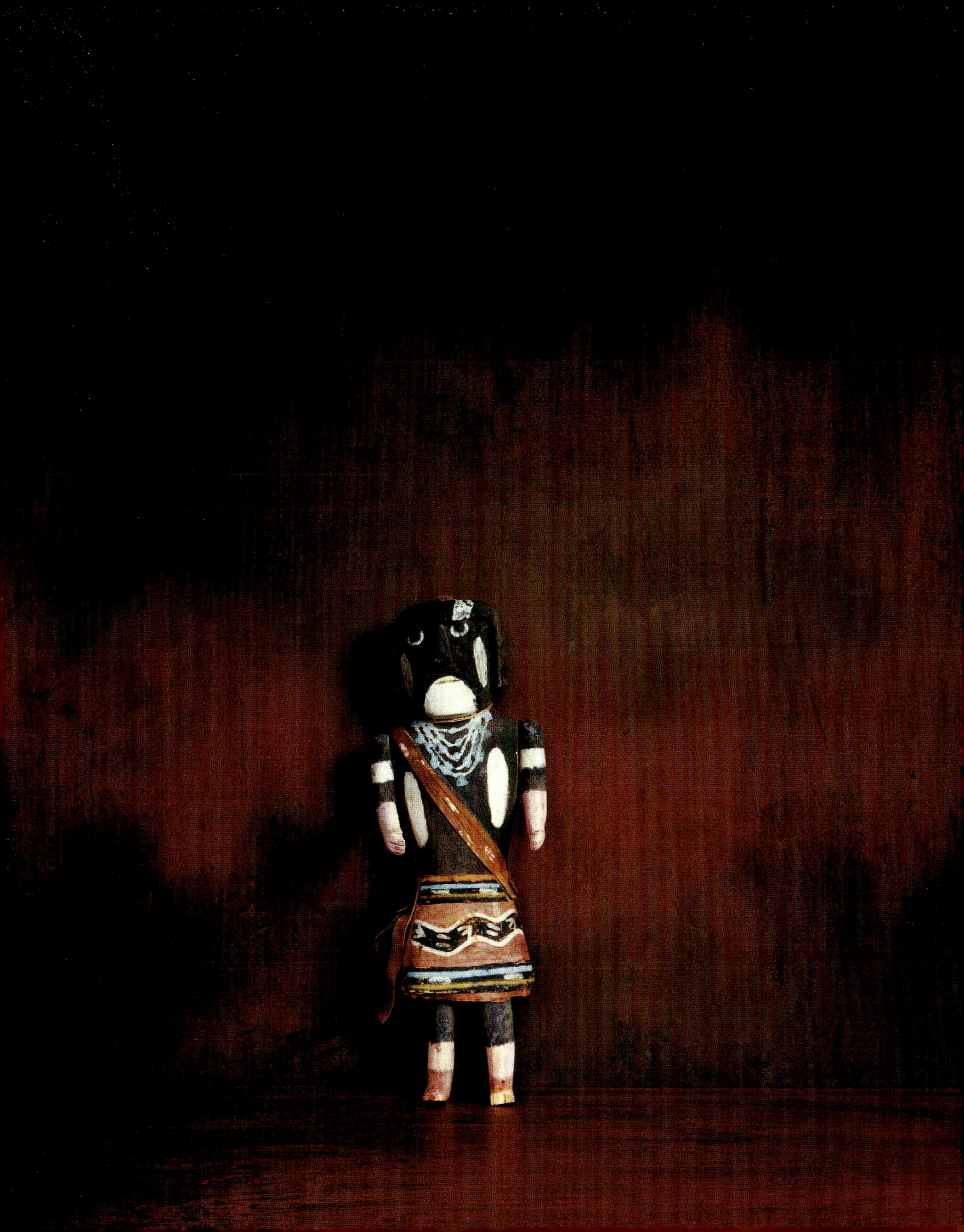

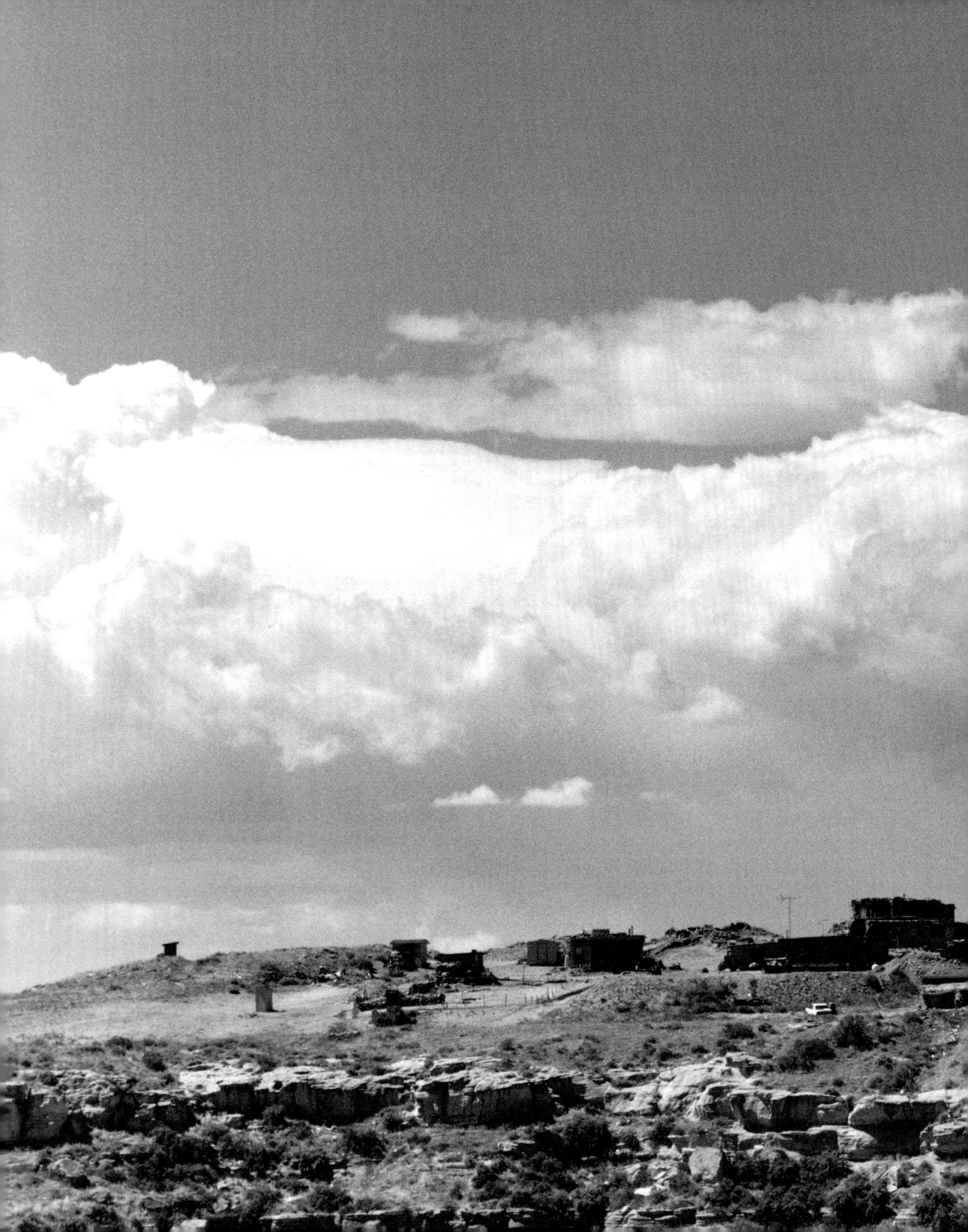

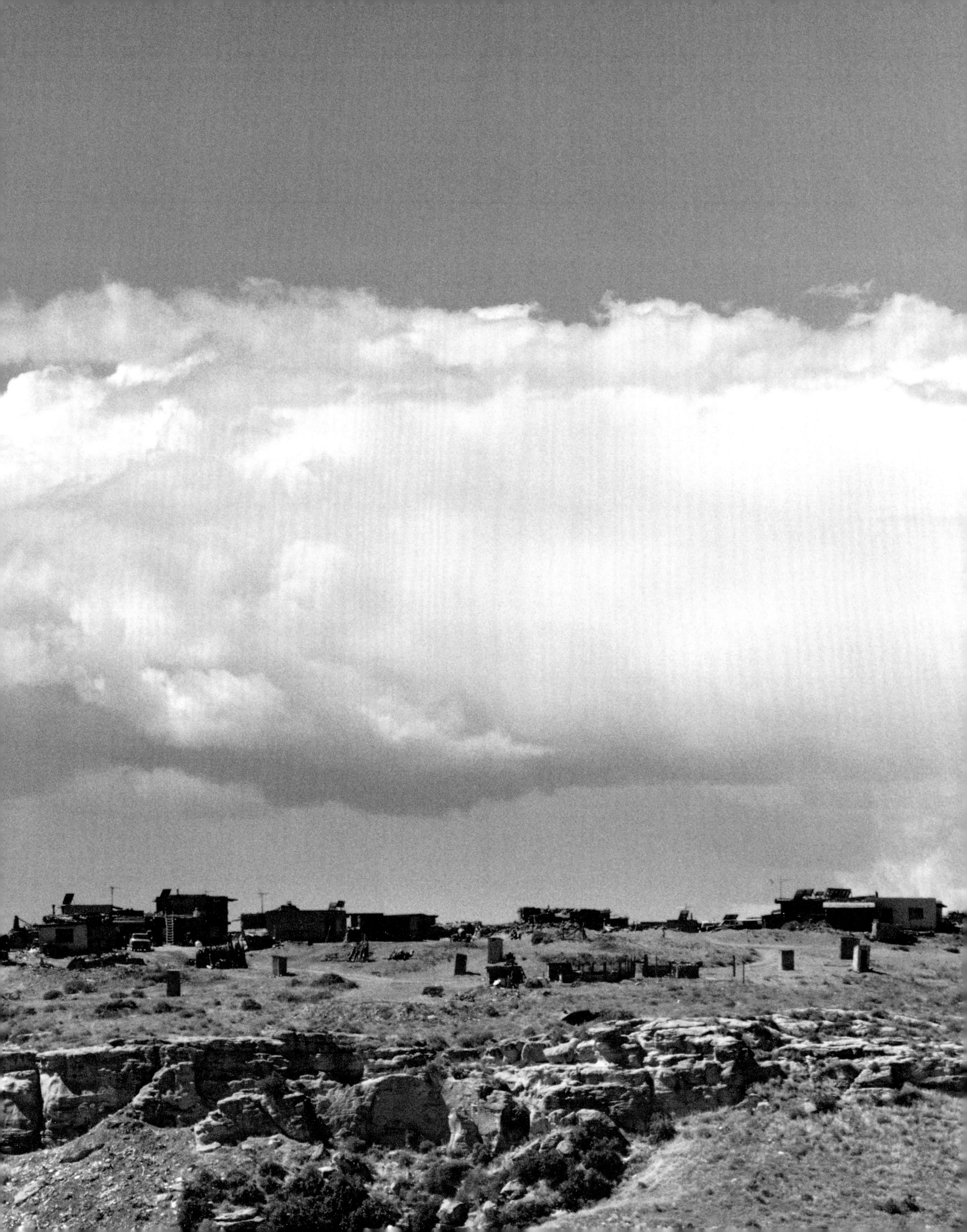

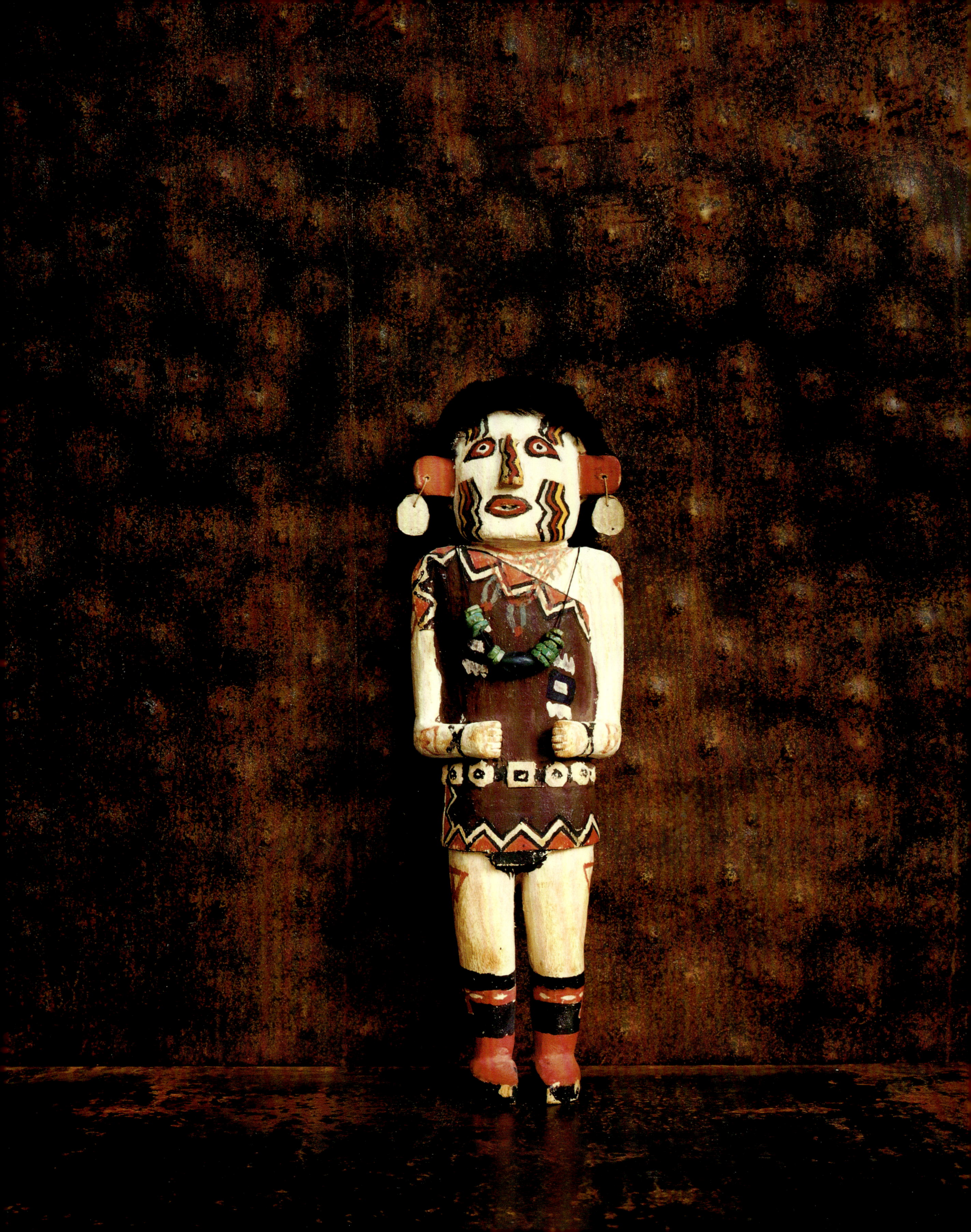

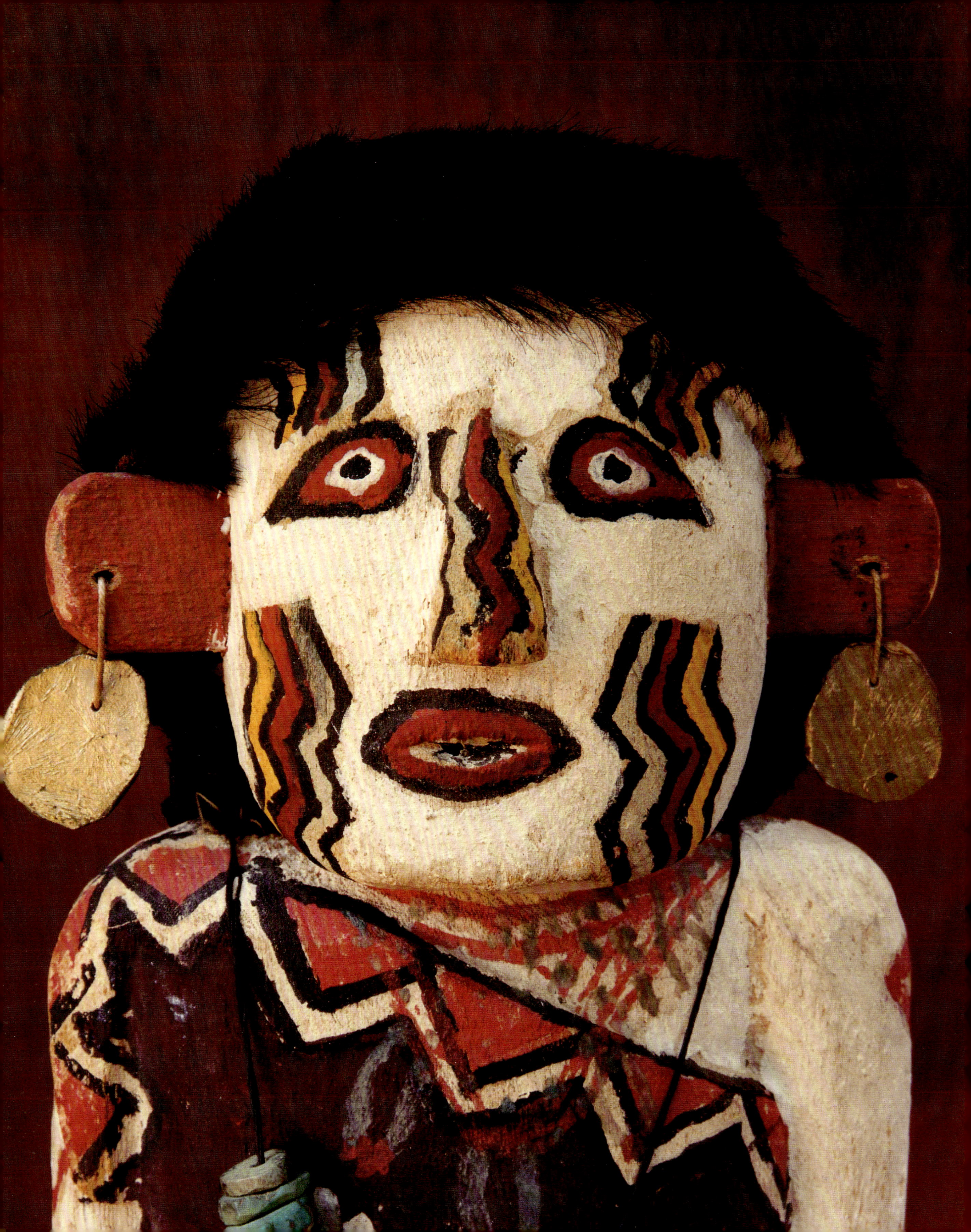

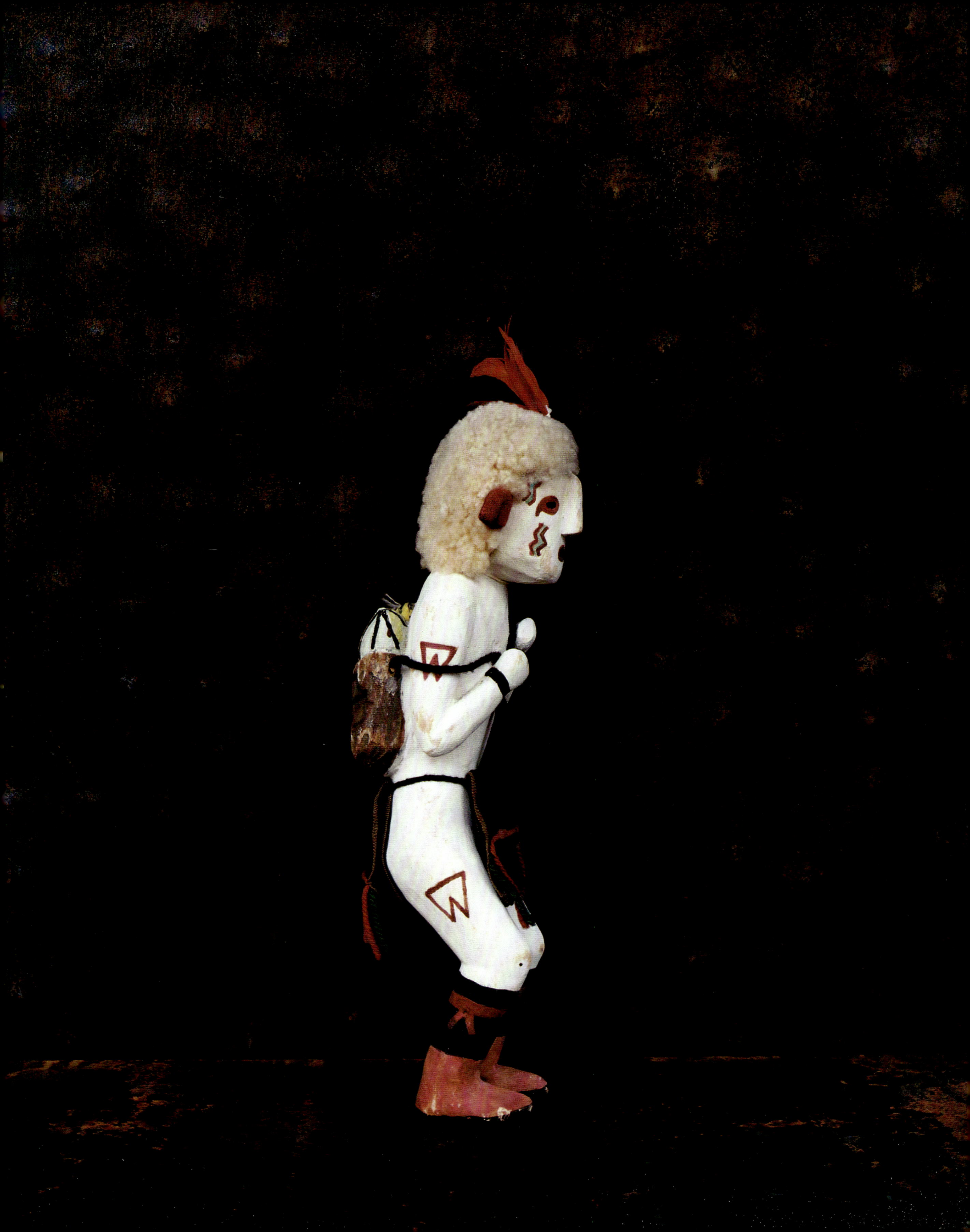

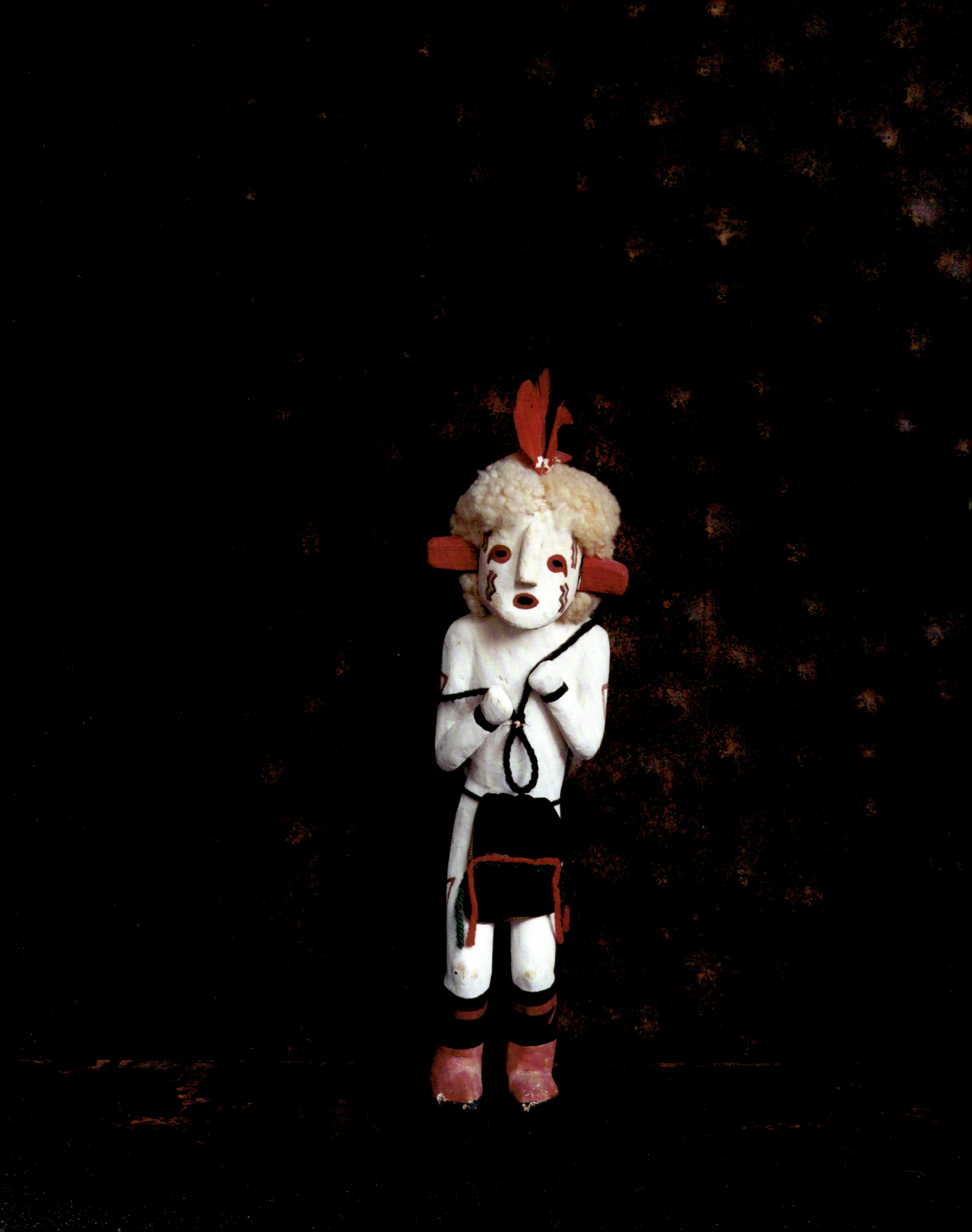

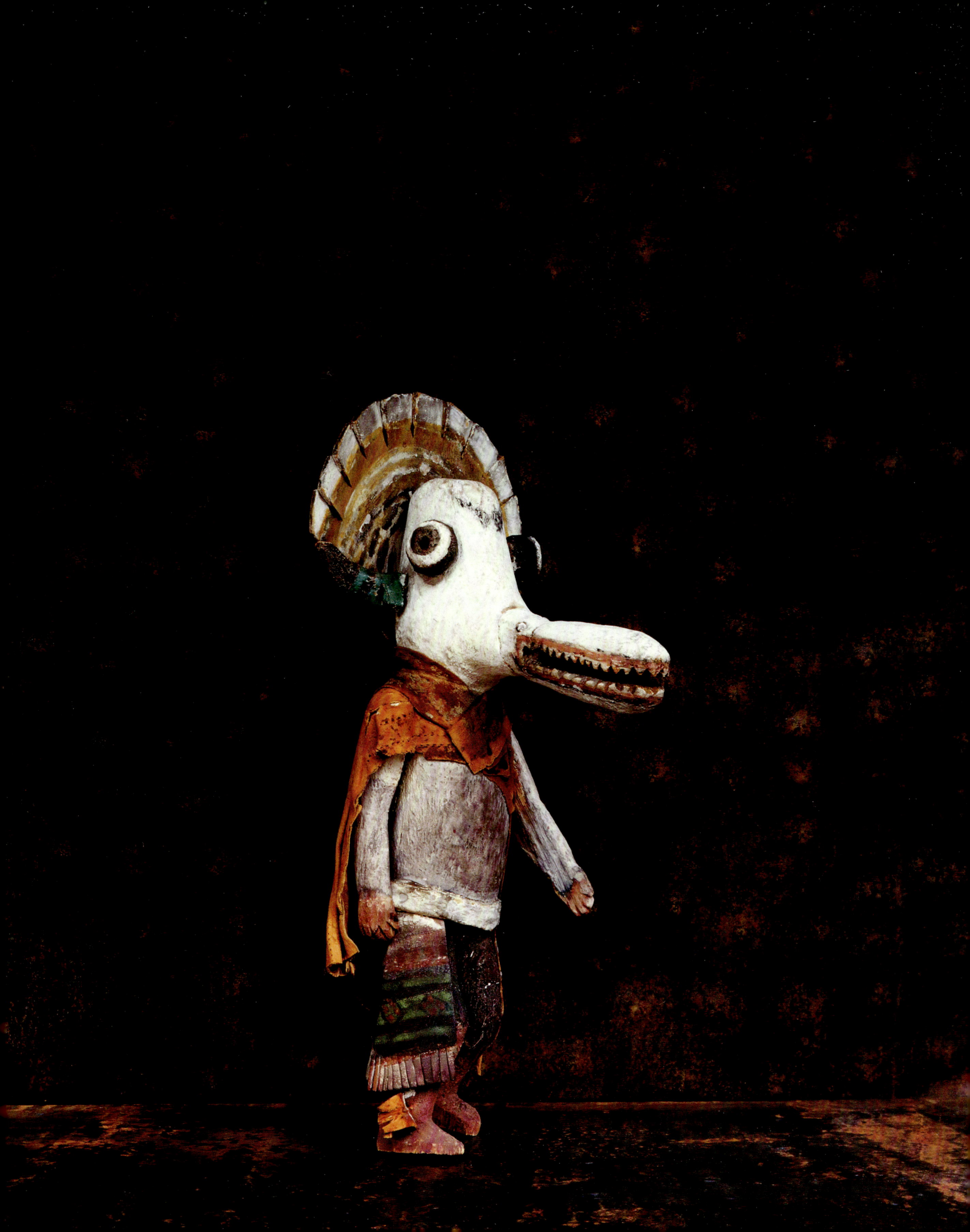

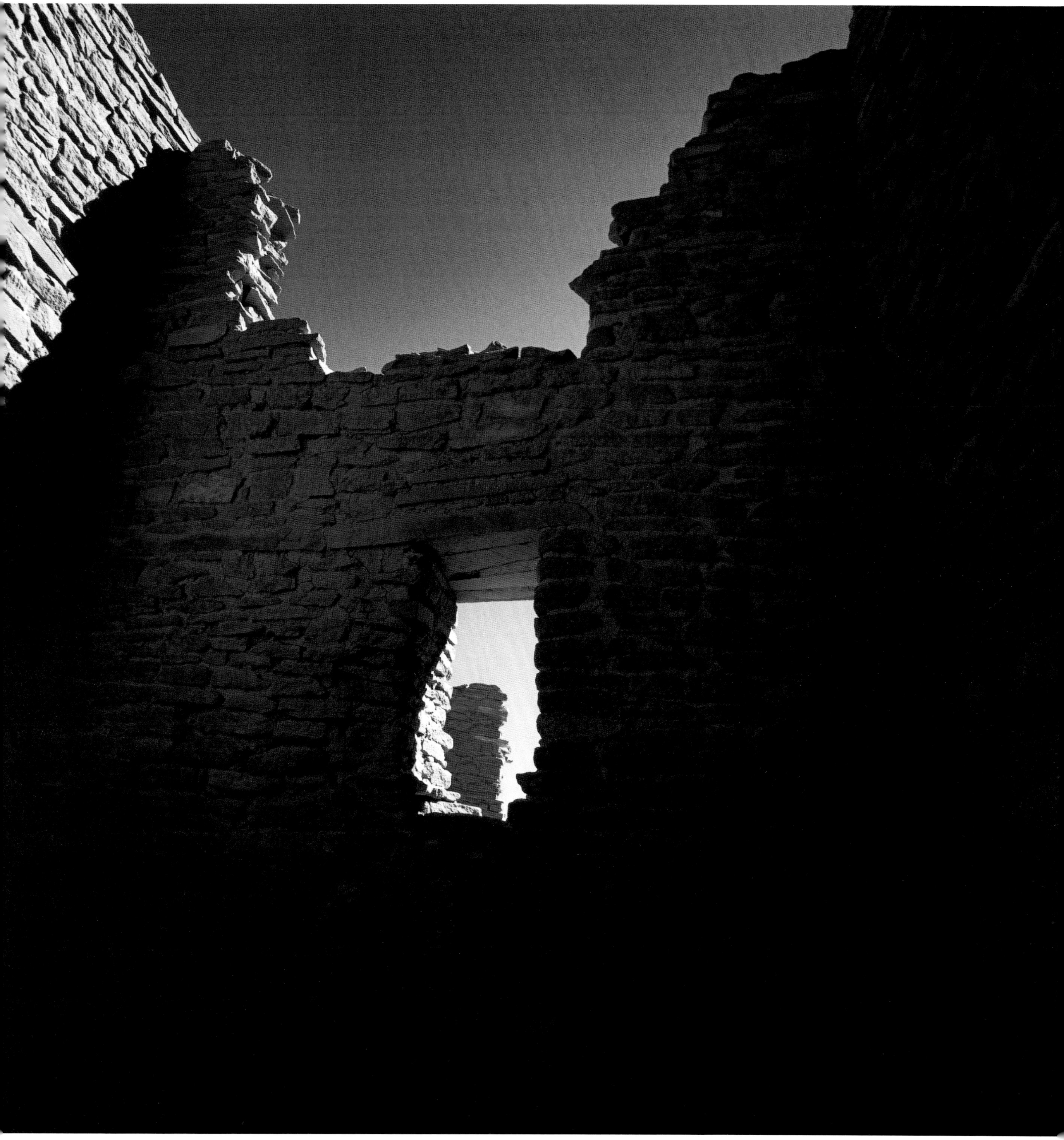

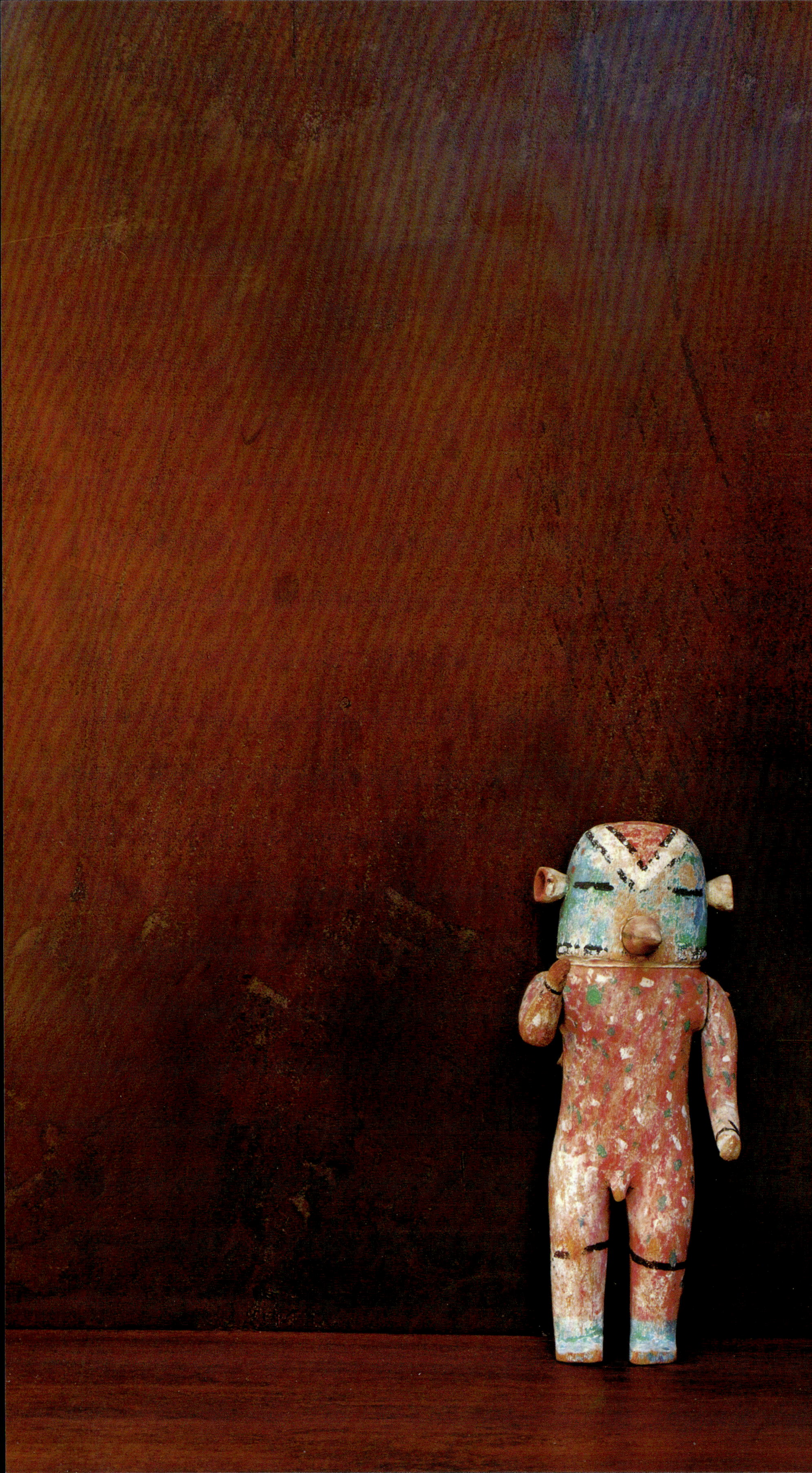

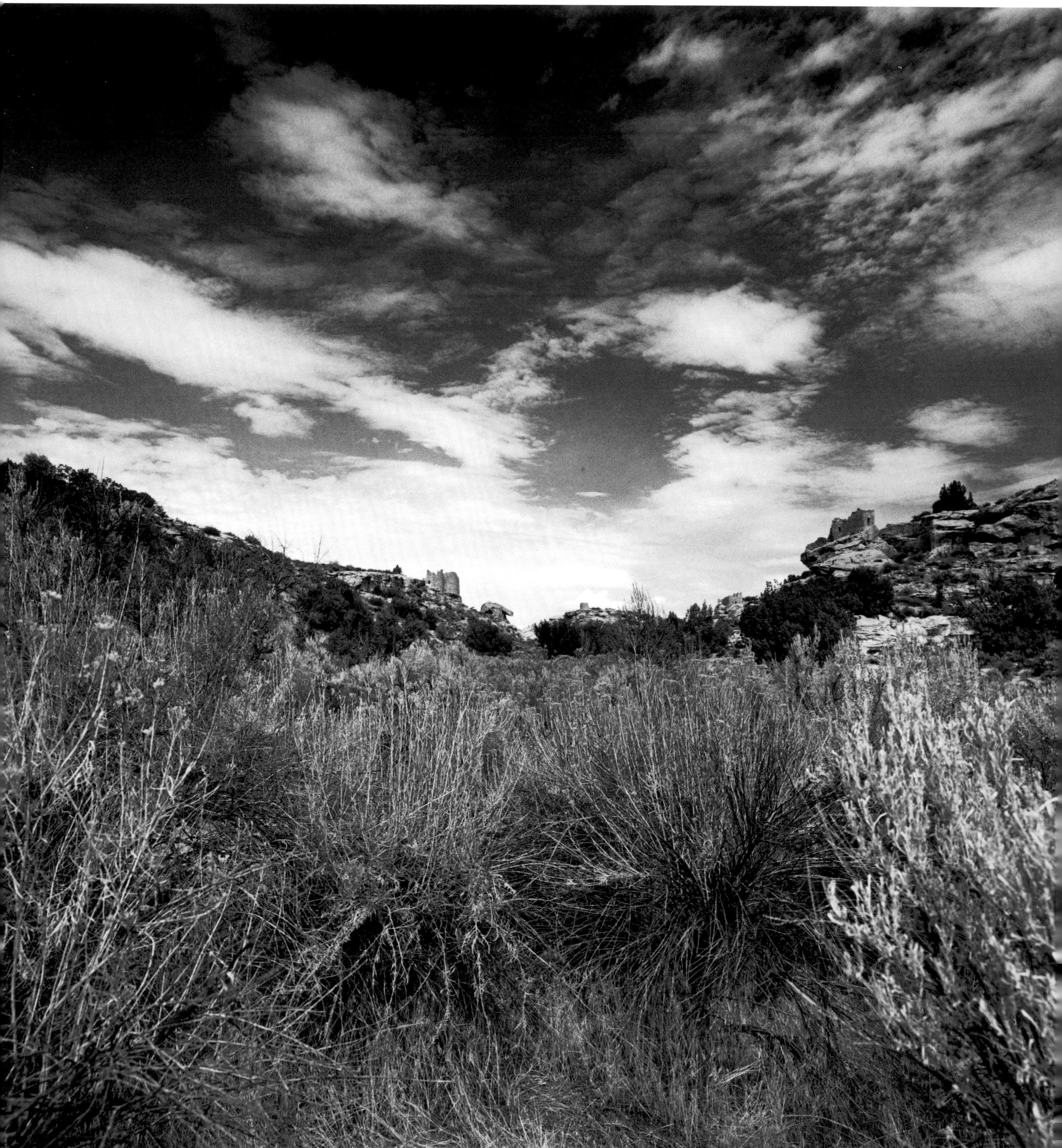

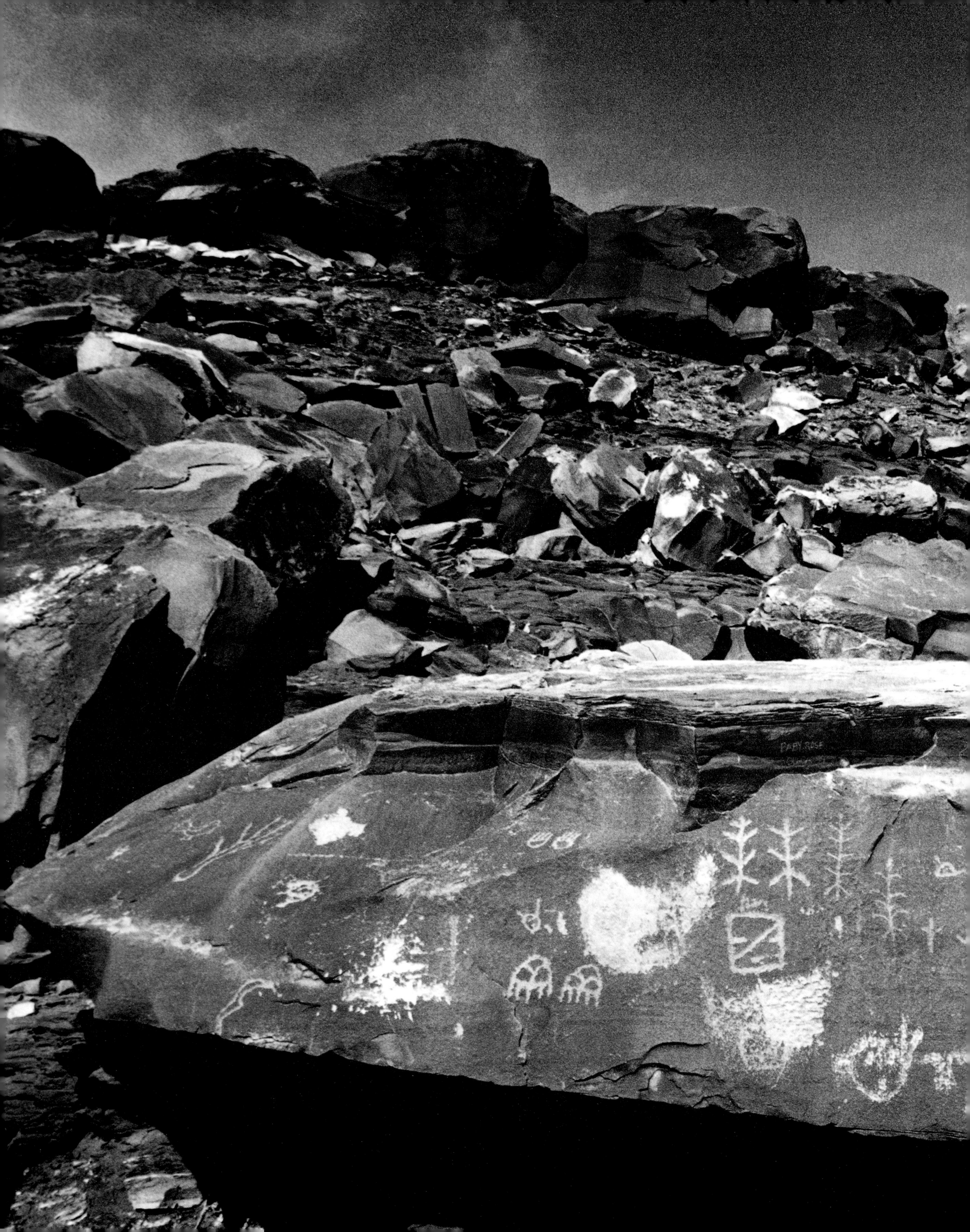

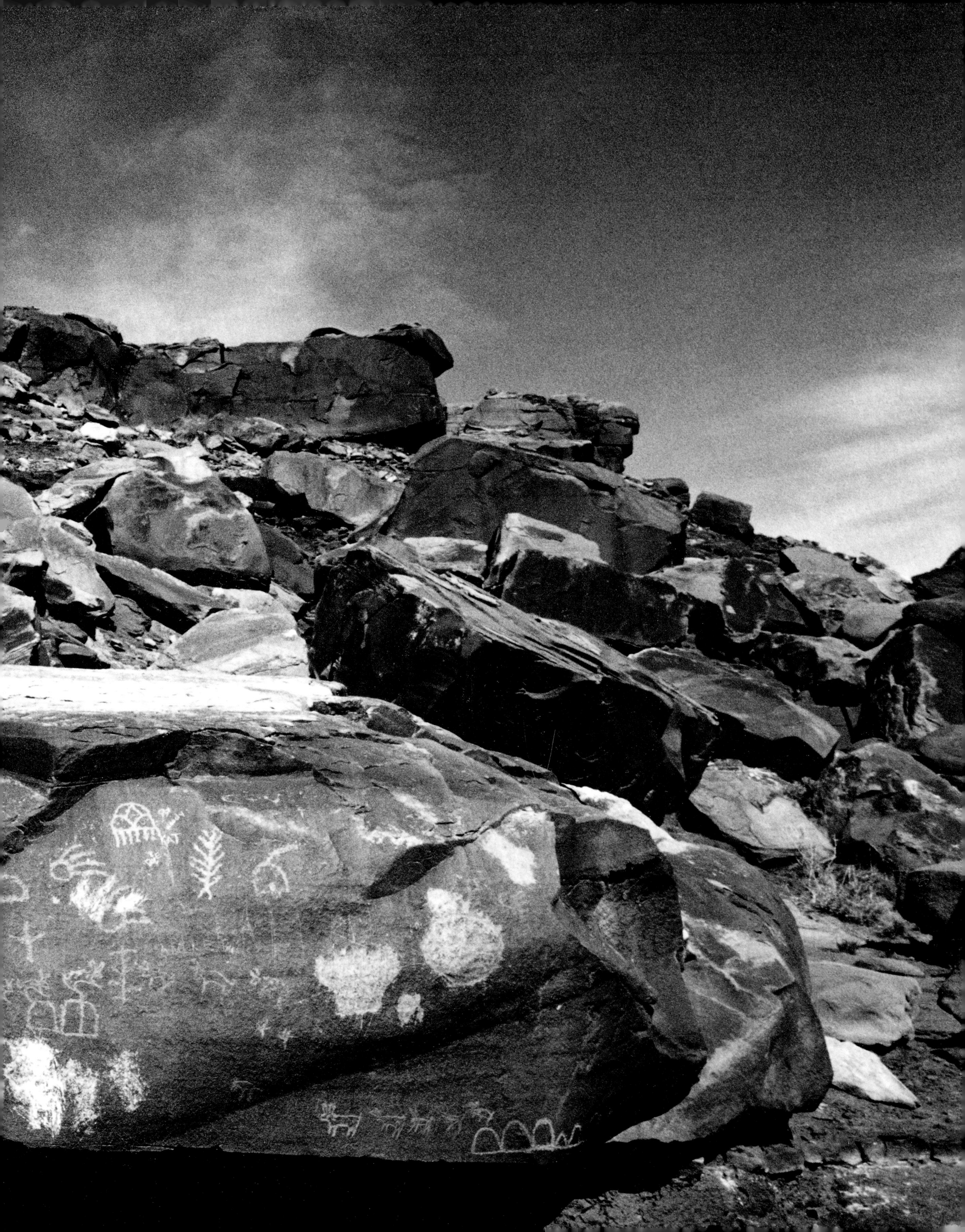

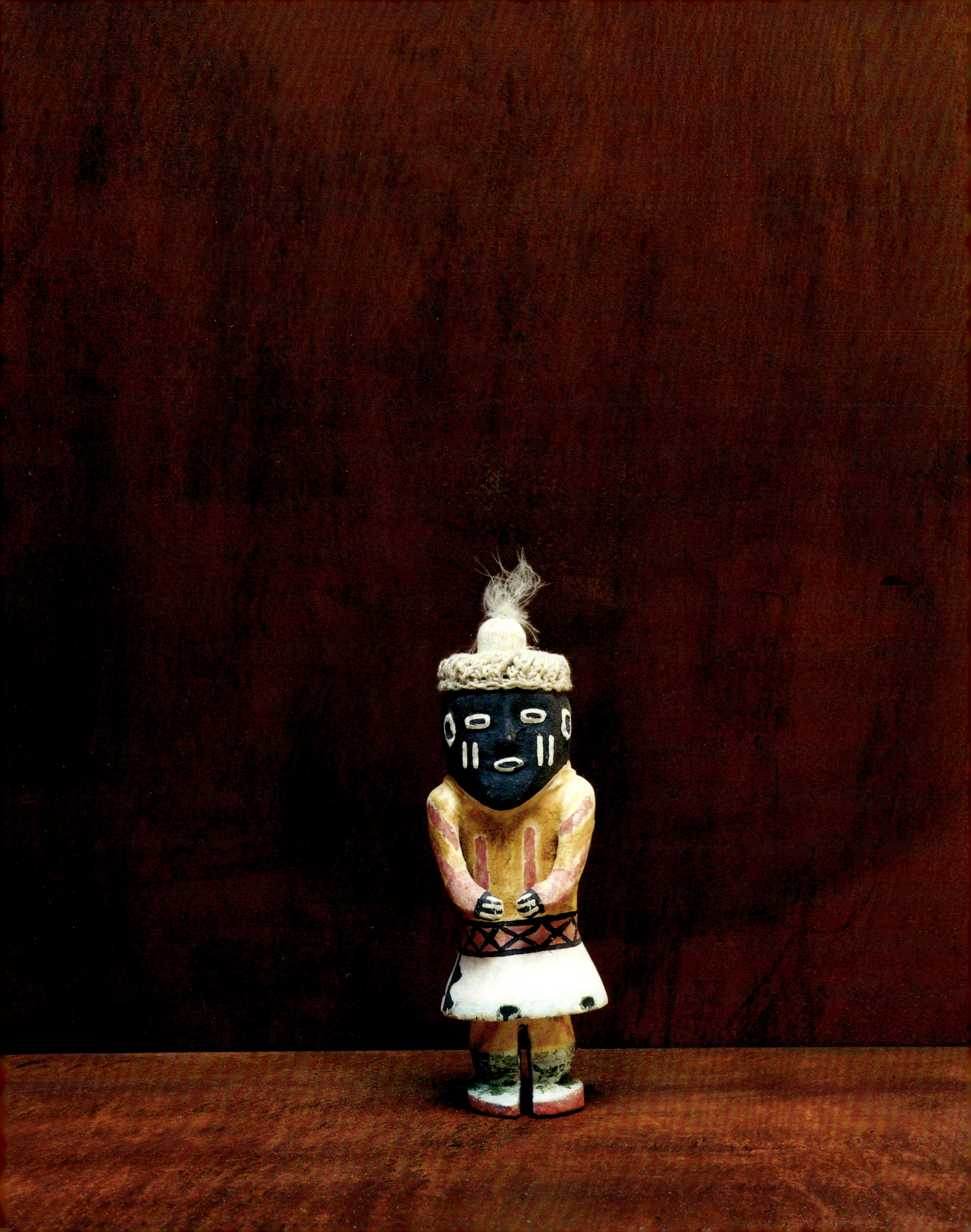

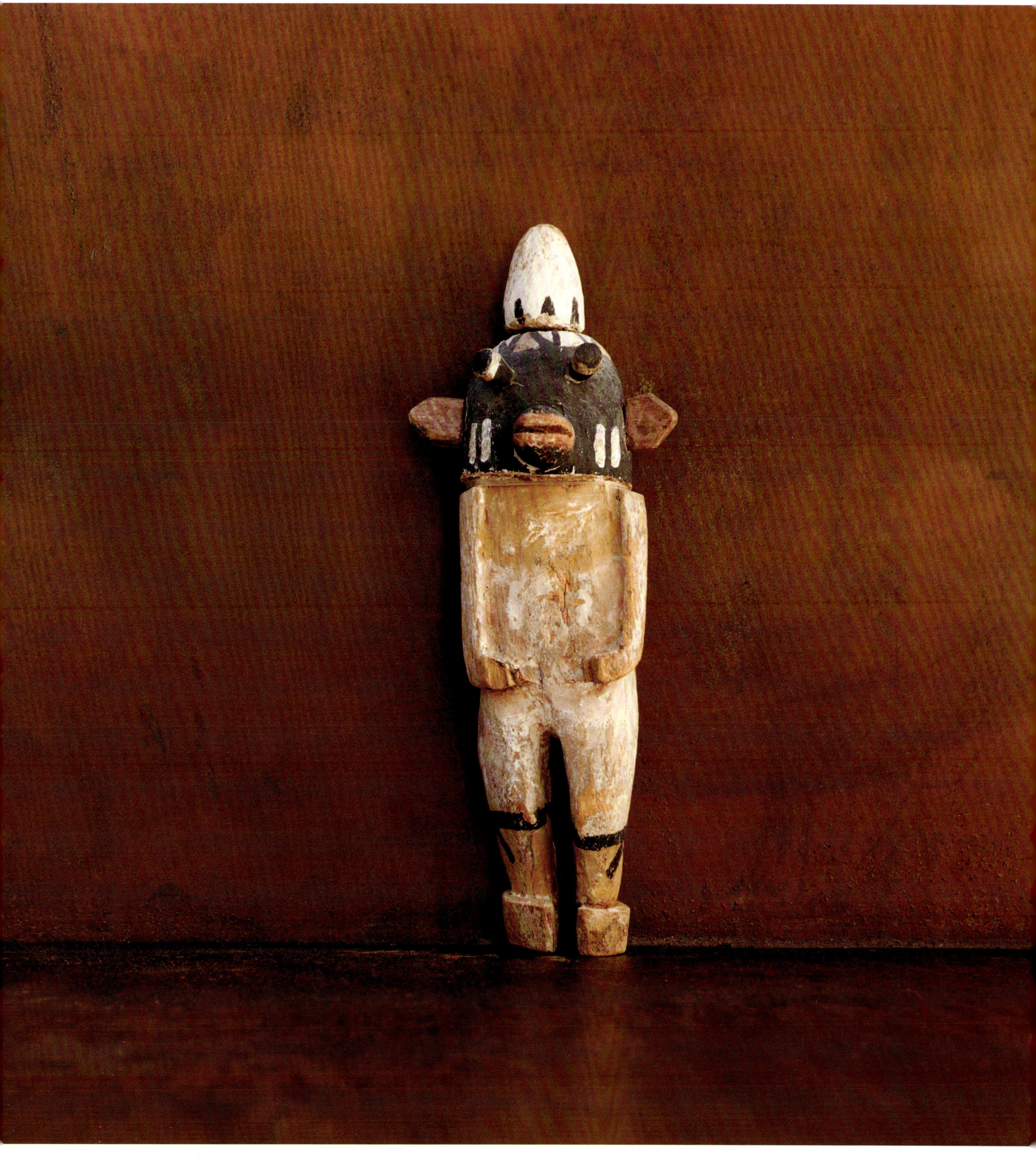

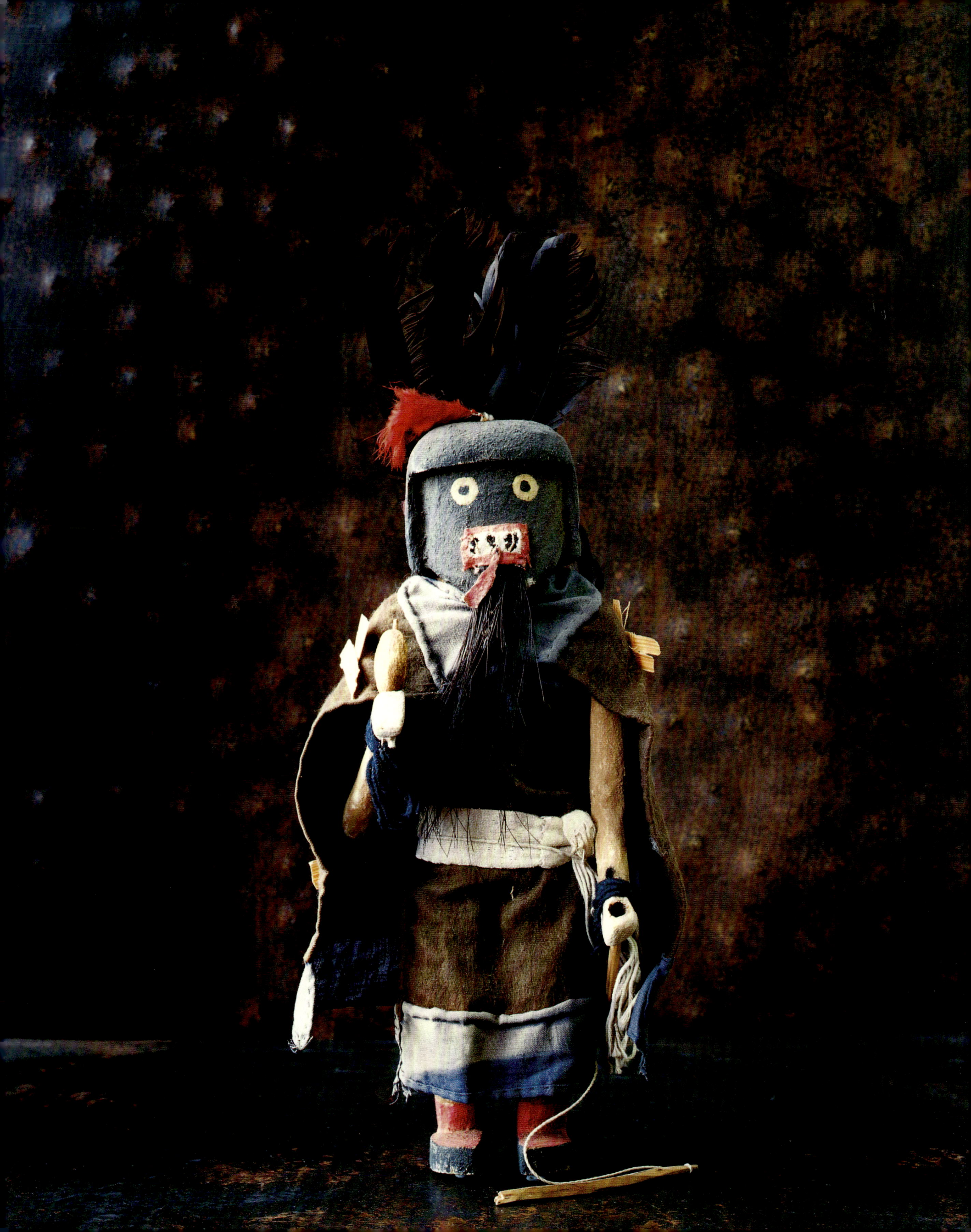

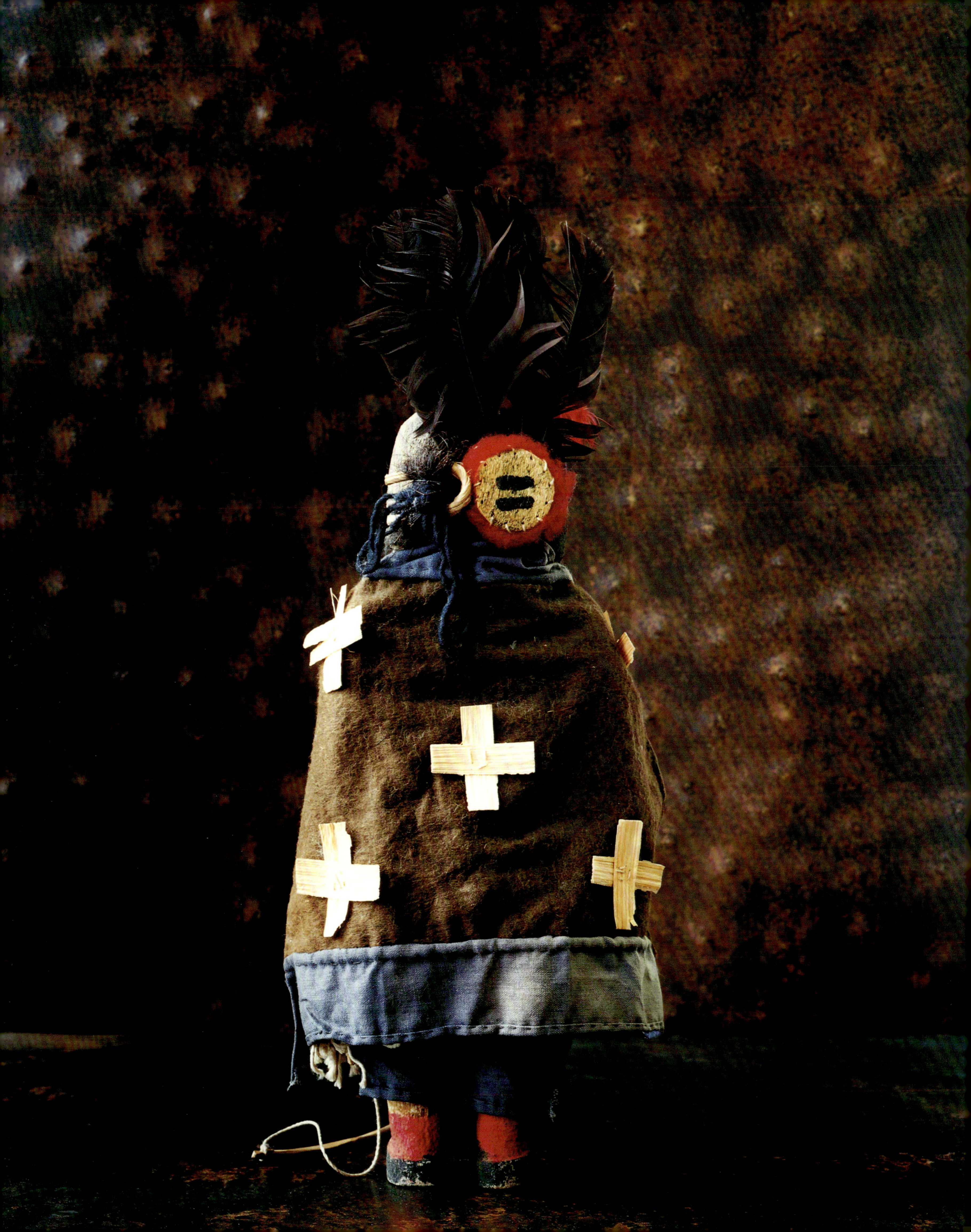

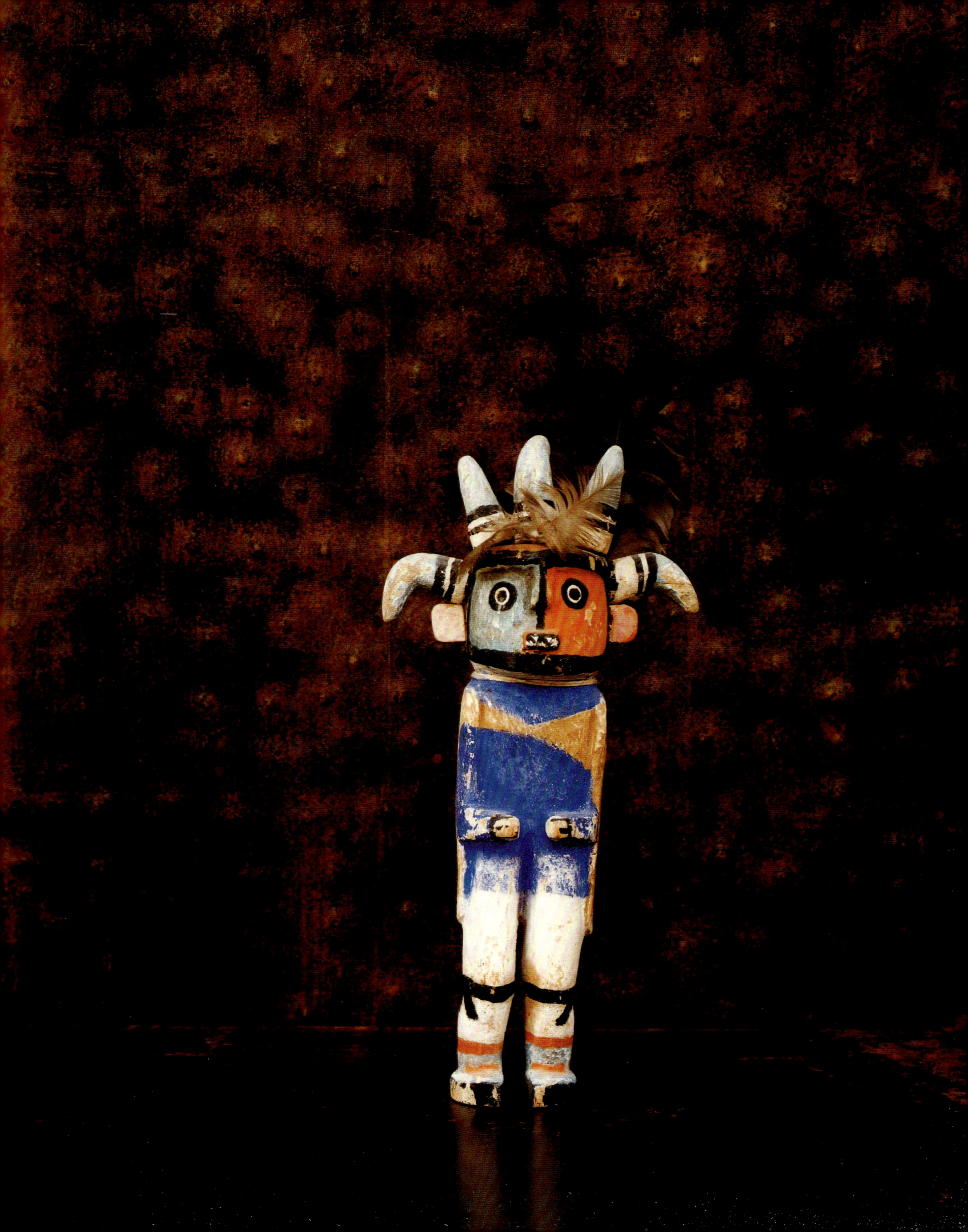

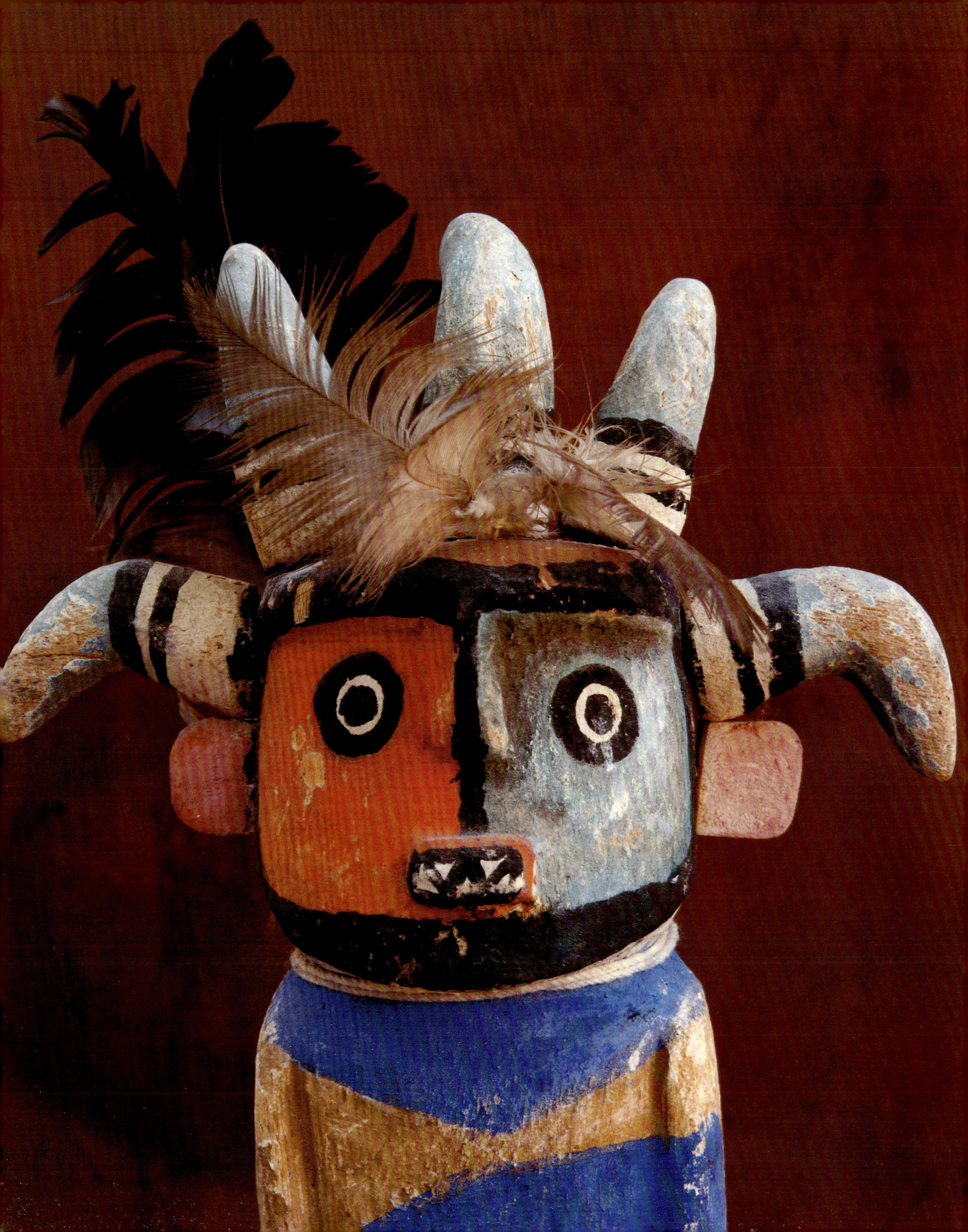

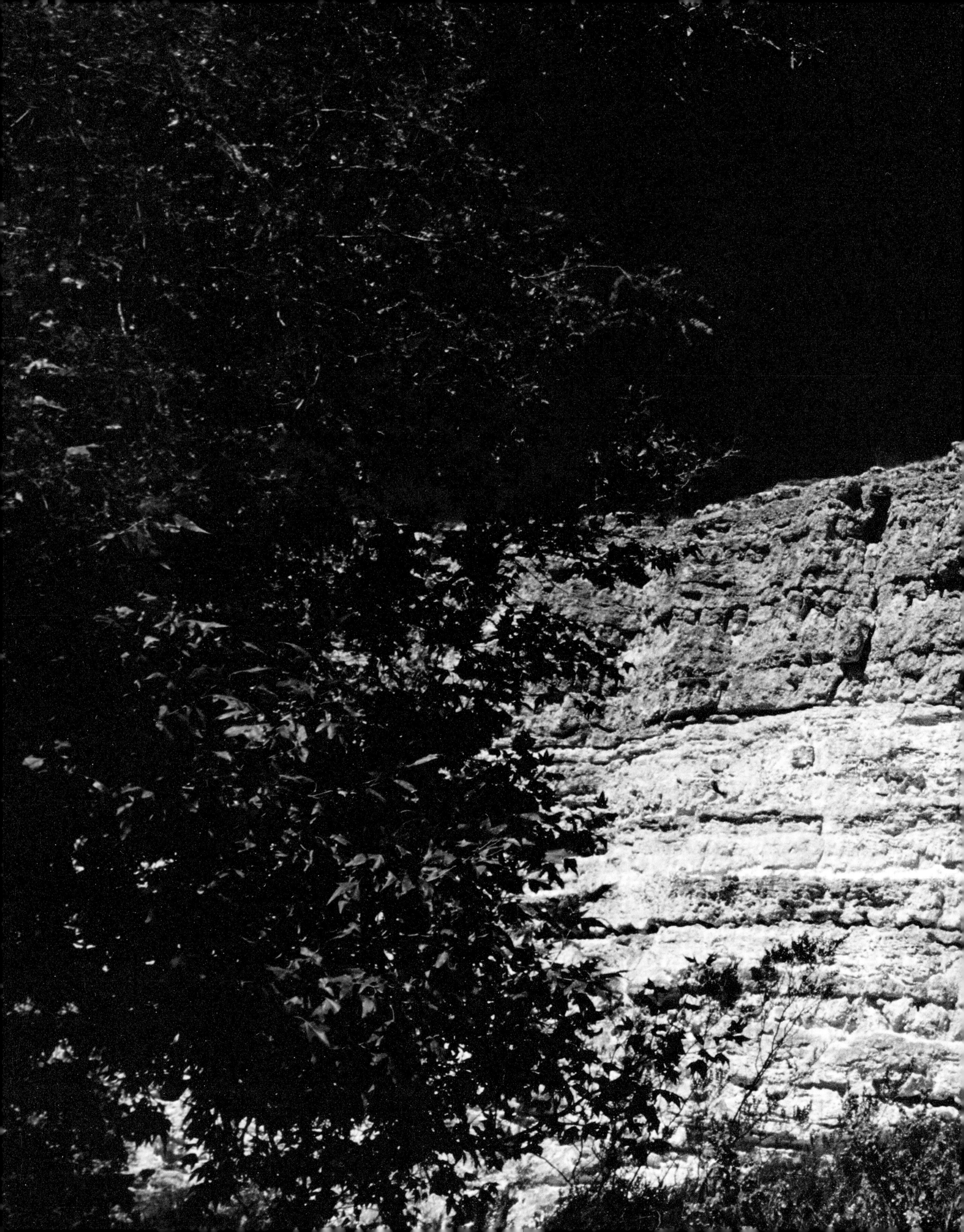

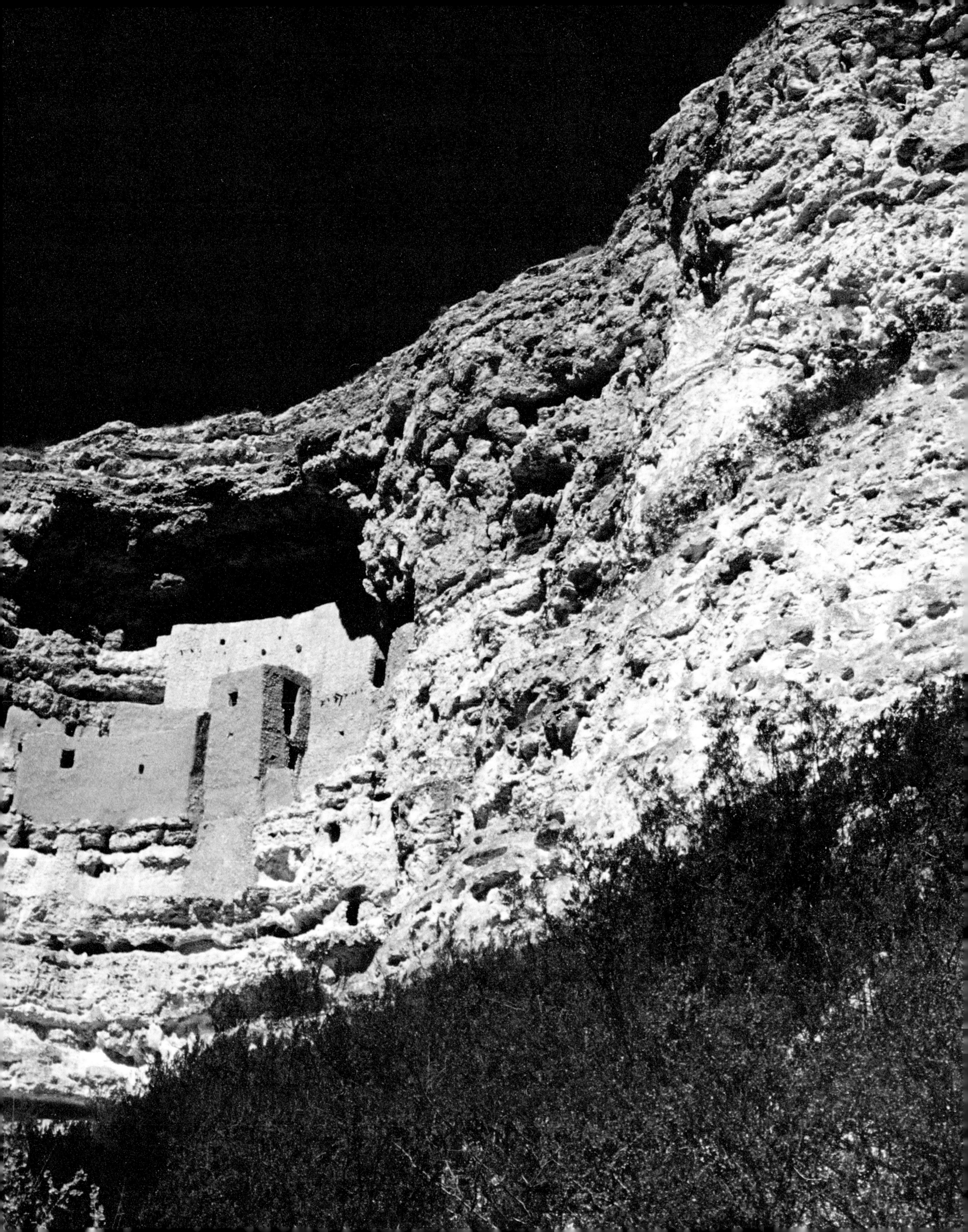

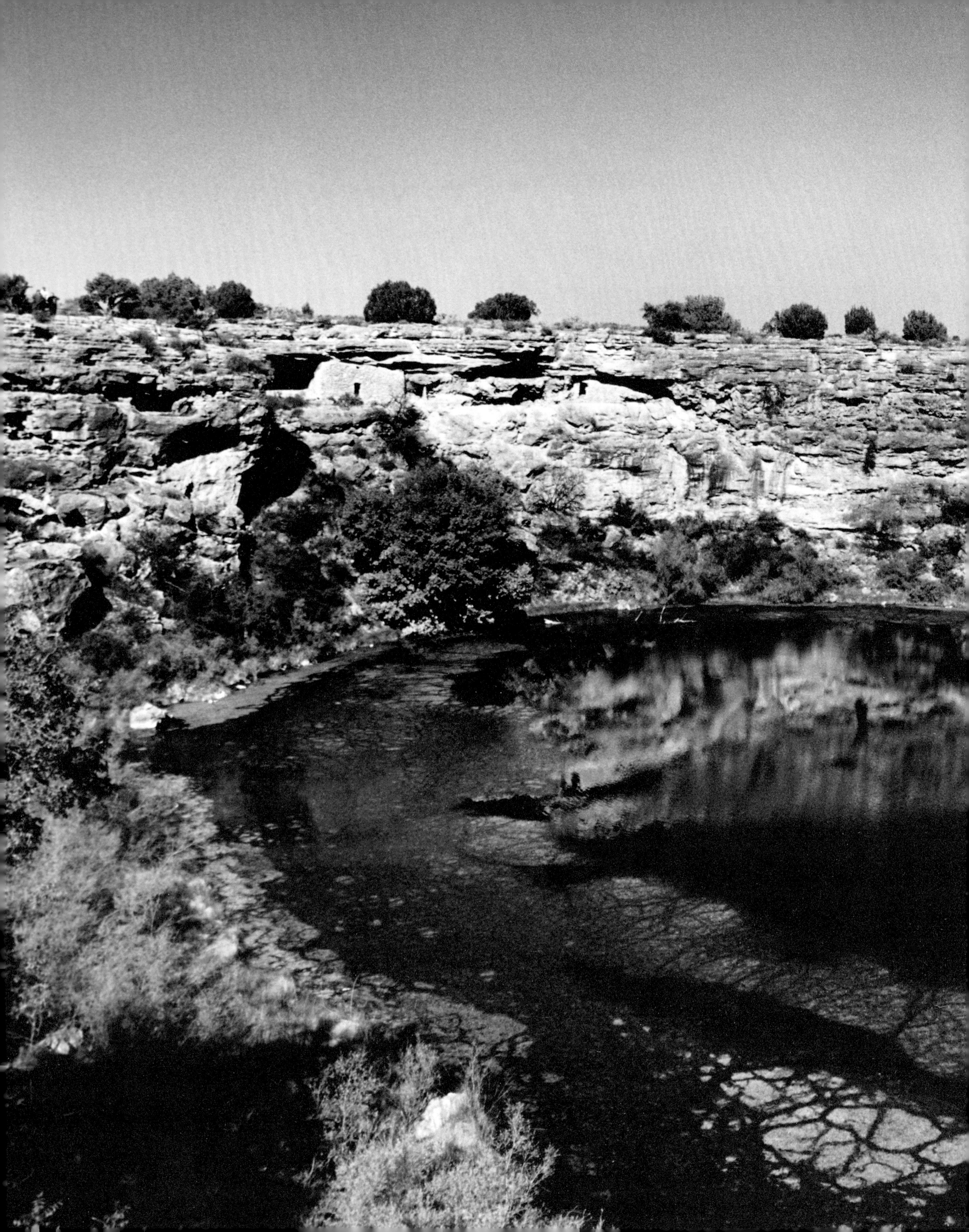

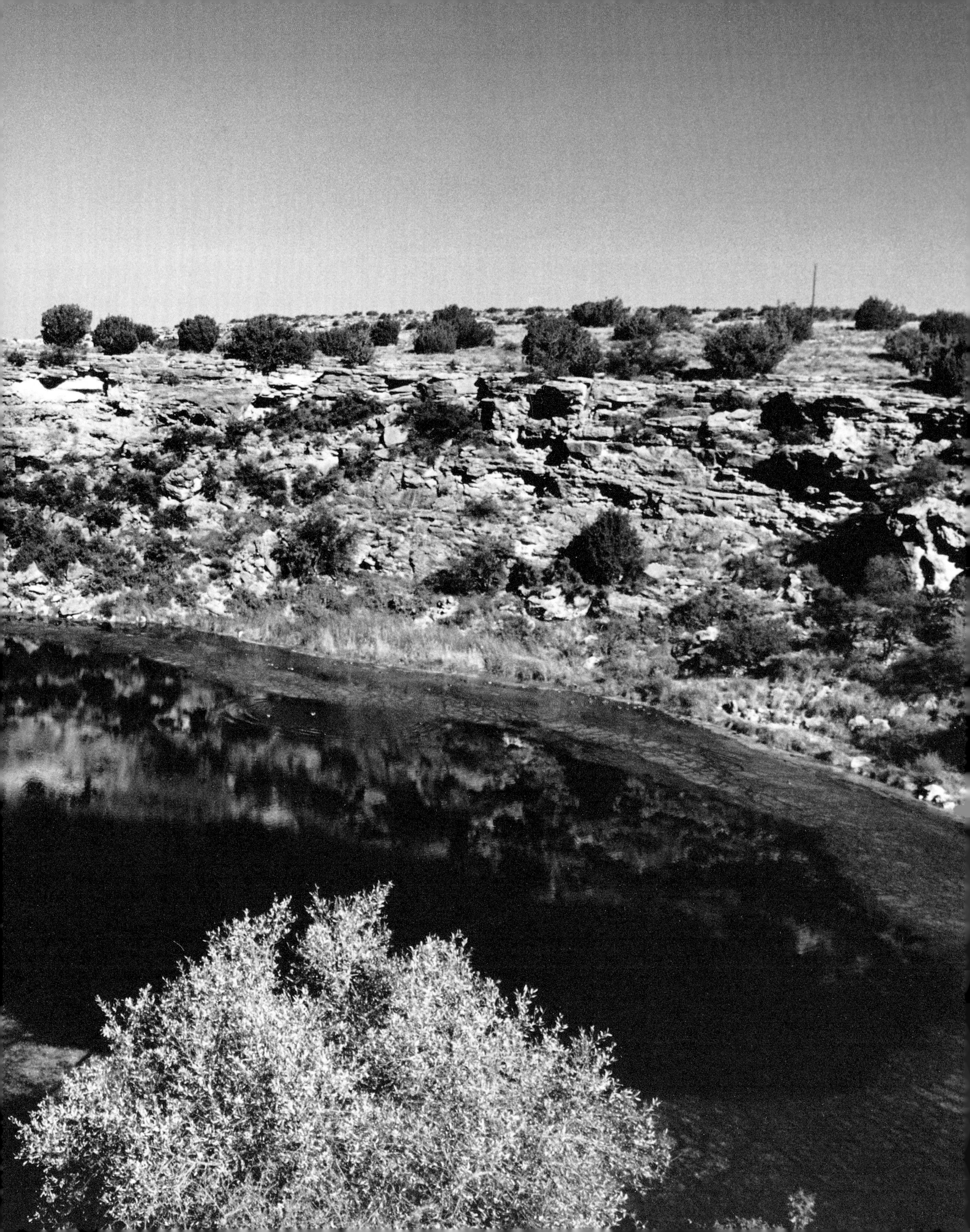

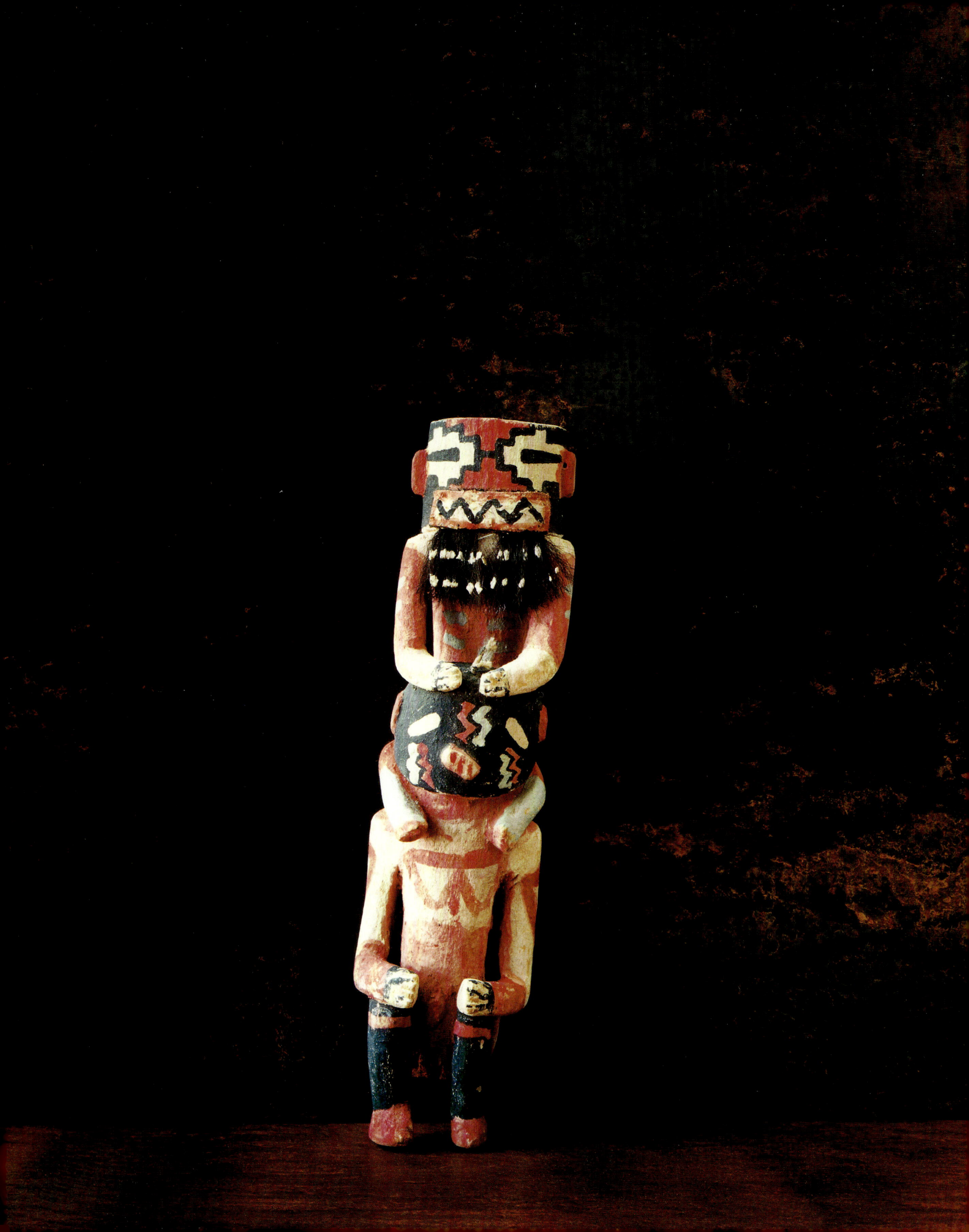

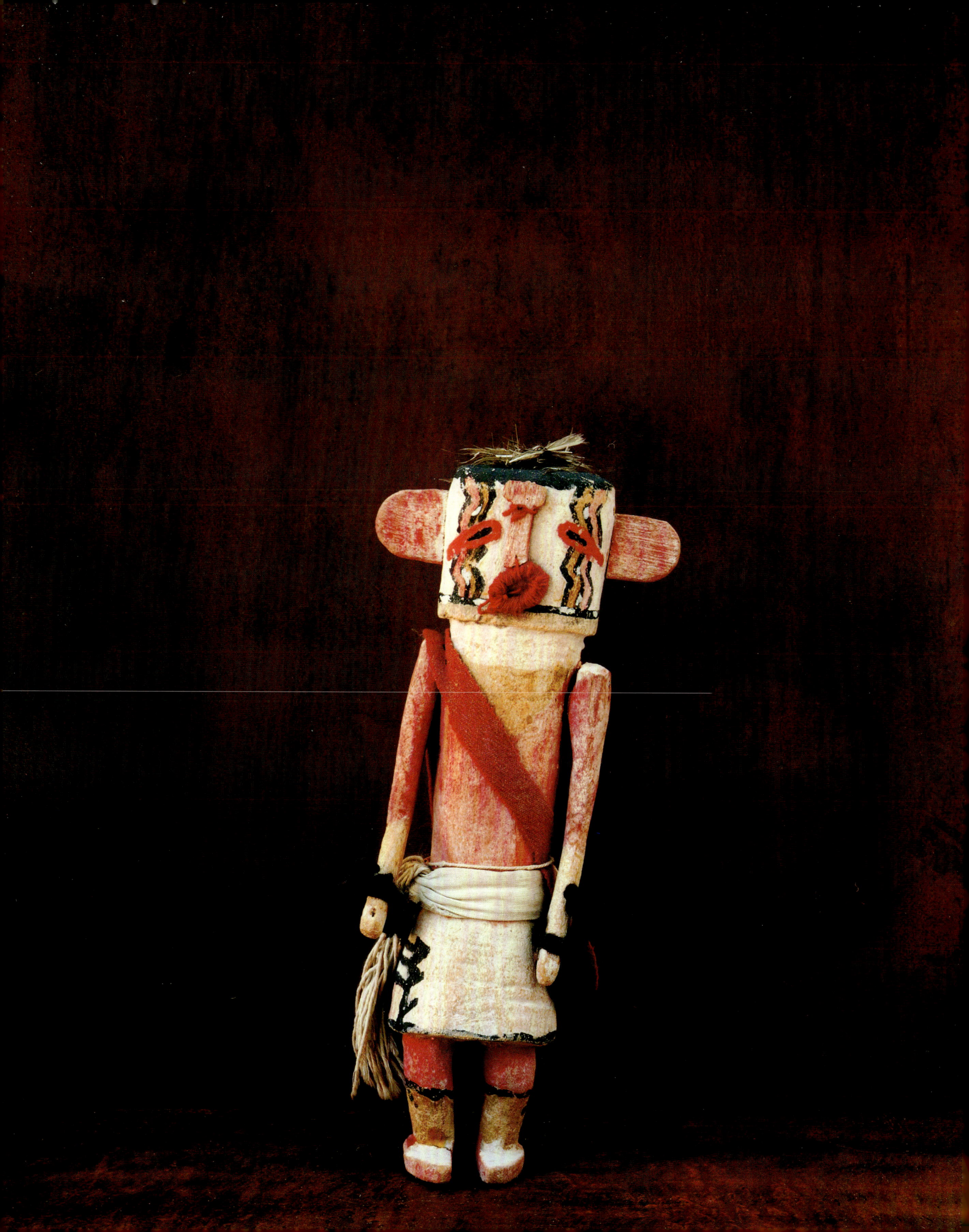

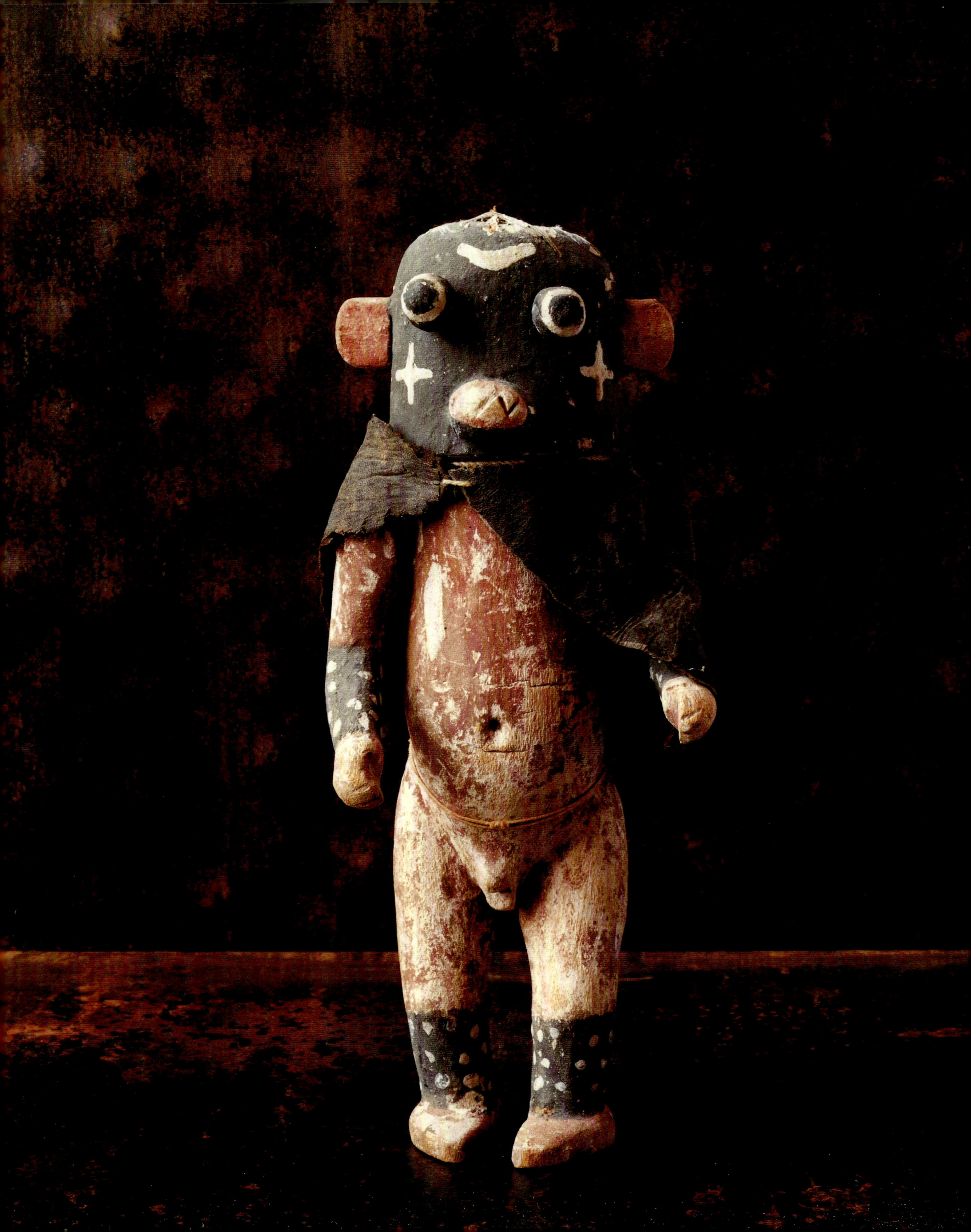

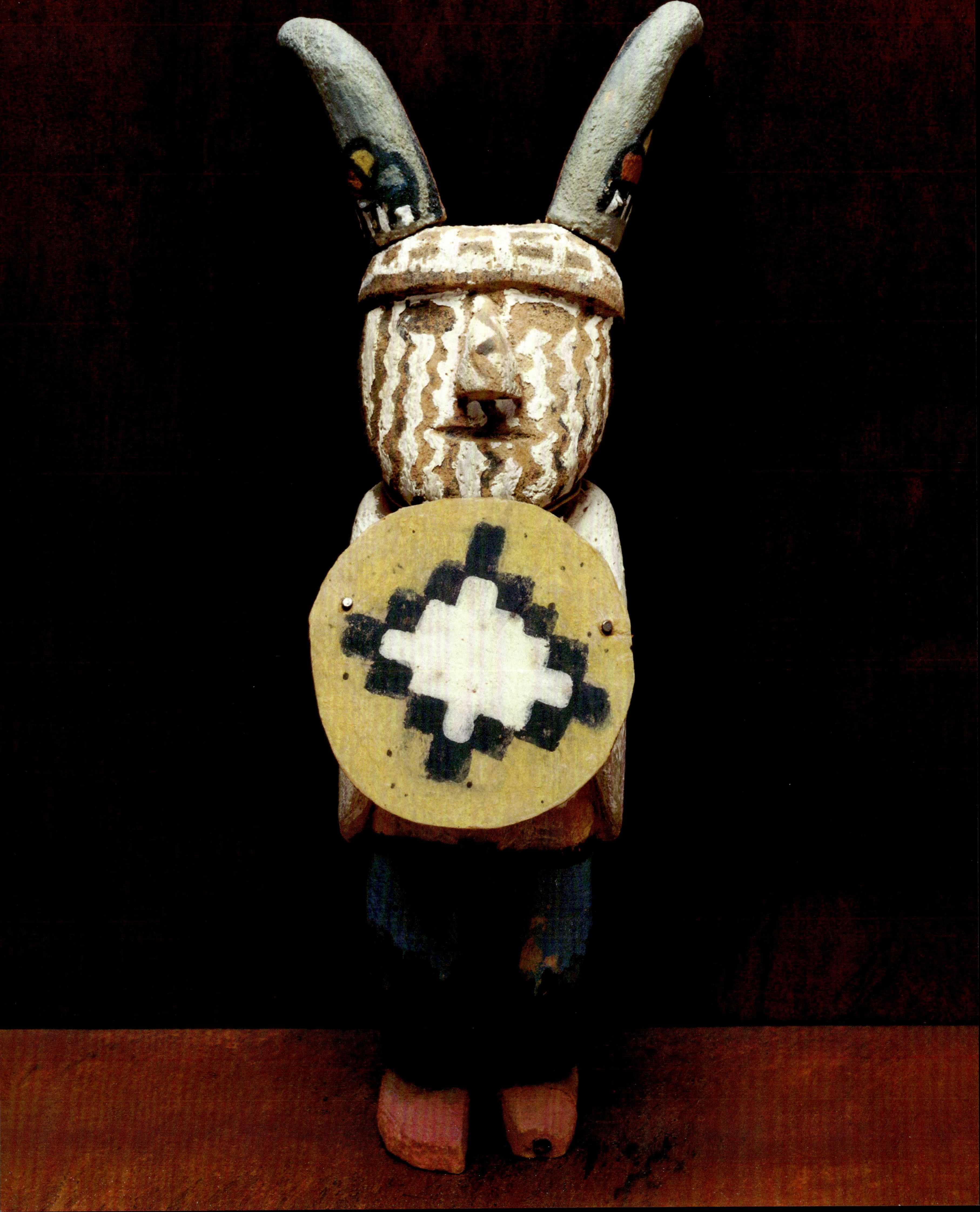

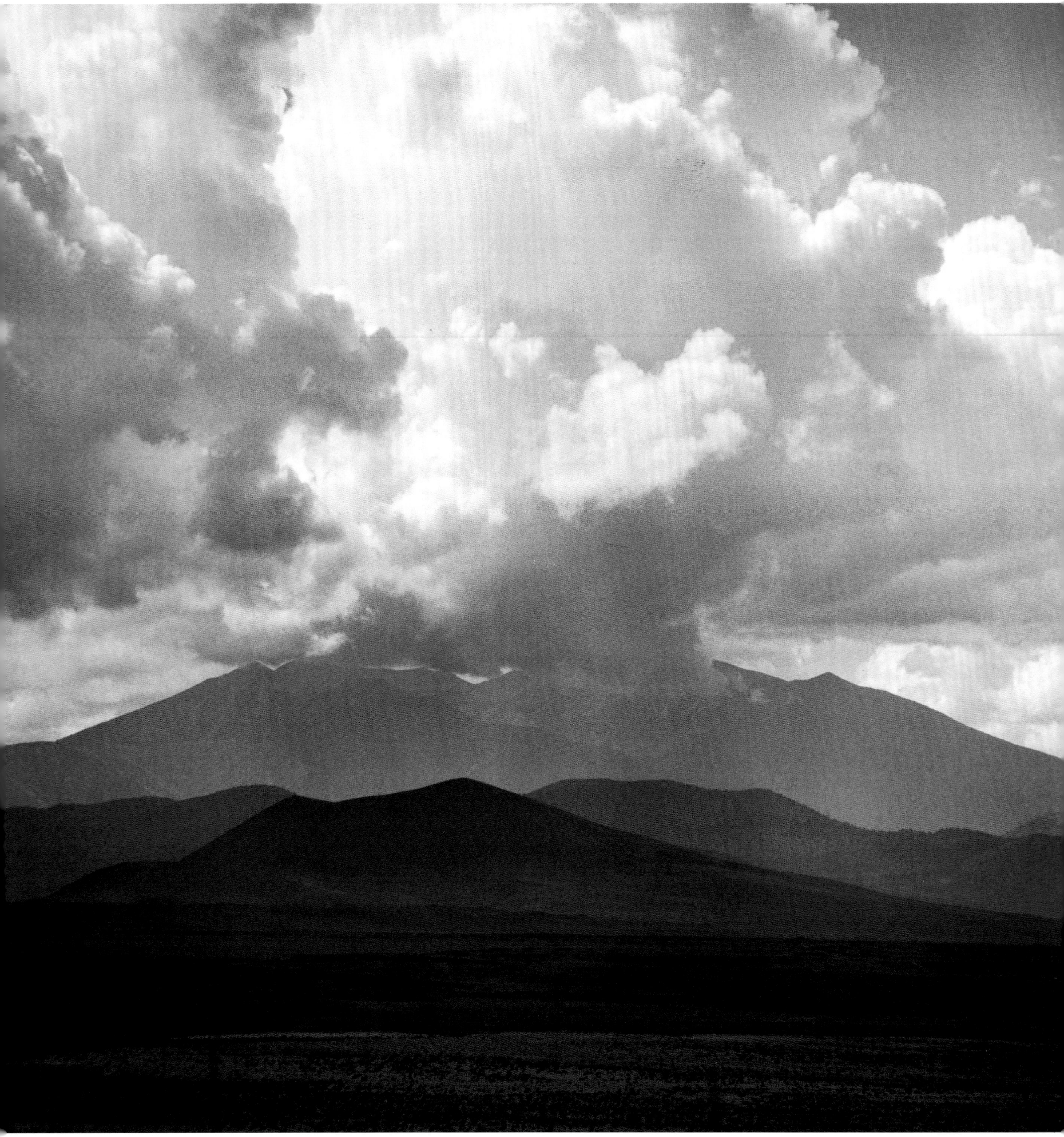

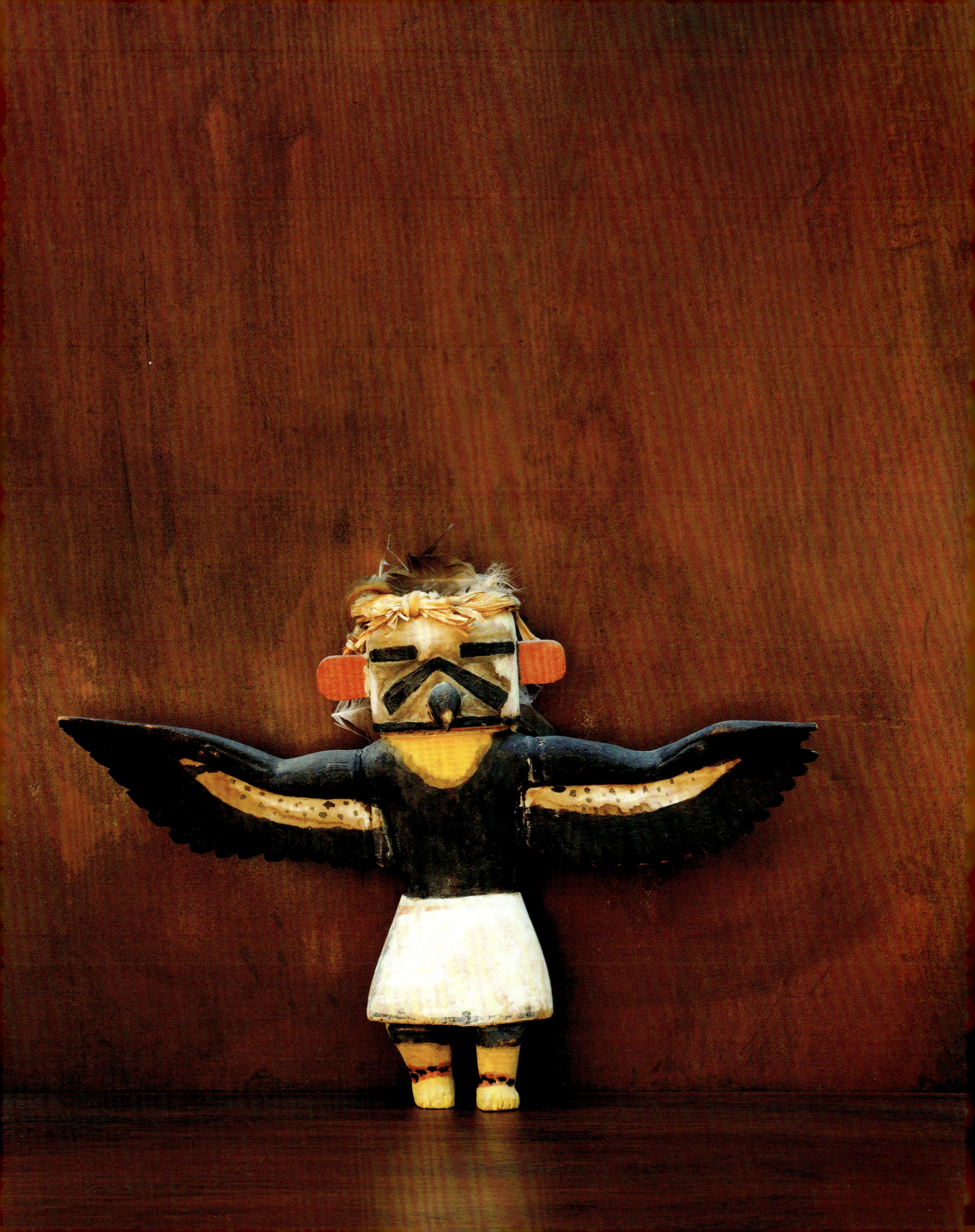

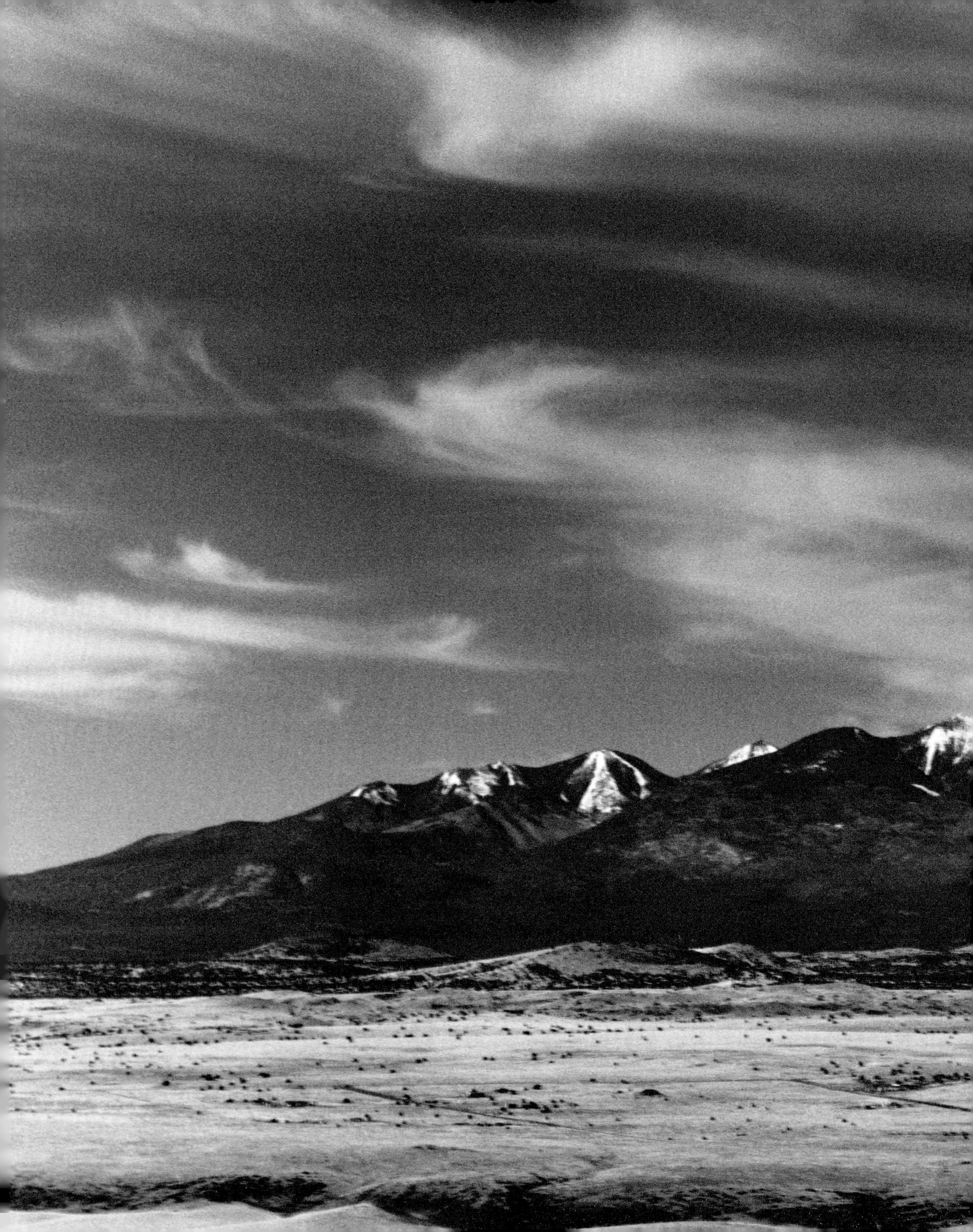

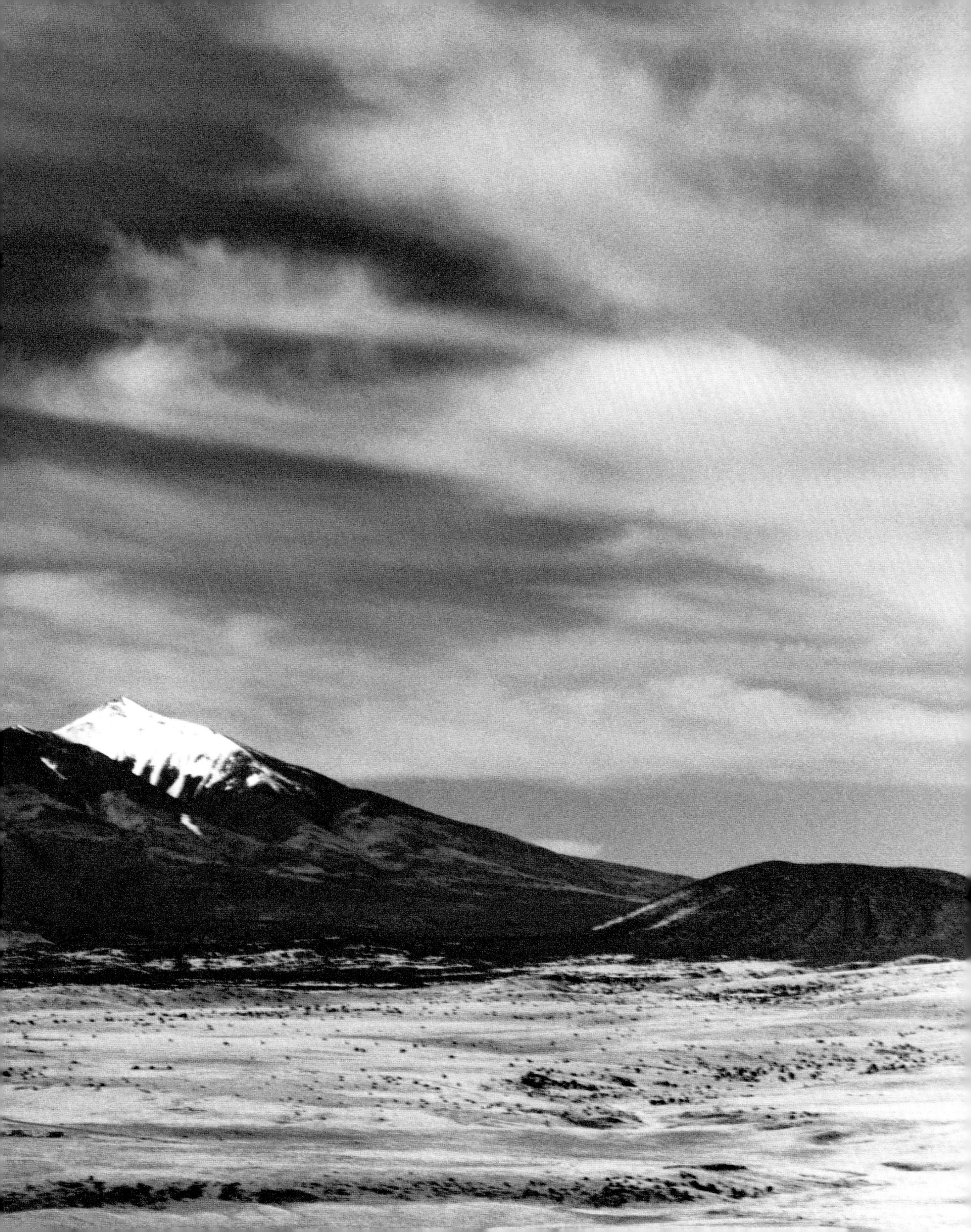

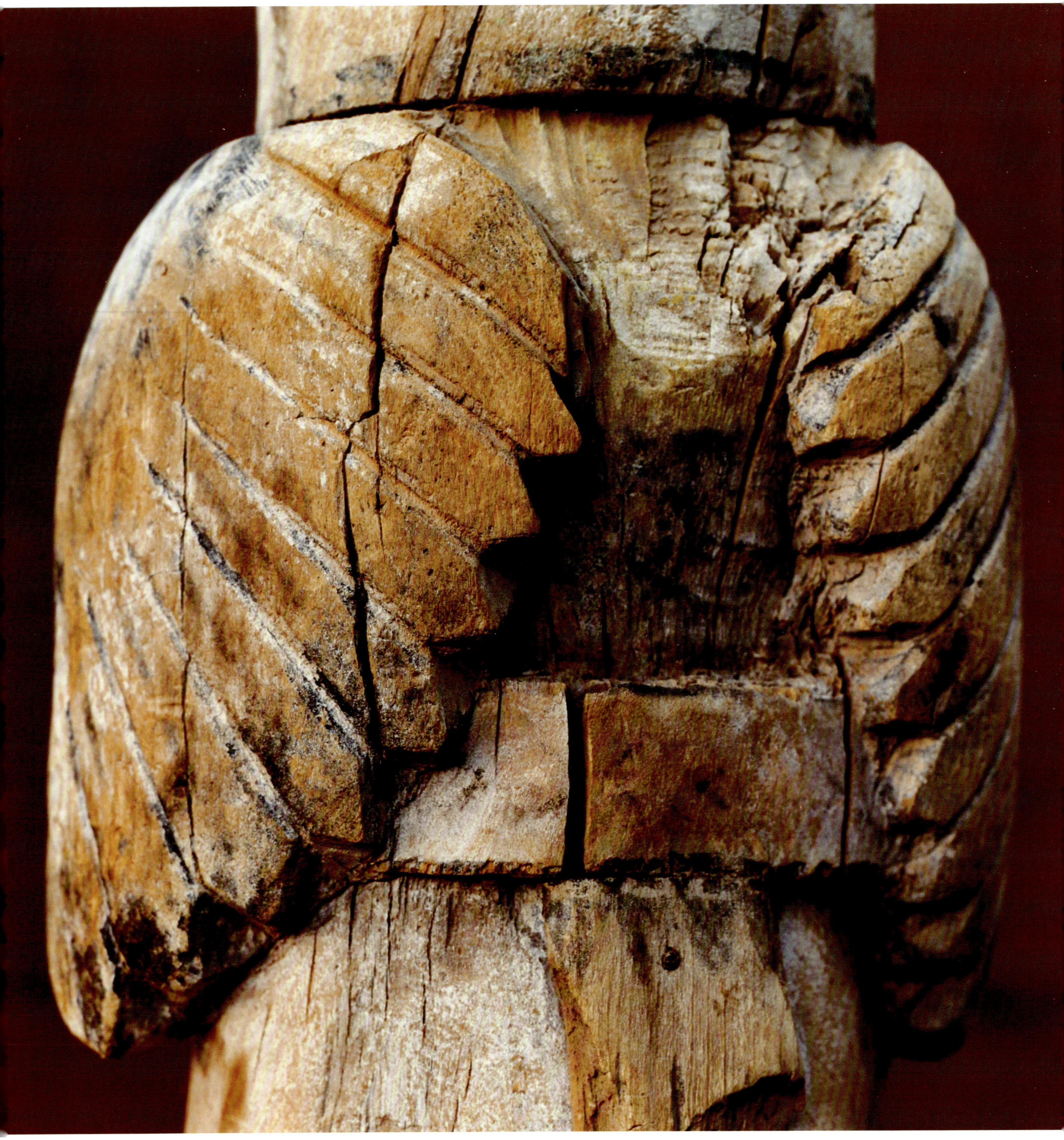

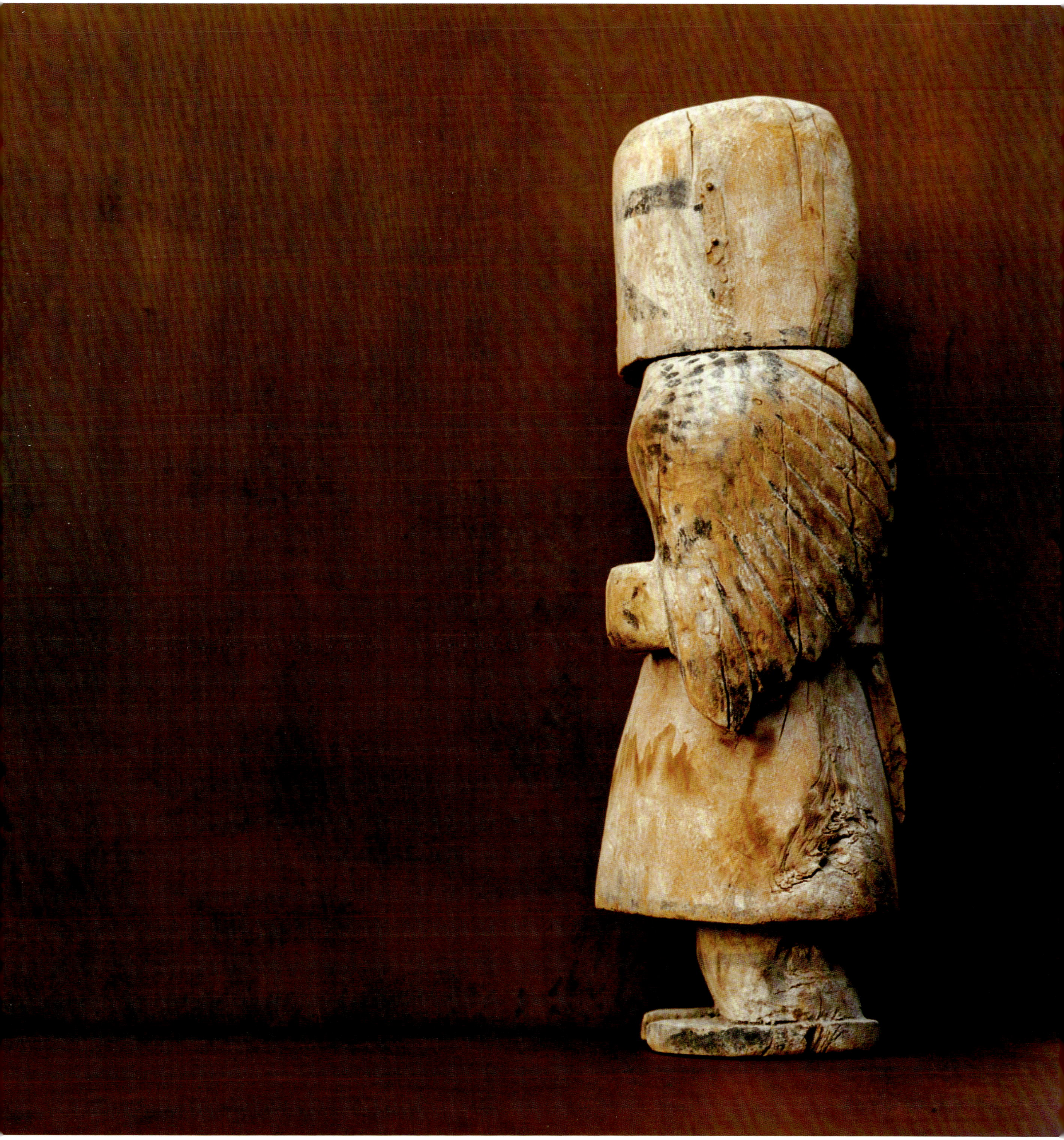

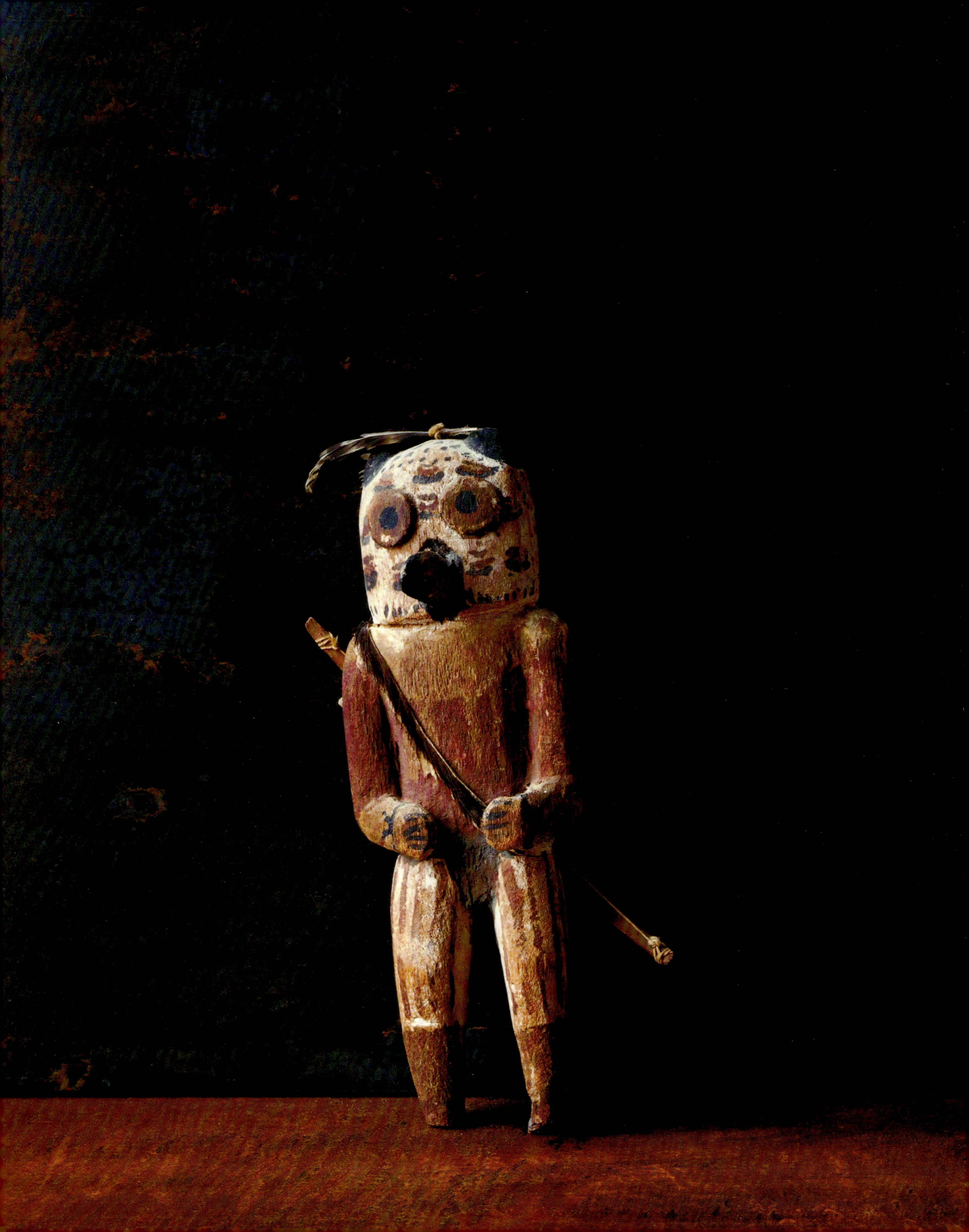

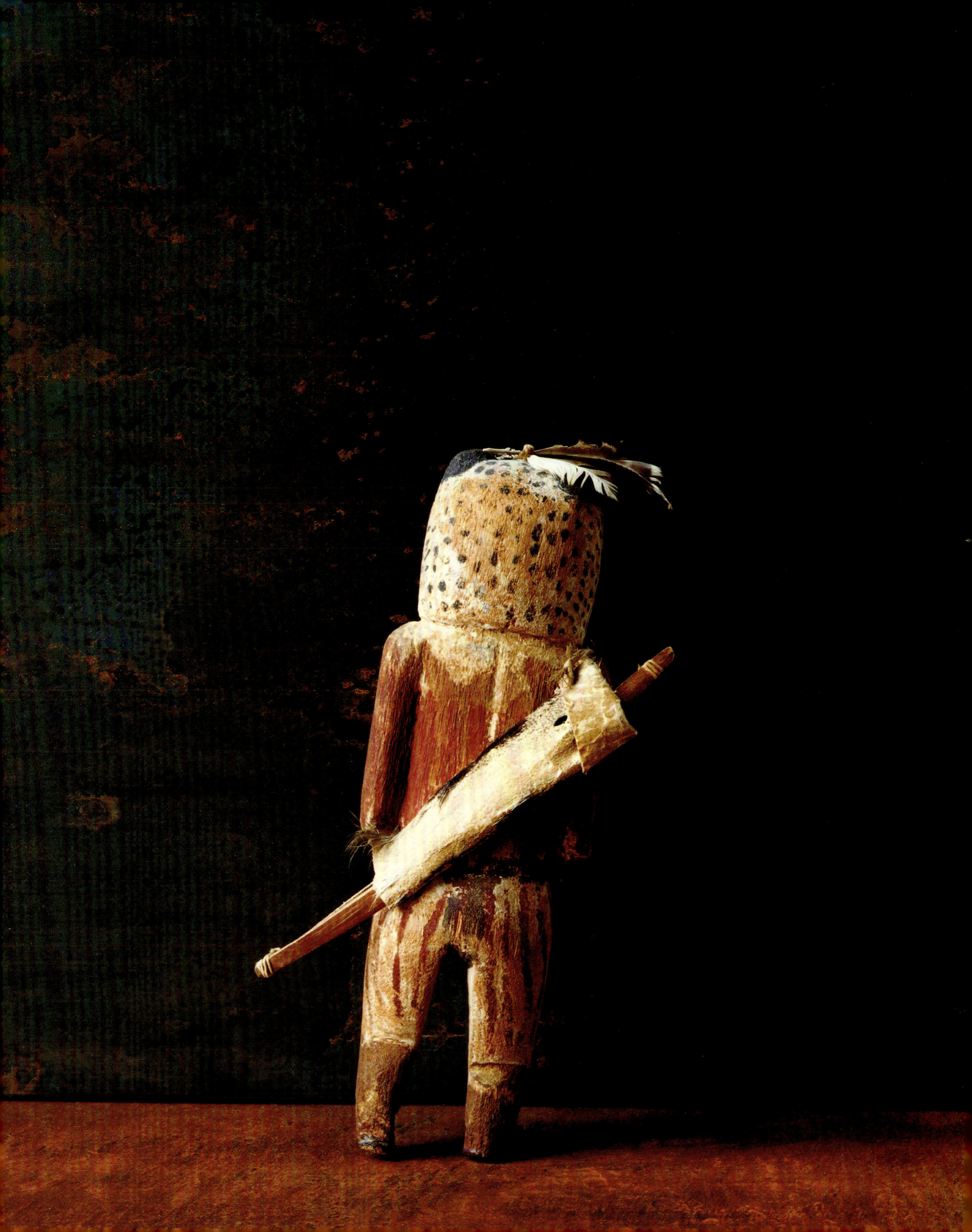

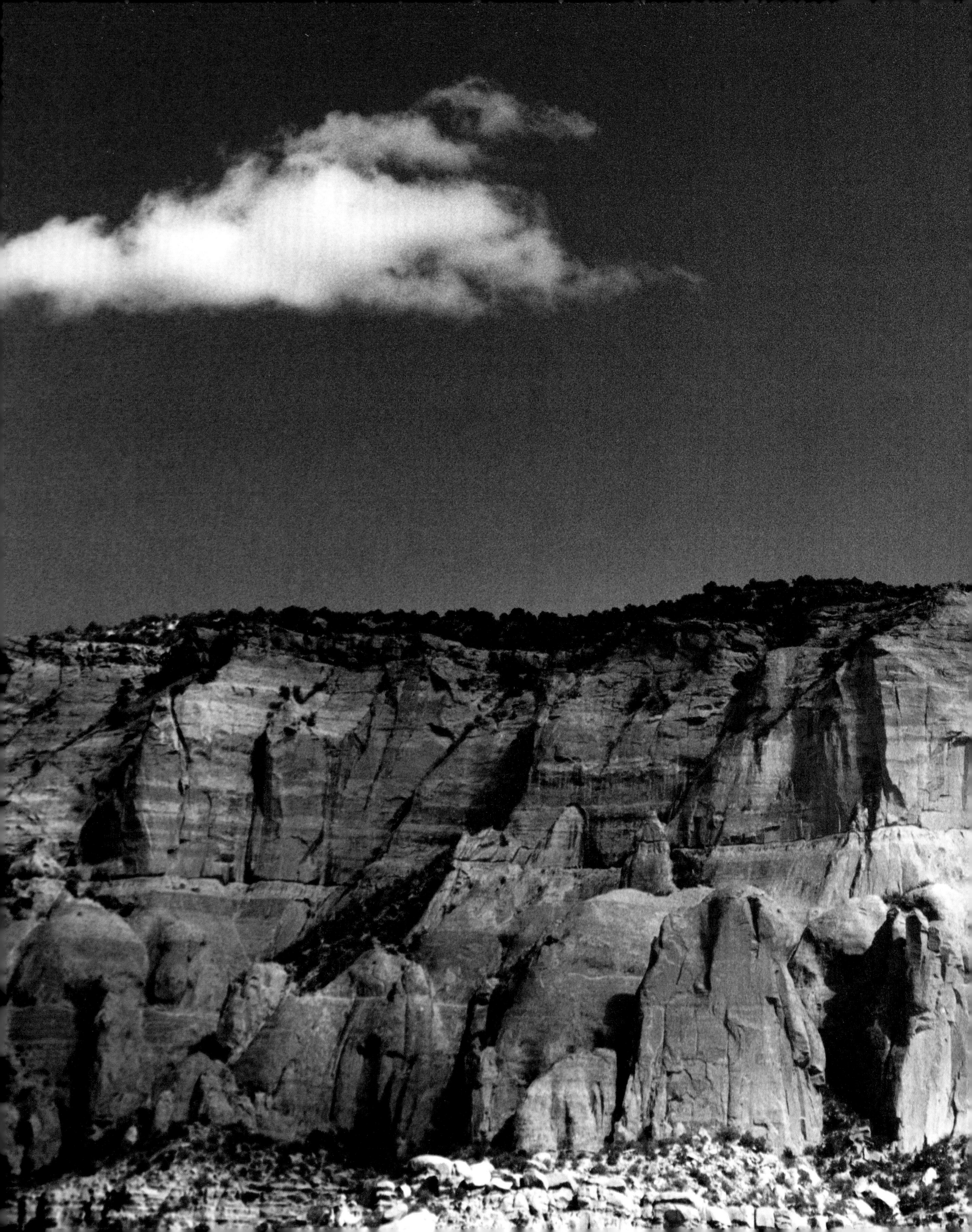

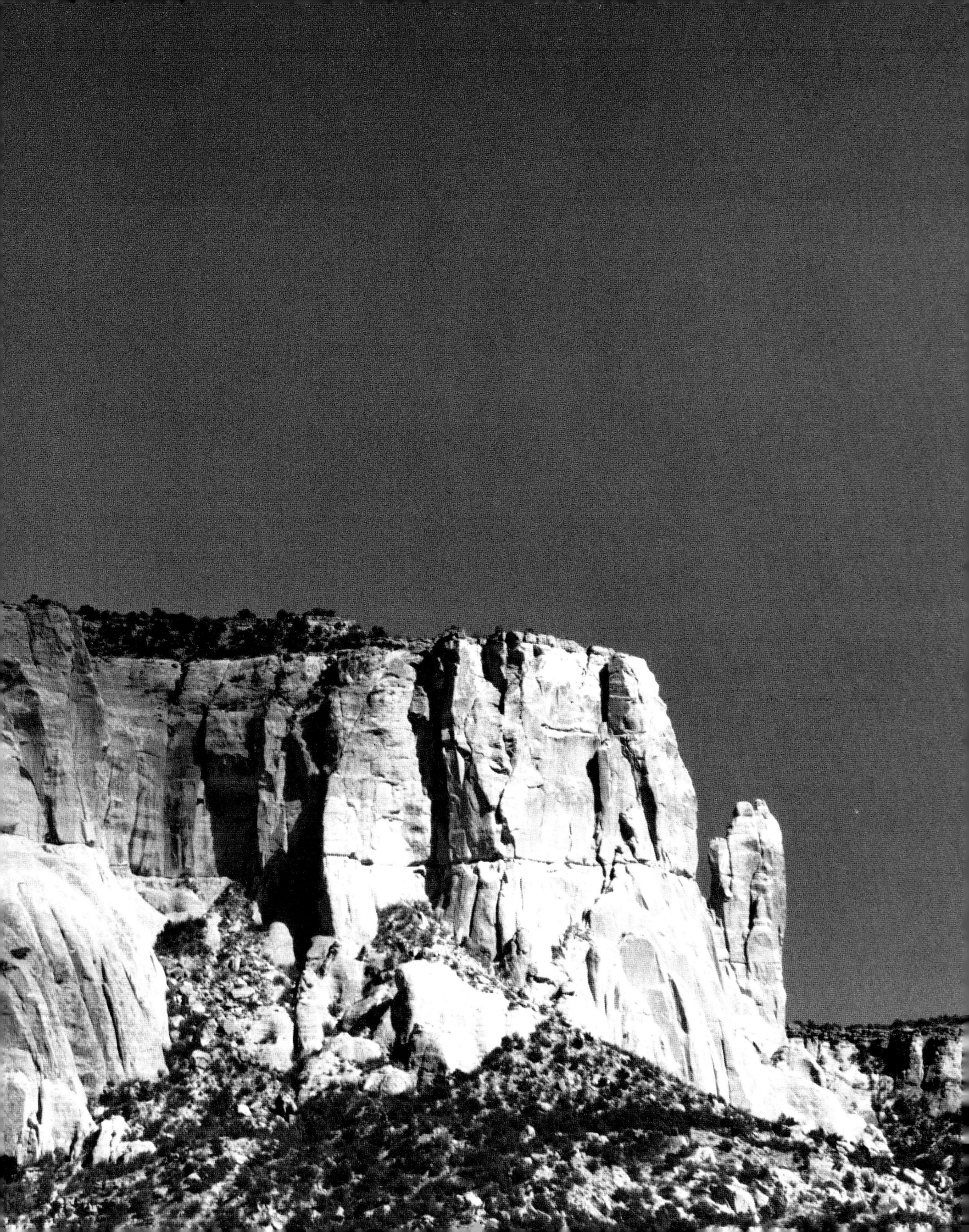

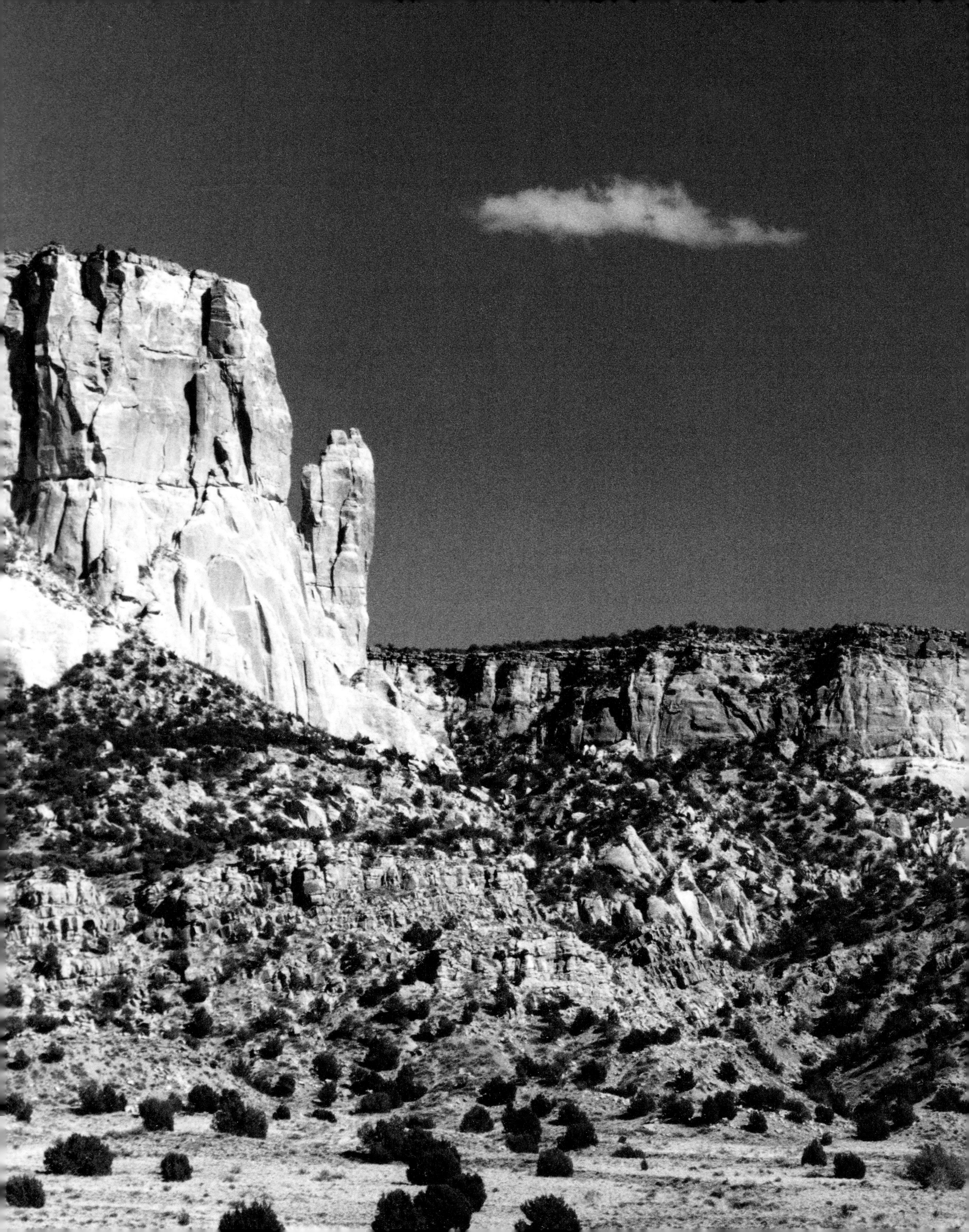

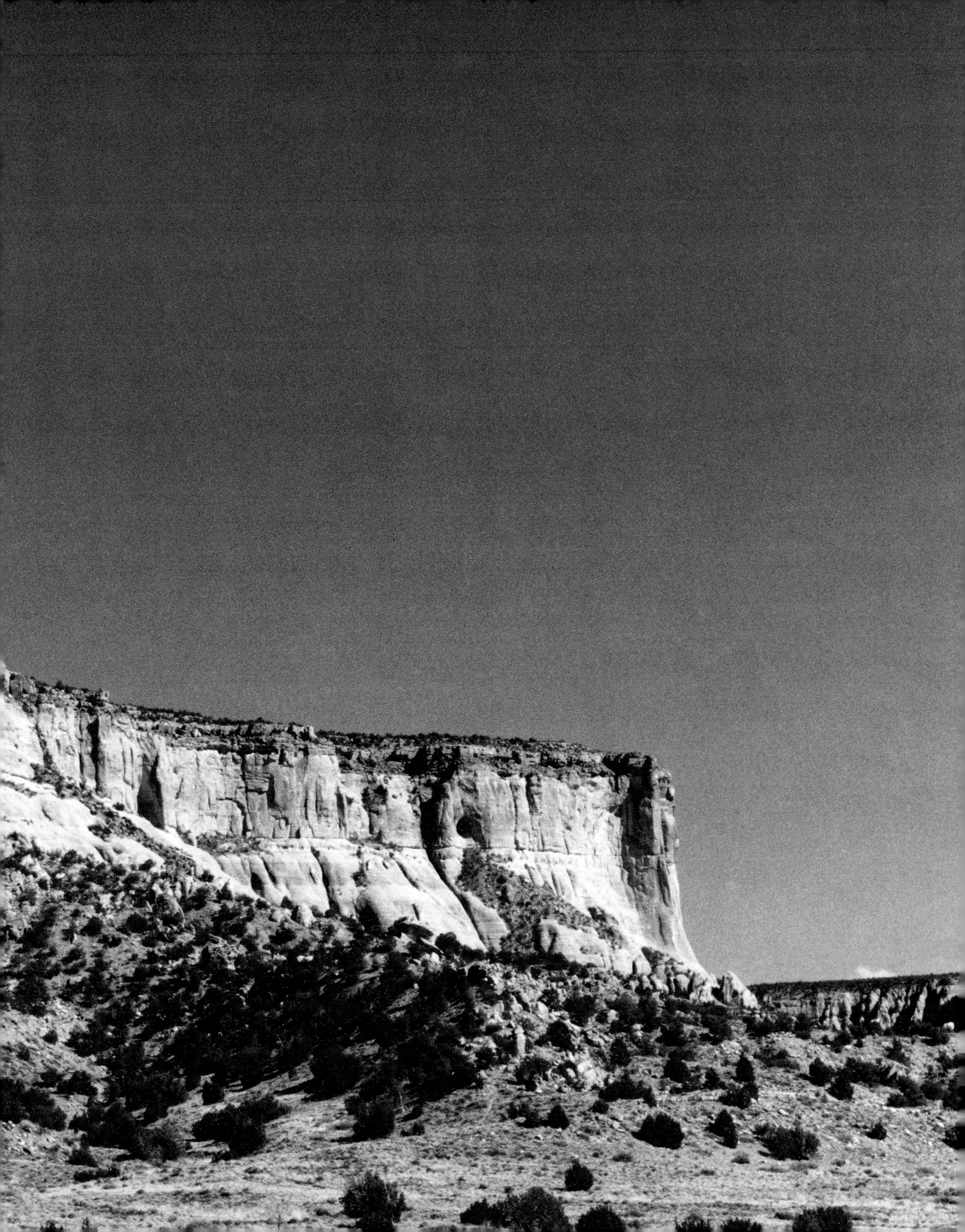

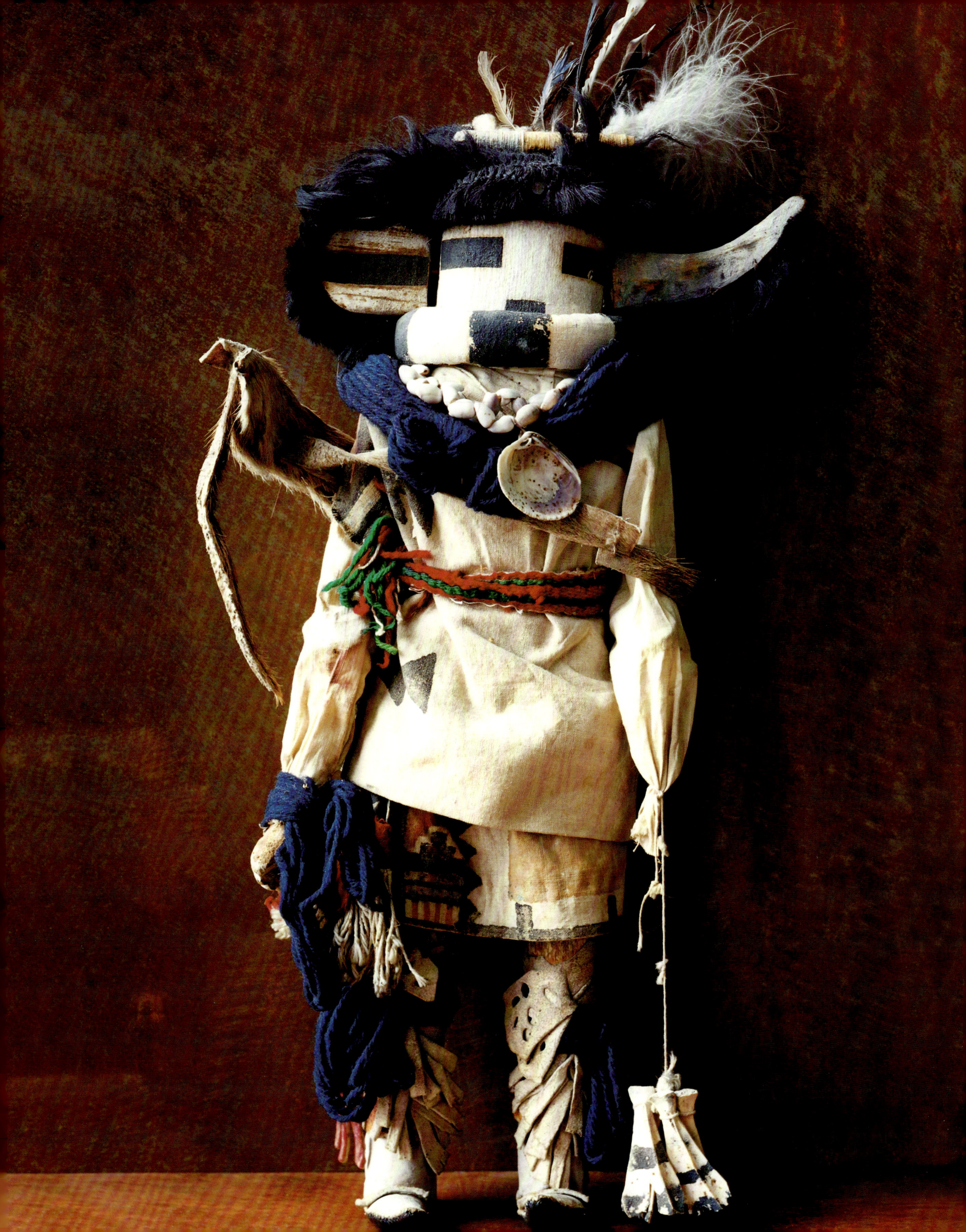

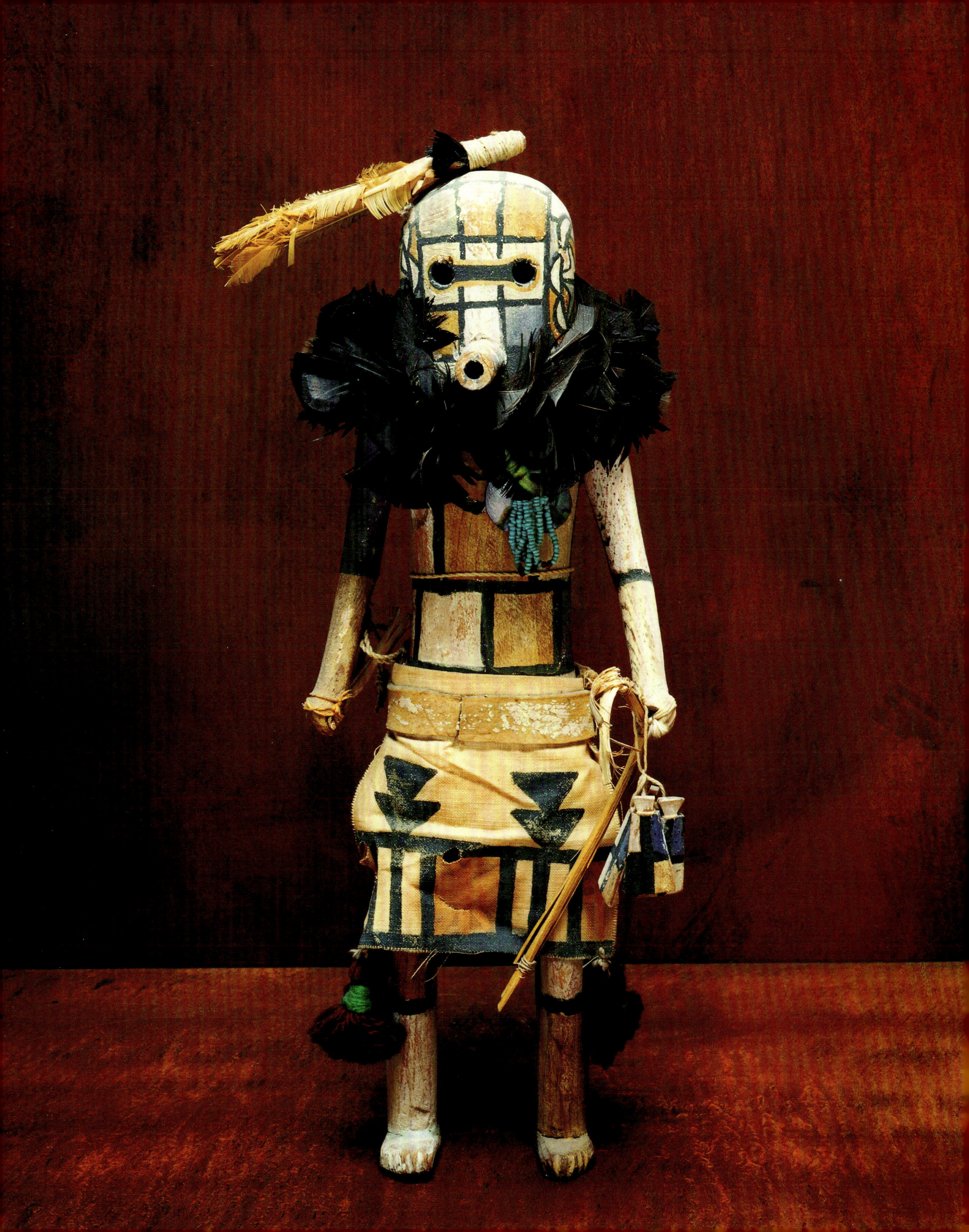

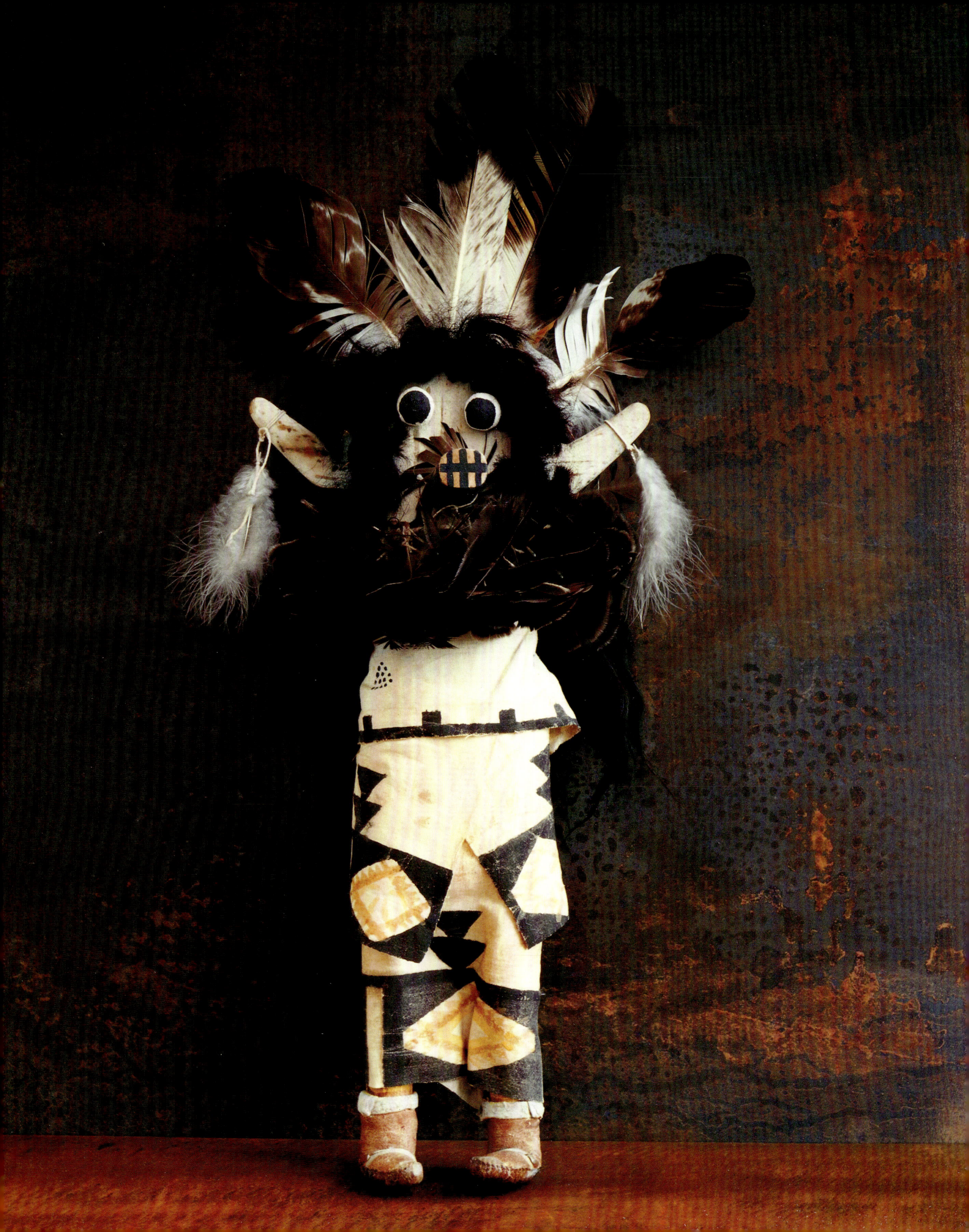

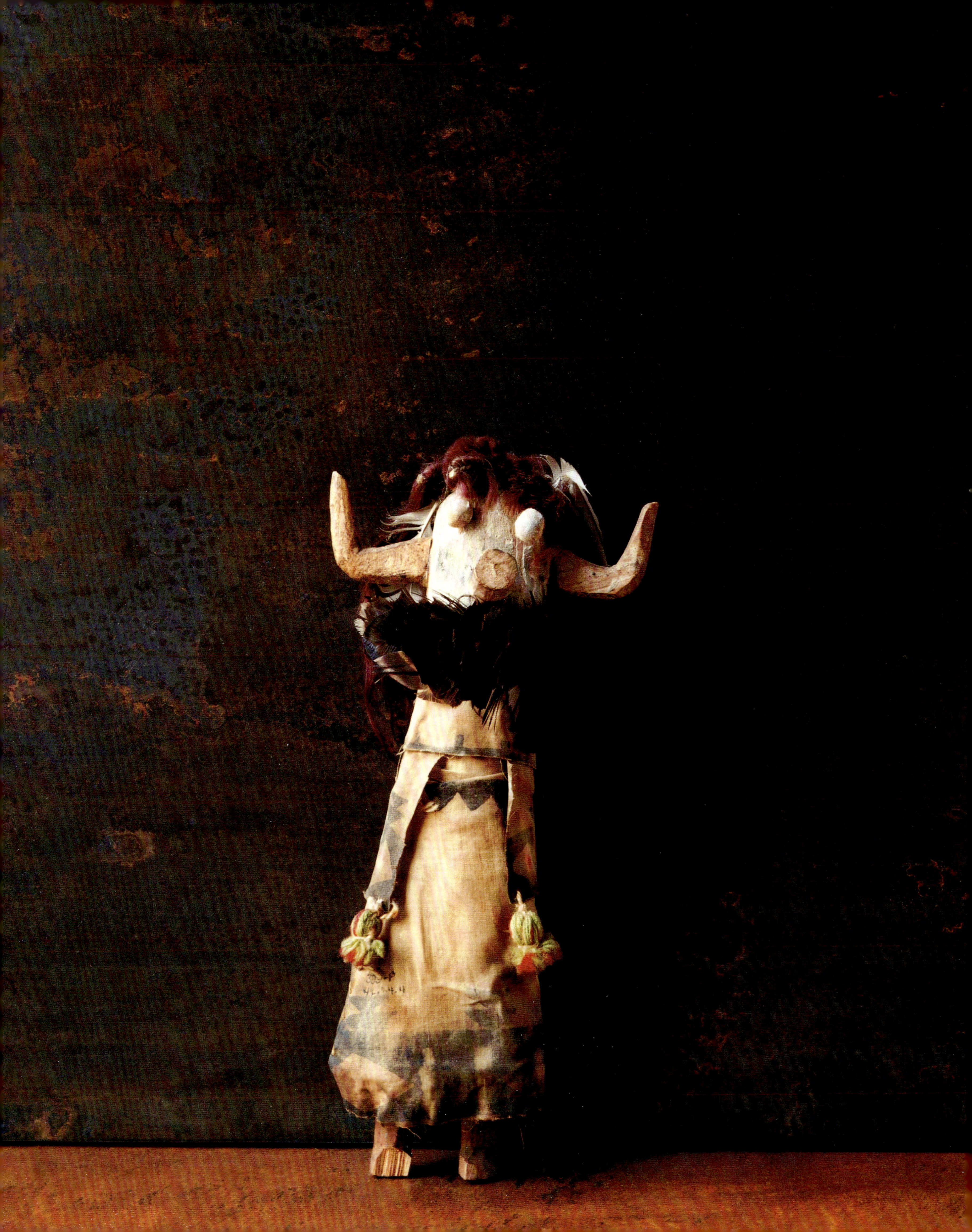

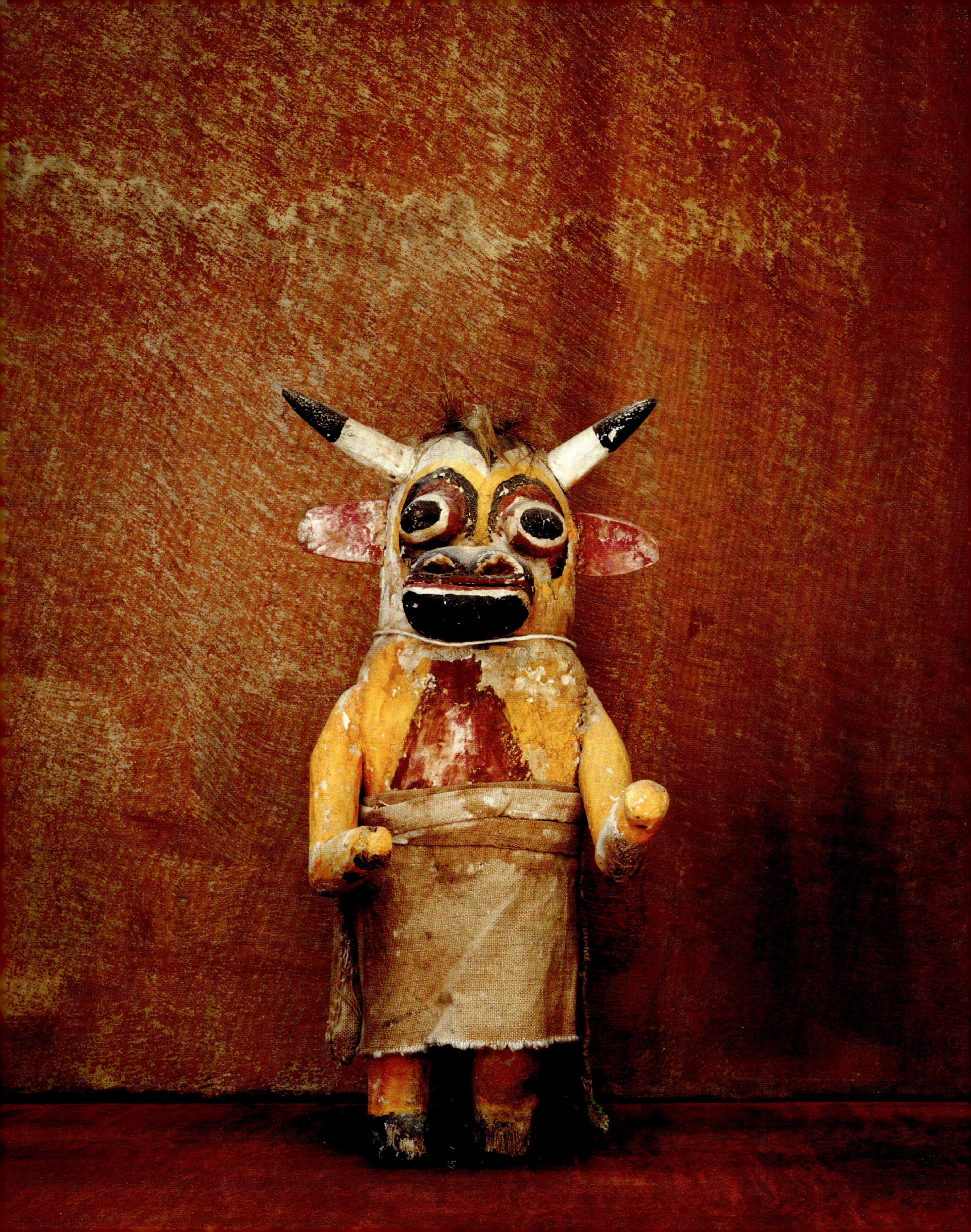

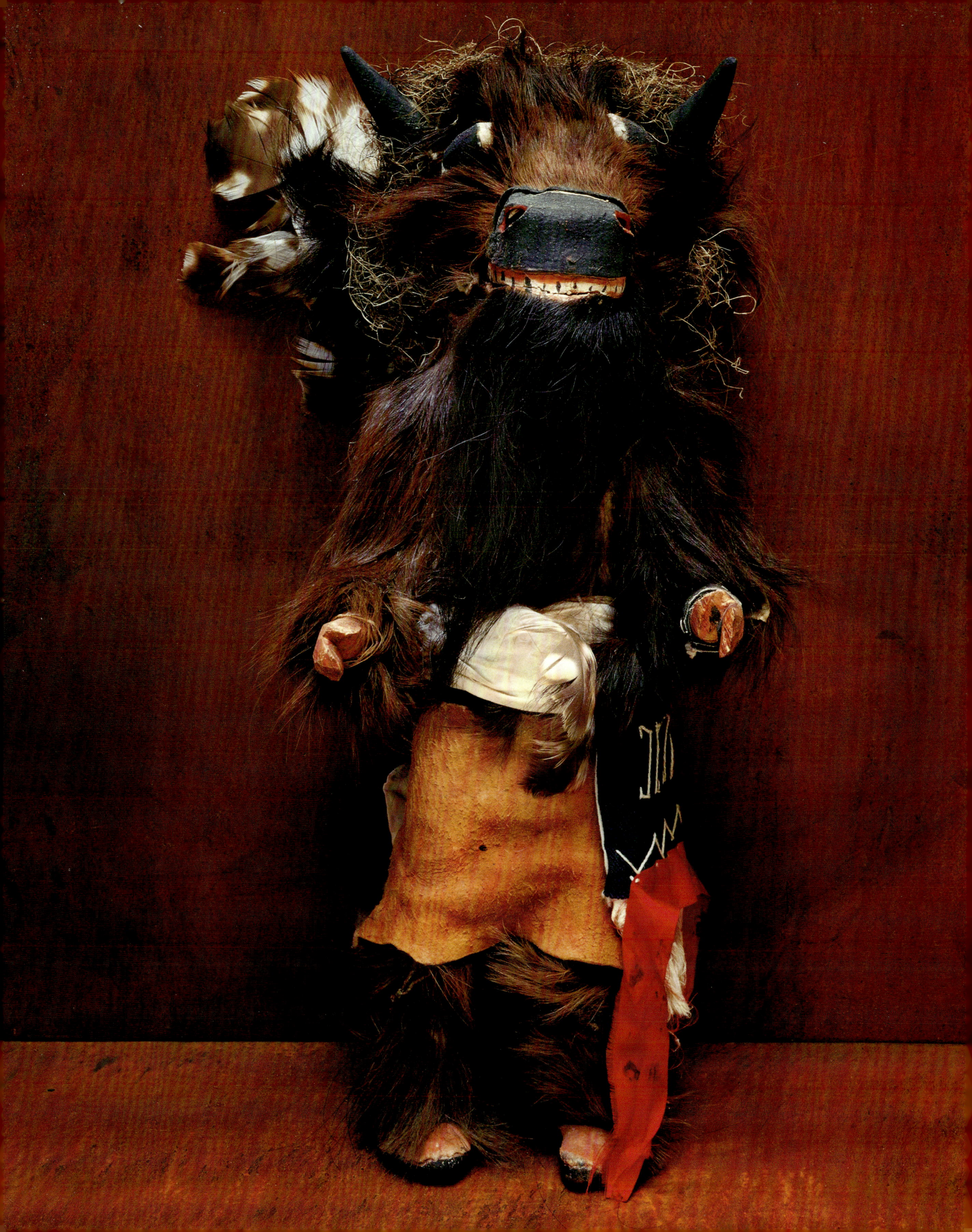

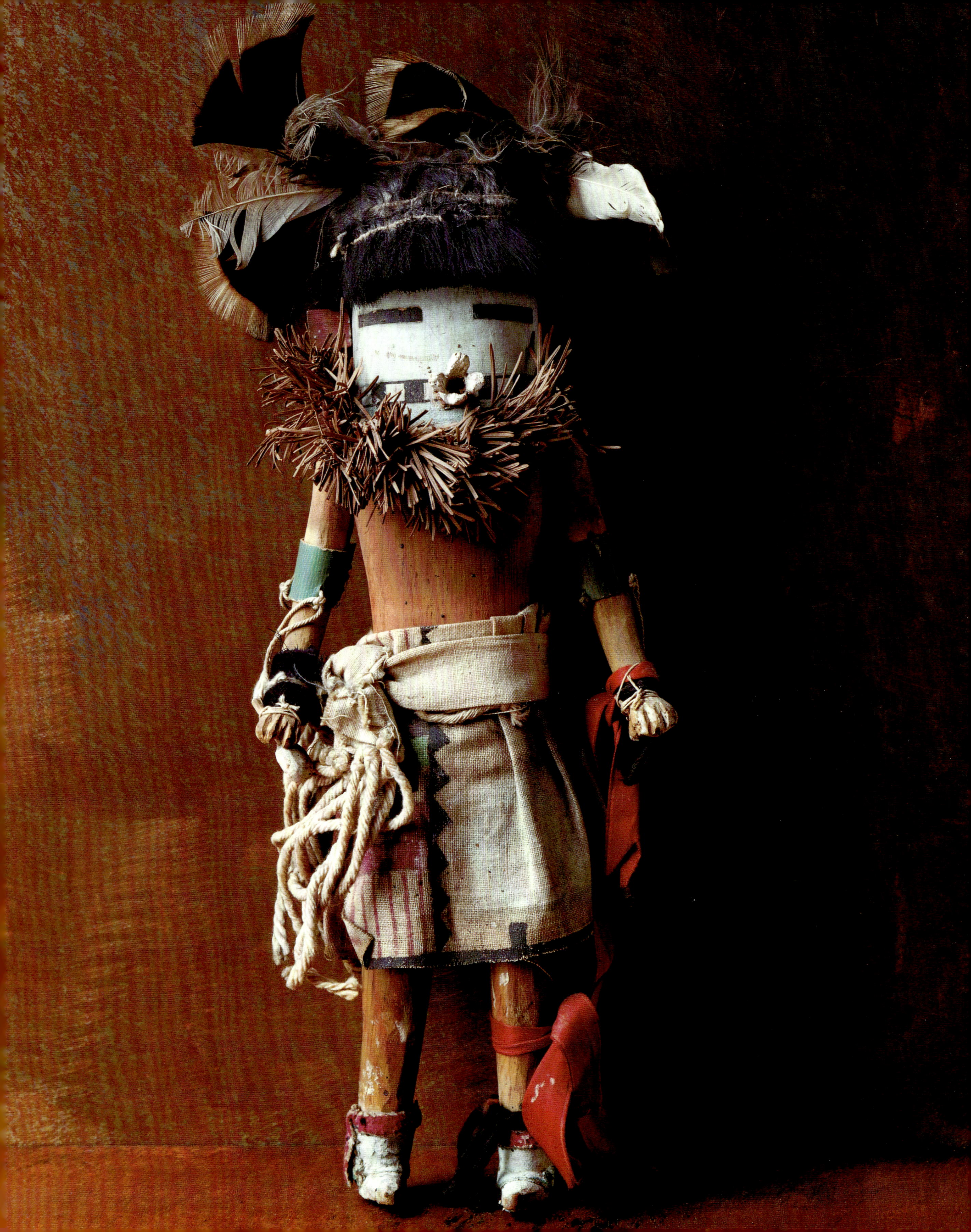

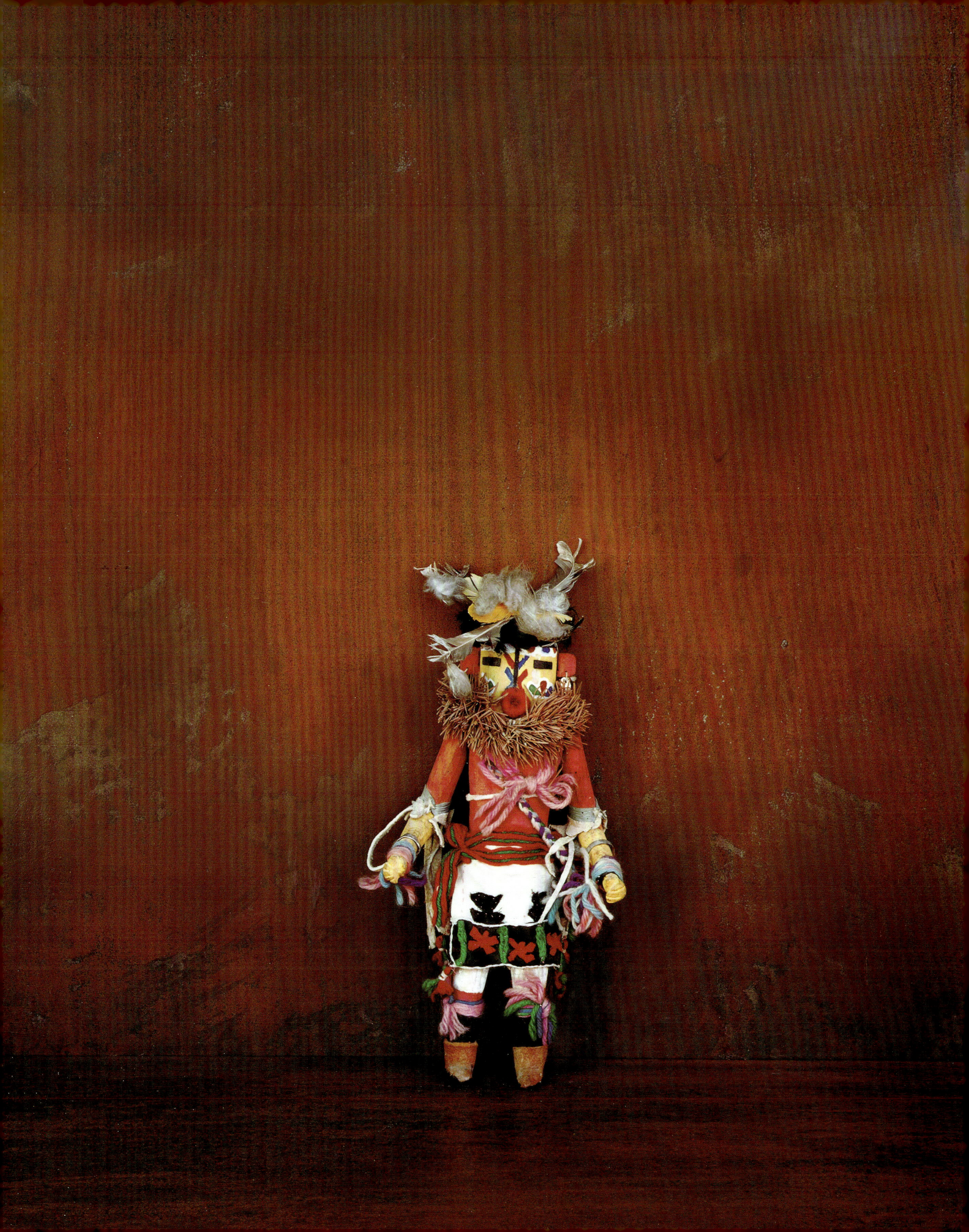

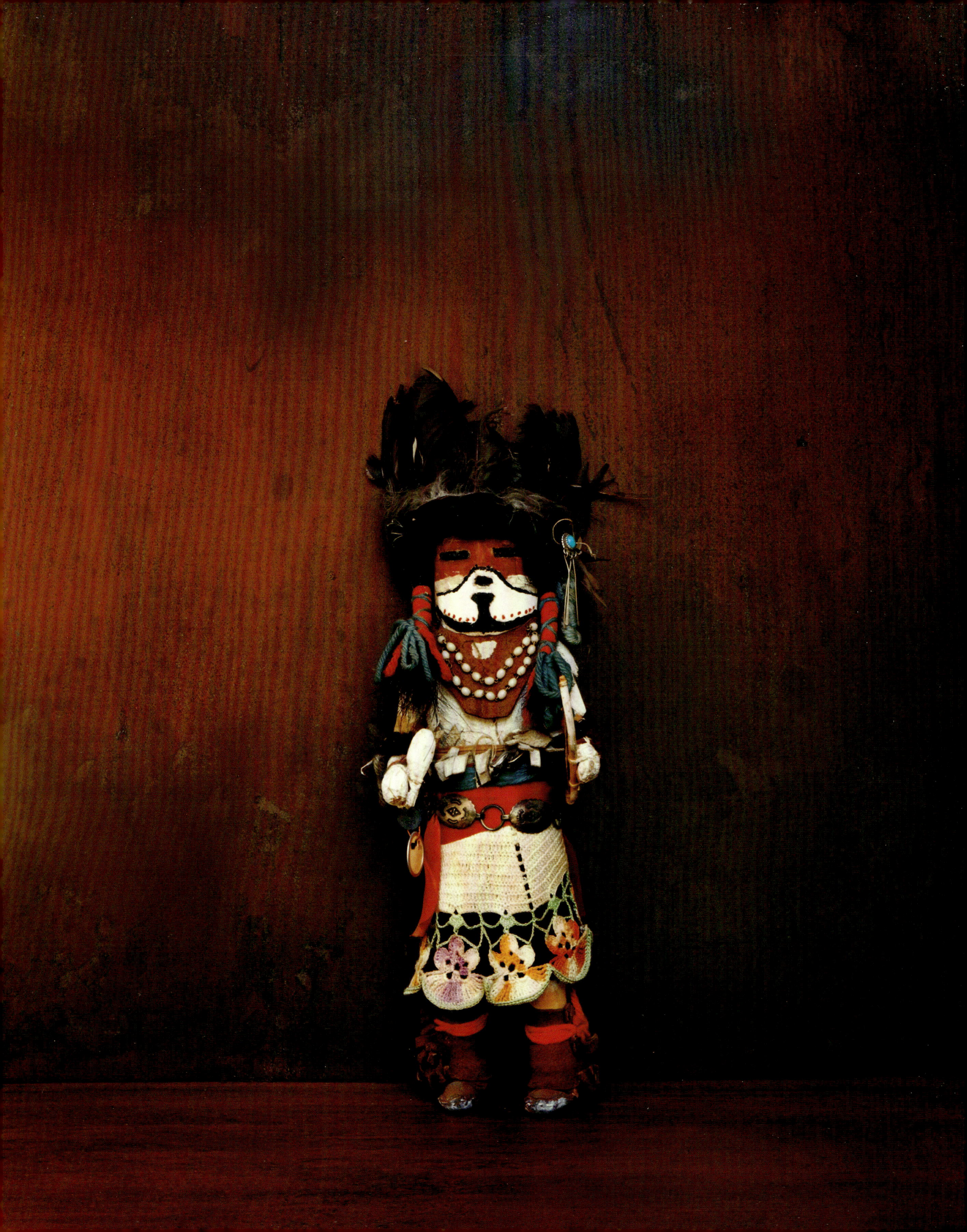

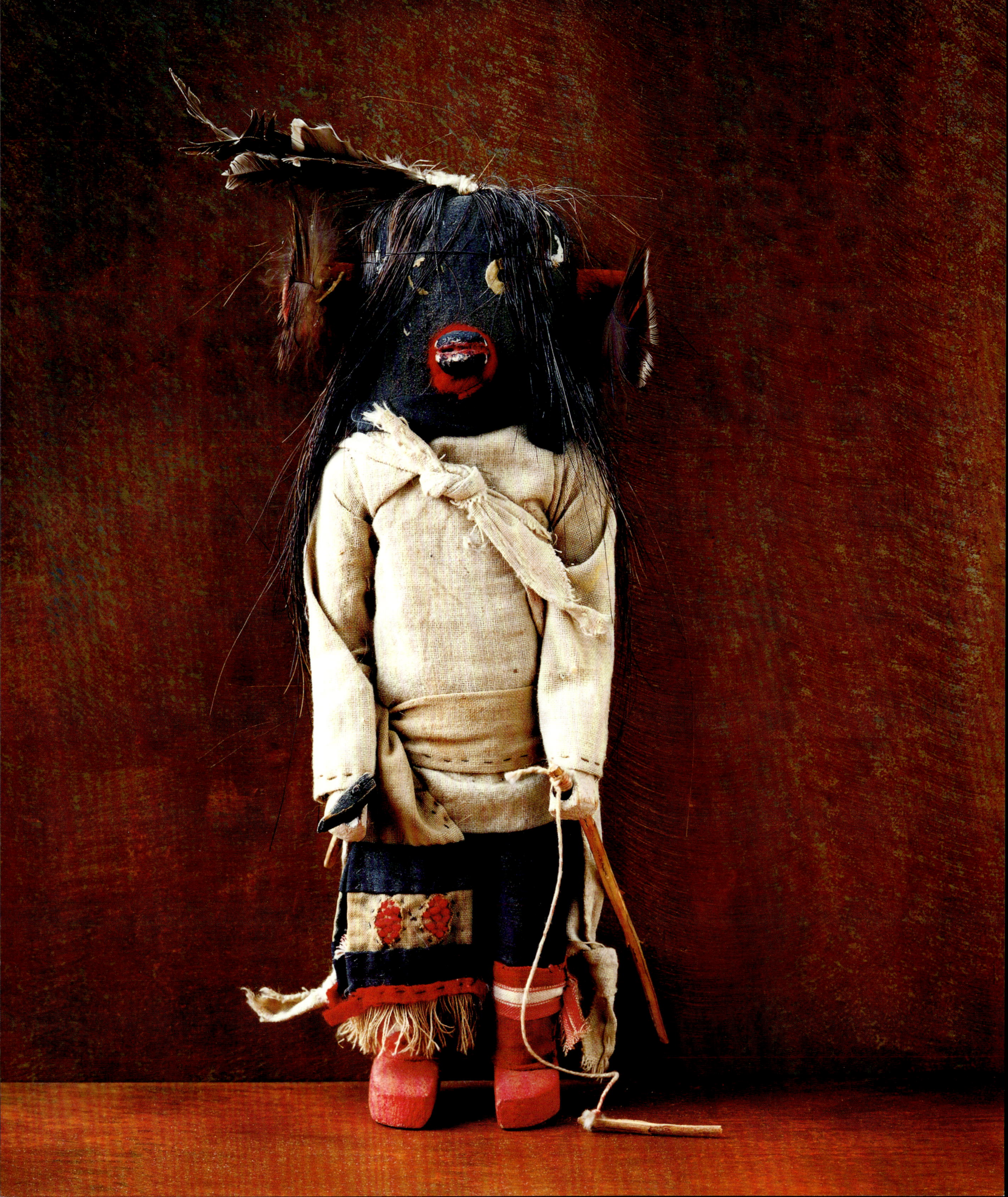

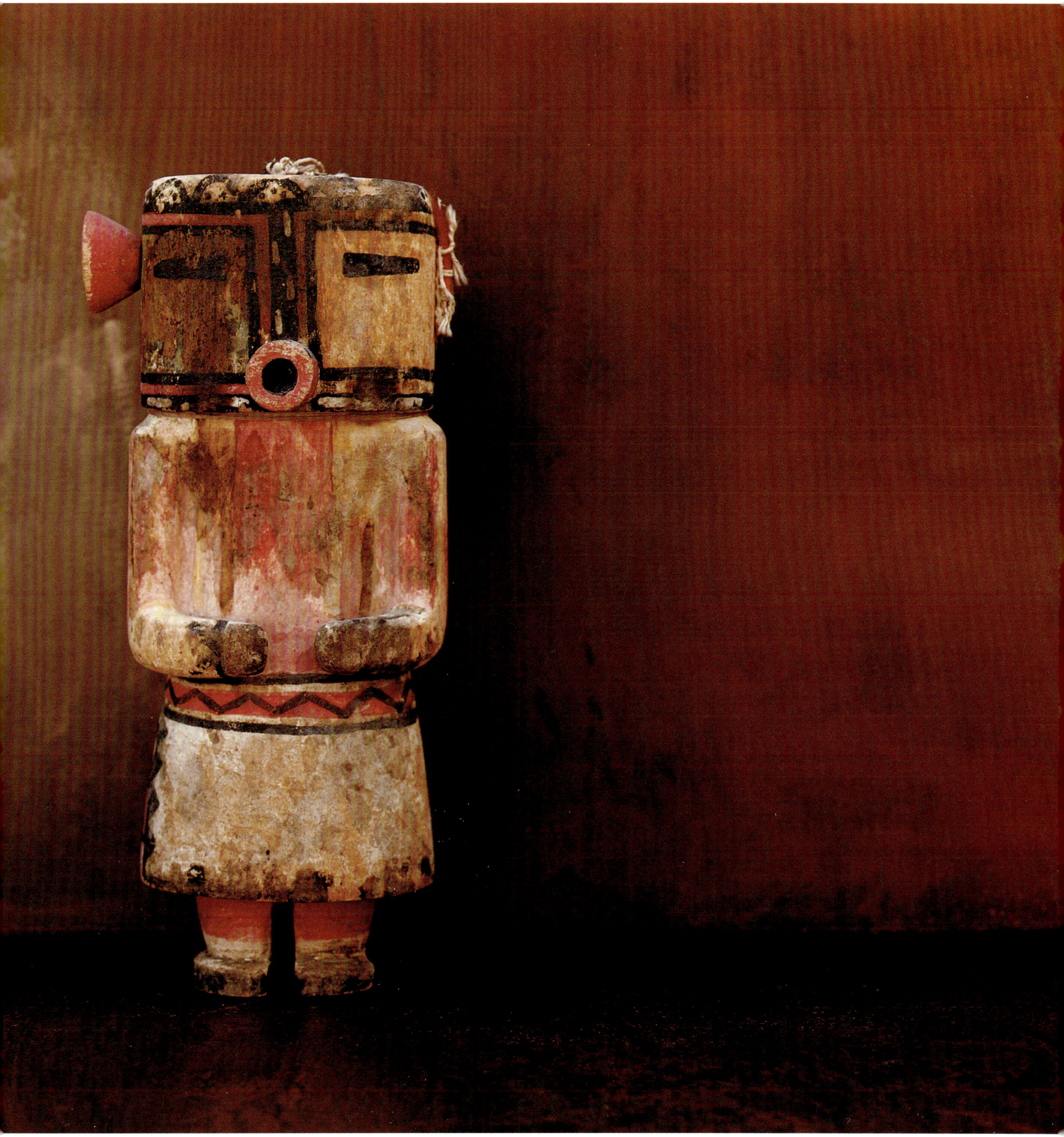

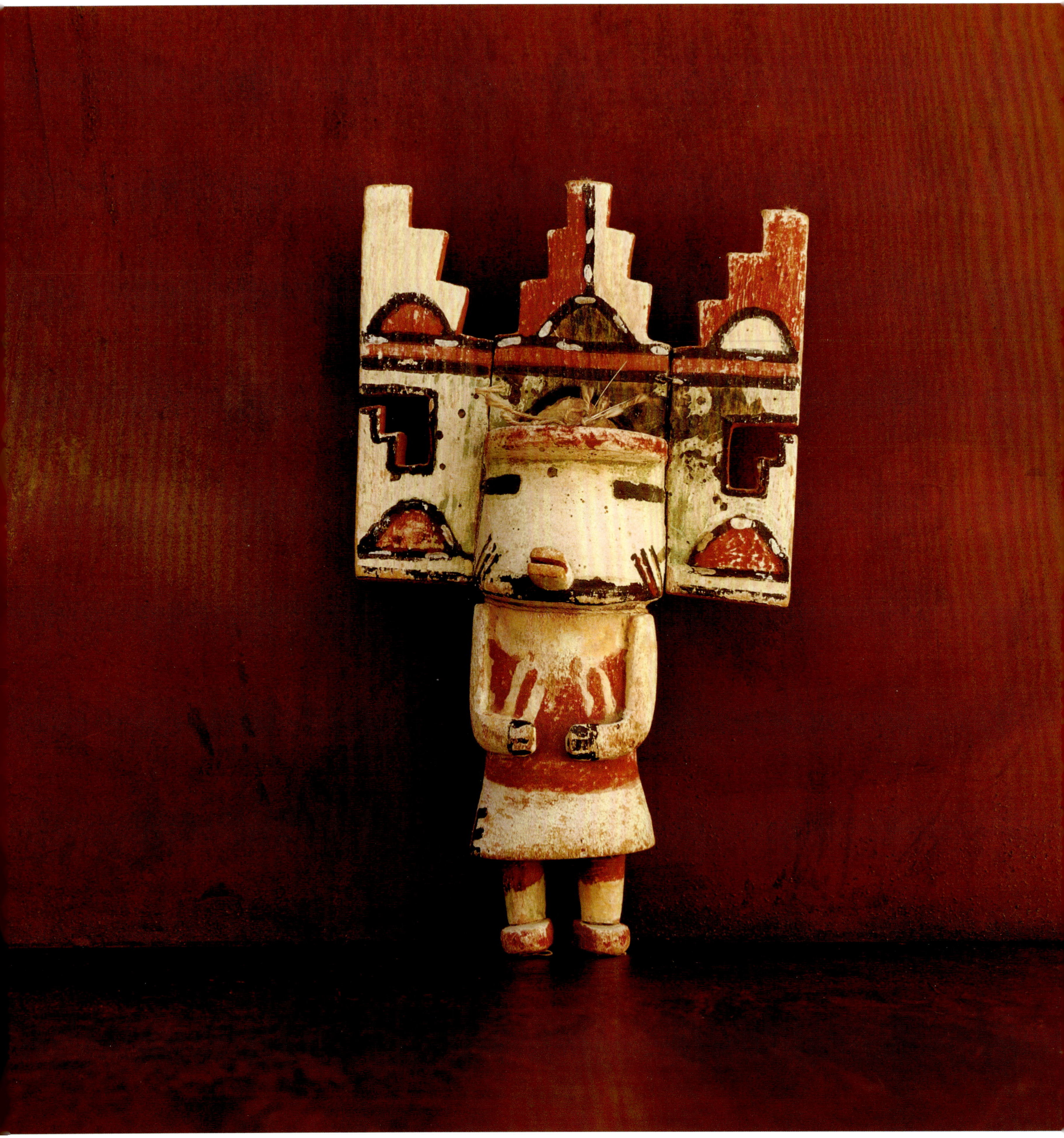

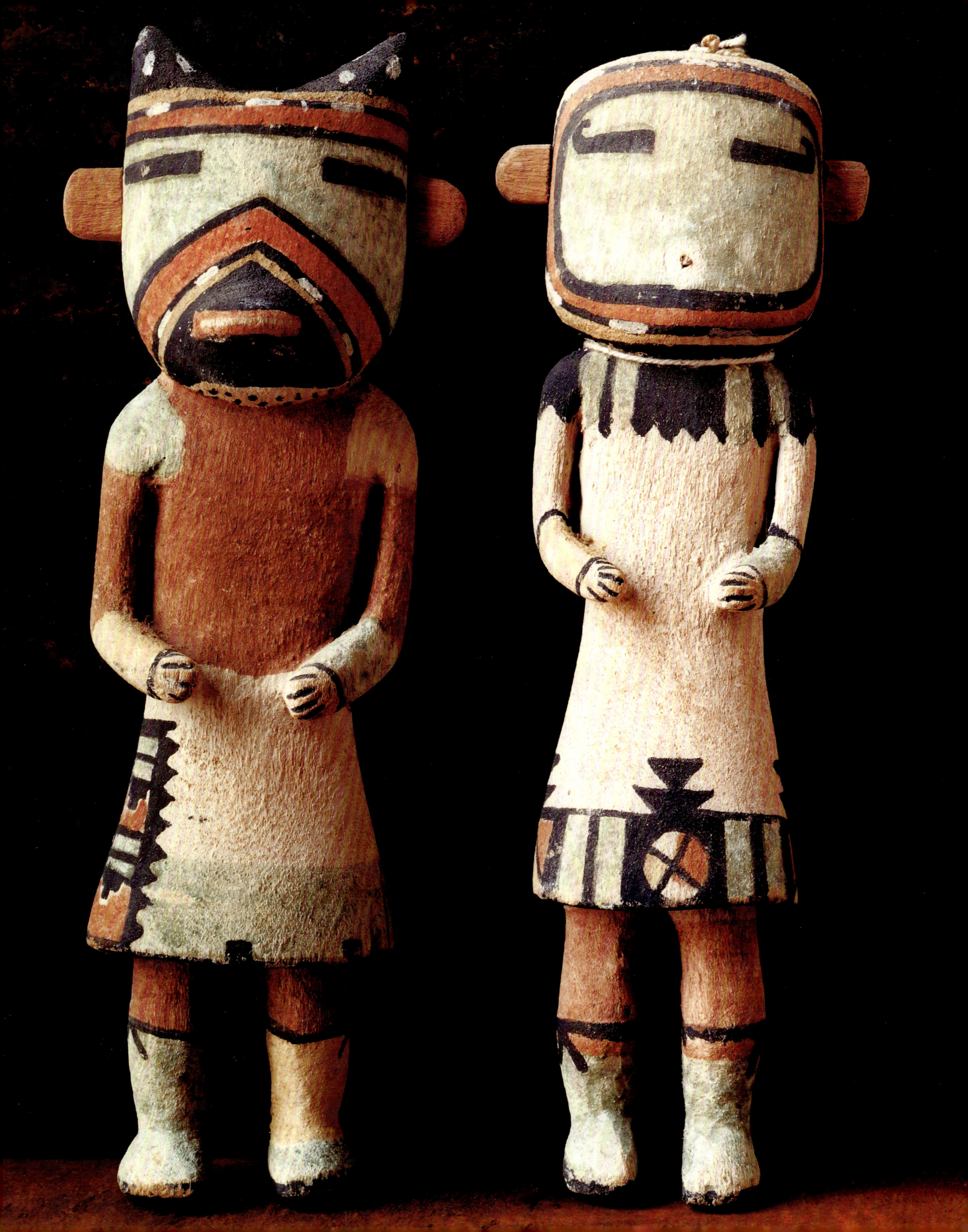

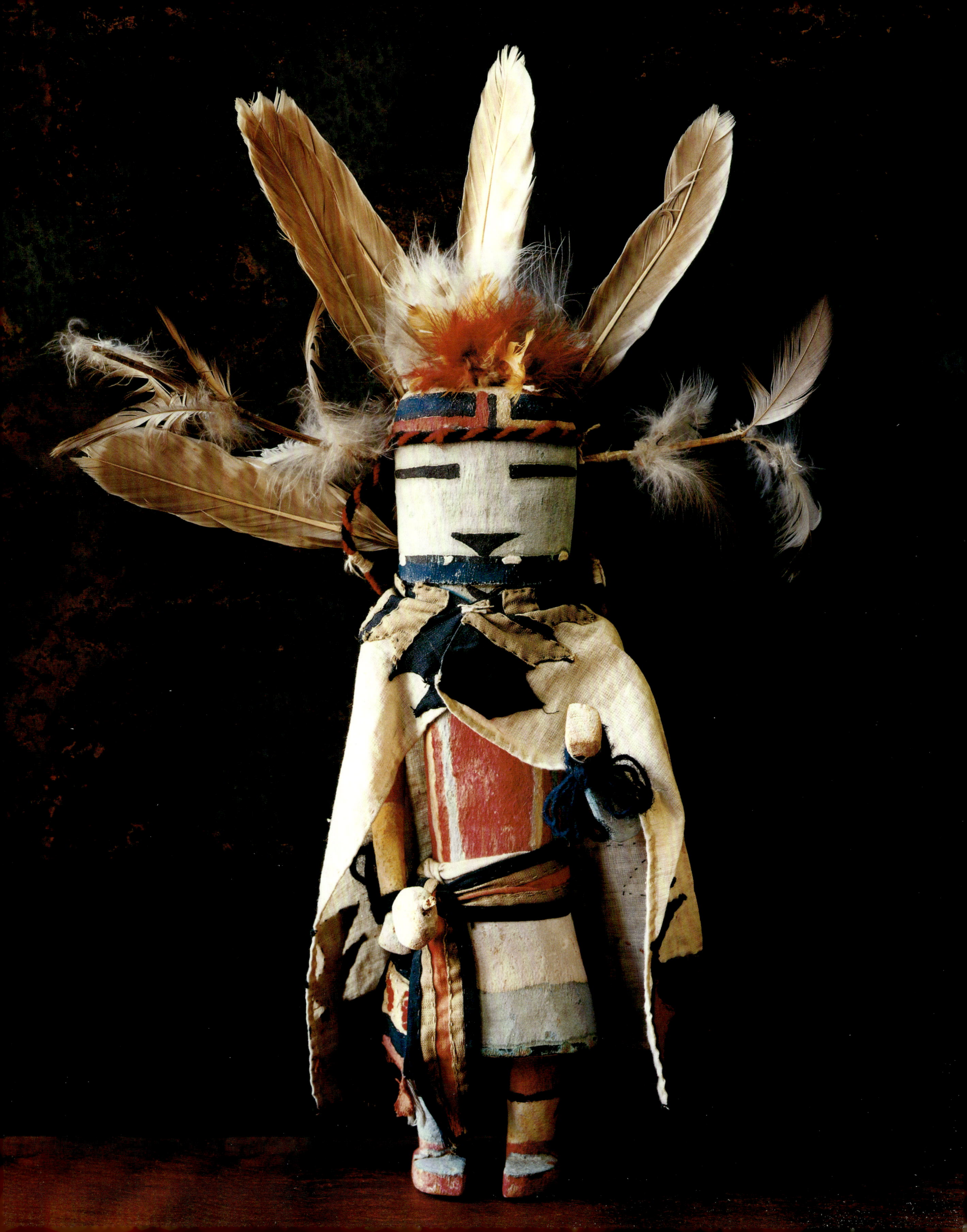

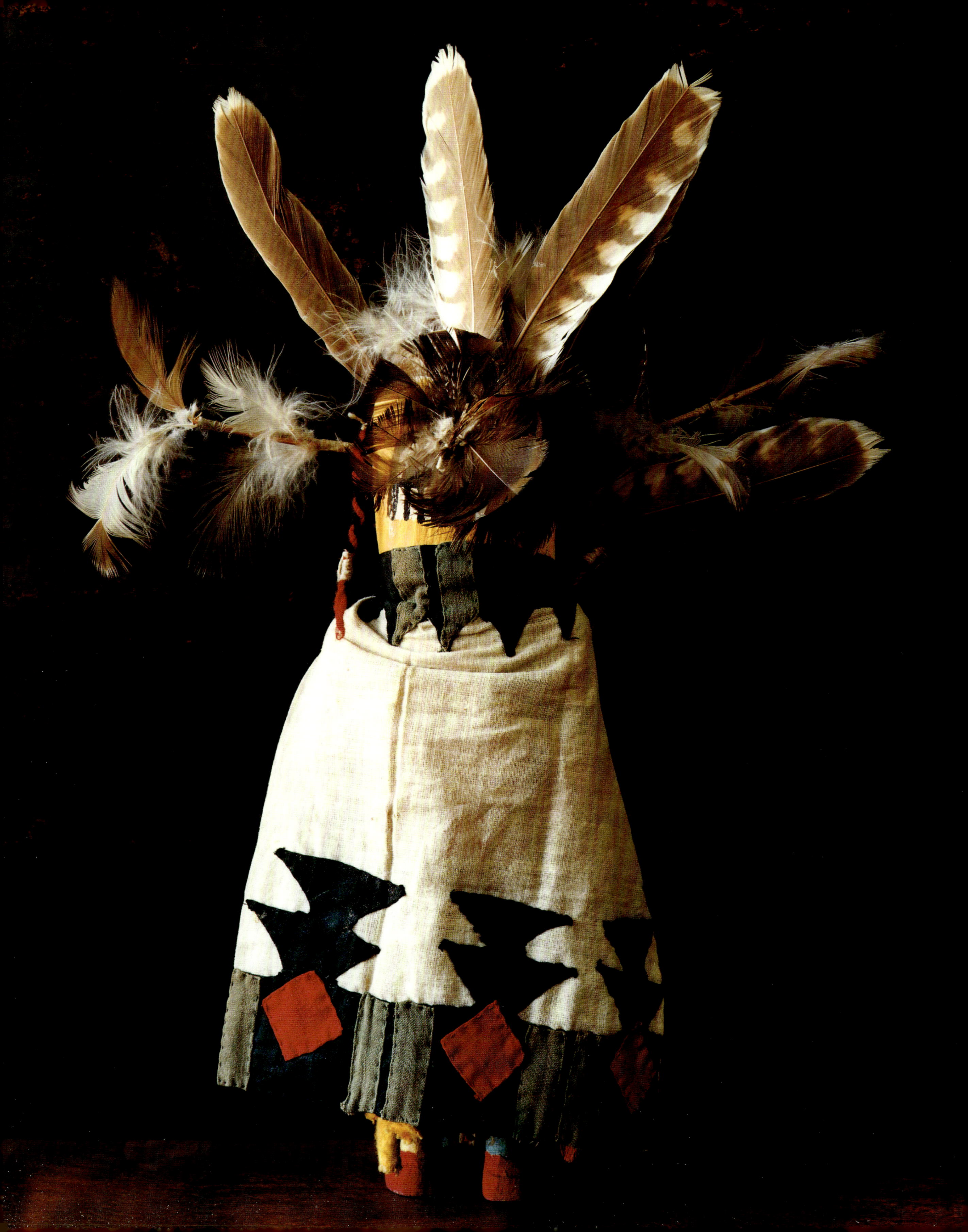

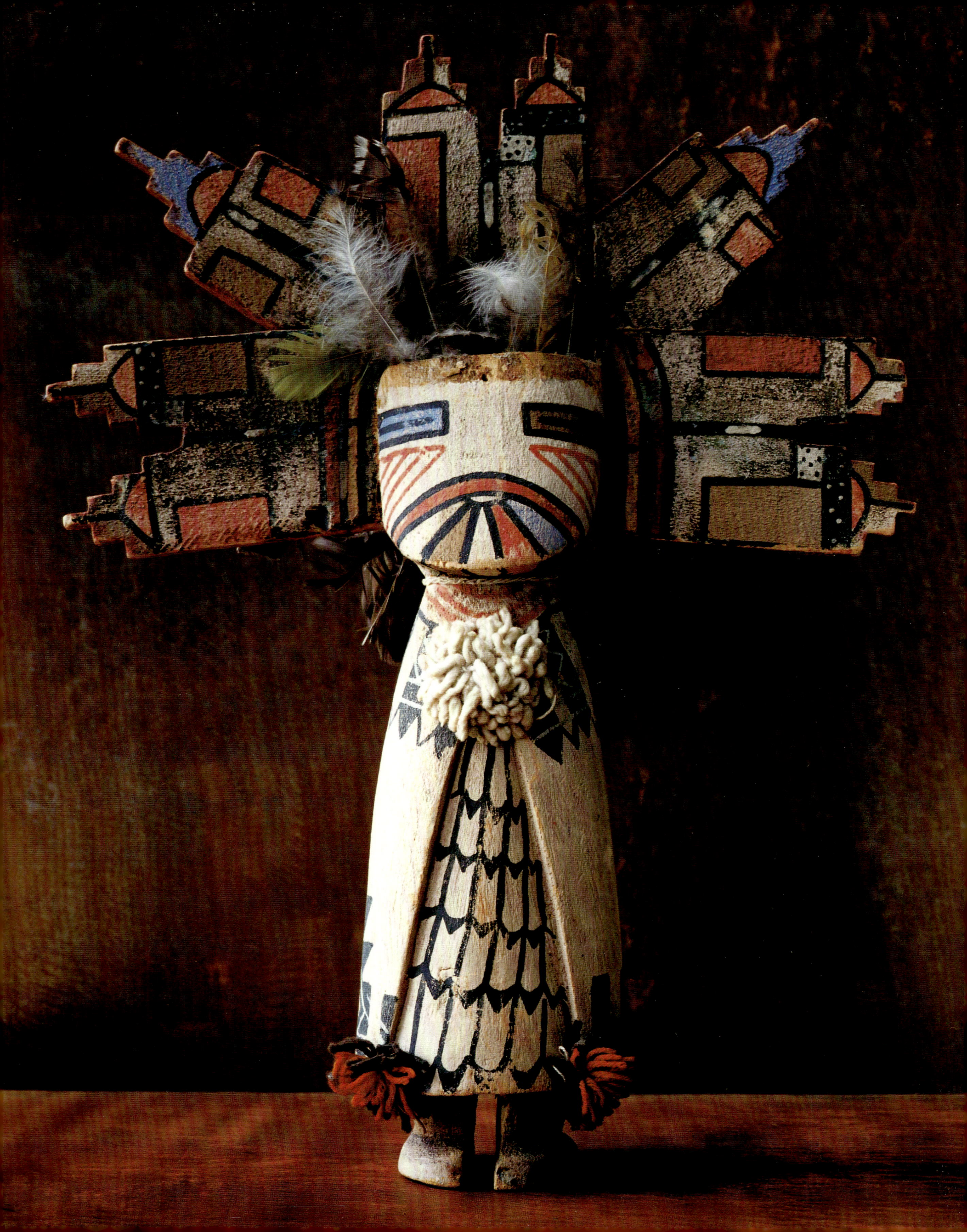

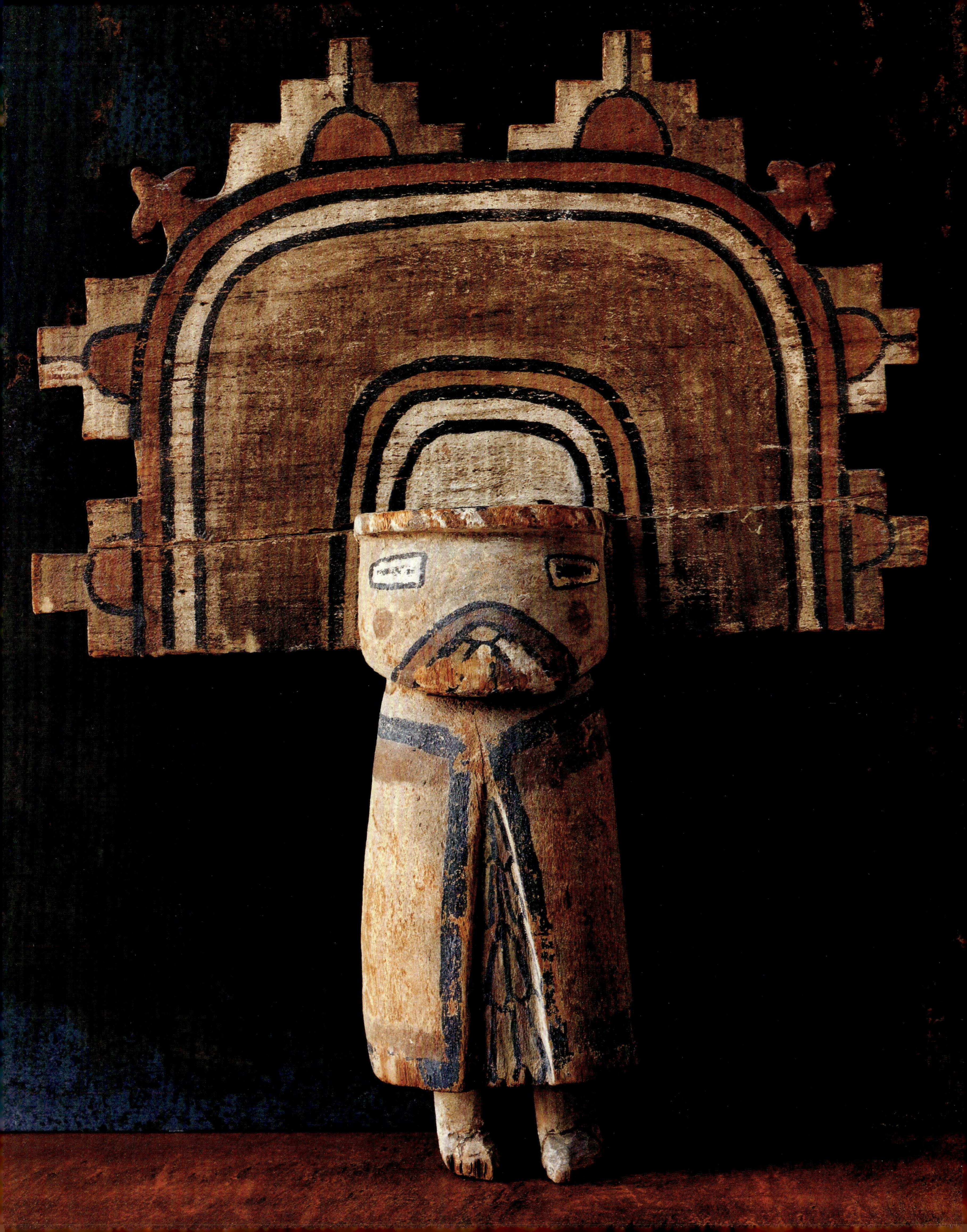

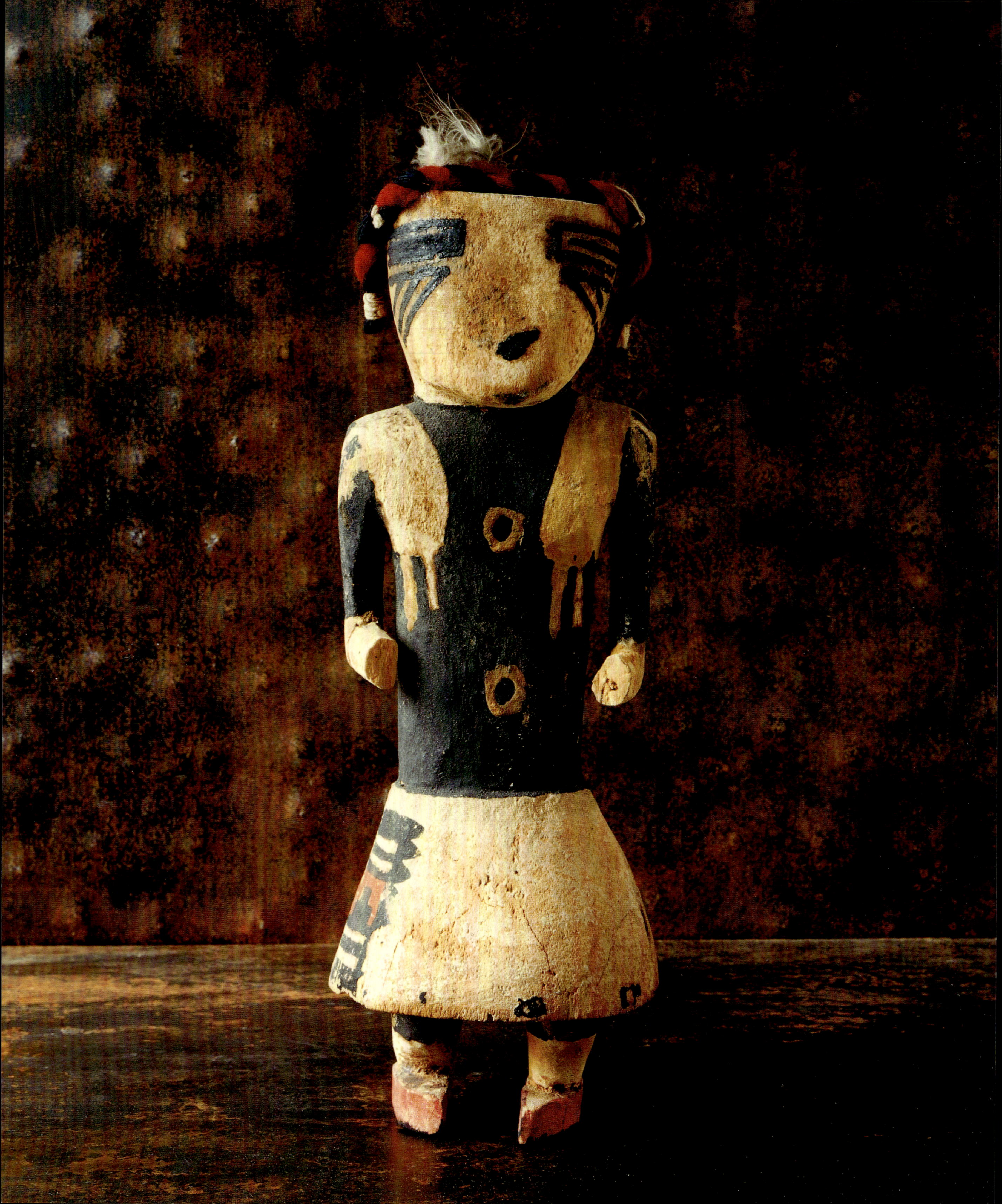

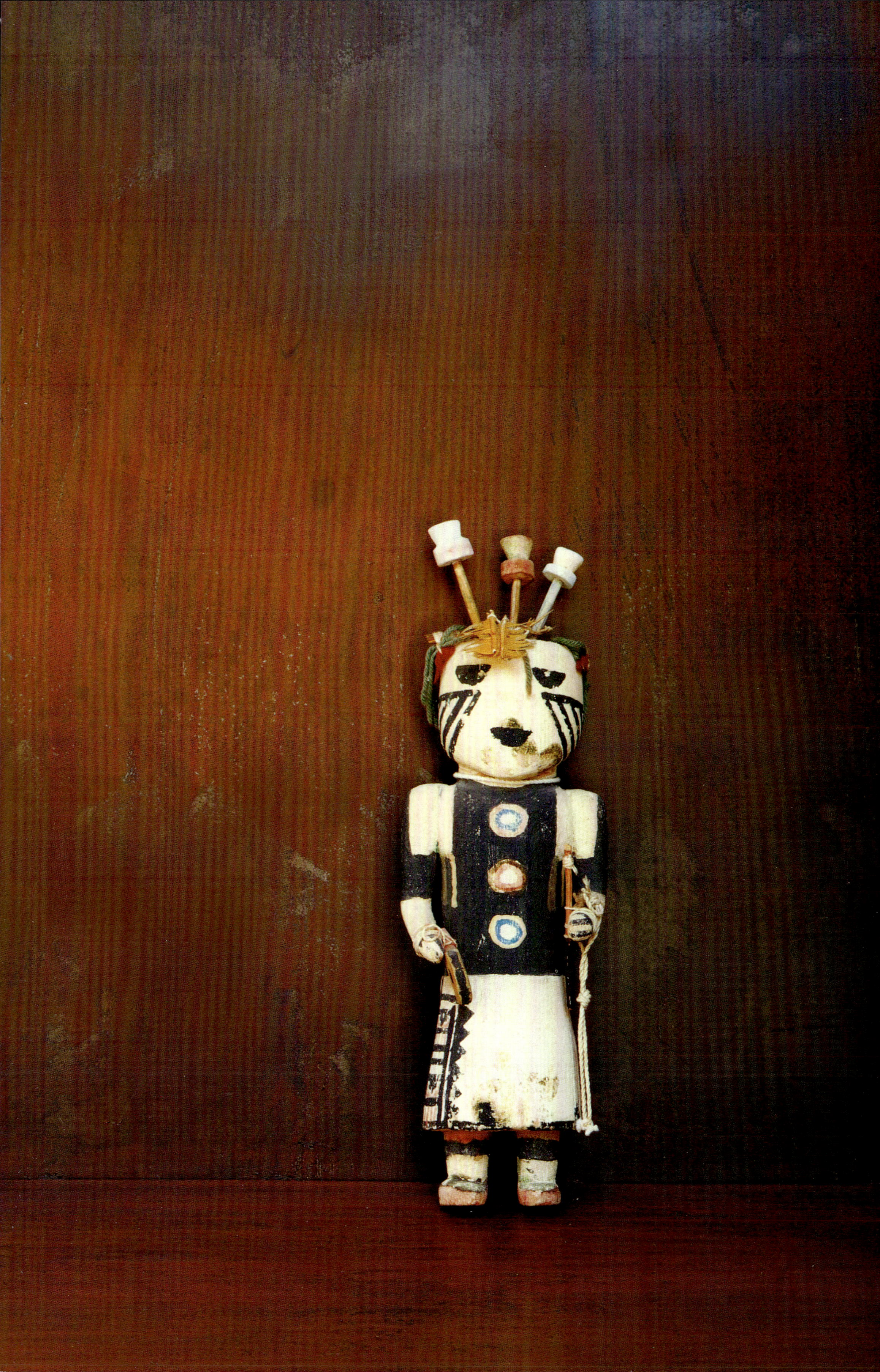

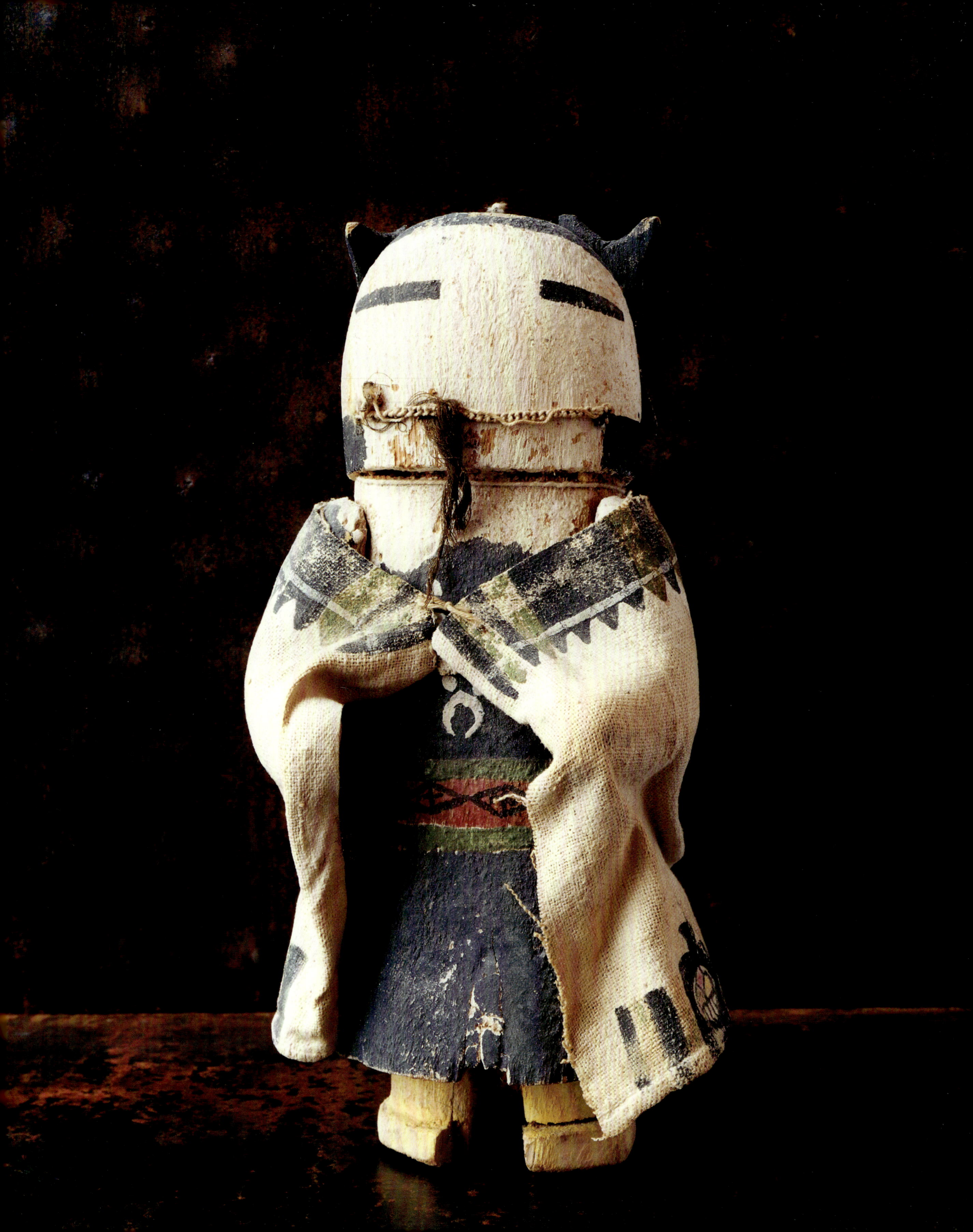

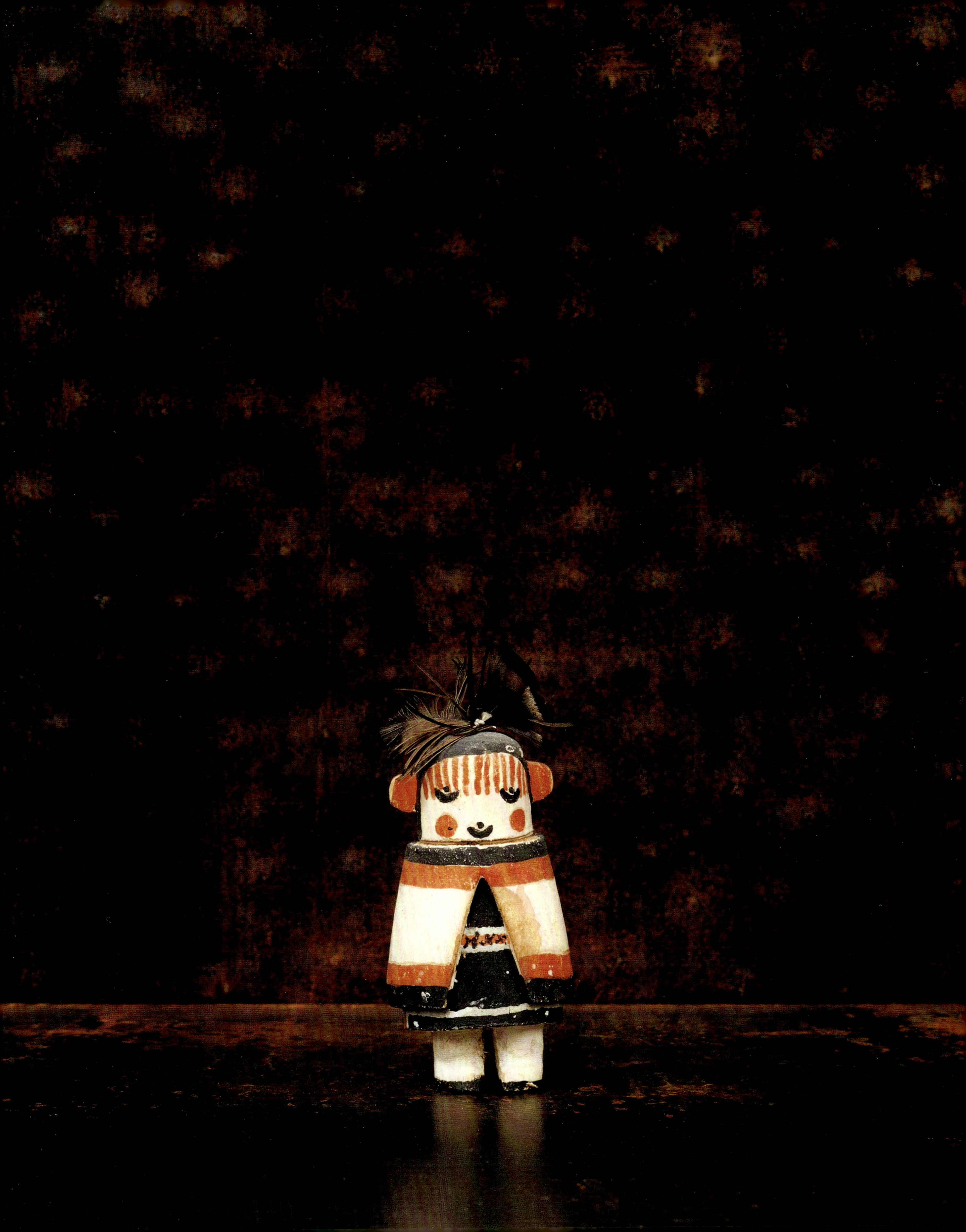

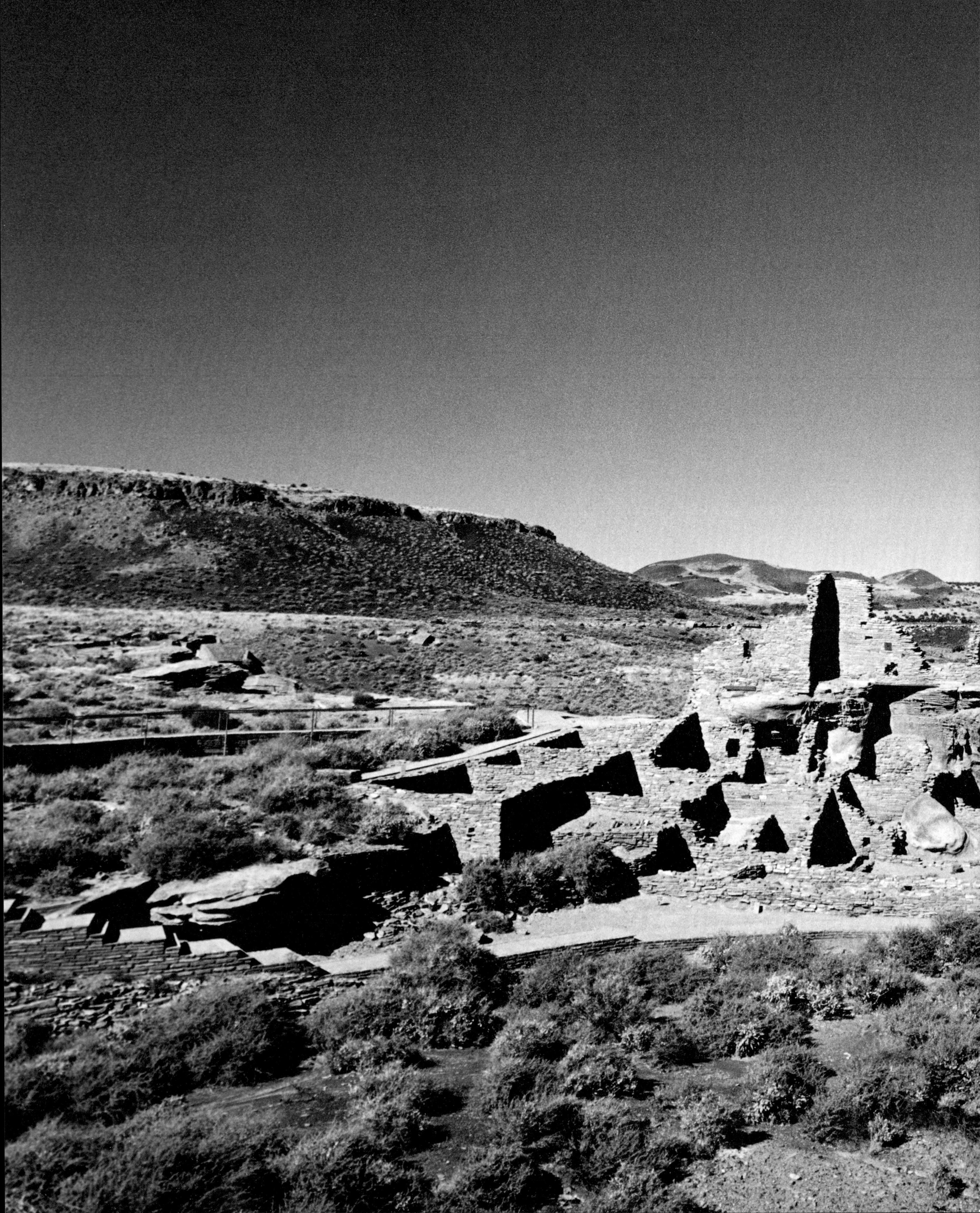

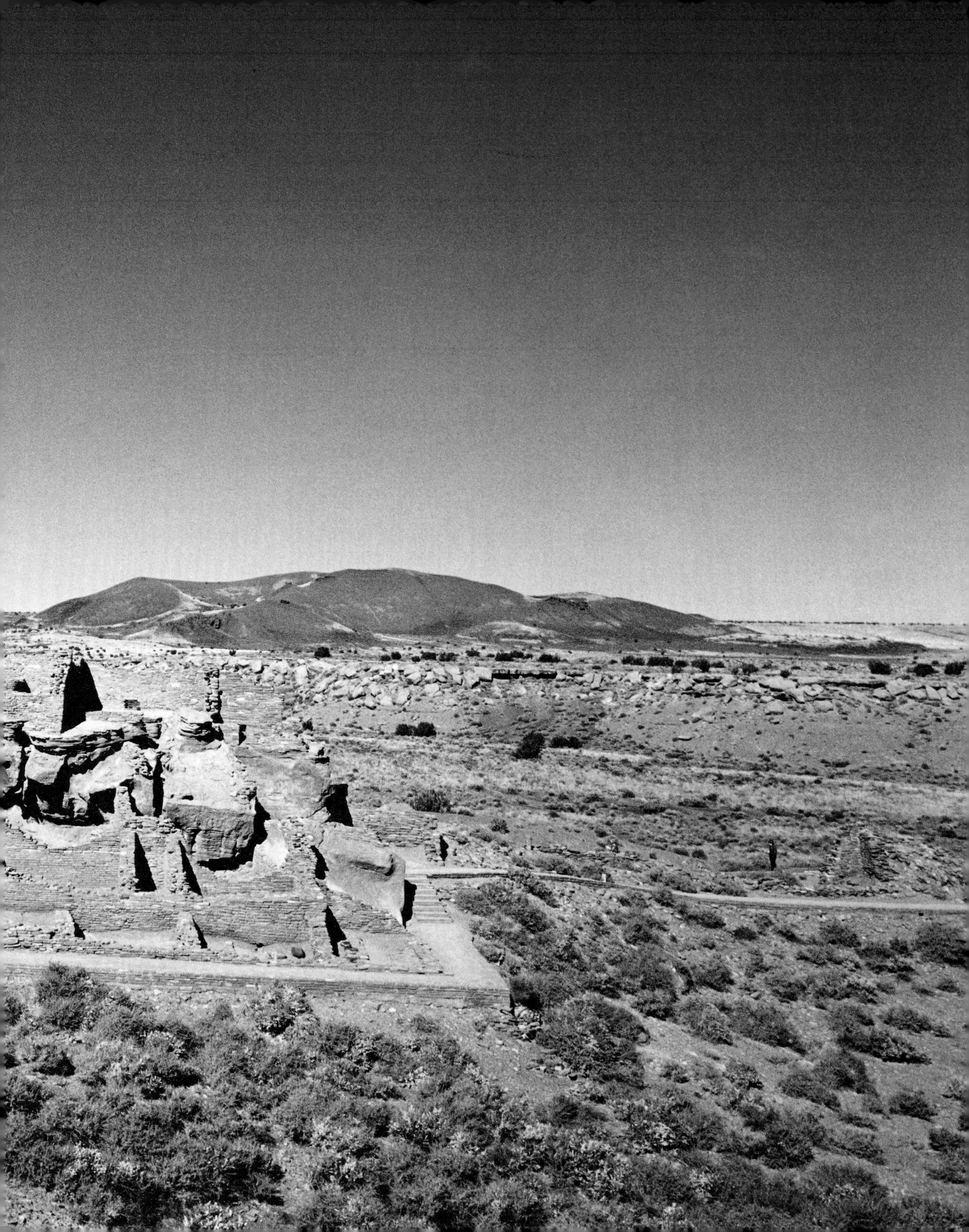

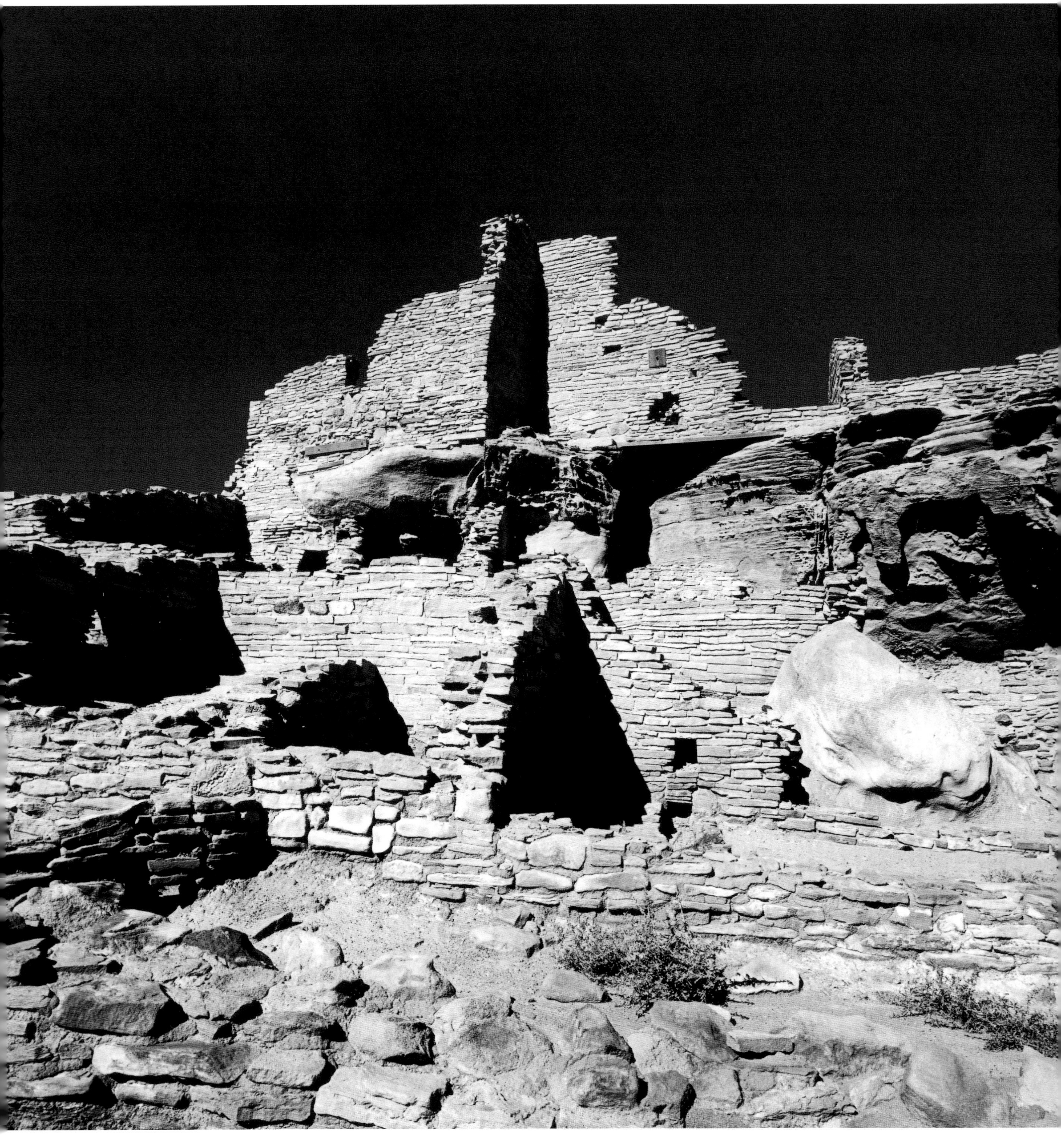

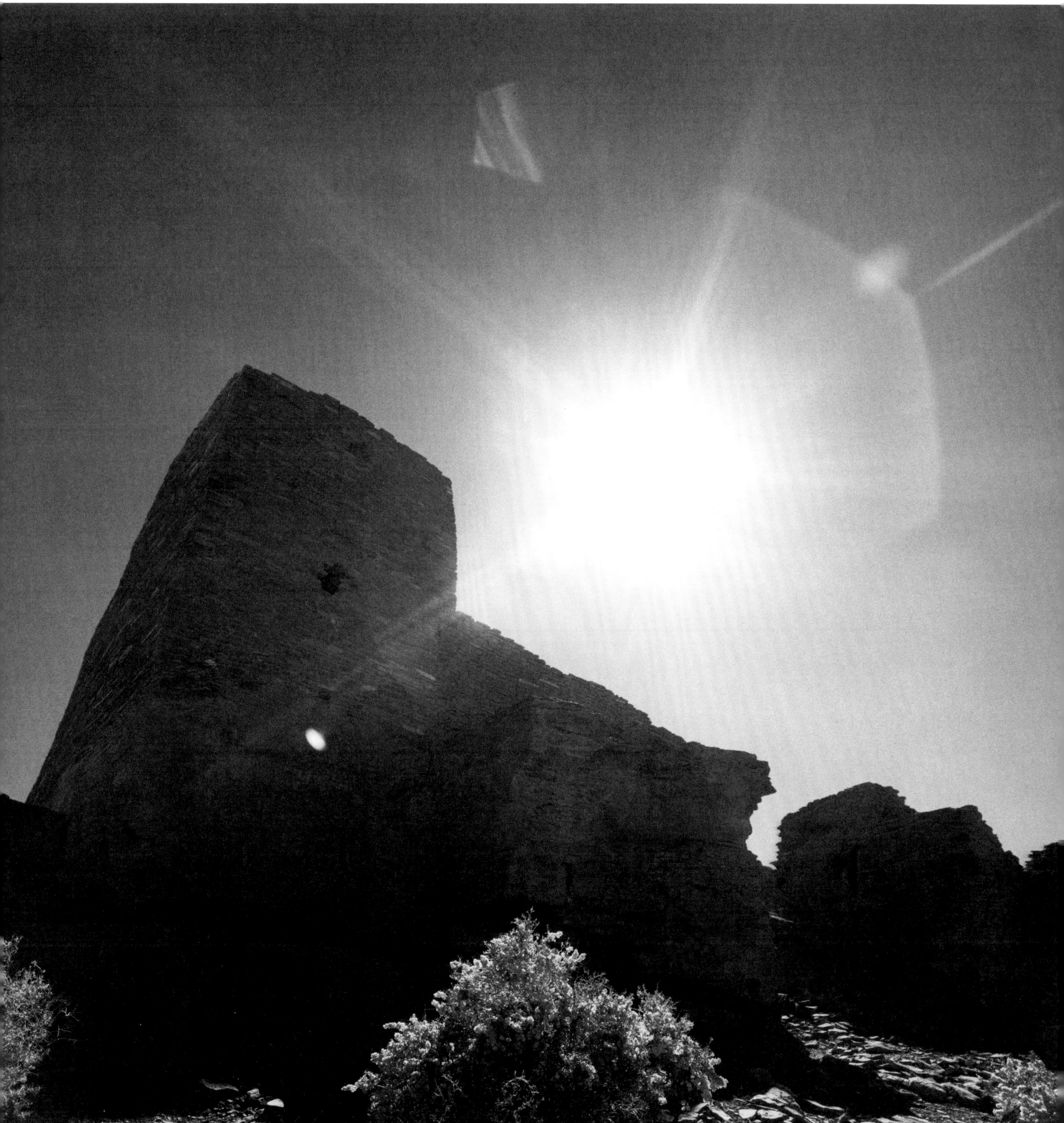

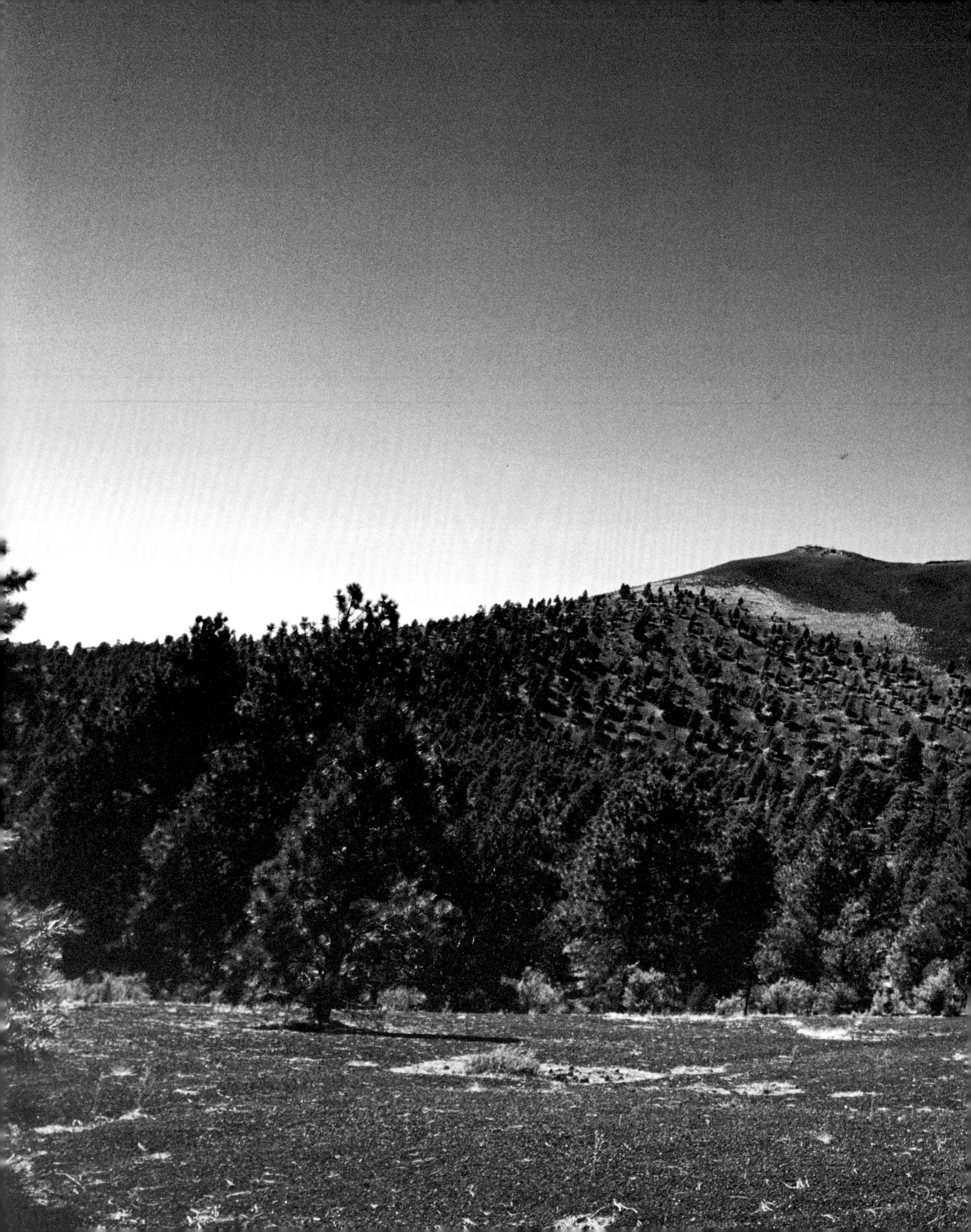

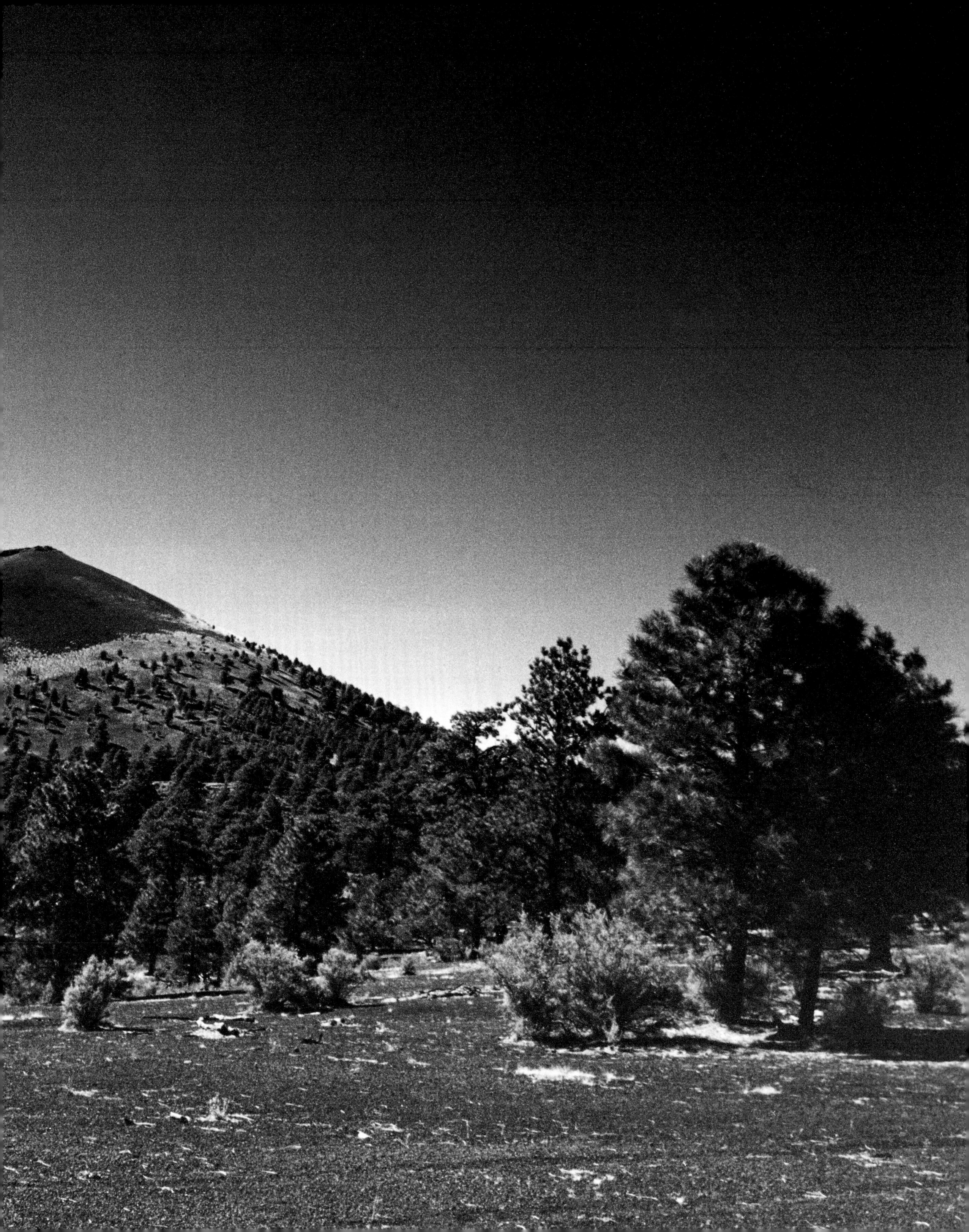

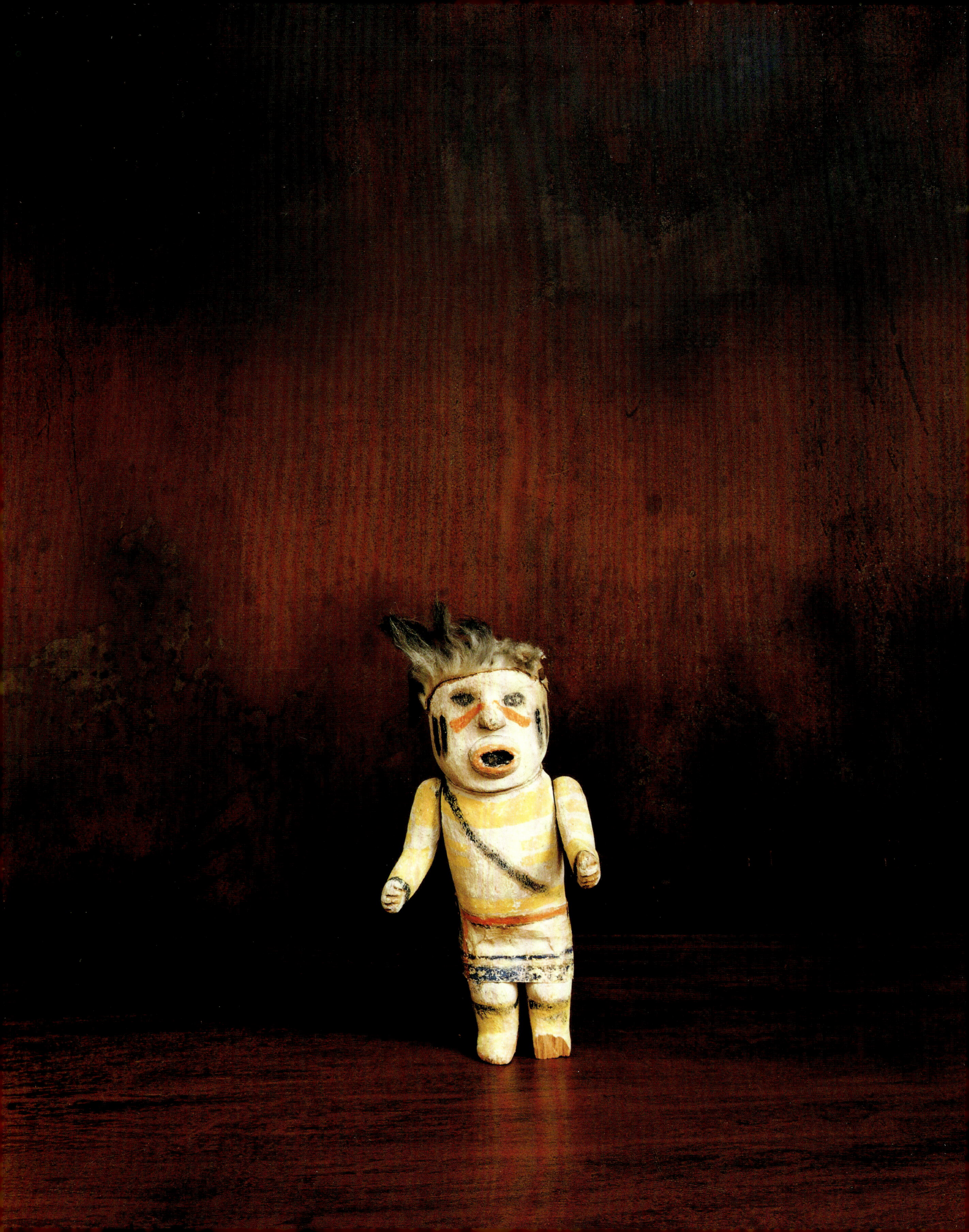

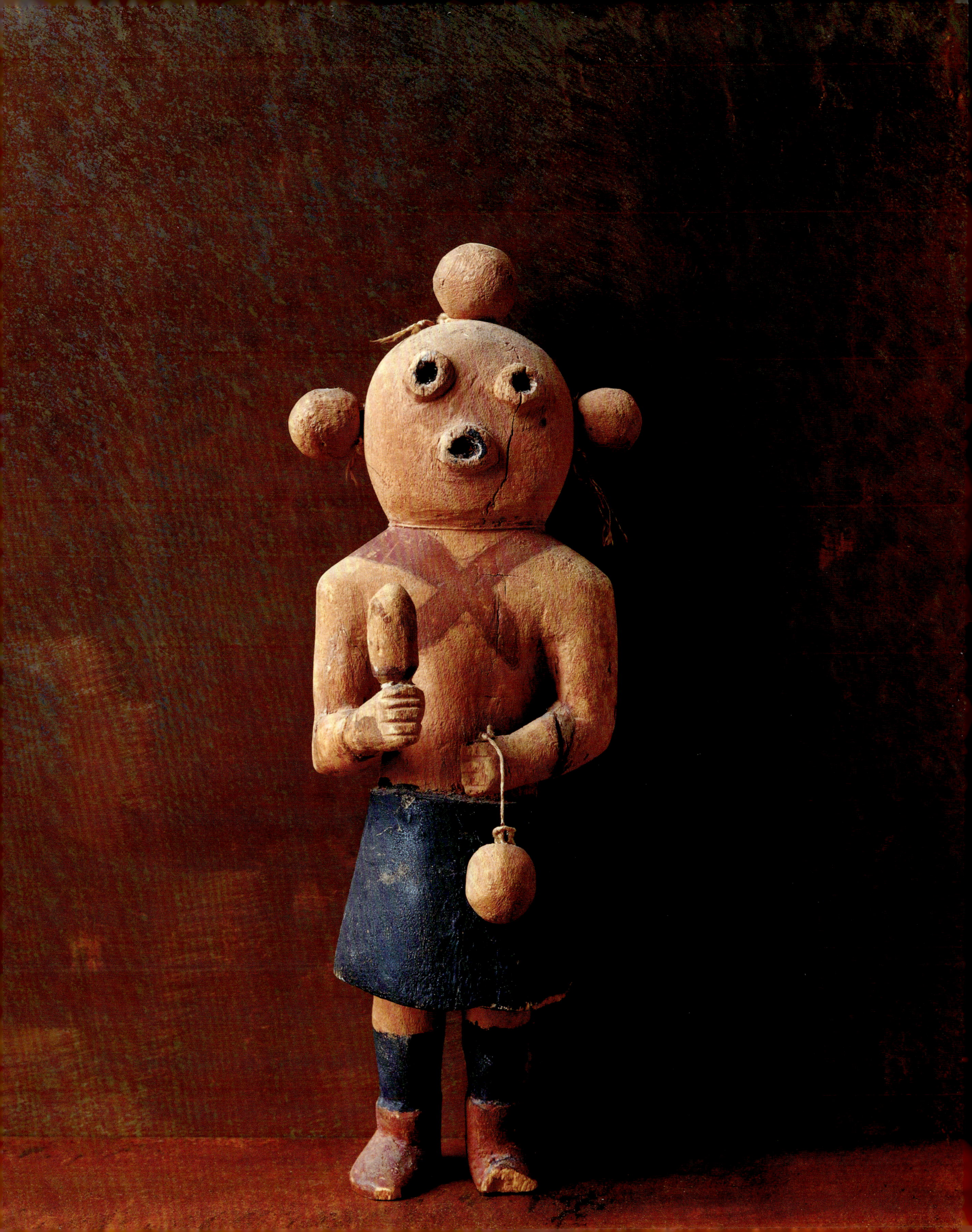

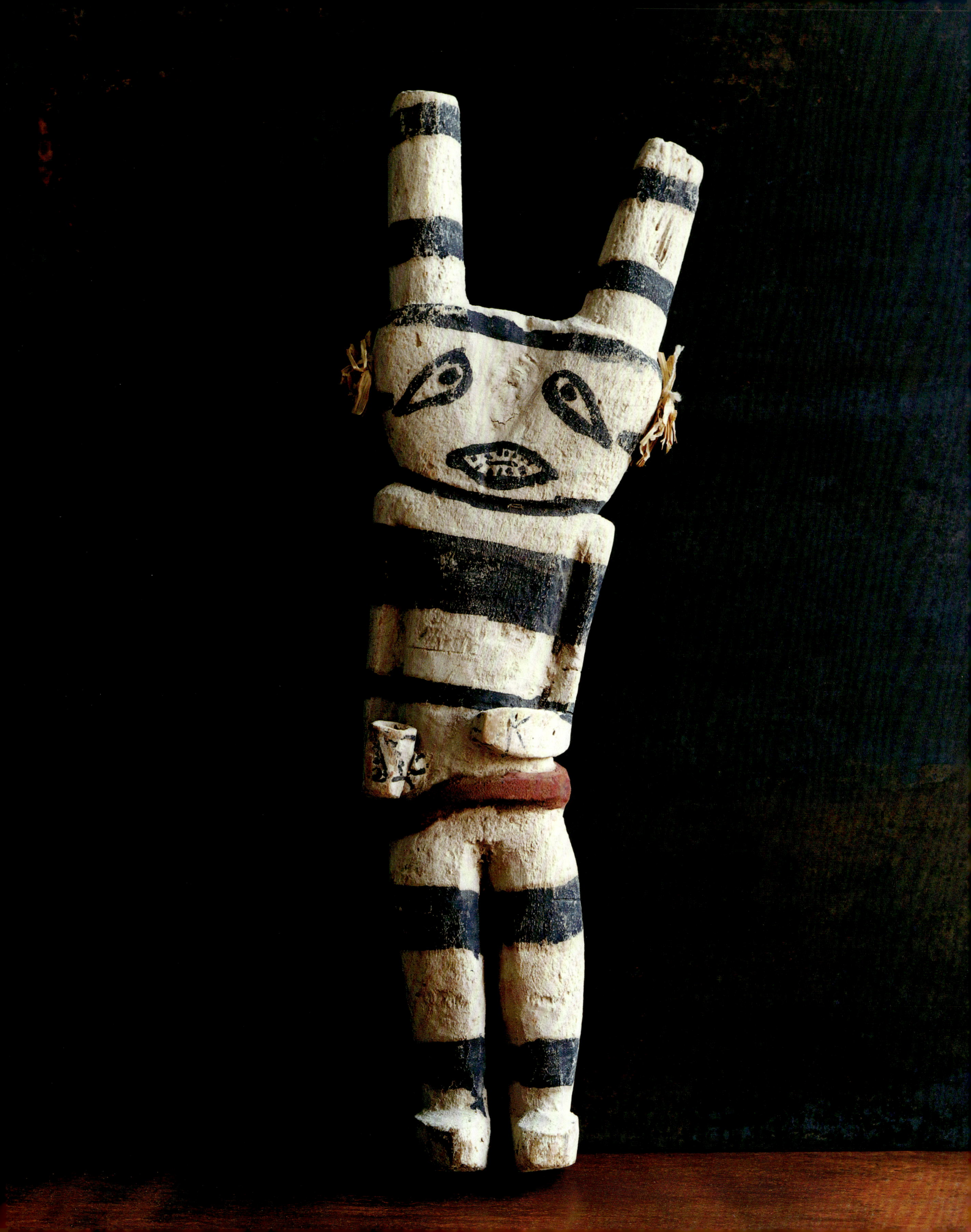

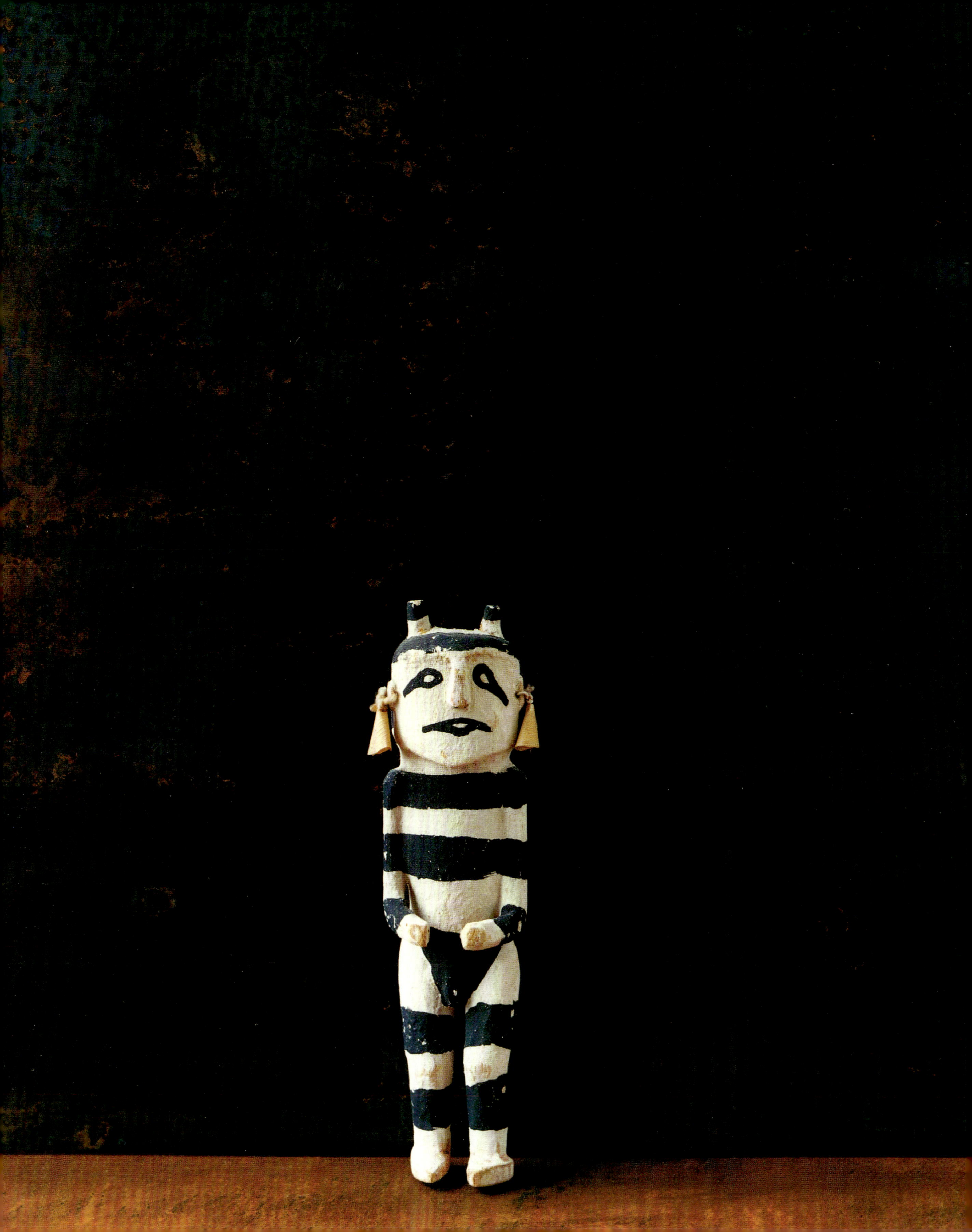

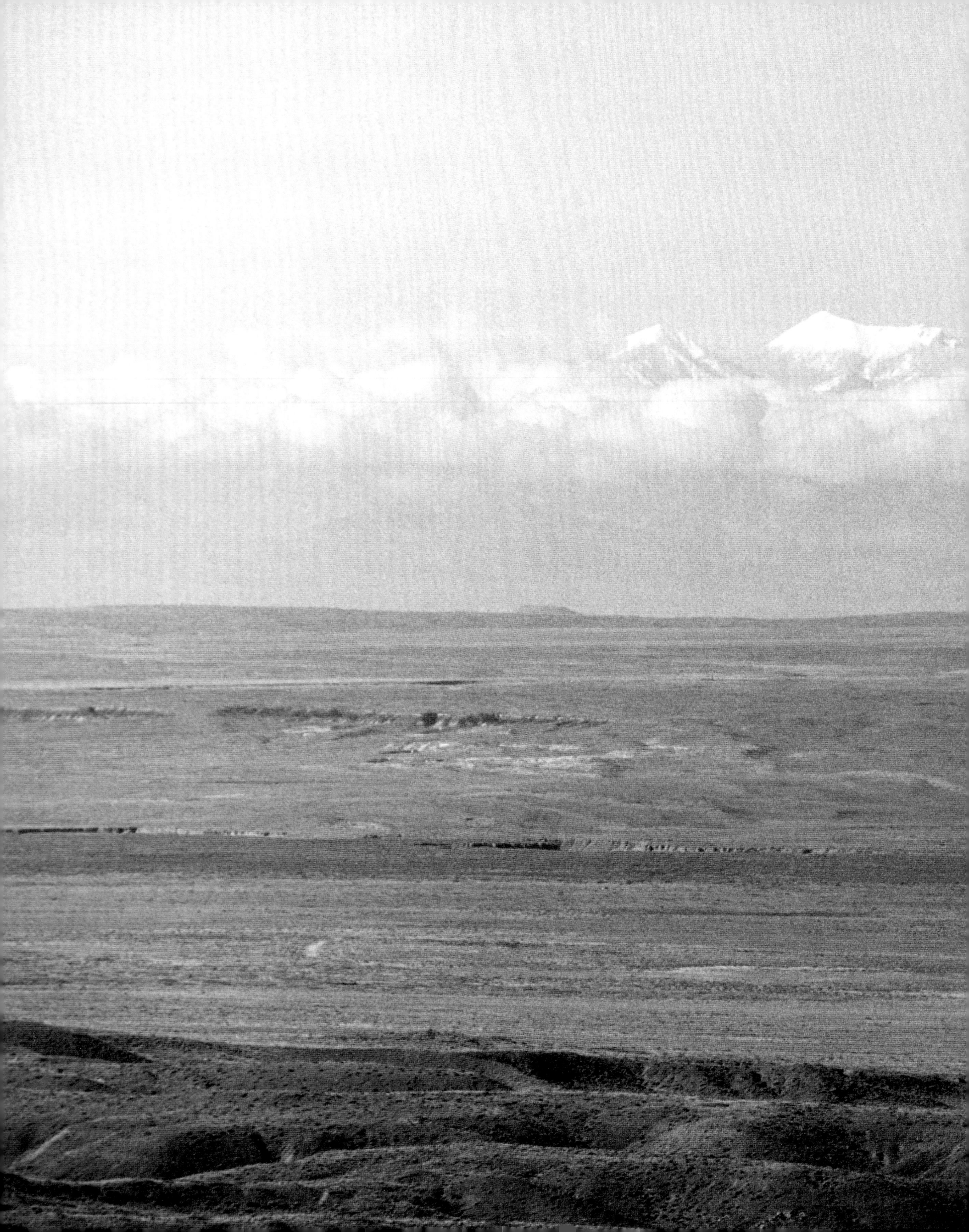

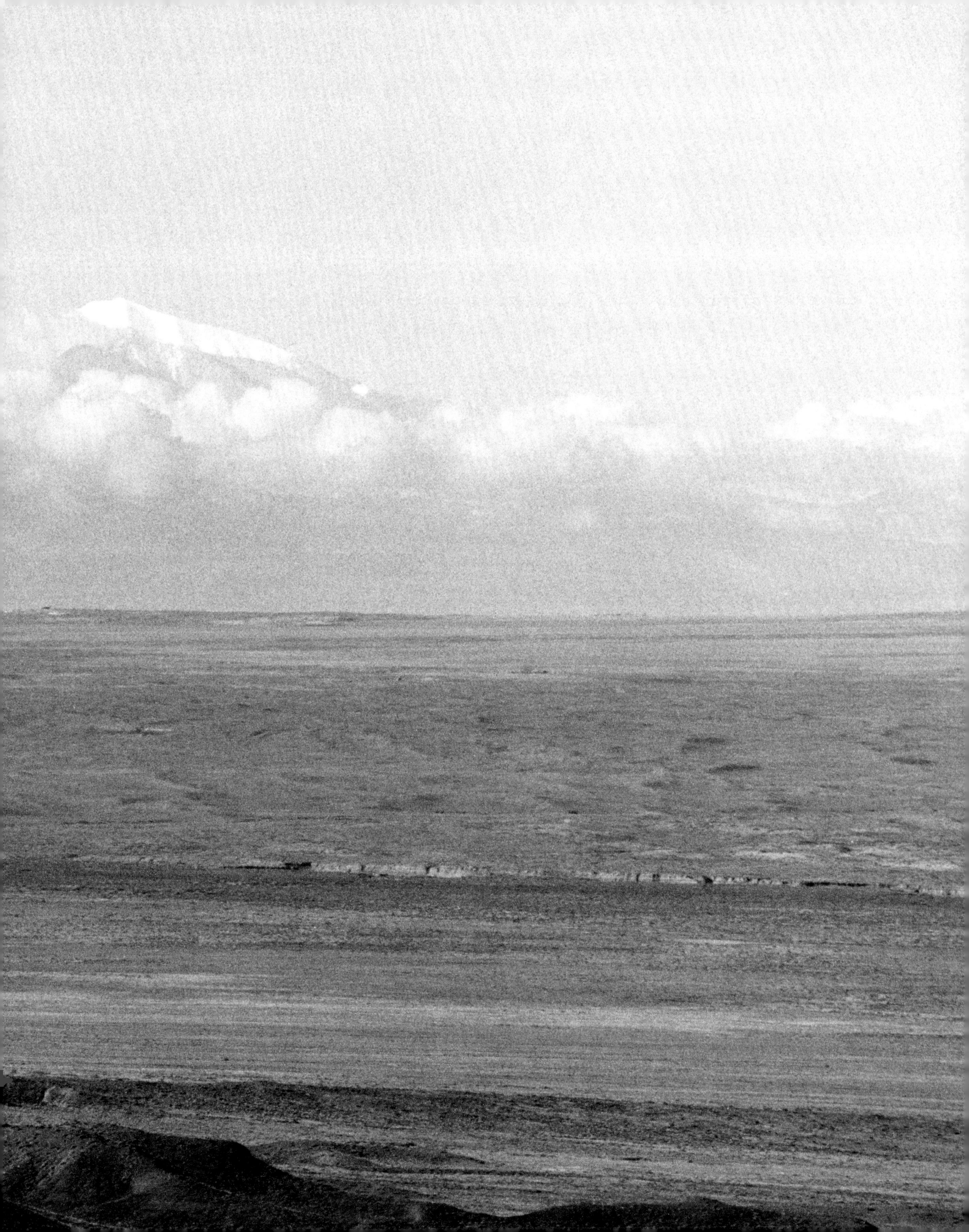

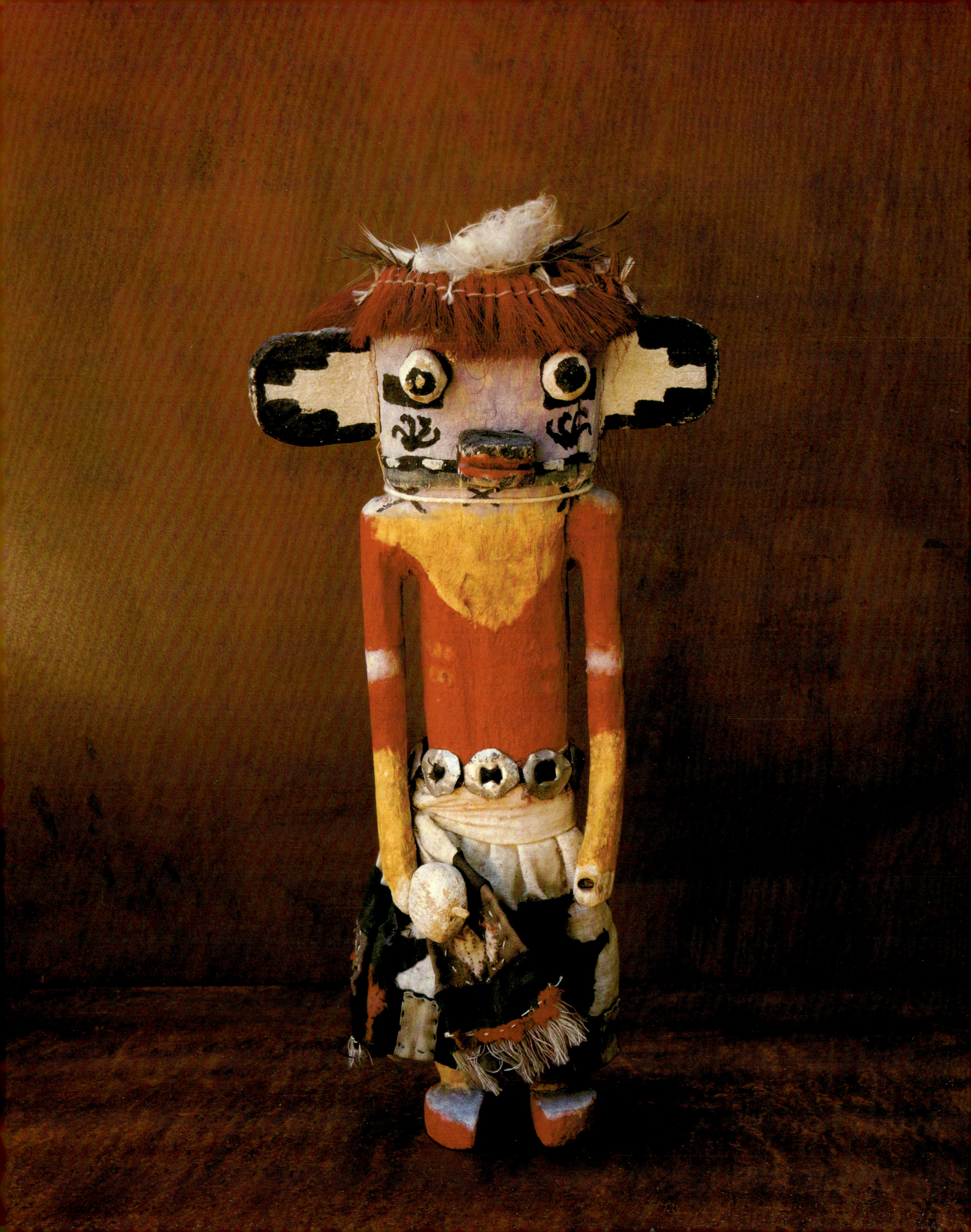

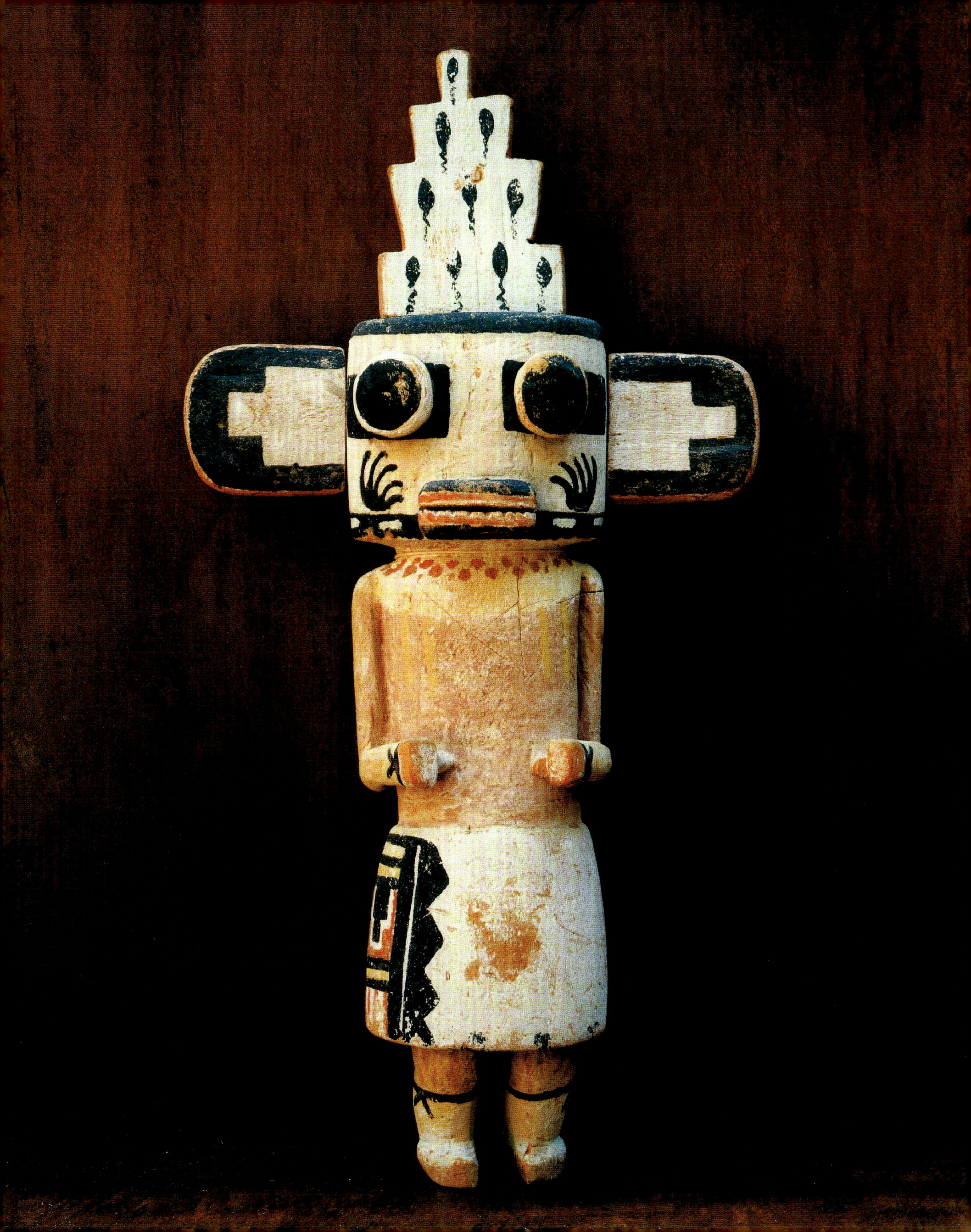

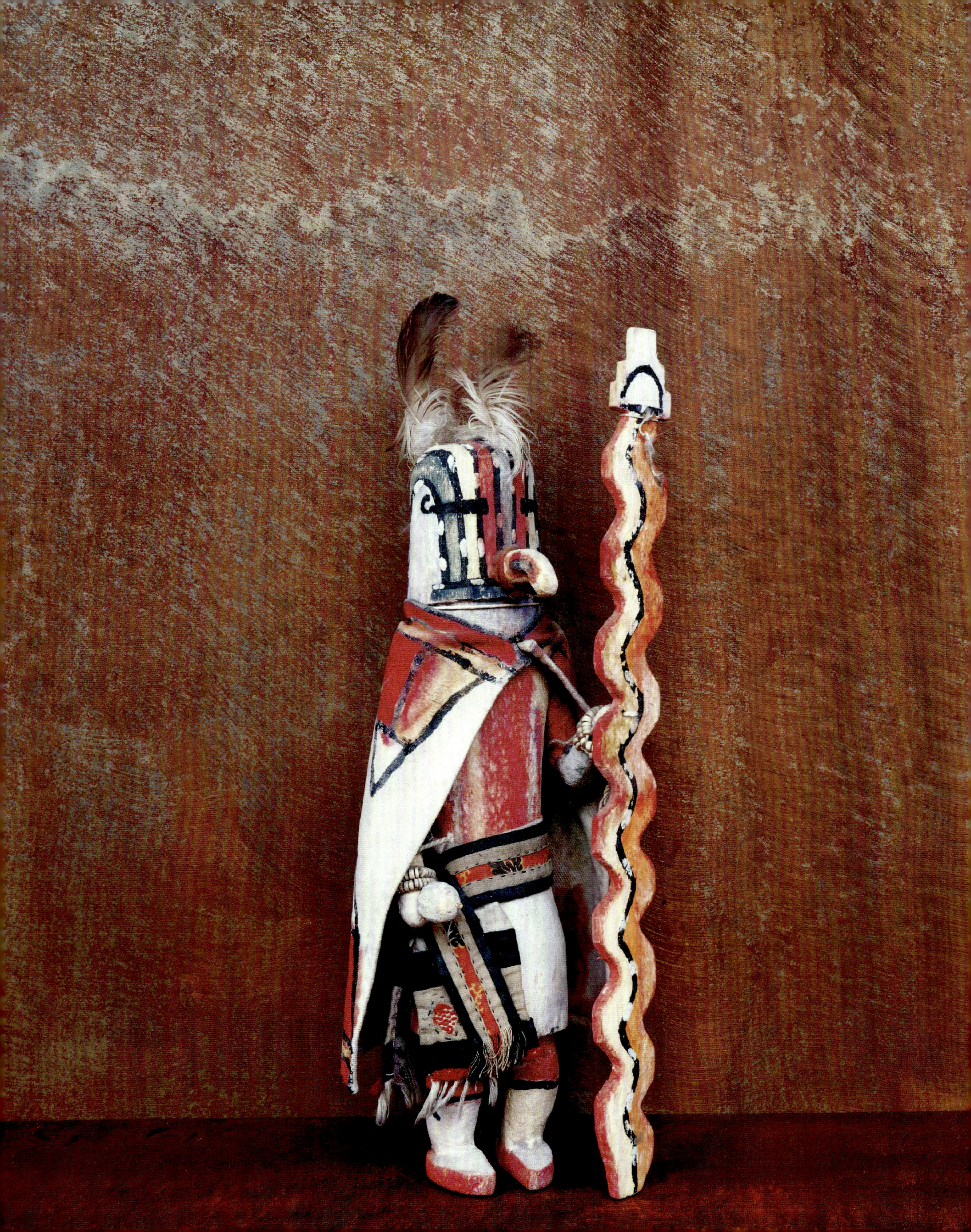

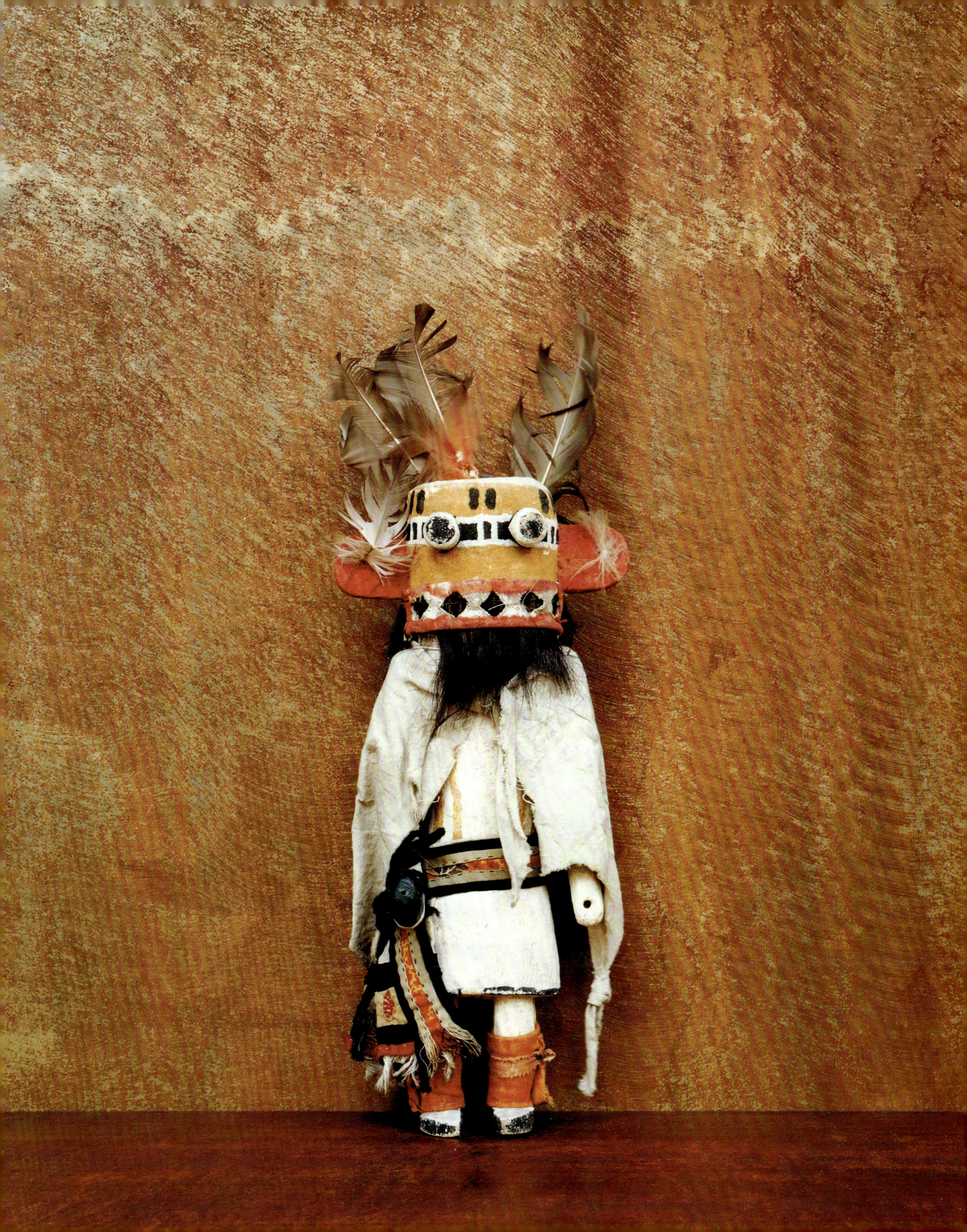

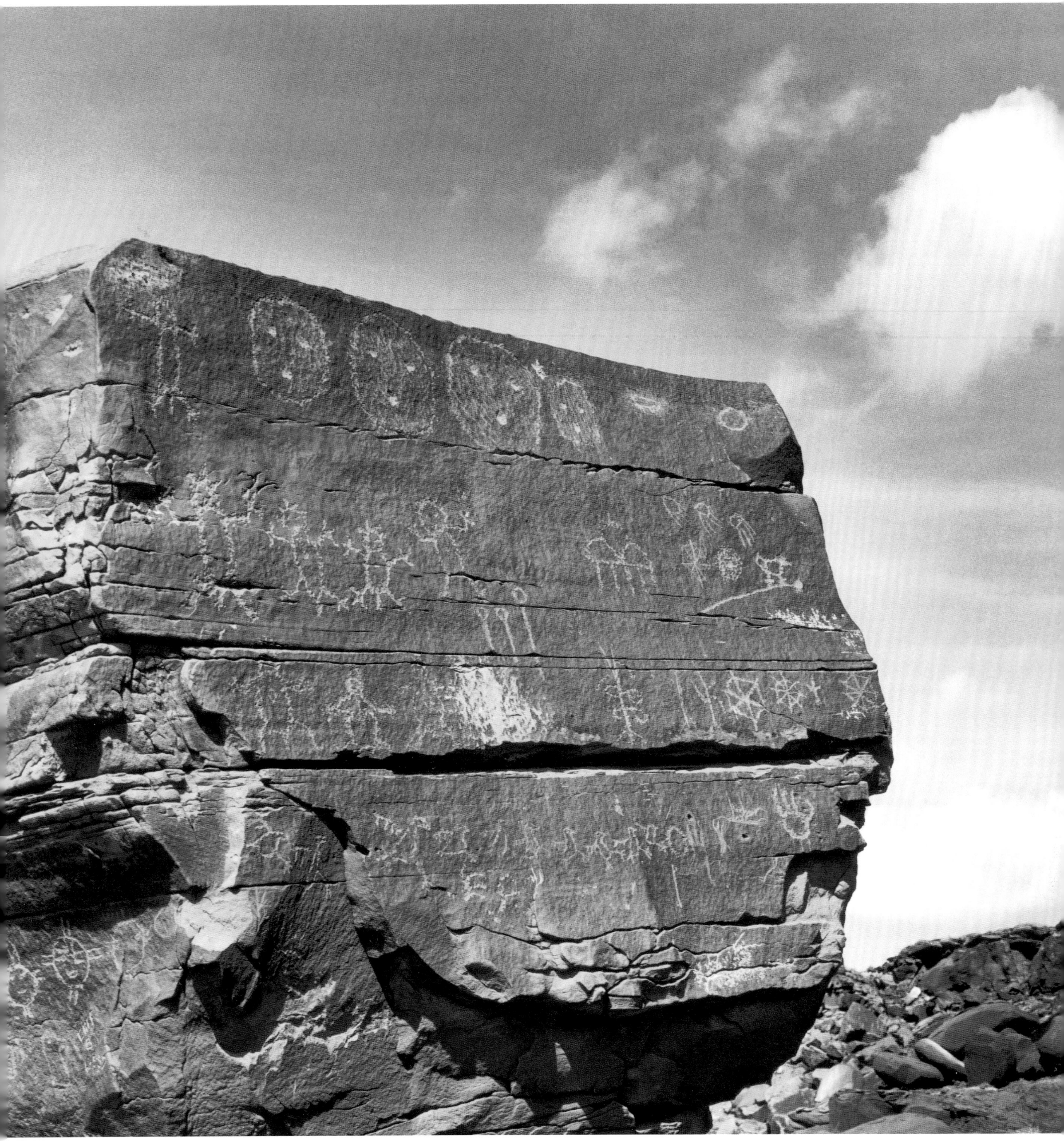

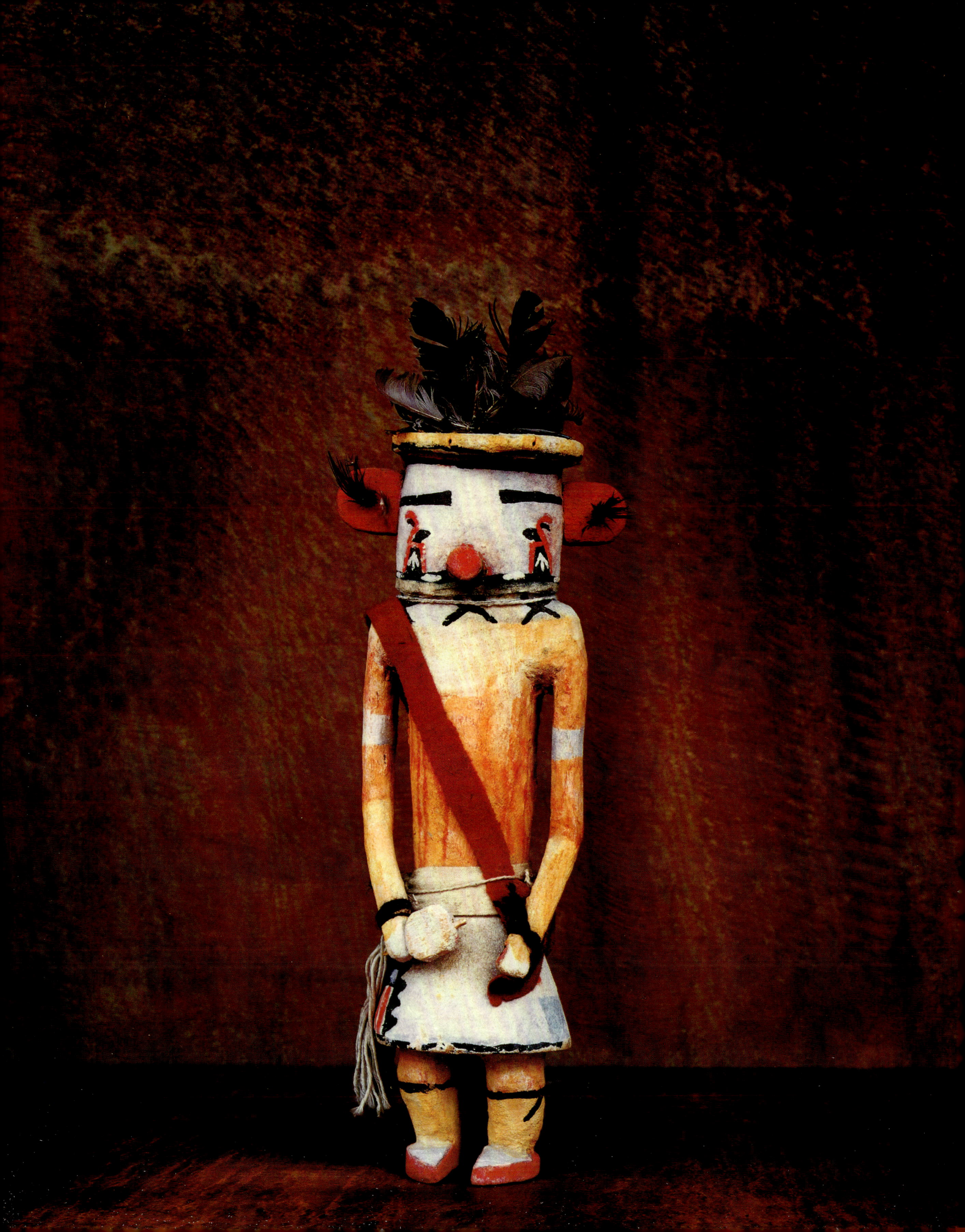

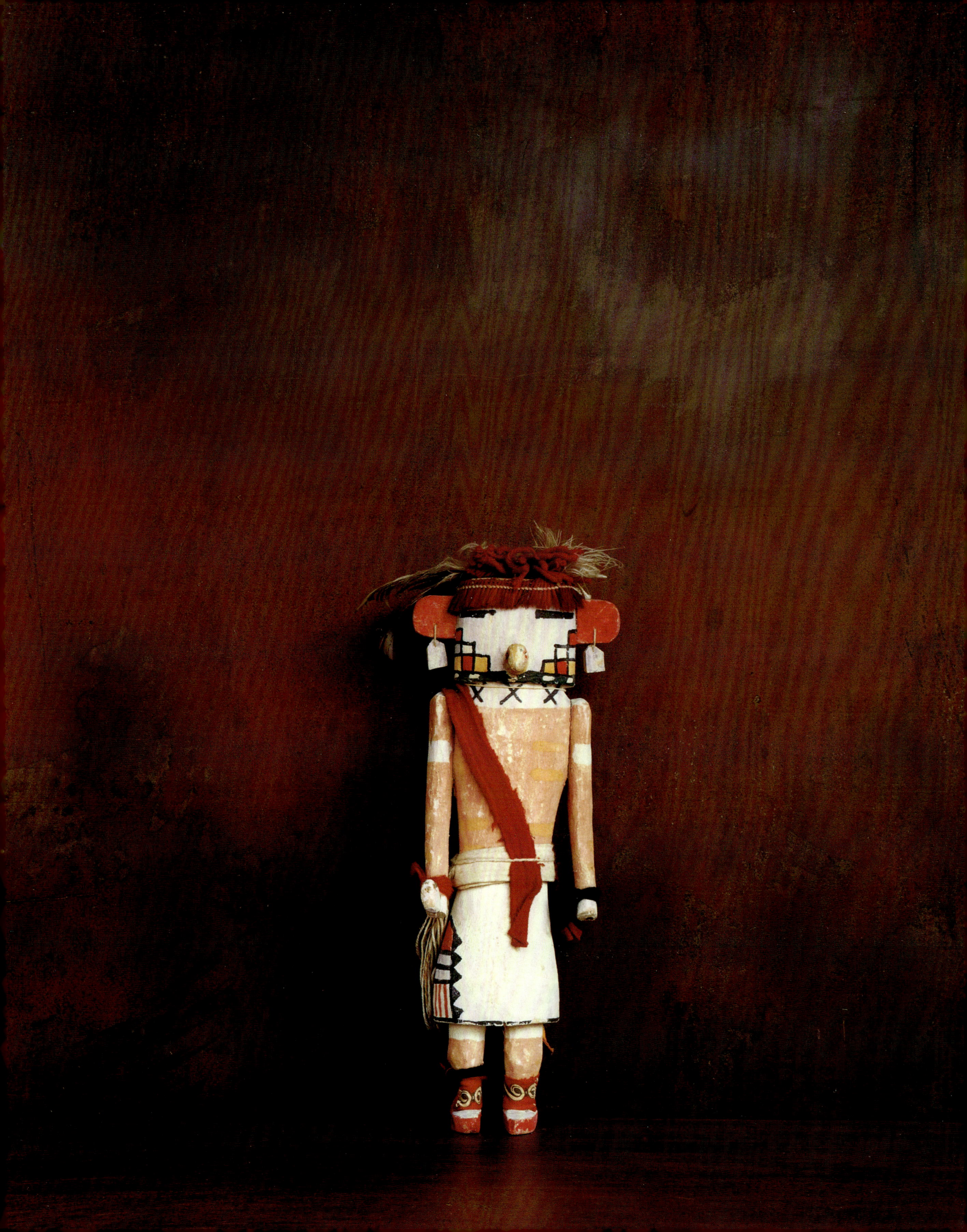

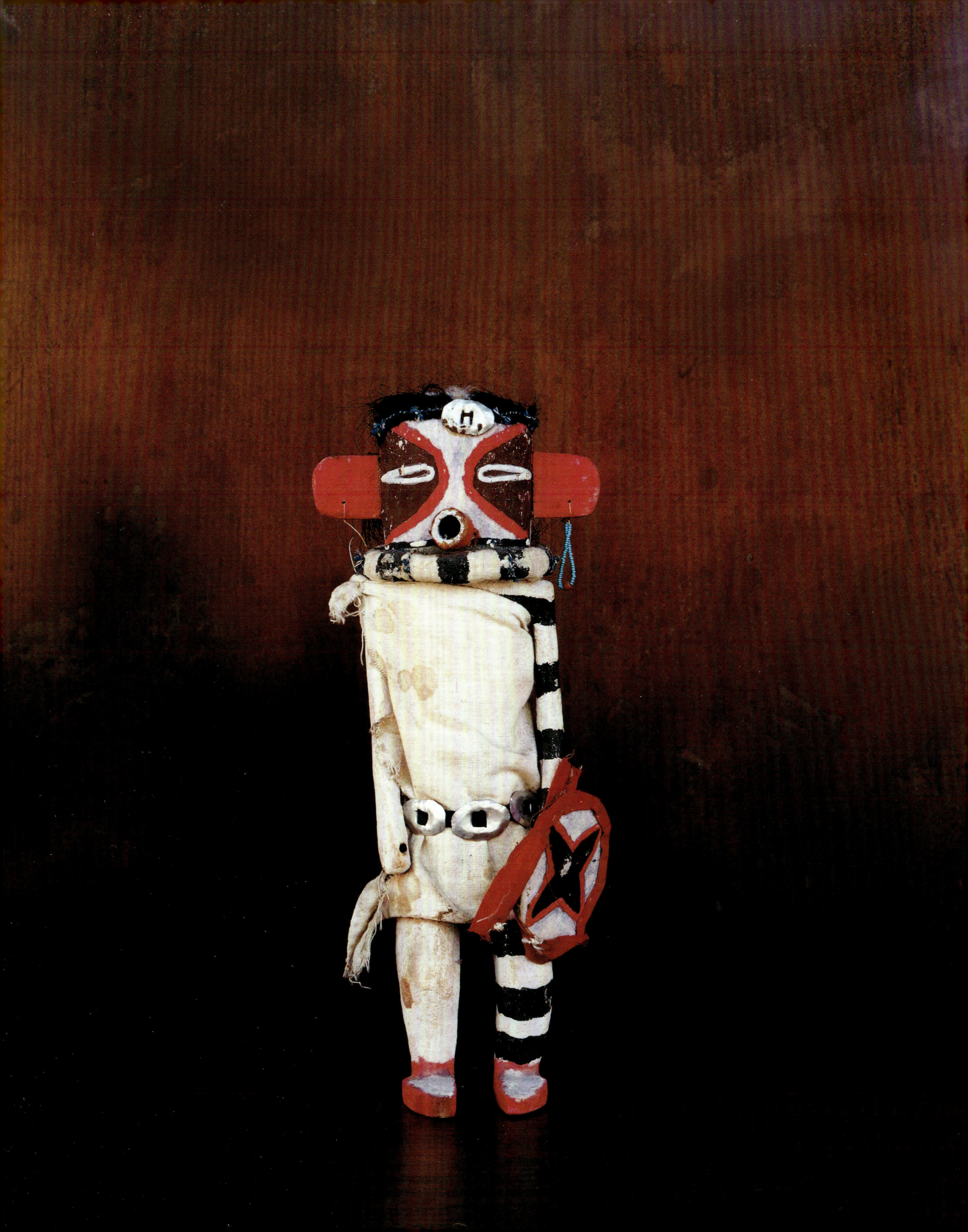

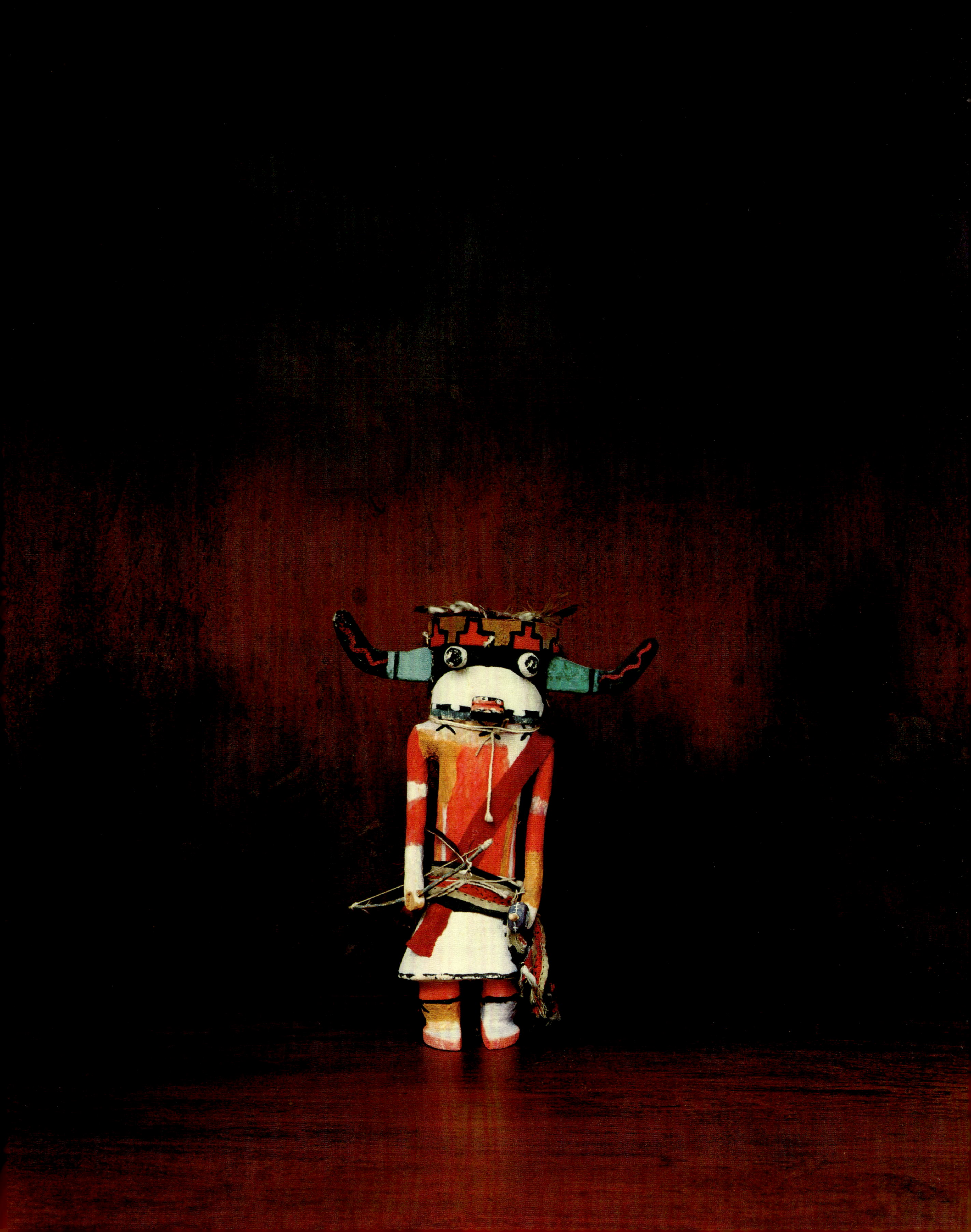

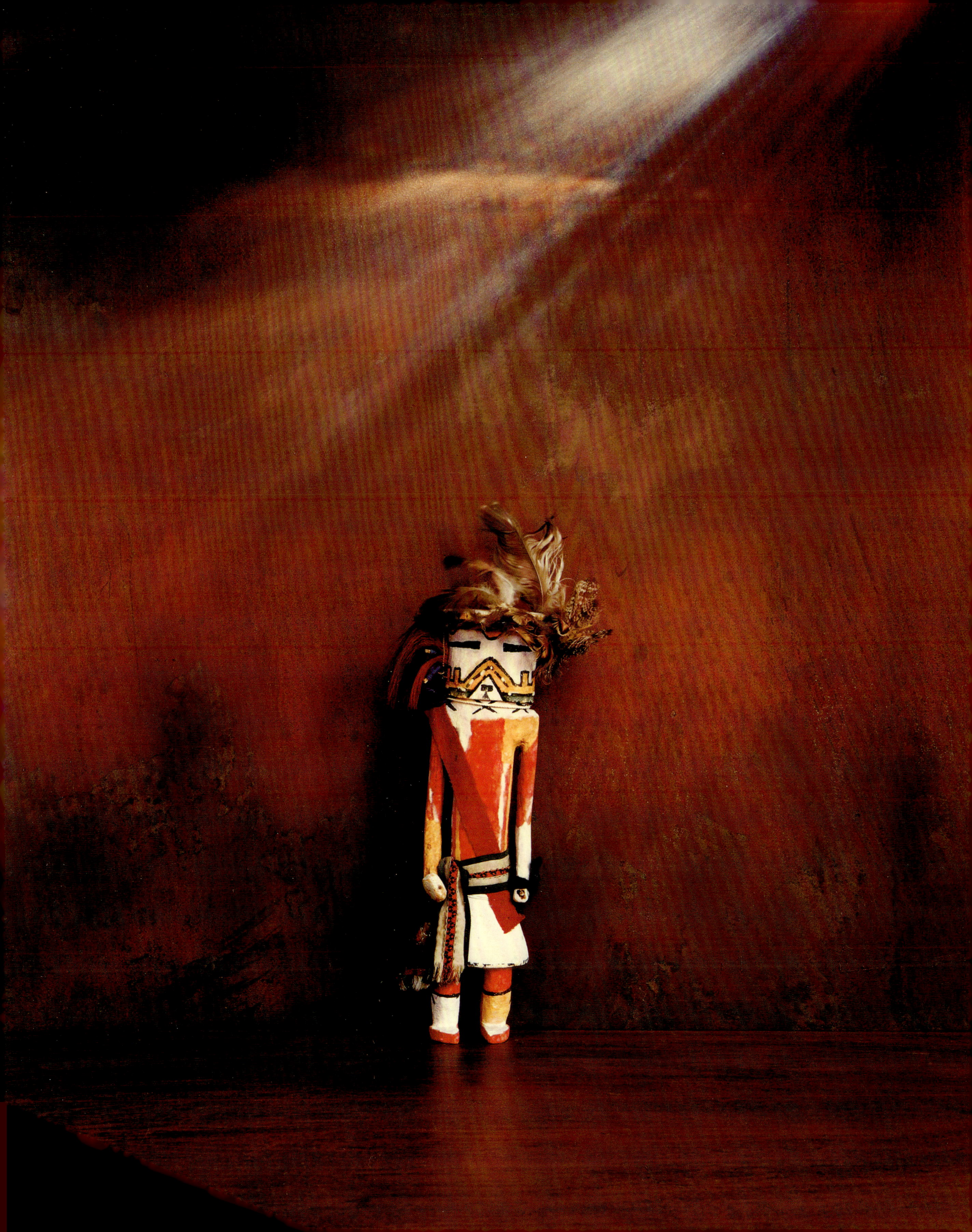

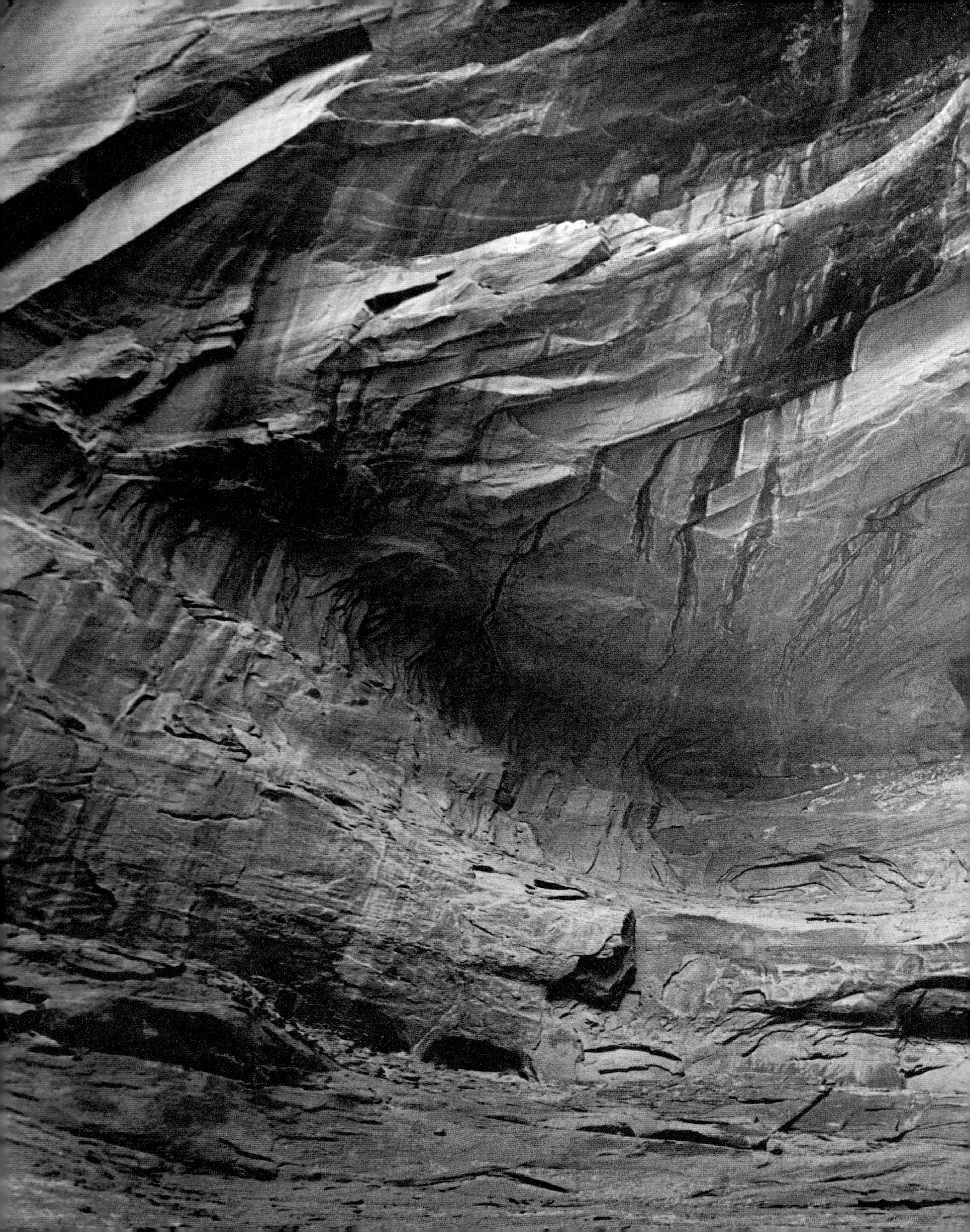

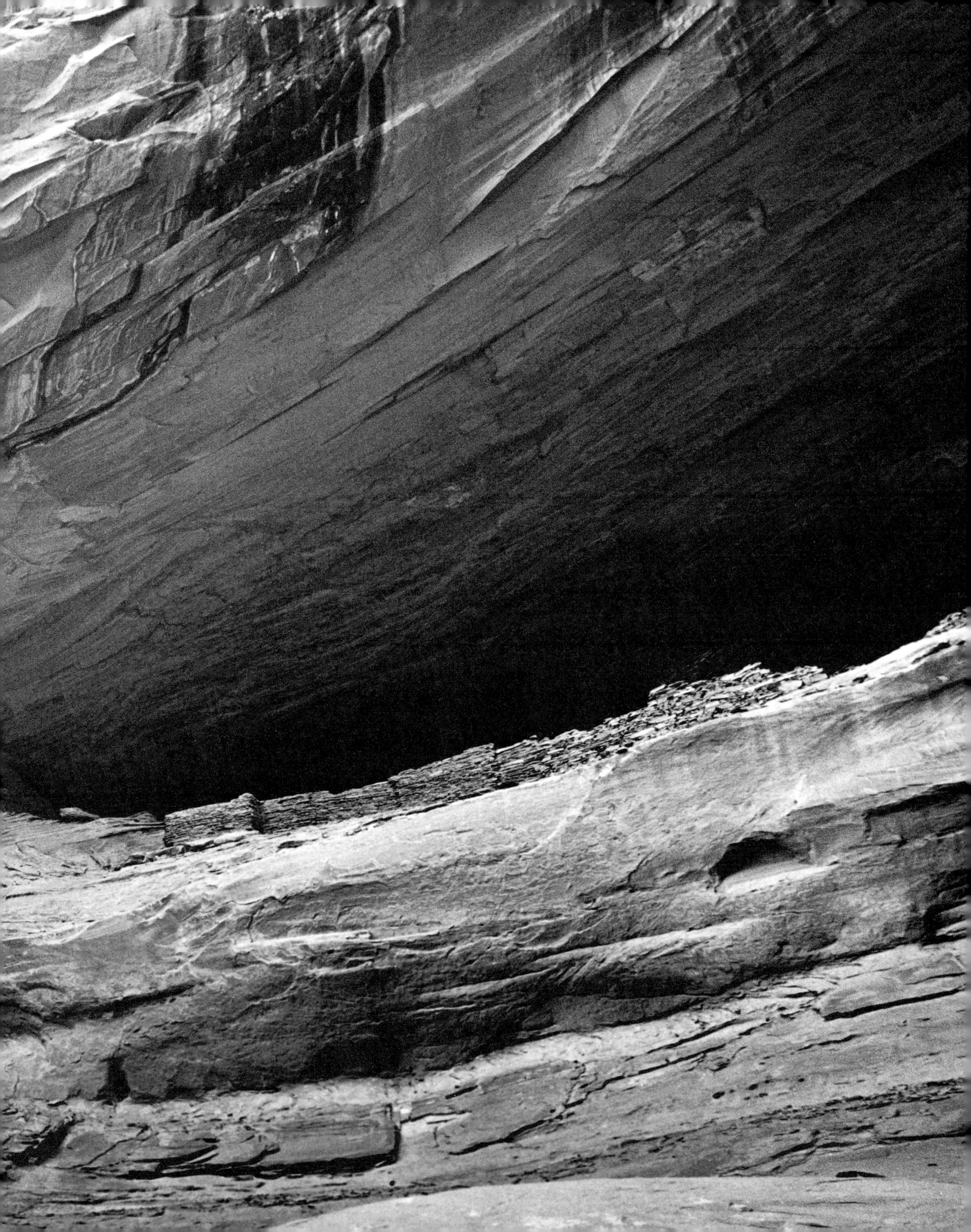

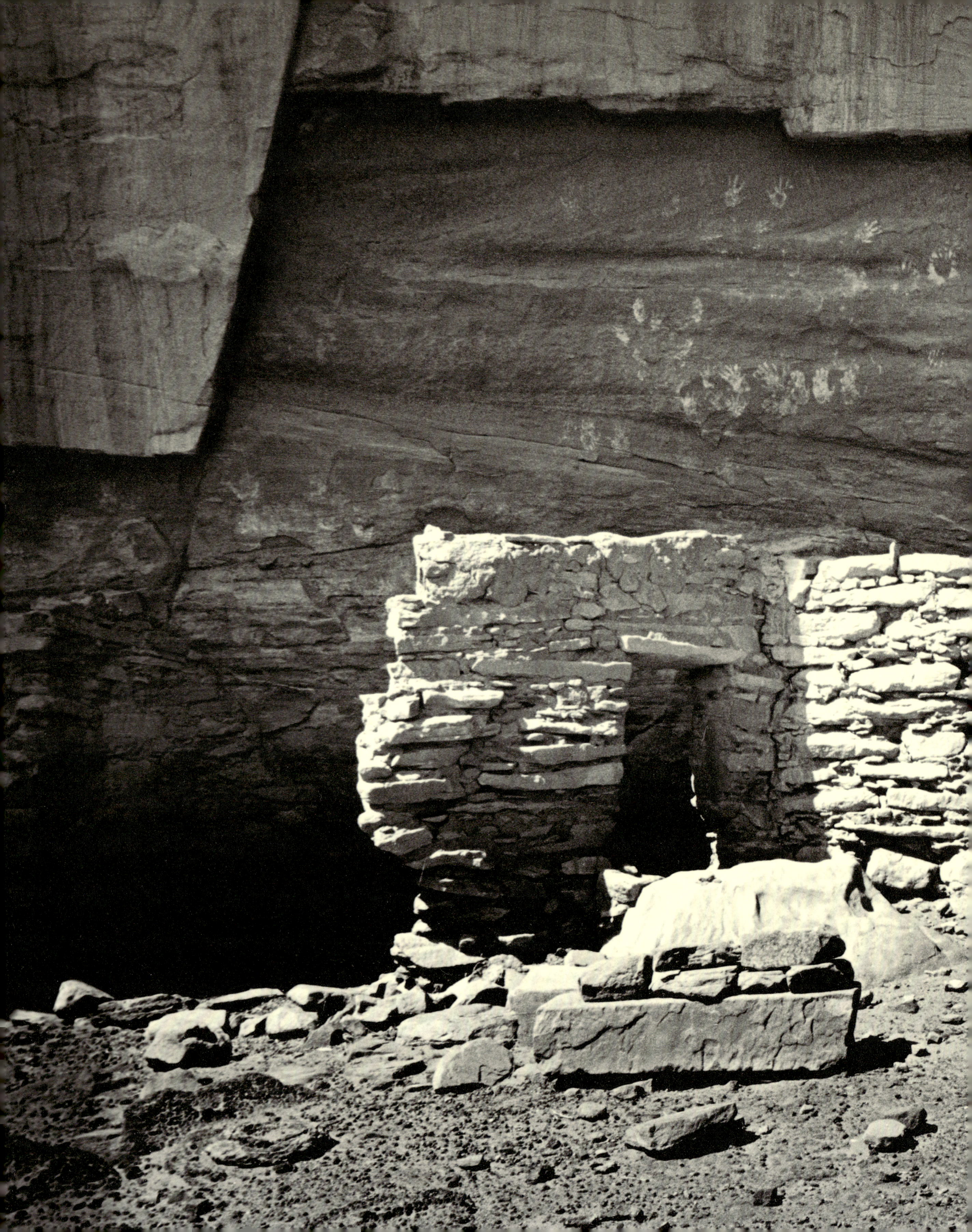

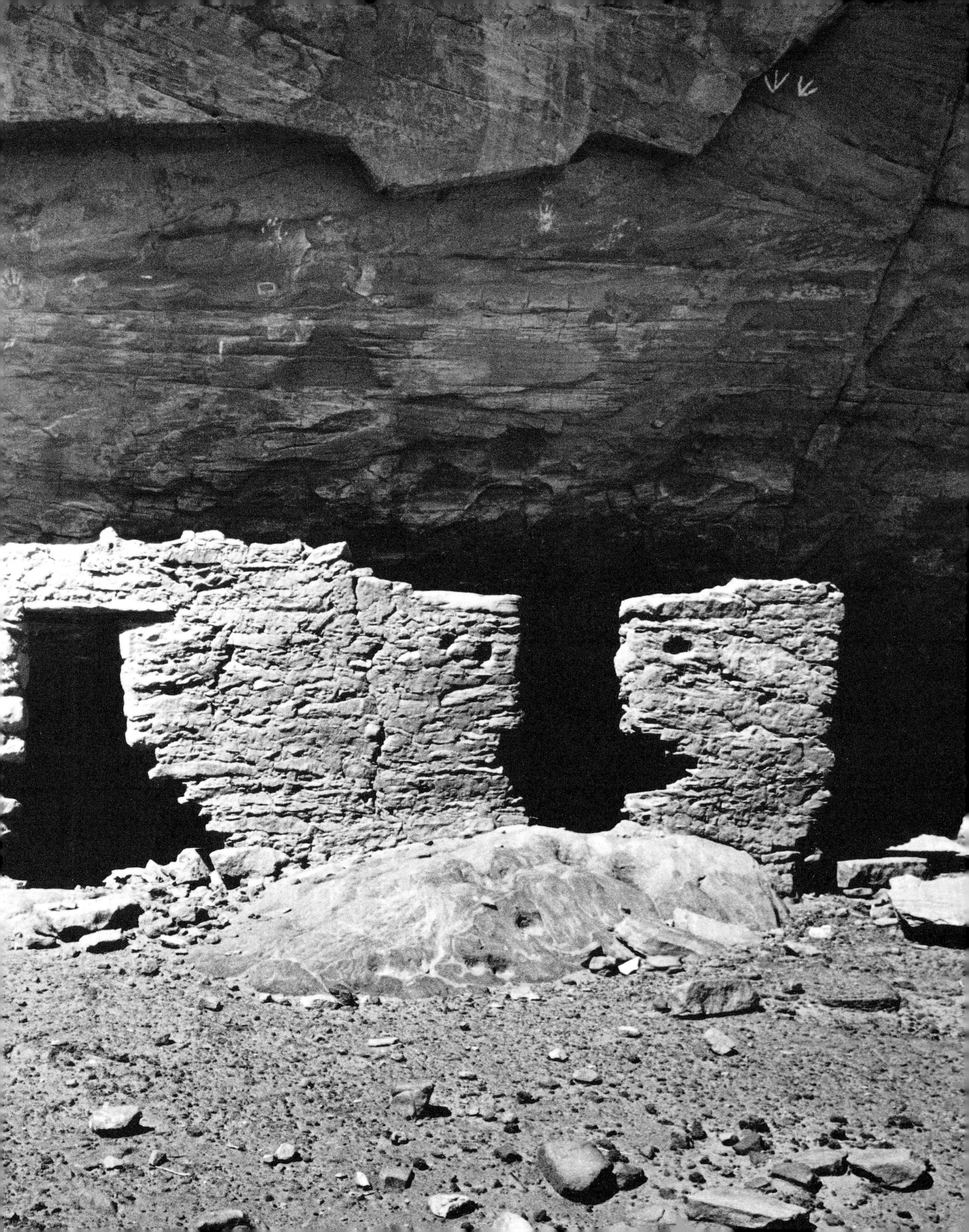

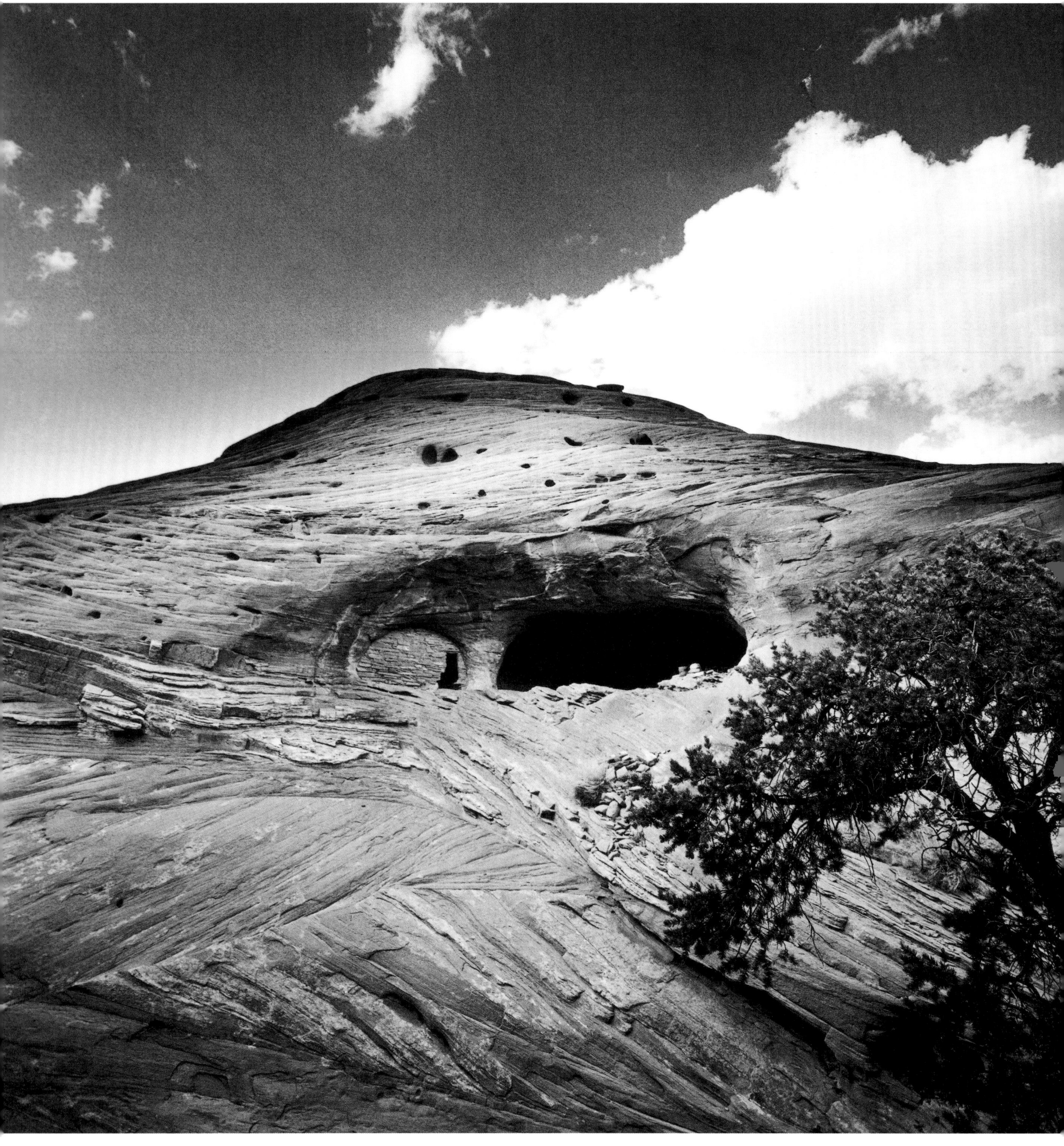

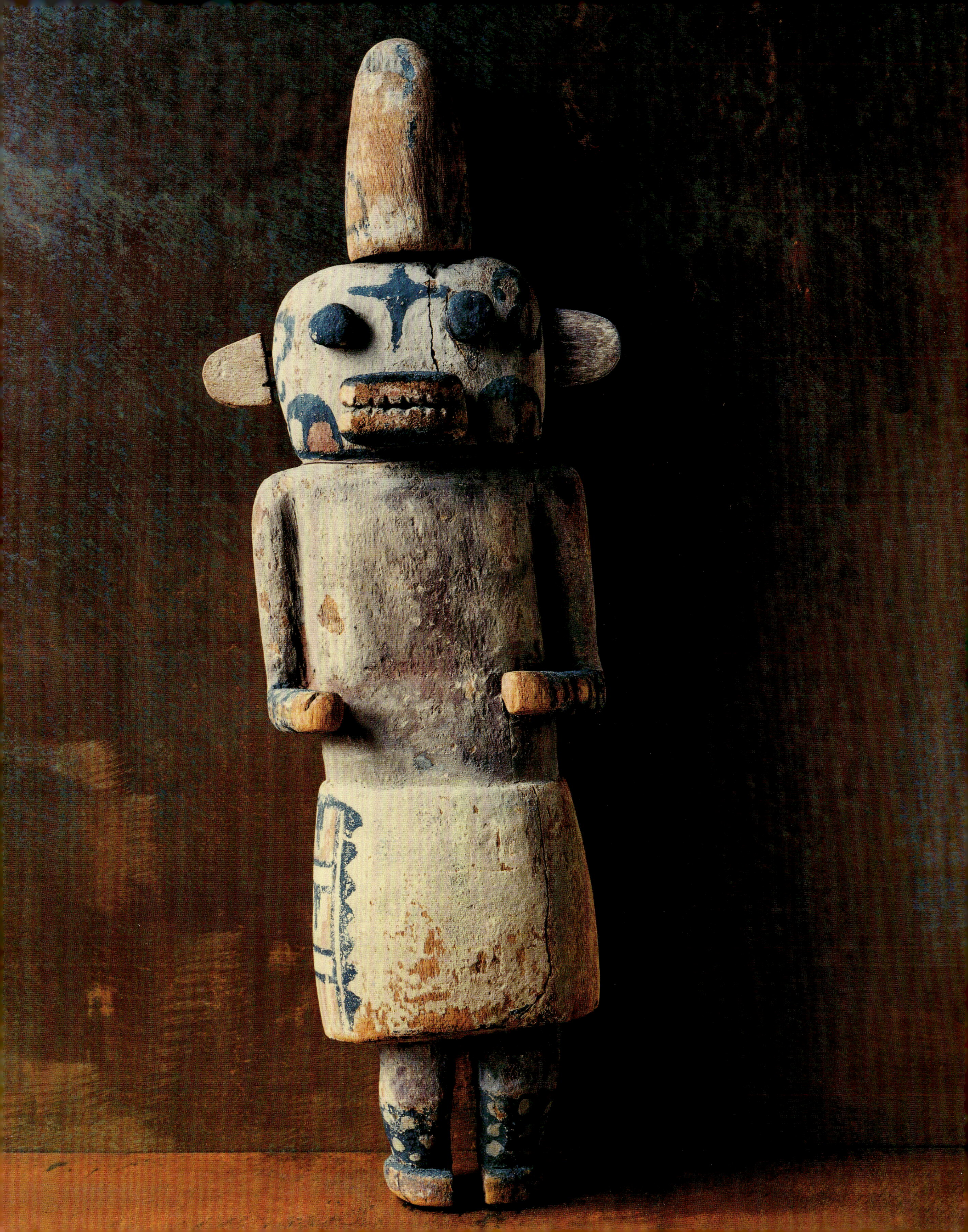

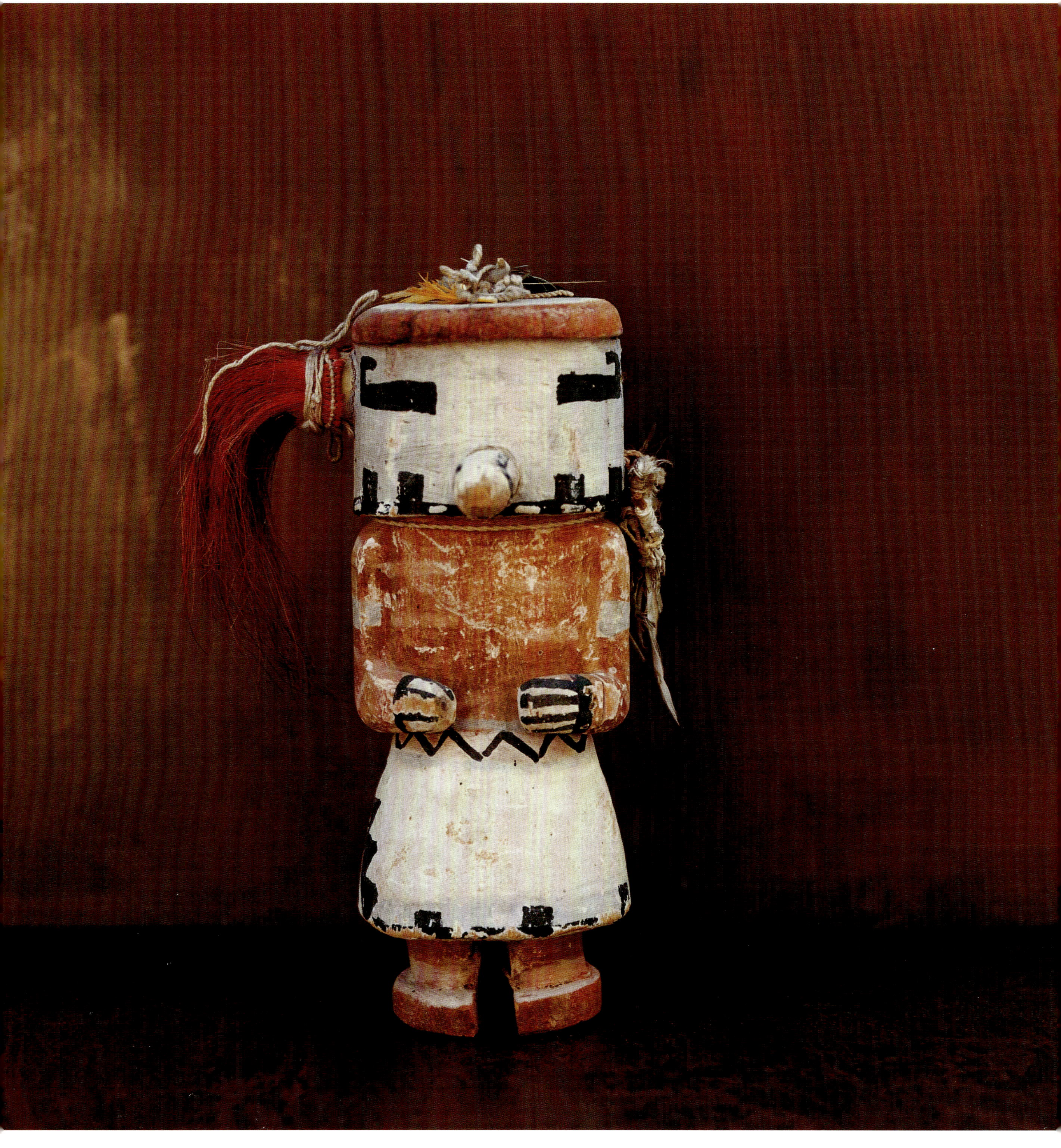

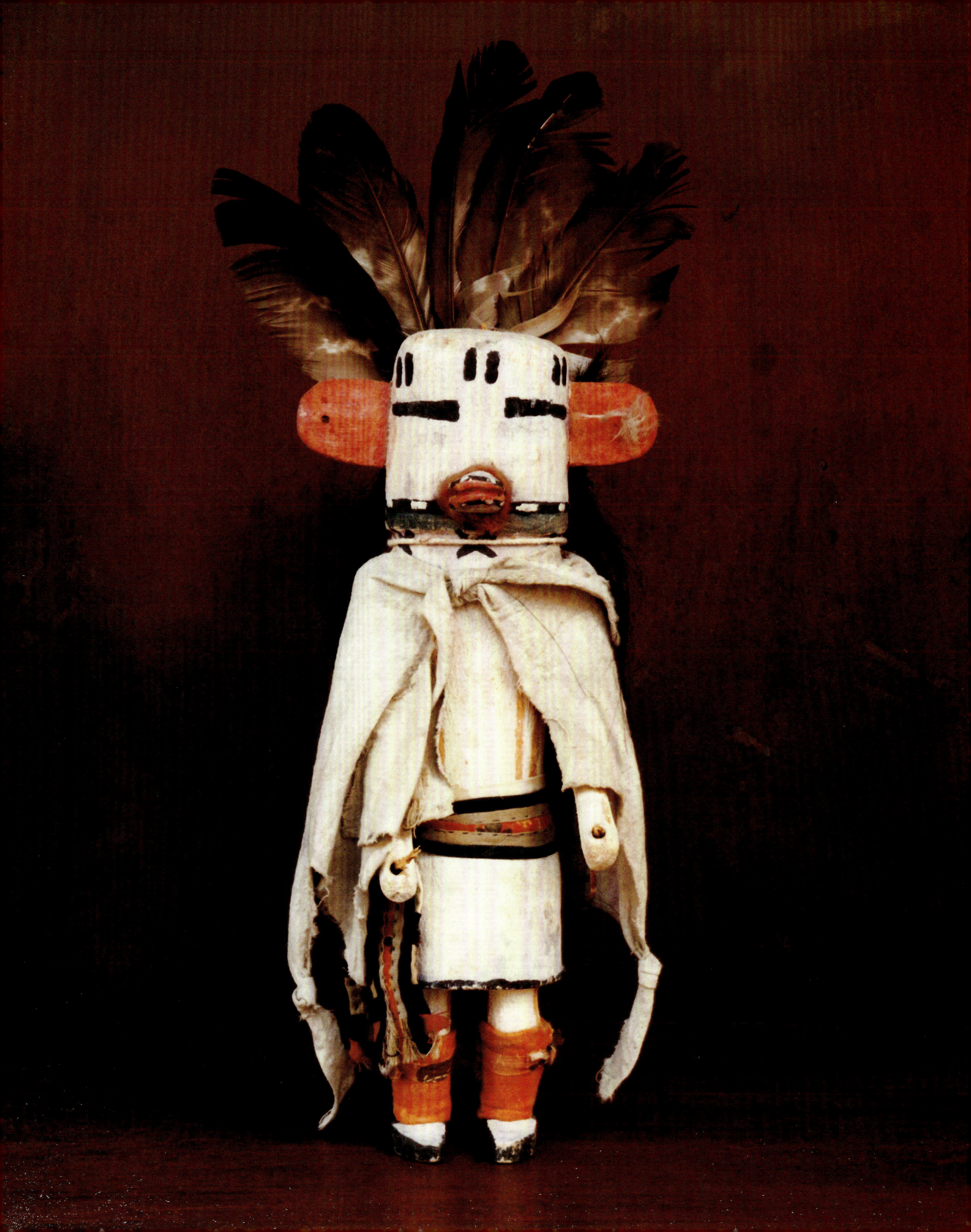

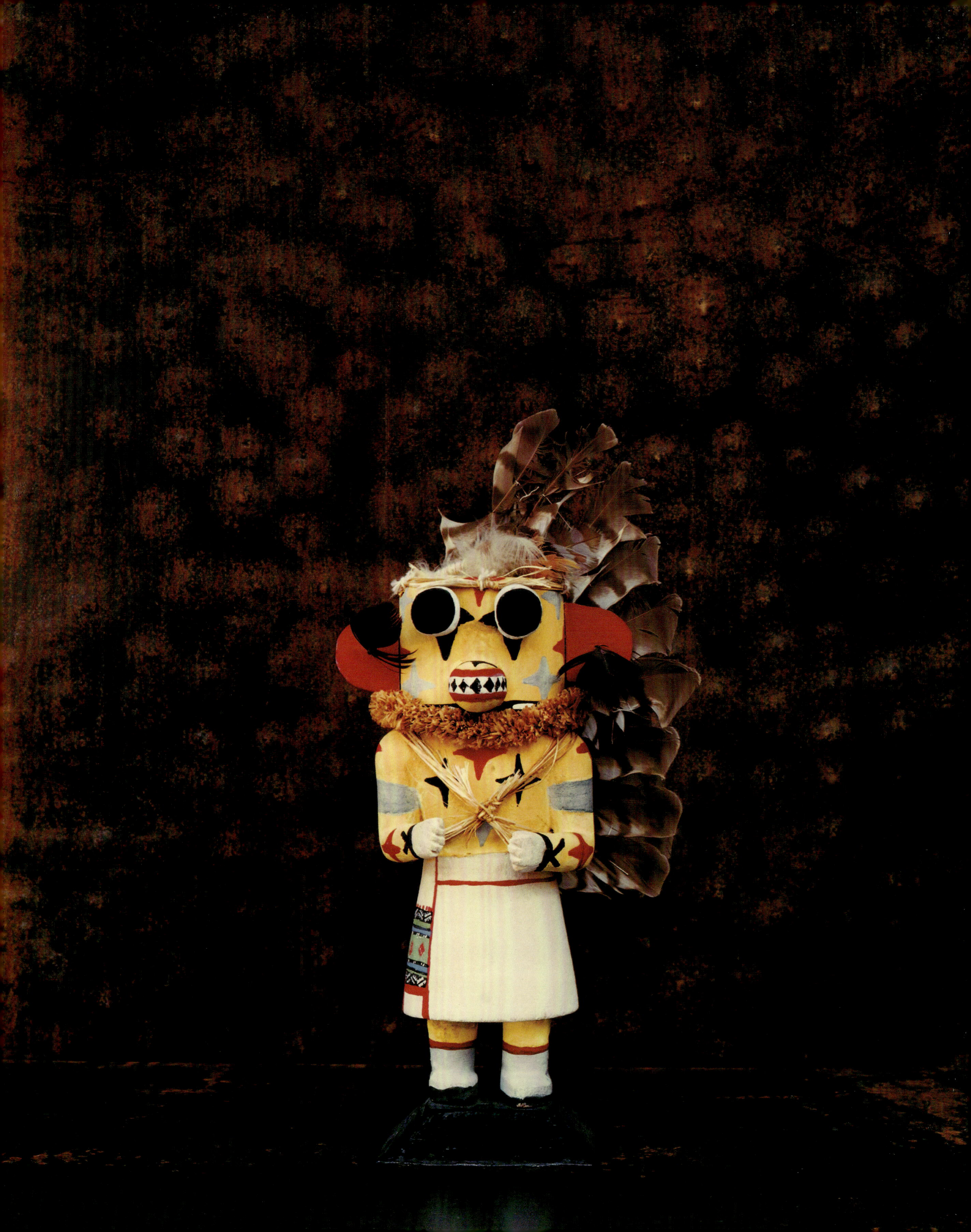

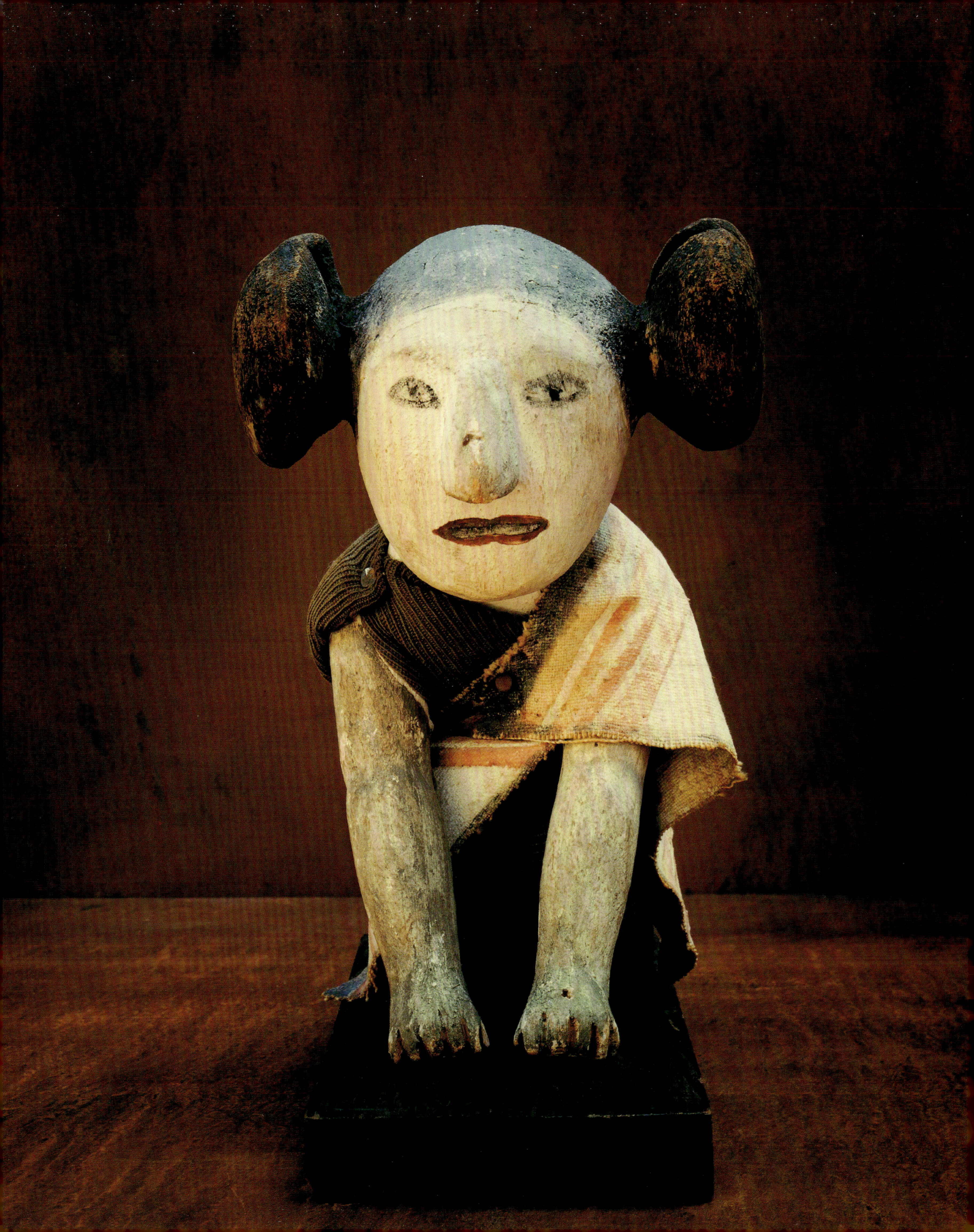

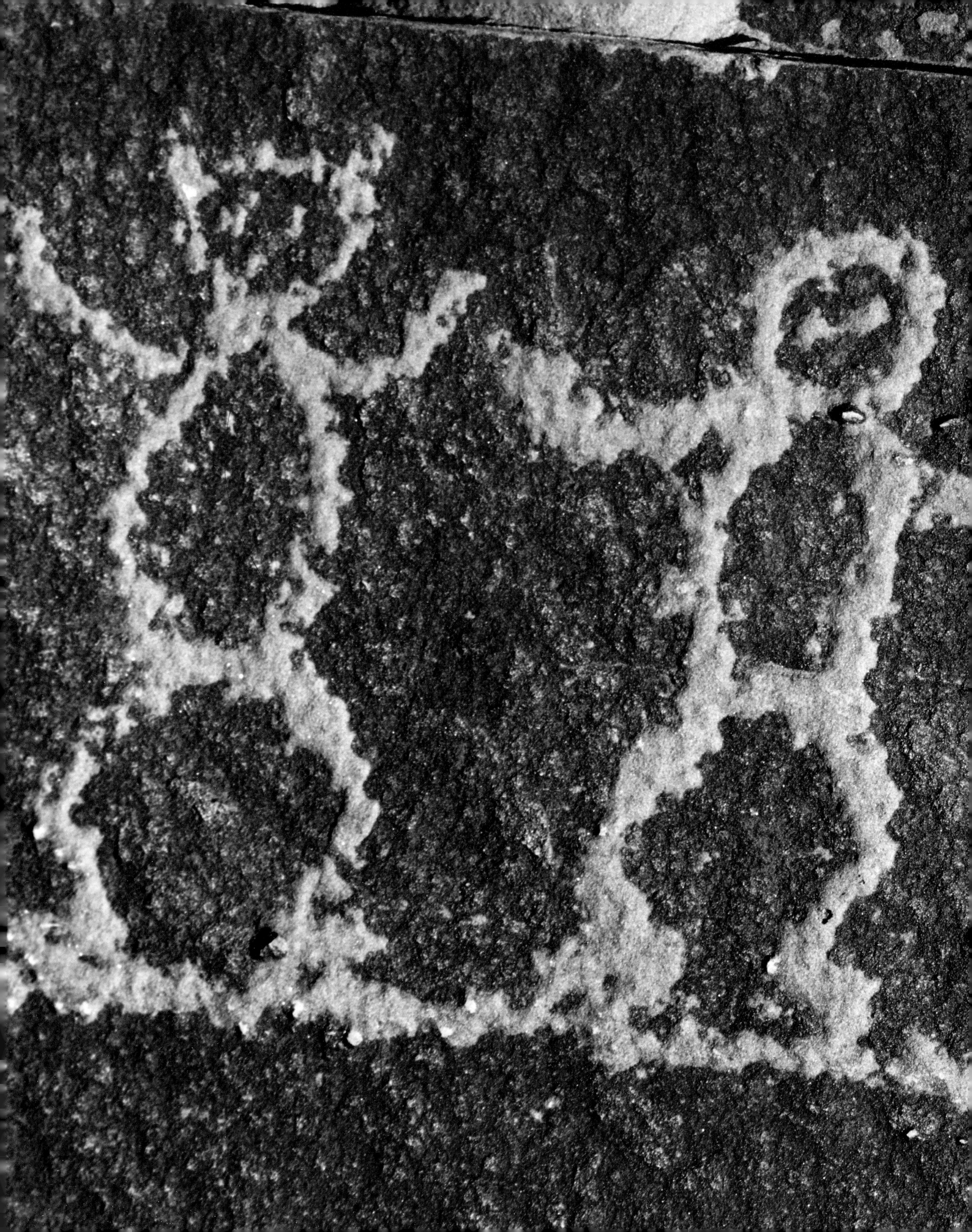

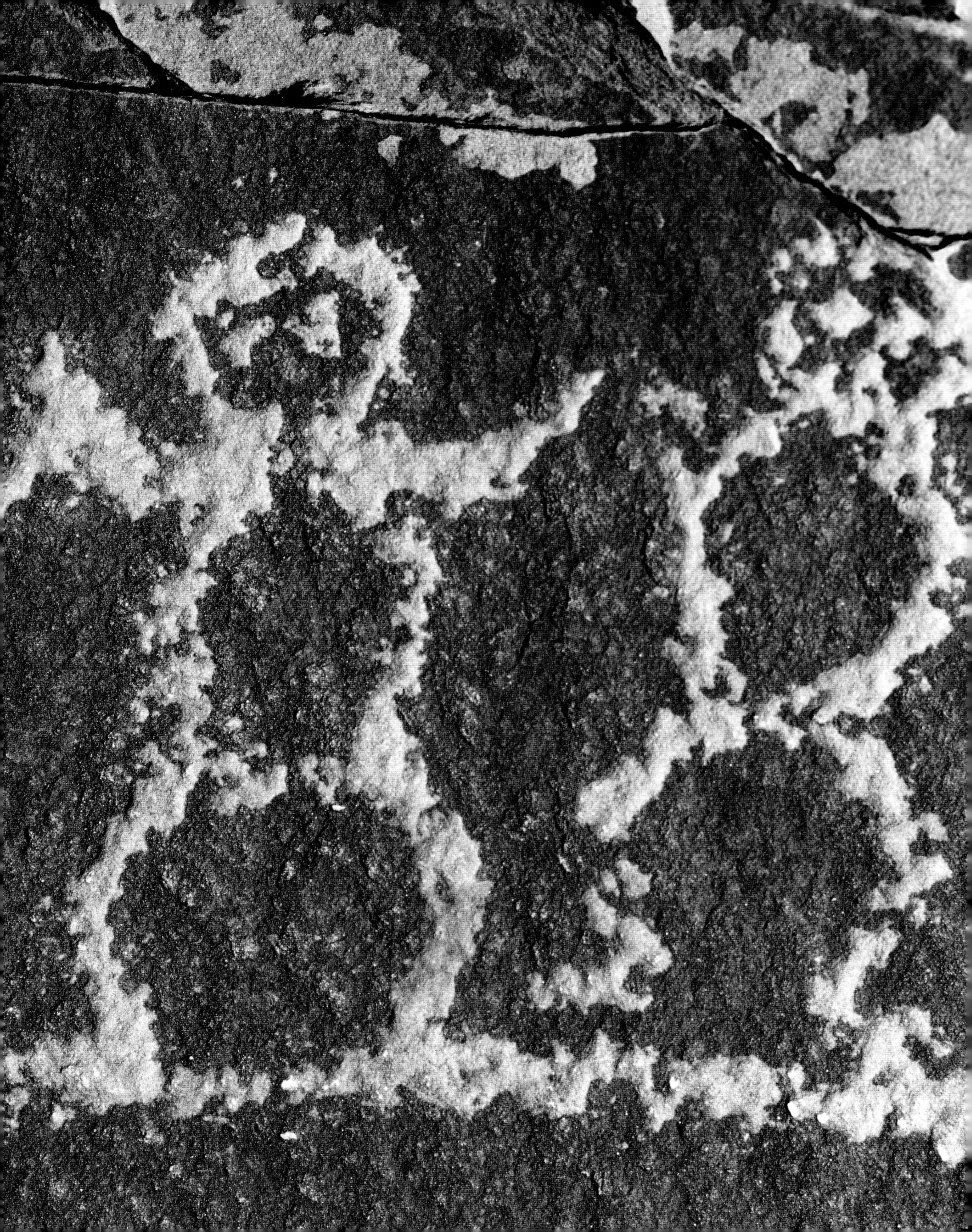

ILLUSTRATED LIST OF PLATES

The captions and identifications of figures are the work of Barton Wright. Landscape identifications are the work of Barton Wright and Andrea Portago. Dates are from museum records, private collectors, or Barton Wright. Information on provenance is the research of Andrea Portago. Photographs of Hopi and Zuni carved figures and landscapes by Andrea Portago were made 1999–2004.

Most of the kachinas were photographed using a 4 × 5 Toyo field camera fitted with 150mm and 210mm lenses, using ready load Fuji NPS 160 film. A few of the kachinas were also photographed with a Nikon F2 35mm camera. The landscapes primarily were shot with a Hasselblad 903SWC using Kodak Tri-X 400 film. A few landscapes were also shot with a Nikon F2 and 28/50mm zoom lens, using Kodak Plus-X 125 film. Most landscapes were shot using a red filter.

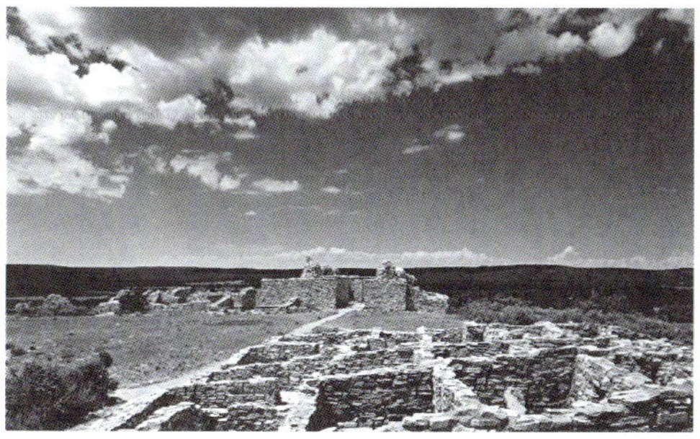

PLATE 1

GRAN QUIVIRA, SALINAS PUEBLO MISSION, NEW MEXICO. Gran Quivira is the largest and most important of the three Salinas Pueblo Missions, which also include **Abó** and **Quarai**. Building of the Roman Catholic Church at Gran Quivira, known as the **San Isidro Mission**, was started in 1629 and completed in 1636; San Isidro is one of the earlier churches built by the Spaniards. The great significance of this site as it relates to the kachina cult is the physical evidence of the confluence of the two cultures. In the foreground are the ruins of the Indian dwellings. Although the Franciscan missionaries banned the Kachina Society, the Indians continued their religious rites in secret.

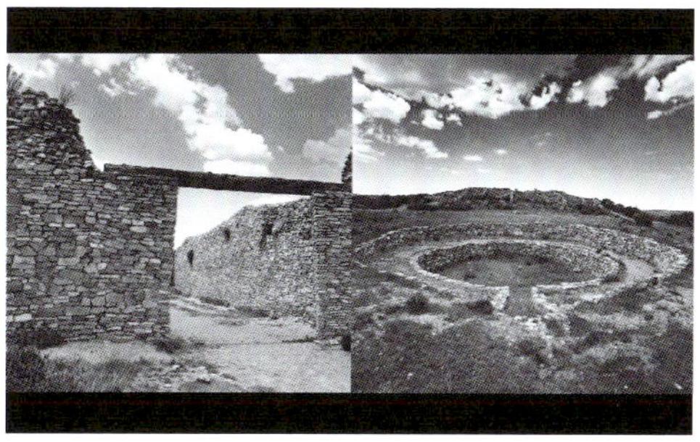

PLATE 2

GRAN QUIVIRA, SALINAS PUEBLO MISSION, NEW MEXICO. Entrance to the mission church San Isidro.

PLATE 3

GRAN QUIVIRA, SALINAS PUEBLO MISSION, NEW MEXICO. The base of an ancient kiva, a religious building where clan initiations and ceremonies took place. Also a place where the men retired to make kachinas and other ritual objects and to weave the garments they needed.

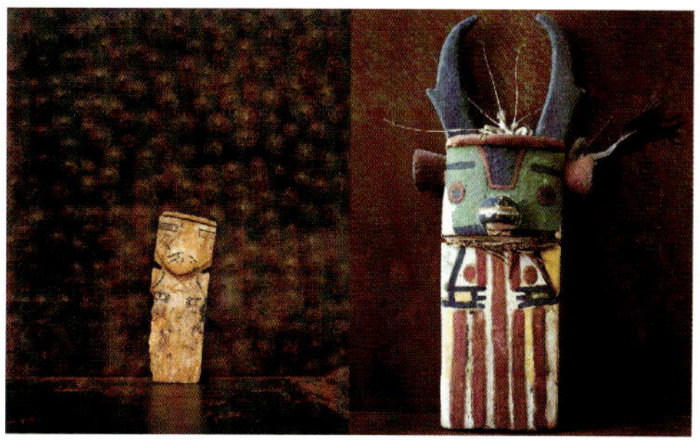

PLATE 4

The flat dolls given to Hopi infants have been in use for generations. This particular **Shalako Mana,** a **Hisot Puchtihu** or Ancient Flat Doll, was found buried beneath several renovated floors in a Hopi home.

Hopi, ca. 1880 or possibly earlier

The Museum of Northern Arizona, Flagstaff, Arizona

PLATE 5

Small flat kachina dolls, *puchtihu,* are given to the very young. **Chop,** the Antelope Kachina, is one that prevents spasms and can increase the number of animals.

Hopi, ca. late 1800s

Purchased in 1901 by American Museum of Natural History (AMNH)from the Fred Harvey Company during the Museum's Hyde Expedition, which was sponsored by the brothers Talbot and Frederick Hyde of New York. Mennonite missionary and ethnologist Henry R. Voth, who lived in Oraibi from 1893 to 1902, originally collected the kachinas from this group, which later were sold by Fred Harvey.

The American Museum of Natural History, New York, New York
AMNH Catalogue no. H/15381

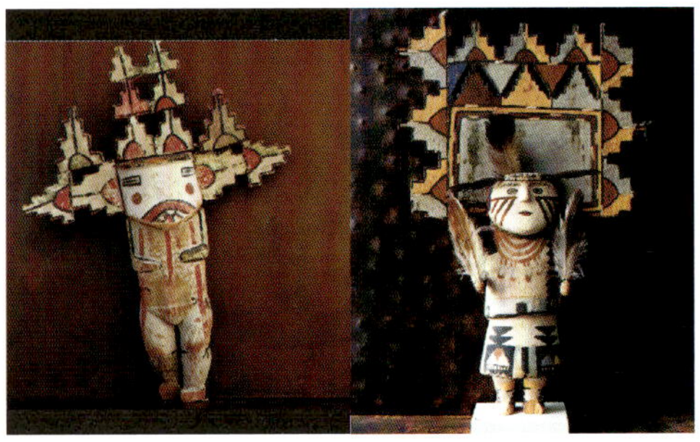

PLATE 6

The more ancient figure of the **Shalako Mana** is always carved completely nude. Whether she functions as a supernatural associated with reproduction rather than rainfall is not known.

Hopi, ca. 1880 or possibly earlier

Acquired by art dealers Stephen Langtang and John Kidd in the late 1960s or early 1970s from a woman who was a member of the Shaker community at Hancock Village in New Hampshire. Later sold to dealer Bob Ashton, who sold it to dealer Phillip Holstein, who sold it to dealer Alex Acevedo, who consigned it to Sotheby's, where it was bought by dealer/artist/collector Alan Kessler.

Alan Kessler Collection, Santa Fe, New Mexico
Private Collection

PLATE 7

Palhik' Mana is a society figure who appears unmasked on First and Second Mesas but is masked on Third Mesa. This very important person is not considered to be a kachina and is always performed by a woman.

Hopi, ca. late 1800s to early 1900s

Purchased for the Museum by AMNH ethnologist Dr. Clark Wissler as part of a large group of mixed artifacts from the Fred Harvey Indian Store in the Grand Canyon in 1910. Mennonite missionary and ethnologist Henry R. Voth, who lived in Hopi from 1893 to 1902, originally collected the kachinas in this group, known as the Voth Collection.

The American Museum of Natural History, New York, New York
AMNH Catalogue no. 50/9321

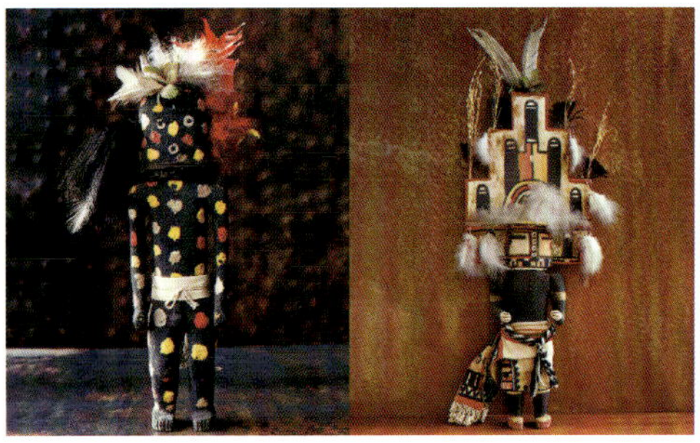

PLATE 8

Kokoshori is the younger brother of the Hemis Kachina. He represents the germinating spirit of corn, and the colored spots represent all the different kinds of corn.

Hopi, ca. late 1800s early 1900s

Purchased for the Museum by AMNH ethnologist Dr. Clark Wissler as part of a large group of mixed artifacts from the Fred Harvey Indian Store in the Grand Canyon in 1910. Mennonite missionary and ethnologist Henry R. Voth, who lived in Hopi from 1893 to 1902, originally collected the kachinas in this group, known as the Voth Collection.

The American Museum of Natural History, New York, New York
AMNH Catalogue no. 50/9614

PLATE 9

One of the more beautiful kachinas, **Hemis** is the one that brings the harvest of the first corn. All of the symbols on it are associated with rain or moisture. Both the Hopi and the Zuni have a Hemis-type kachina. The kachinas differ mainly in the decoration of their tabletas.

Hopi, ca. early 1900s

Purchased for the Museum by AMNH ethnologist Dr. Clark Wissler as part of a large group of mixed artifacts from the Fred Harvey Indian Store in the Grand Canyon in 1910. Mennonite missionary and ethnologist Henry R. Voth, who lived in Hopi from 1893 to 1902, originally collected the kachinas in this group, known as the Voth Collection.

The American Museum of Natural History, New York, New York
AMNH Catalogue no. 50/9328

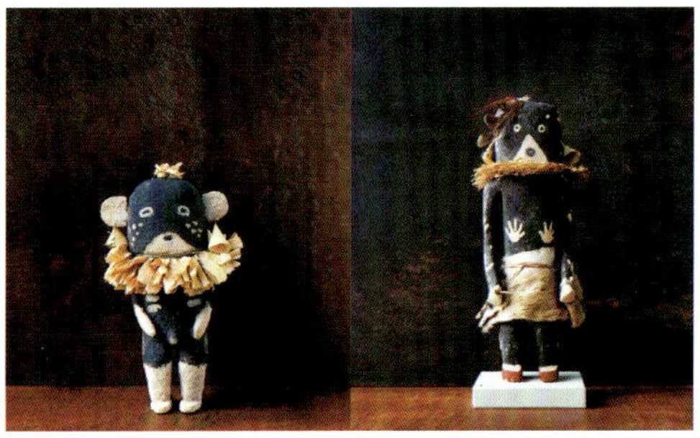

PLATE 10

One of the kachinas that is associated with the initiation of children into the Kachina Society on Second Mesa is **Sivuk'china**. Because he appears only in the kivas he is seldom seen by outsiders.

Hopi, ca. late 1800s

Purchased by AMNH from the Fred Harvey Company in 1901. Mennonite missionary and ethnologist Henry R. Voth, who lived in Hopi from 1893 to 1902, originally collected the kachinas in this group.

The American Museum of Natural History, New York, New York
AMNH Catalogue no. H/15404

PLATE 11

Mastop appears in the Soyal or Winter Solstice Ceremony. He comes as a pair and is also known as the Death Fly Kachina.

Hopi, ca. late 1800s to early 1900s

Purchased for the Museum in 1910 by AMNH ethnologist Dr. Clark Wissler, as part of a large group of mixed artifacts known as the Voth Collection, from the Fred Harvey Indian Store in the Grand Canyon. Mennonite missionary and ethnologist Henry R. Voth, who lived in Hopi from 1893 to 1902, collected the kachinas in this group.

The American Museum of Natural History, New York, New York
AMNH Catalogue no. 50/9428

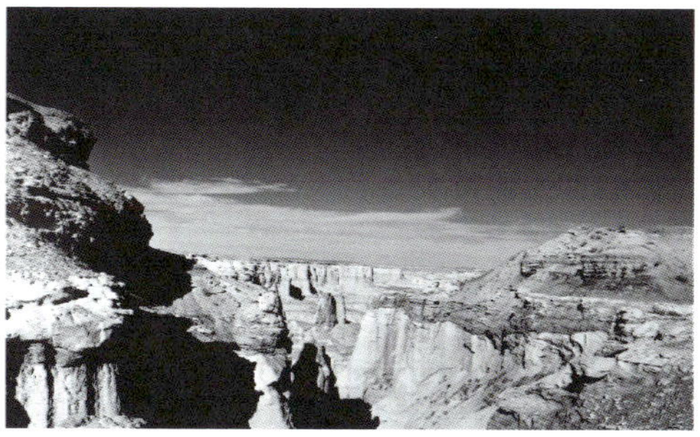

PLATE 12

COAL CANYON, ARIZONA. There are many legends about this place hidden in the high desert plains. It is an area where the Hopi hunt for the eagles that furnish the feathers for their kachinas and ceremonies.

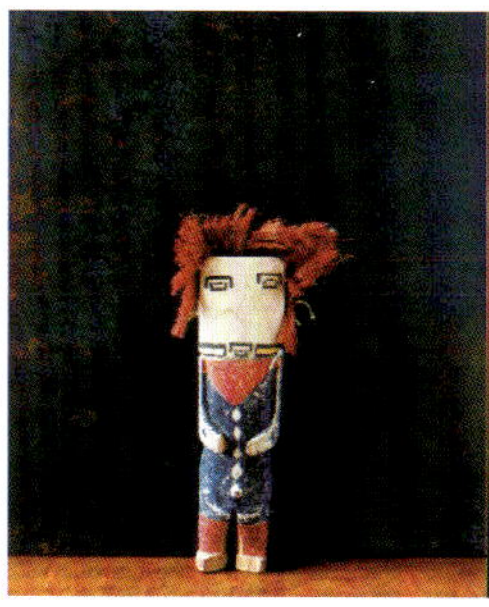

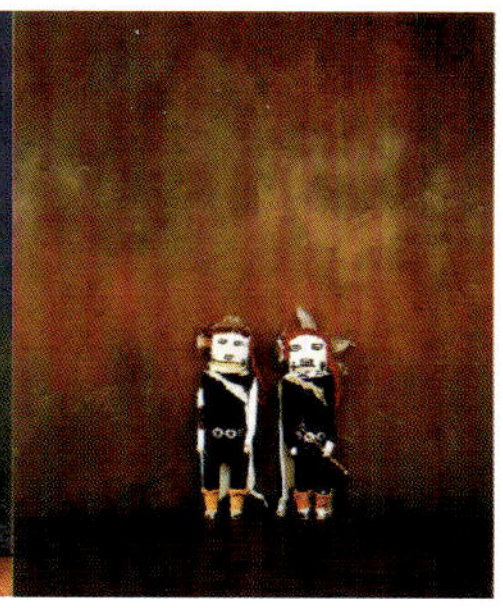

PLATE 13

One of the more consistent kachinas to appear are the **Tasap Yeibichai**, or the Navajo Talking Gods. They come to encourage the Tasap Kachinas when they dance. They are a Hopi kachina inspired by a Navajo Yeibichai Ceremony.

Hopi, ca. late 1800s

Purchased by AMNH from the Fred Harvey Company in 1901. Mennonite missionary and ethnologist Henry R. Voth, who lived in Hopi from 1893 to 1902, originally collected the kachinas in this group.

The American Museum of Natural History, New York, New York
AMNH Catalogue no. H/15377

PLATE 14

A Hopi version of the Navajo **Yeibichai**, Talking Gods or Navajo Grandfathers. When the Hopi make this doll it represents a kachina that comes in the Navajo dance. It can behave in a clownish way.

Hopi, ca. 1890–1900

Gifts of Clay Lockett to MNA in 1967.

The Museum of Northern Arizona, Flagstaff, Arizona
figure on left: MNA Catalogue no. E3764
figure on right: MNA Catalogue no. E3759

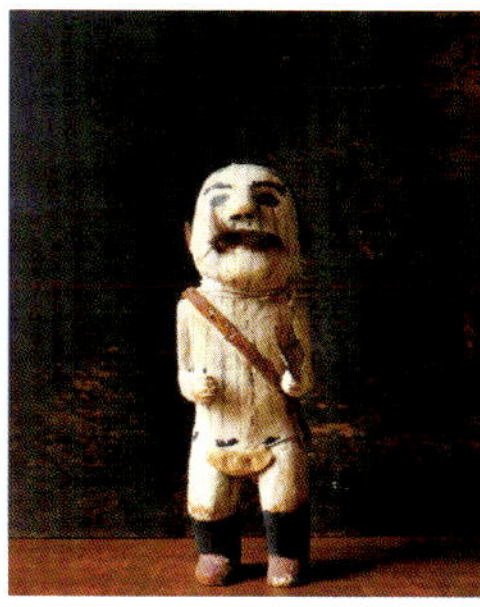

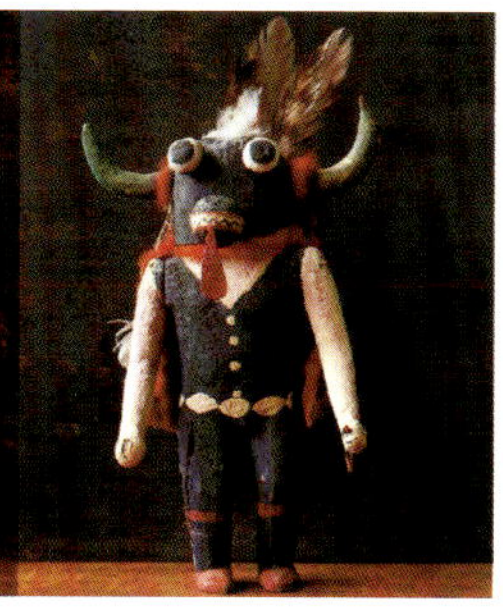

PLATE 15

This is **Tasavu**, a clown who comes as a caricature of the Hopi's neighbors, the Navajo. It is not a kachina. When it appears it behaves in ways that present the worst attributes of the Navajo to the great amusement of the Hopi audience at the dance.

Hopi, ca. early 1900s

George Terasaki Collection, New York, New York

PLATE 16

The Hopi have a family of ogres that visit the villages in early spring and threaten to eat the children unless they are ransomed with substitute food. This kachina, **Nataska Na'amu**, is the hunter or father of the ogres.

Hopi, ca. late 1800s to early 1900s

Purchased for the Museum by AMNH ethnologist Dr. Clark Wissler as part of a large group of mixed artifacts from the Fred Harvey Indian Store at the Grand Canyon in 1910. Mennonite missionary and ethnologist Henry R. Voth, who lived in Hopi from 1893 to 1902, collected the kachinas in this group, known as the Voth Collection.

The American Museum of Natural History, New York, New York
AMNH Catalogue no. 50 /9318

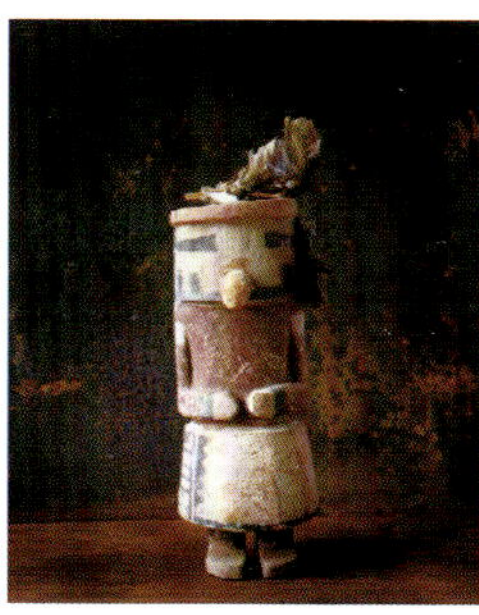

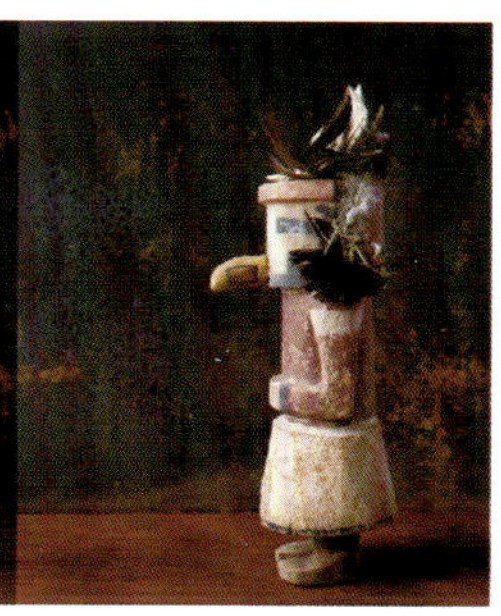

PLATES 17 and 18

The **Tasap Kachina** is a visualization by the Hopi of their nearby neighbors, the Navajo. The kachina is a representation both of those people and one of their more important ceremonies, the Yeibichai performance.

Hopi, ca. 1920s

George Terasaki Collection, New York, New York

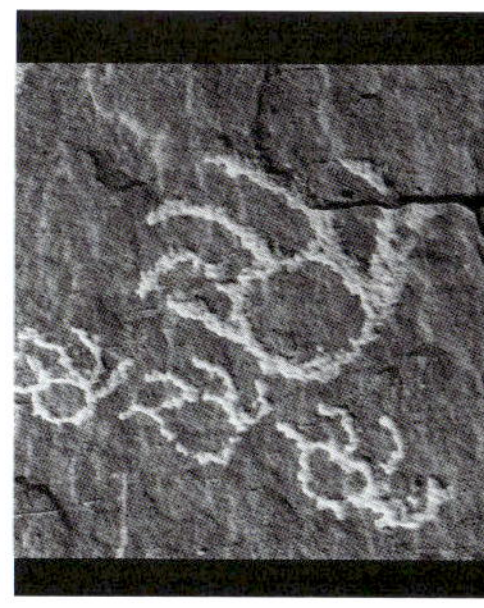

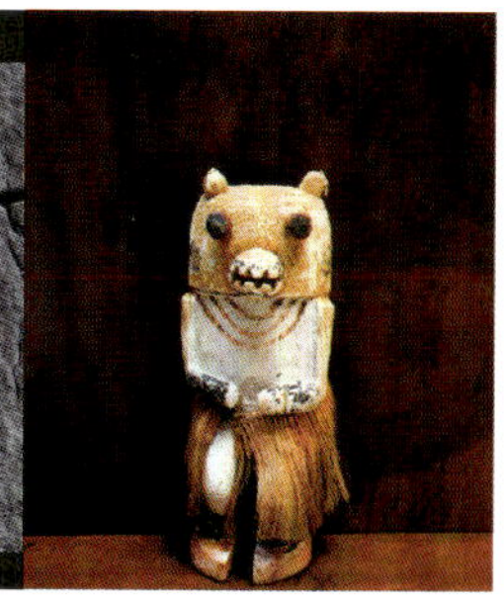

PLATE 19

BADGER CLAN PETROGLYPH. A collection of badger tracks signifying that people from the Badger Clan had passed through here. A great many kachinas and ceremonies were brought by the Badger Clan when they came to Hopi.

PLATE 20

Hon, the Bear Kachina, is a powerful one. He controls medicines of many varieties as well as efficacy. He is the spirit partner of the Bear Clan that controls many of the villages on the Hopi mesas.

Hopi, ca. late 1800s

Morningstar Gallery, Santa Fe, New Mexico

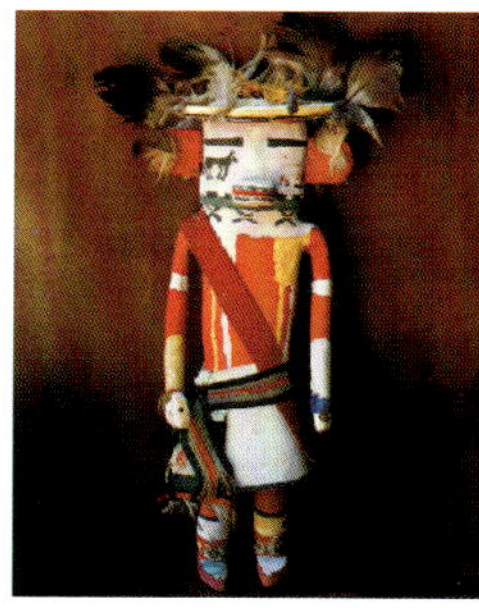

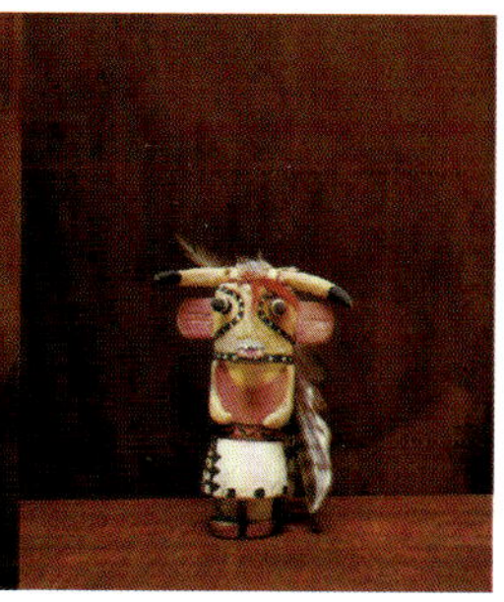

PLATE 21

The **Kavai-i Kachina** is one that postdates the arrival of the Spaniards bringing horses. His name is a Hopi version of the word *caballo.* His appearance is a hope for the increase of horses.

Hopi, ca. 1890–1900

Gift of Clay Lockett to MNA in 1967.

The Museum of Northern Arizona, Flagstaff, Arizona
MNA Catalogue no. E3830

PLATE 22

Like the Zuni the Hopi acquired their herds from the Spanish and adapted their word *vacas* to refer to them. In Hopi this term changed to **Wakas** but the intent is the same, to increase their herds of cattle.

Hopi, ca. 1920s

The School of American Research, Santa Fe, New Mexico
SAR Catalogue no. 1980-1-19

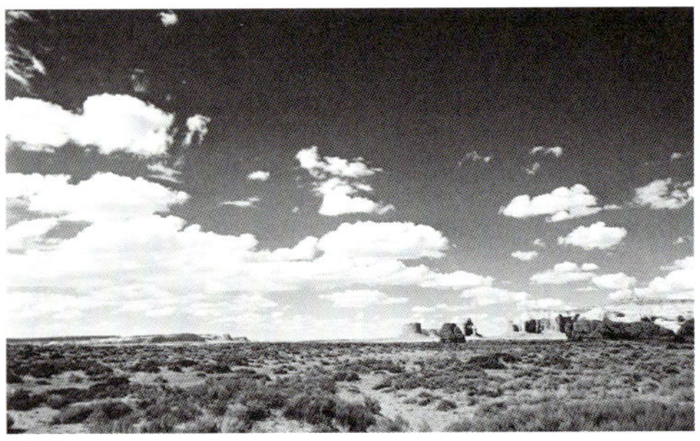

PLATE 23

MYSTERY VALLEY, UTAH. Mystery Valley is the much lesser known valley adjacent to Monument Valley. Now part of Navajoland, it was previously populated by an earlier people known as the Anasazi. Today a Navajo guide can be hired to take visitors to see the many ancient dwellings and storage places found deep within this almost secret desert valley with areas of quicksand and homes that are often inaccessibly high up within rock formations.

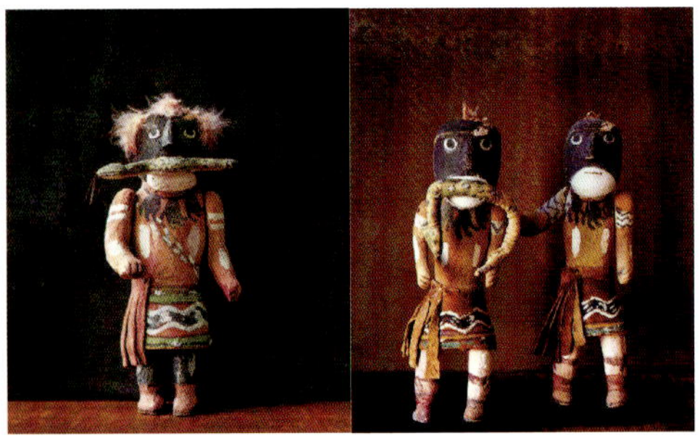

PLATE 24

Awahiya is a very important kachina for he represents the spirit that guards the entrance into the Underworld, the home of the dead and the supernaturals. He is called the Assistant Chief of the Underworld and always dresses as a Snake Dancer.

Hopi, ca. 1910

Gift of Edmund R. Brill to AMNH in 1970.

Given as a gift to Edmund Brill of New York by Tony Luhan, a Taos Pueblo Indian and husband of Mabel Dodge Luhan. Originally acquired by Tony Lujan from Taos Pueblo in 1927.

The American Museum of Natural History, New York, New York
AMNH Catalogue no. 50.2/6651

PLATE 25

When the **Chusona**, Snake Dancers, come, they dance in pairs. The lead person holds a snake in his mouth, and the one behind him uses a feather wand to distract the snake if it becomes too active.

Hopi, ca. 1910s to 1940s

Emily Fischer Landau Collection, Galisteo, New Mexico

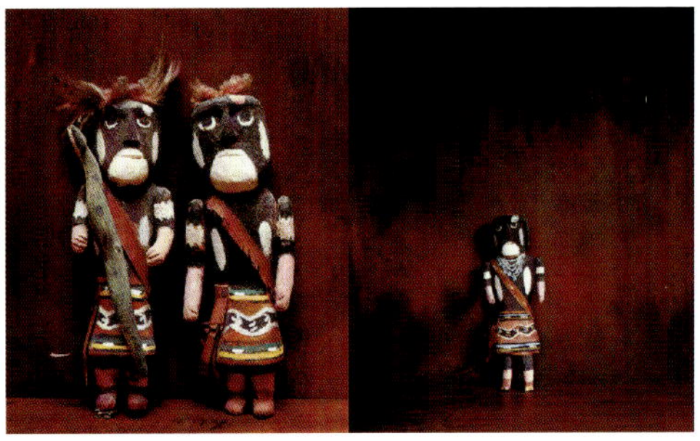

PLATE 26

Every other year in August the Snake Dancers, **Chusona**, who are not kachinas, appear. They have received wide attention because they dance with live snakes in their mouths. This sacred performance links snakes and lightning and thus rain in the minds of the Hopi.

Hopi, ca. 1910s to 1940s

Gift of the Elizabeth White Estate, which also bequeathed the current School of American Research grounds and housing, her former home. Elizabeth White was a founding member of the Laboratory of Anthropology, the Old Santa Fe Association, Santa Fe Indian Market, and the Indian Arts Fund that began the collection that forms the basis for the Indian Arts Research Center collection.

The School of American Research, Santa Fe, New Mexico
left figure: SAR Catalogue no. 1978-1-116
right figure: SAR Catalogue no. 1978-1-115

PLATE 27

Another version of **Chusona**.

Hopi, ca. 1910s to 1940s

Gift of Clay Lockett to MNA in 1967.

The Museum of Northern Arizona, Flagstaff, Arizona
MNA Catalogue no. E3753

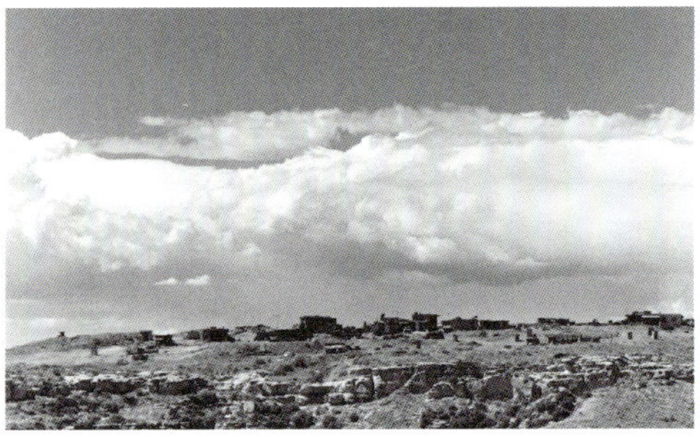

PLATE 28

OLD ORAIBI, HOPI. Old Oraibi is the oldest inhabited village in the United States. It was a village settled from the older village of Shungopovi when two brothers quarreled about ceremonial duties.

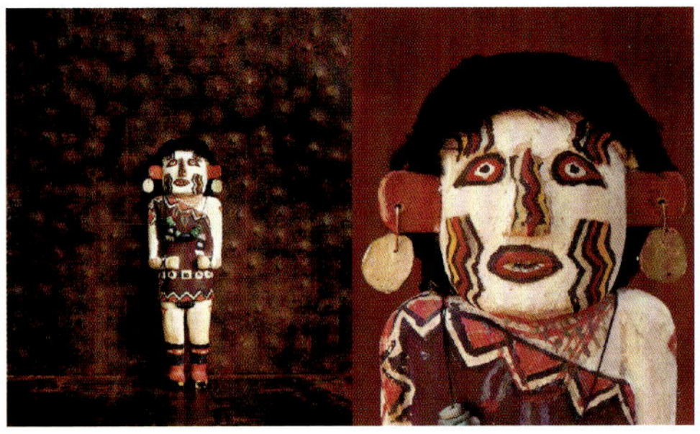

PLATES 29 and 30

The **Kwivi Heheya** or Flashy Heheya is merely a fancy or gaudily dressed Heheya. There are a number of Heheyas, and the actions of this one are sometimes like the Kuwan Heheya, who appears during the Niman Ceremony.

Hopi, ca. 1920s

Gift of Elizabeth Compton Hegemann in 1961.

Originally from the McGill Collection.

The Museum of Northern Arizona, Flagstaff, Arizona
MNA Catalogue no. E3870

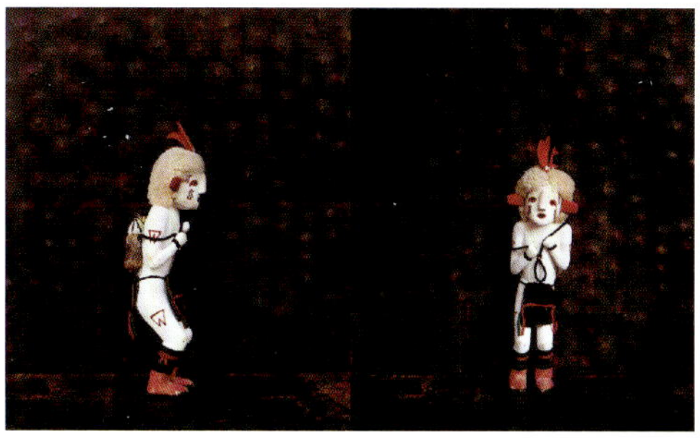

PLATES 31 and 32

Heheya comes in a variety of forms. This one is usually referred to as a Harvester Kachina because he carries farm produce in a large basket on his back. He usually appears as a single dancer at the side of a line of kachinas.

Hopi, ca. 1920s

Gift of Clay Lockett to MNA in 1967.

The Museum of Northern Arizona, Flagstaff, Arizona
MNA Catalogue no. E3870

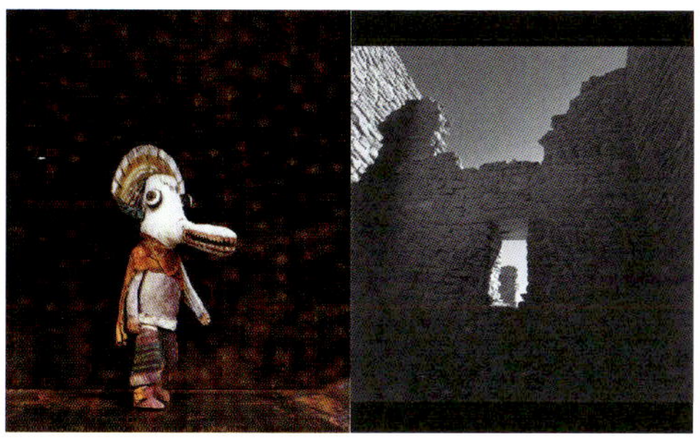

PLATE 33

Among the ogre family are several who have enormous mouths and are said to be able to eat a child with one bite. They come in different colors, and this one, **Wiharuma**, is white. He likes fat.

Hopi, ca. 1920s

Bequest of Earle R. Forrest to MNA in 1969.

The Museum of Northern Arizona, Flagstaff, Arizona
MNA Catalogue no. E4427

PLATE 34

Doorway at village of WUPATKI, ARIZONA.

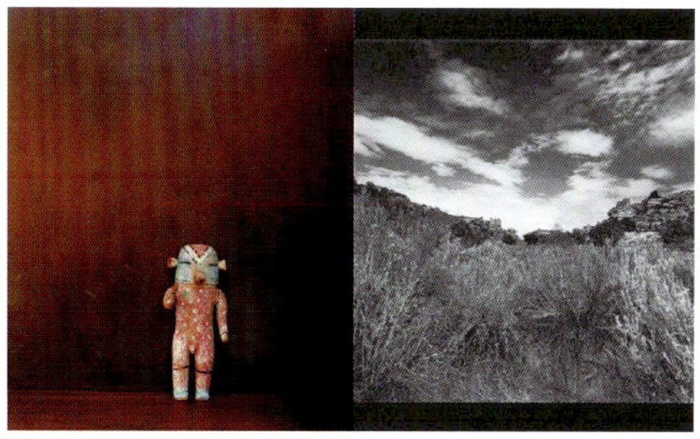

PLATE 35

The Hummingbird Kachina, **Tocha**, comes in dances held both in the kiva and outdoors in the plaza. He can serve either as an individual or part of a group. The hummingbird is a harbinger of springtime and is thought of as a warrior because of its pugnacious attitude.

Hopi, ca. late 1800s

Richard and Nedra Matteucci Collection, Santa Fe, New Mexico

PLATE 36

HOVENWEEP, FOUR CORNERS AREA, UTAH. The lonely ruins of Hovenweep lie on a deserted mesa belying the importance of the area as the center of the Anasazi culture. The earliest kivas or ceremonial structures are known from this area.

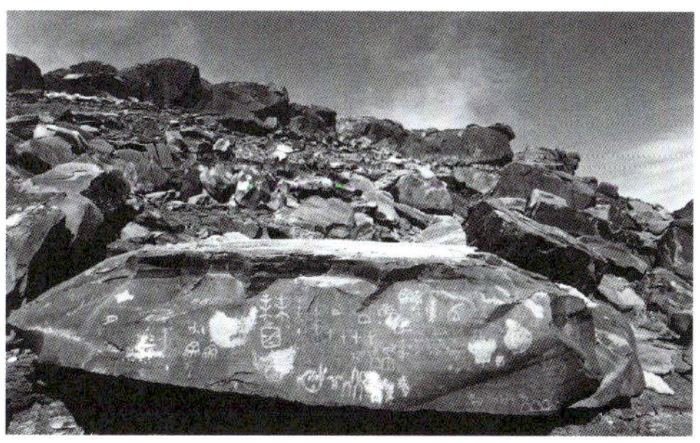

PLATE 37

CLAN ROCKS, NAVAJOLAND, NORTHERN ARIZONA. Clan Rocks was one of the Ancients' most important stopping places along an arduous trip on foot as the various clans made their way to gather salt along the Colorado River deep within the Grand Canyon's floor. As each passed they placed a symbol of their clan on the rocks.

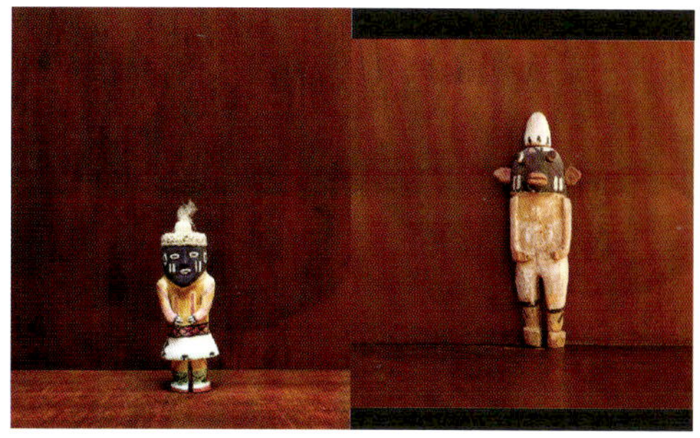

PLATE 38

Pookonghoya is the eldest of the Two Little War Gods. He and his brother Palungahoya are the equivalent of mischievous boys. They can perform heroic deeds but most of the time they are playing with a ball.

Hopi, ca. late 1800s to early 1900s

Part of the SAR Collection originally housed in the Museum of New Mexico.

The School of American Research, Santa Fe, New Mexico
SAR Catalogue no. 1980-1-6

PLATE 39

Palungahoya is the younger of the Two Little War Gods, the brother of Pookonghoya.

Hopi, ca. 1880–1890

Private Collection

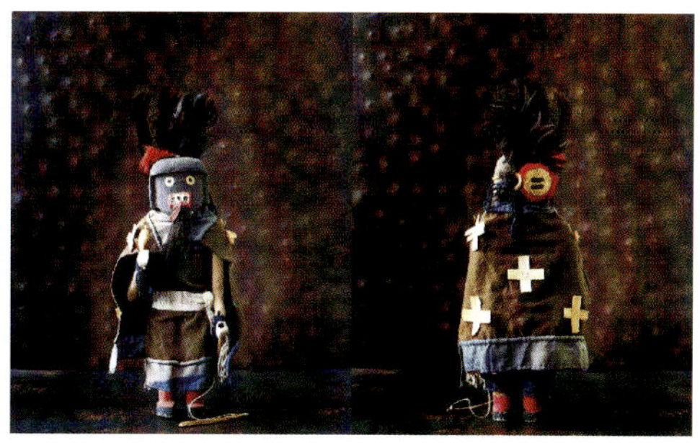

PLATES 40 AND 41

This kachina represents a maiden who with her hair half dressed took up bow and arrow and fought off an enemy attacking while the men were in the field. She is the powerful warrior maiden **He-é-é**.

Hopi, ca. late 1800s to early 1900s

Purchased for the Museum by AMNH ethnologist Dr. Clark Wissler, as part of a large group of mixed artifacts known as the Voth Collection, from the Fred Harvey Indian Store at the Grand Canyon in 1910. Mennonite missionary and ethnologist Henry R. Voth, who lived in Hopi from 1893 to 1902, collected the kachinas in this group.

The American Museum of Natural History, New York, New York
AMNH Catalogue no. 50/9432

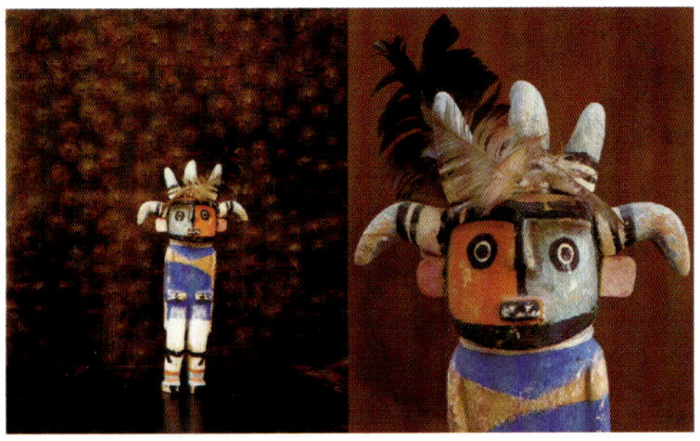

PLATES 42 AND 43

When the warrior maid **Pohaha** of the Tewa returned from fighting off the enemy, her face changed from that of a woman to the kachina Naleucala. The kachina can appear in the Powamu, or Mixed Dance.

Hopi, ca. pre-1940

Gift of Clay Lockett to MNA in 1967.

The Museum of Northern Arizona, Flagstaff, Arizona
MNA Catalogue no. E3795

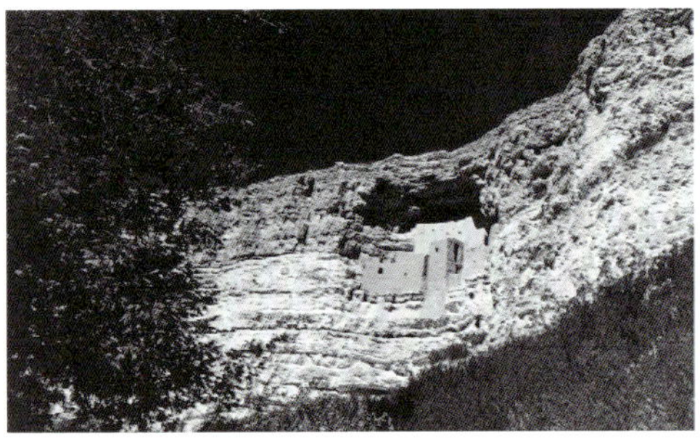

PLATE 44

MONTEZUMA'S CASTLE, ARIZONA. Montezuma's Castle is a place of refuge because enemy people often beset the Sinagua people who farmed and lived in this valley. It is the village closest to the all-important Montezuma's Well, where the kachinas come and go.

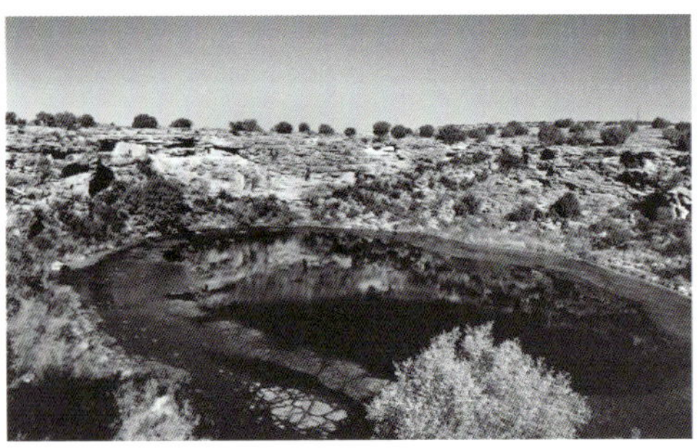

PLATE 45

MONTEZUMA'S WELL. Both for the Ancients and present-day Hopi and Zuni, the belief system is that there is tremendous fluidity between the world we see and live in and the Netherworld. The Indians believe that there is constant coming and going between these two mirrored realities. The significance of Montezuma's Well is that it is a spring, which is one place of exit and entry between the two worlds.

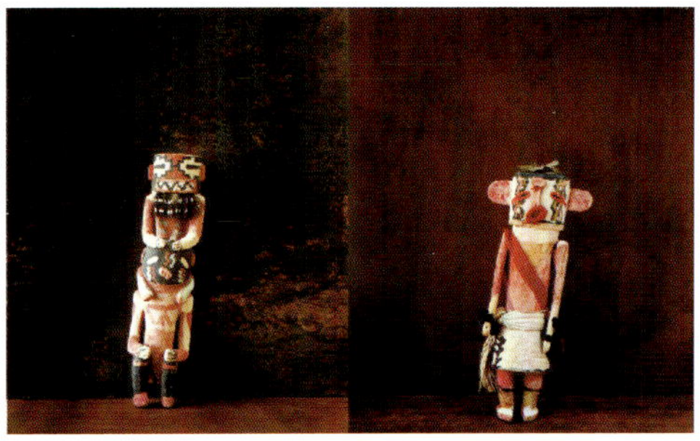

PLATE 46

Hilili on top of Aheya Motaqa. Hilili is a guard kachina, and **Heheya Aumutaka** often comes as a clownlike helper. A reason for this doll carved as sitting on the shoulders of another is not known.

Hopi, ca. late 1800s

Purchased by AMNH from the Fred Harvey Company in 1901. Mennonite missionary and ethnologist Henry R. Voth, who lived in Hopi from 1893 to 1902, originally collected the kachinas in this group.

The American Museum of Natural History, New York, New York
AMNH Catalogue no. H/15384

PLATE 47

There are some kachinas identical in appearance that come to dance as a group in the plaza. The **Kuwan Heheya** who may come as Niman, or home-going kachinas, is such a group.

Hopi, ca. 1901 or earlier

Purchased for MNA by E. B. Danson through the Collector's Club, from Martha Voth Dyck. Martha Voth Dyck was the daughter of Henry R. Voth, a Mennonite missionary who lived at Oraibi. The chief of Old Oraibi originally gave this doll to Martha's aunt in 1901 while she was visiting there. When her aunt died, Martha acquired the doll.

The Museum of Northern Arizona, Flagstaff, Arizona
MNA Catalogue no. E7371

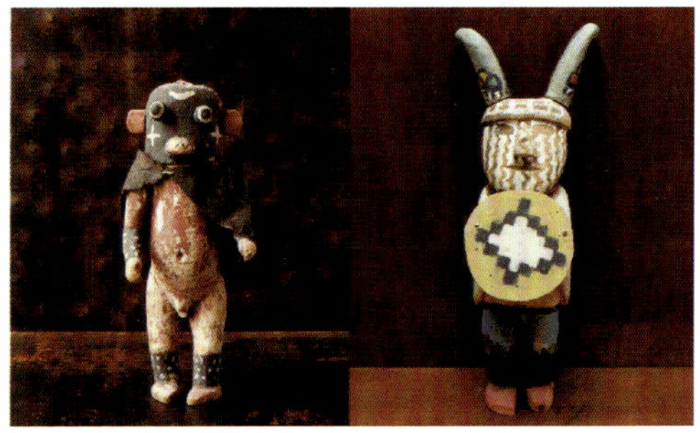

PLATE 48

The little naked doll characterizes **Chaveyo**, the Child Hunter, who is one of the most fearsome of beings to the children. If a youngster misbehaves badly enough, this kachina may come looking for him unless he changes his ways.

Hopi, ca. late 1800s

One of the kachinas from Jo Mora's Collection. Jo Mora was an artist and photographer who lived and worked in Polacca, at Hopi, from 1902 to 1904.

George Terasaki Collection, New York, New York

PLATE 49

Ahl Taka is not a kachina but rather a priest. He is a member of the Ahl or Two-Horned Society and appears during ceremonies when that group is called upon to assist other societies.

Hopi, ca. 1920s

The School of American Research, Santa Fe, New Mexico
SAR Catalogue no. C324

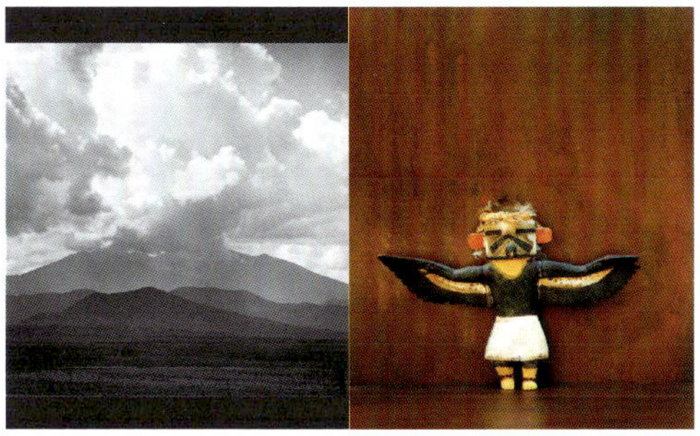

PLATE 50

SAN FRANCISCO PEAKS with clouds. The clouds hide not only the kachinas within but also the faces of the Hopi grandmothers and all the others who live in the Netherworld.

PLATE 51

One of the most favored kachinas of the Hopi is **Kwahu**, the Eagle Kachina. Its appearance is limited to the kivas, apparently never being seen in the plaza dances. It brings an increase in the number of eagles.

Hopi, ca. 1920s

Tony Berlant Collection, Santa Monica, California

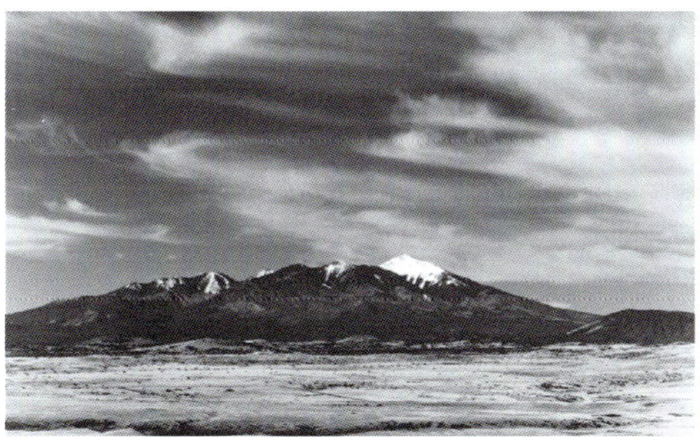

PLATE 52

SAN FRANCISCO PEAKS, FLAGSTAFF, ARIZONA. The San Francisco Peaks are where most kachinas live during the six months when they are not visiting the pueblos.

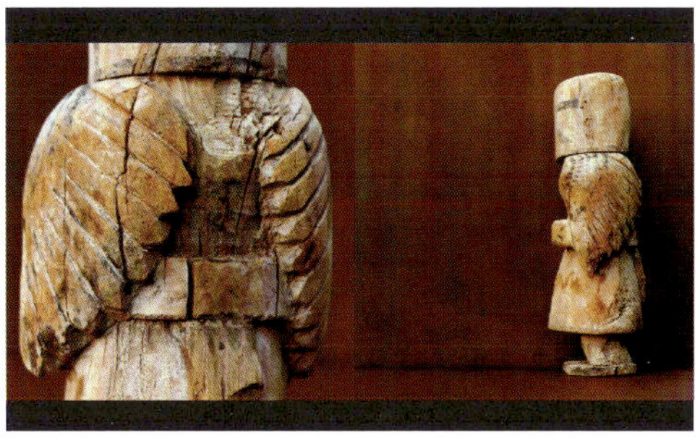

PLATES 53 and 54

This **Hisot Kwahu** is an ancient doll. This one has been left outside, subject to considerable weathering. Its purpose has not changed, and if the need were great enough it could be patched, repainted, and given again.

Hopi, ca. 1880 or possibly earlier

This rare kachina once belonged to New Mexico native and rodeo legend "Queenie," Fern Sawyer, a member of the Cowgirl Hall of Fame. Fern bought the doll in 1959 from a dealer on East Palace Avenue in Santa Fe.

Private Collection

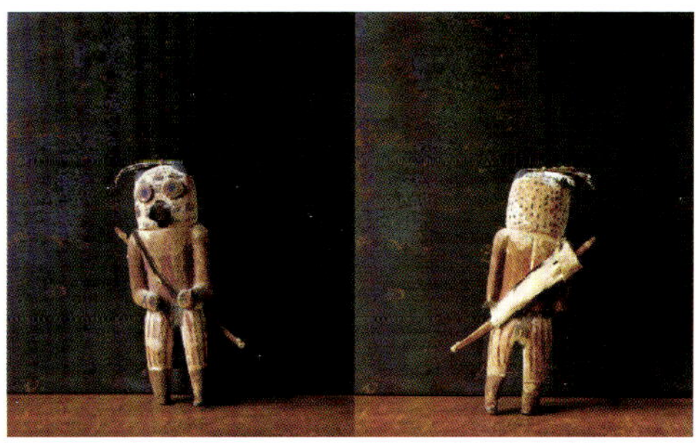

PLATES 55 and 56

The Great Horned Owl Kachina, **Mongwu**, comes to chastise the clowns when their behavior becomes too outrageous. The doll usually has a wing mounted on either side of his head, which produces a fearsome appearance.

Hopi, ca. late 1800s or possibly earlier

George Terasaki Collection, New York, New York

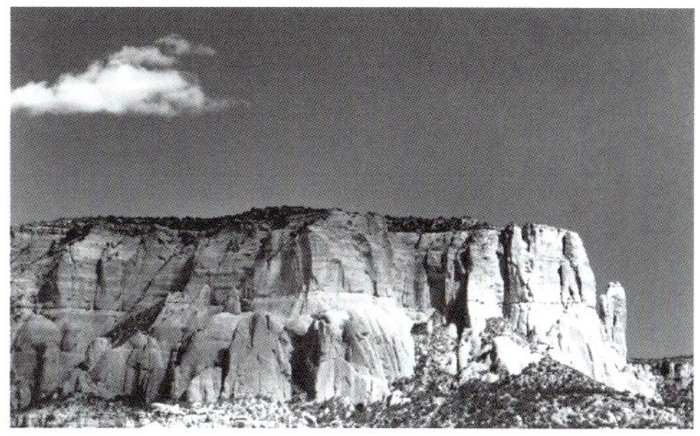

PLATE 57

ZUNI, NEW MEXICO. TOWAYALLANE MESA. The Mesa watches over present-day Zuni. Legend has it that an enormous feathered serpent flooded the world and the villagers fled to the top of Towayallane to escape the flood. As the water continued to rise and the village faced destruction, a young boy and girl volunteered to sacrifice themselves by going into the water. As they did so they were turned to stone, forever becoming a part of Towayallane. They stand way over on the right at the end of the mesa.

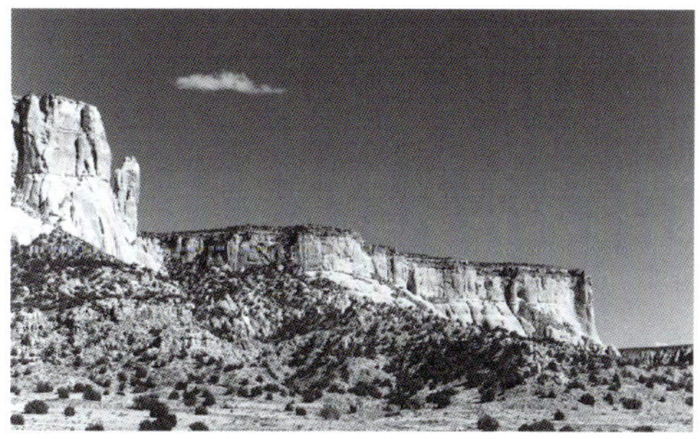

PLATE 58

TUWAYALLANE MESA. Boy/Girl legend is just in from the left side under the lone cloud.

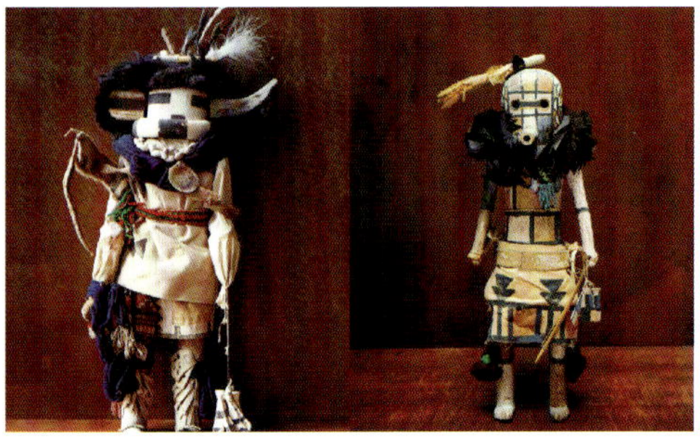

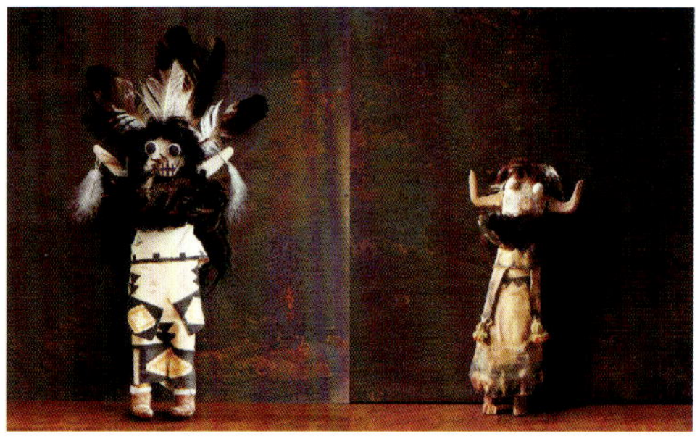

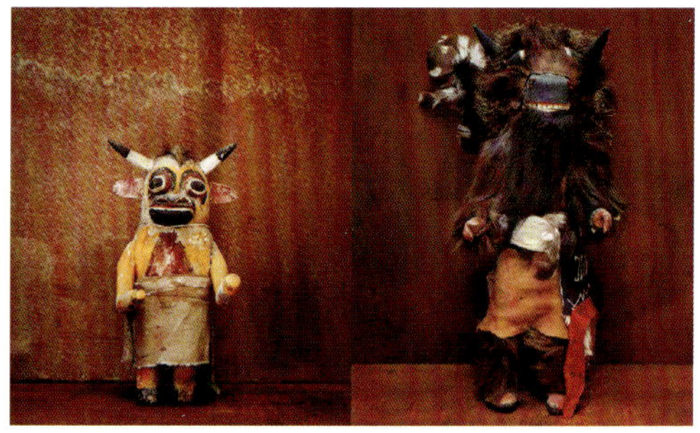

PLATE 59

The chief or ritual father of the kachinas at Zuni is **Saiatasha**. He is also called the Long Horn Kachina. He leads a group of kachinas around the village from one location to another to plant prayer feathers for the good of the people.

Zuni, ca. late 1800s to early 1900s

Collected by Professor Alfred L. Kroeber for AMNH in 1915. While on a one-year sabbatical from the University of California, Dr. Kroeber asked to join one of AMNH's southwestern expeditions. Dr. Clark Wissler of AMNH put Kroeber in charge of the work at Zuni.

The American Museum of Natural History, New York, New York
AMNH Catalogue no. 50.1/9166

PLATE 60

Salimopaiya, the Seed Warrior from the nadir, is a guard at Zuni for the more sacred kachinas. He runs barefoot with anklets of evergreens and a yucca whip in each hand to strike those who come too close or who interfere in any way.

Zuni, ca. pre-1940s

Gift of Elinor Gregg in 1964.

School of American Research, Santa Fe, New Mexico
SAR Catalogue no. IAF.C323

PLATE 61

There are six **Shalako** that come in winter at Zuni. They are impressive ten-foot-tall figures who take part in an extensive ceremony. They bless new houses and houses that have been rebuilt for them. They dance in them in the early morning hours.

Zuni, ca. early 1900s

Collected by Professor Alfred L. Kroeber for AMNH in 1915. While on a one-year sabbatical from the University of California, Dr. Kroeber asked to join one of AMNH's southwestern expeditions. Dr. Clark Wissler of AMNH put Kroeber in charge of the work at Zuni.

The American Museum of Natural History, New York, New York
AMNH Catalogue no. 50.1/9165

PLATE 62

Shalako Kachina.

Zuni, ca. late 1800s

Private Collection

PLATE 63

The Zuni acquired cattle from the Spaniards. To increase their herds they have a kachina, **Wakashi**, Cow Kachina, who comes and dances in groups in the village plaza. There is a related form at Hopi.

Zuni, ca. late 1800s

Richard and Nedra Matteucci Collection, Santa Fe, New Mexico

PLATE 64

No buffalo ever roamed near either Hopi or Zuni but among the eastern pueblos they were important. In consequence the **Mosairu Kachina** has made its way into the pantheon of all pueblos to aid in the increase of the animal.

Zuni, ca. 1910–20s

Purchased in Gallup, New Mexico, in 1925 for the Indian Arts Institute in Santa Fe, New Mexico, by the Institute's curator, Kenneth Chapman. The Indian Arts Institute was part of the original School of American Research in Santa Fe.

School of American Research, Santa Fe, New Mexico
SAR Catalogue no. IAF.C2

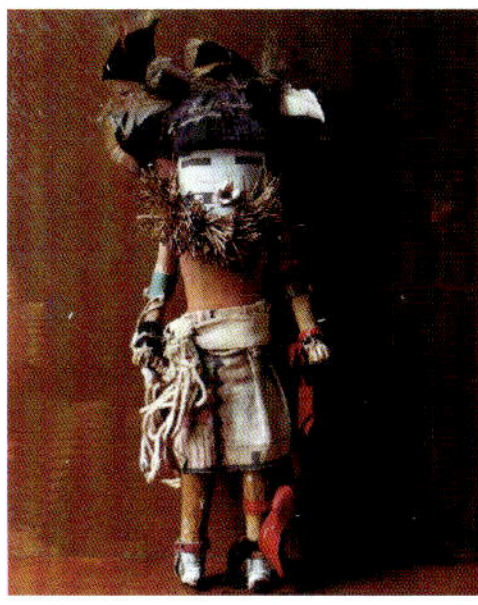
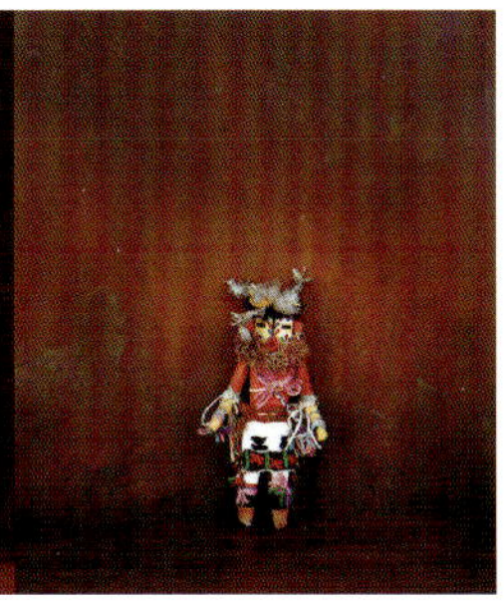
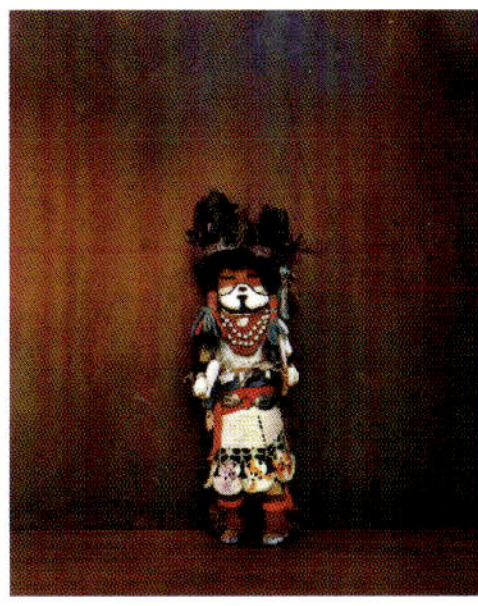
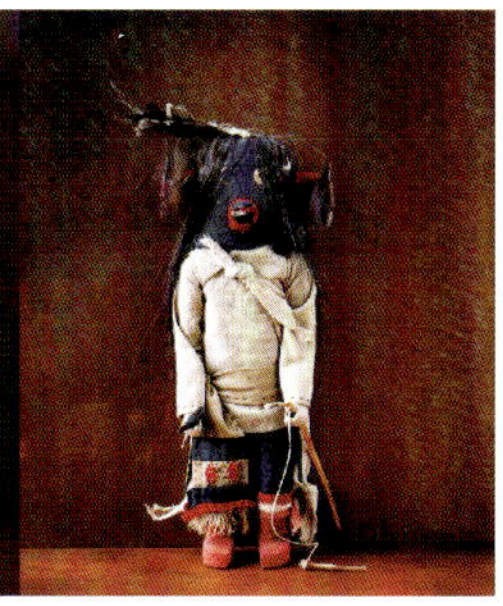
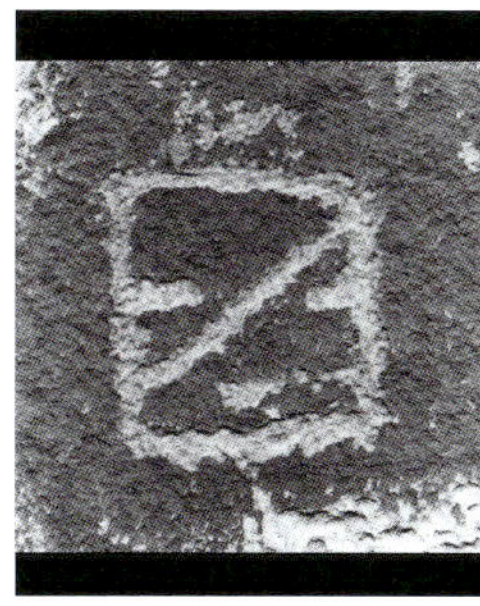
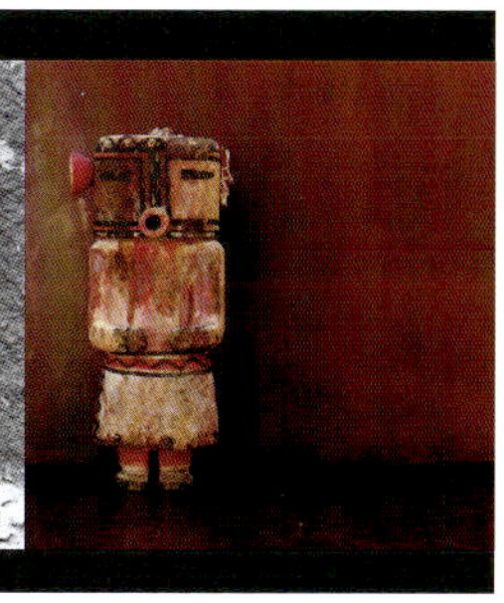

PLATE 65

The Zuni kachina **Kanatshu** is thought of as a gentle dancer who comes in the winter. He usually dances with other kachinas like Kokokshi and at other times comes in a set. He is thought to be equivalent to the Hopi Talavai-i Kachina.

Zuni, ca. 1920s

George Terasaki Collection, New York, New York

PLATE 66

Another of the Zuni kachinas that appears in the winter dances is **Nahalisho**. He is a dancer who comes as a group. Usually he wears four turkey feathers set at right angles on his crown as punishment for sneaking out and hunting turkeys at night.

Zuni, ca. late 1800s

Acquired by gift from Thomas L. Woodard, trader and owner of Woodard's Indian Arts, Gallup, New Mexico. Collected ca. 1900, brought into Woodard's ca. 1920. Part of the Austin Ladd Collection.

The Museum of Northern Arizona, Flagstaff, Arizona
MNA Catalogue no. E6558

PLATE 67

The Zuni have a dance they call **Komanshi**, Comanche Dance. Started in relatively recent times it is equivalent to that of other pueblos, including the Hopi. The costume is quite elaborate with a full war bonnet when danced.

Zuni, ca. early 1900s

Richard and Nedra Matteucci Collection, Santa Fe, New Mexico

PLATE 68

The Zuni **Hilili** is a ubiquitous kachina; he appears in Hopi, Zuni, Acoma, and Laguna, as well as other pueblos to the east. He is a guard or a warrior and usually accompanies other kachinas. At times he is equated with witches.

Zuni, ca. early 1900s

Purchased in 1910 by AMNH ethnologist Dr. Clark Wissler, as part of a large group of mixed artifacts known as the Voth Collection, from the Fred Harvey Indian Store at the Grand Canyon. Mennonite missionary and ethnologist Henry R. Voth, who lived in Hopi from 1893 to 1902, collected the kachinas in this group.

The American Museum of Natural History, New York, New York
AMNH Catalogue no. 50/9430

PLATE 69

KACHINA PETROGLYPH. Many of the petroglyphs of kachinas have faces that are distinguishable: in this instance **Ka-a Nas**, the Sunset Crater Kachina or one of the Hilili guards.

PLATE 70

Ma-alo, the Stick Kachina, is one that was very popular in the beginning decades of the twentieth century but in recent years has not appeared. The stick that it usually carries is painted in many colors. It is helpful for growing corn.

Hopi, ca. 1920s

Private Collection

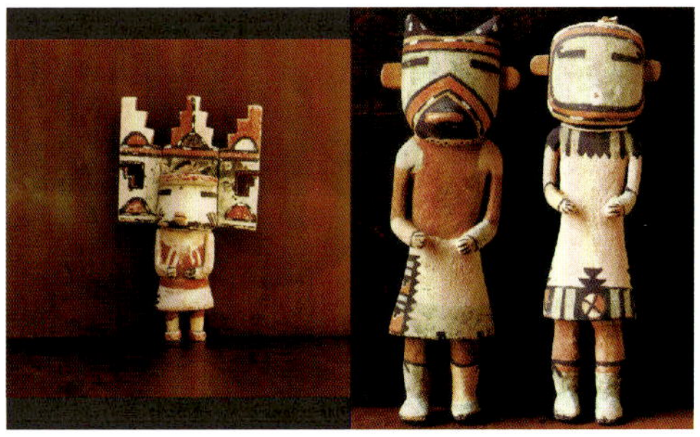

PLATE 71

Laguna is a pueblo that interacts with both Hopi and Zuni. Numerous kachinas or related forms come from there. The Hopi **Sio Sowoya**, from Zuni, is almost identical to the Hopi Kawaika-a Kachina that comes from Laguna.

Hopi, ca. late 1800s

Victor Justice Evans Collection (inscribed on the back side "V. T. Evans, C. 361047, A. 113605, Hopi," the numbers are probably Smithsonian Institution accession numbers).

Alan Kessler Collection, Santa Fe, New Mexico
Private Collection

PLATE 72

The left figure is that of a very old kachina, **Owa**, frequently misidentified as Quoi-a. The right-hand figure is that of **Saitaka**, the Smiling Man. Both kachinas can appear in a Mixed Dance.

Hopi, ca. late 1800s to early 1900s

Kachinas from Jo Mora's Collection. Jo Mora was an artist and photographer who lived and worked in Polacca, at Hopi, from 1902 to 1904.

George Terasaki Collection, New York, New York

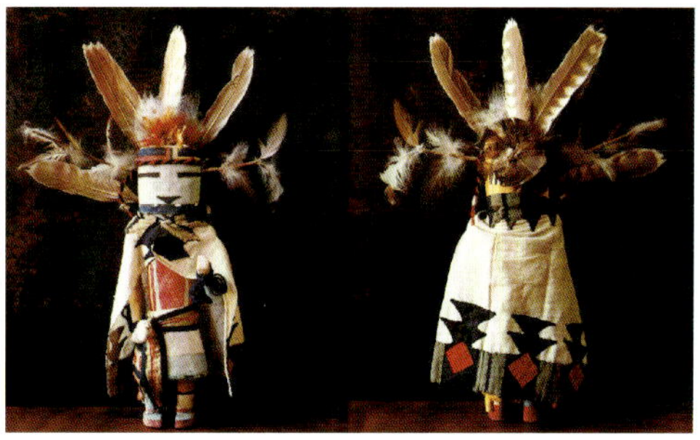

PLATES 73 and 74

Nakiachop, the Silent Kachina or Shalako Warrior, is one that seldom appears today. He is one of the old kachinas and is purported to be the one who performed the extremely dangerous Ladder Dance on the cliff edge.

Hopi, ca. late 1800s to early 1900s

Purchased for the Museum in 1910 by AMNH ethnologist Dr. Clark Wissler, as part of a large group of mixed artifacts known as the Voth Collection, from the Fred Harvey Indian Store at the Grand Canyon. Mennonite missionary and ethnologist Henry R. Voth, who lived in Hopi from 1893 to 1902, collected the kachinas in this group.

The American Museum of Natural History, New York, New York
AMNH Catalogue no. 50/9433

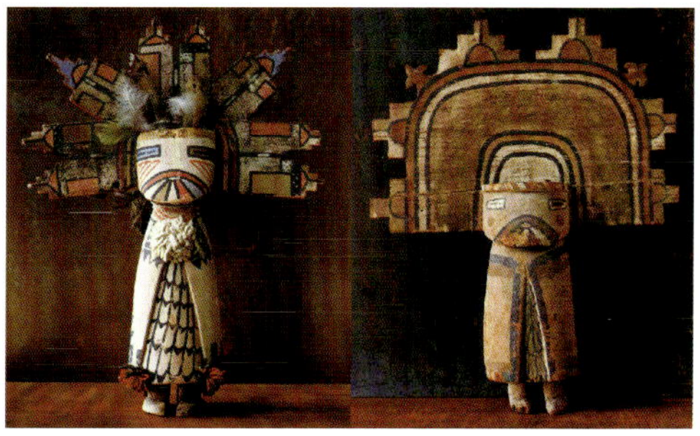

PLATE 75

Two Shalako kachinas appear at Hopi, a male and a female. Even though he does not have the usual pink face, this doll is the male, or **Shalako Taka**, wearing the traditional blue boots.

Hopi, ca. late 1800s to early 1900s

Purchased for the Museum in 1910 by AMNH ethnologist Dr. Clark Wissler, as part of a large group of mixed artifacts known as the Voth Collection, from the Fred Harvey Indian Store at the Grand Canyon. Mennonite missionary and ethnologist Henry R. Voth, who lived in Hopi from 1893 to 1902, collected the kachinas in this group.

The American Museum of Natural History, New York, New York
AMNH Catalogue no. 50/9333

PLATE 76

Shalako Mana is the female form that accompanies the Shalako Taka, although a man always takes the part. She wears a full-length skirt made entirely of eagle feathers. She is called upon in times of drought.

Hopi, ca. 1875

George Terasaki Collection, New York, New York

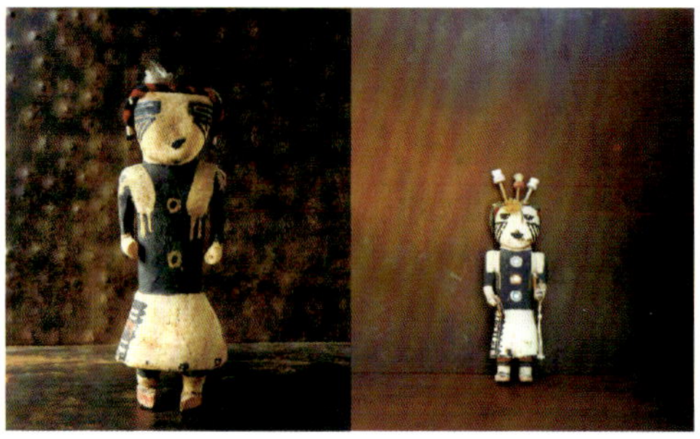

PLATES 77 and 78

The Flute Kachina, **Lenang**, is an important one for he is associated with the bringing of water, particularly to the springs that formerly furnished all the water for the Hopi villages.

Hopi, ca. late 1800s or possibly earlier

George Terasaki Collection, New York, New York
Lenang Kachina on the right: ca. 1910
Richard and Nedra Matteucci Collection, Santa Fe, New Mexico

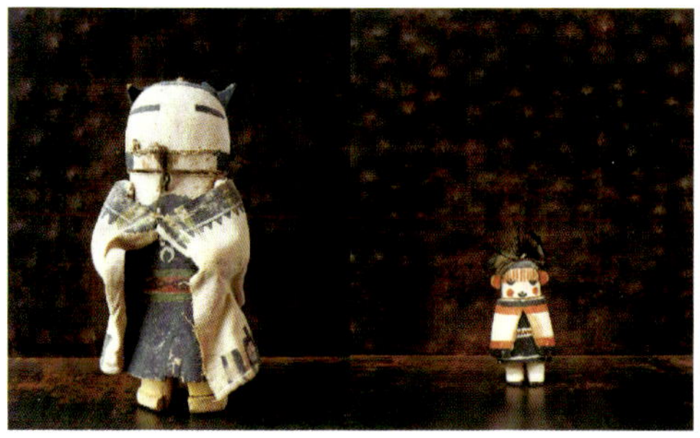

PLATE 79

Alo Mana is a white female kachina that has apparently been derived from Zuni. There is a strong resemblance to the warrior woman, Kothlamana, at that pueblo. At Hopi she may come to make music in the Niman Ceremony.

Hopi, ca. 1880–1900

A kachina from Jo Mora's Collection. Jo Mora was an artist and photographer who lived and worked in Polacca, at Hopi, from 1902 to 1904.

George Terasaki Collection, New York, New York

PLATE 80

Hahai-i Wuhti is the mother of kachinas and surprisingly also of dogs. She is the kindly grandmother yet she comes with her children the ogres or monsters. She tells people how to behave in a thin falsetto voice.

Hopi, ca. 1920s

Gift of Elizabeth Compton Hegemann. Elizabeth Hegemann originally acquired this doll from Carlos Viera, a very early Santa Fe painter, who in 1904 became one of the founding artists of the Santa Fe Art Colony.

The Museum of Northern Arizona, Flagstaff, Arizona
MNA Catalogue no. E2264

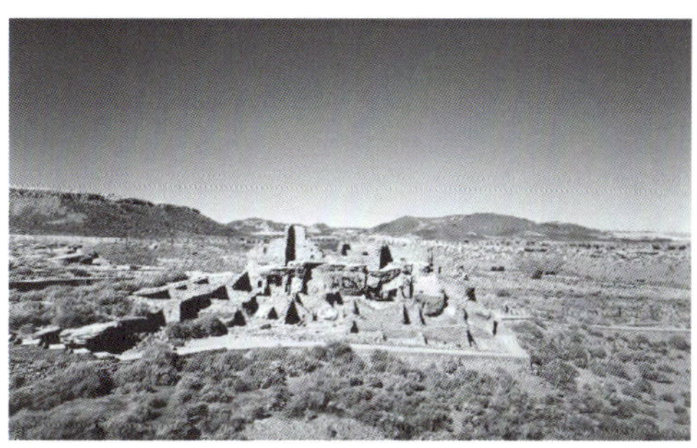

PLATE 81

WUPATKI, ARIZONA. Wupatki is the major village in a cluster of other ruins. The Hopi people maintain a close association with Wupatki. In excavating this ruin several finds were items relating to Hopi clans and the kachina cult.

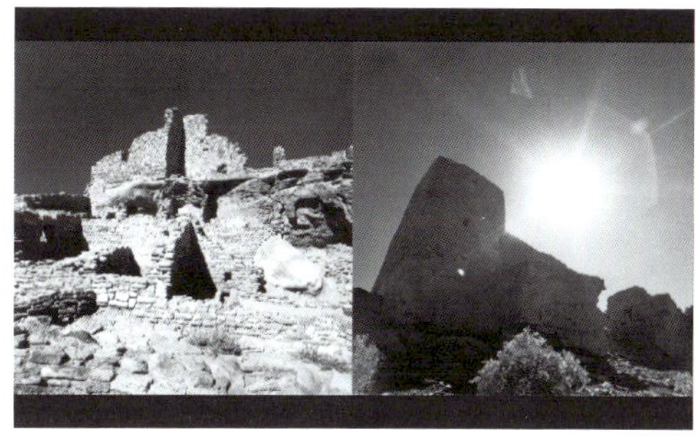

PLATE 82

WUPATKI, ARIZONA. In a desert area, Wupatki was a farming community that utilized the mulch of cinders in Sunset Crater to grow corn in a dry land.

PLATE 83

WUKOKI, ARIZONA. Wukoki, a small village near Wupatki.

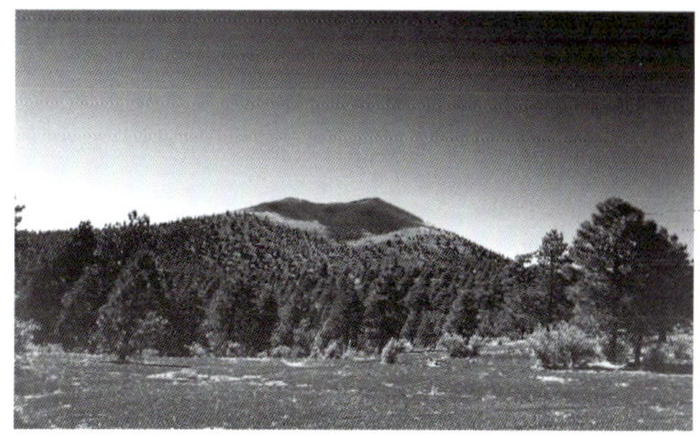

PLATE 84

SUNSET CRATER, ARIZONA. Sunset Crater is a volcano that erupted in 1066. Sunset Crater Kachina presumably lives in the lava caves at its foot.

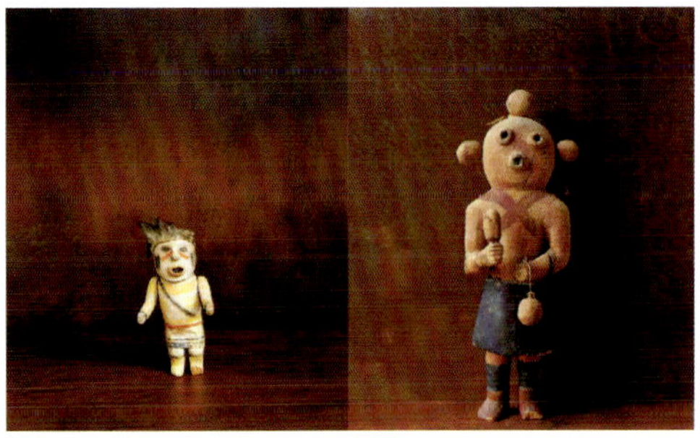

PLATE 85

Ho-é is a clown for the kachinas. He comes during the Bean Dance and behaves as a rambunctious youngster. Sometimes he bedevils the kachinas as they proceed about their business, and at other times he may imitate a neighboring tribal member.

Hopi, ca. 1920s

Carved by Jimmy Kewanwytewa

Jimmy Kewanwytewa is a famous Hopi carver who worked at the Museum of Northern Arizona, Flagstaff, from 1940 to 1965 during the tenure of museum cofounder Dr. Harold S. Colton. Jimmy K's work is cited in many books about kachinas, and his carvings, now mostly in museum collections, are highly prized.

Gift of Elizabeth Compton Hegemann Collection in 1961. One of Elizabeth's husbands was an outpost trader, and they lived for many years at Shonto Trading Post in Navajoland. Elizabeth Hegemann not only lived and traded on the reservation but also wrote about and photographed her many years of living in Hopi/Navajo in her book Navajo Trading Days.

Part of the McGill Collection.
The Museum of Northern Arizona, Flagstaff, Arizona
MNA Catalogue no. E2301

PLATE 86

The **Koyemsi** is a clown figure that is shared by both the Hopi and the Zuni. It is not a kachina but rather an interlocutor between kachinas and men. It behaves as a simpleton one moment and a wise man the next.

Hopi, ca. 1920s

George Terasaki Collection, New York, New York

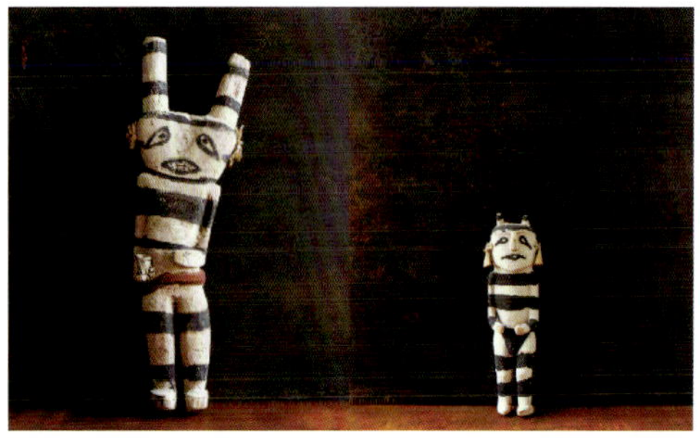

PLATE 87

Koshari.

Hopi, ca. late 1800s, early 1900s

Purchased for the Museum in 1913 by archaeologist Dr. H. J. Spinden on the Museum's Huntington Southwestern Survey expedition.

The American Museum of Natural History, New York, New York
AMNH Catalogue no. 50.1/7532

PLATE 88

The **Koshari** is a clown that was brought by the Tewa when they fled from the Spaniards to the Hopi lands in the early 1700s.

Hopi, ca. early 1900s

Purchased for the Museum in 1910 by AMNH ethnologist Dr. Clark Wissler, as part of a large group of mixed artifacts known as the Voth Collection, from the Fred Harvey Indian Store at the Grand Canyon. Mennonite missionary and ethnologist Henry R. Voth, who lived in Hopi from 1893 to 1902, collected the kachinas in this group.

The American Museum of Natural History, New York, New York
AMNH Catalogue no. 50 9327

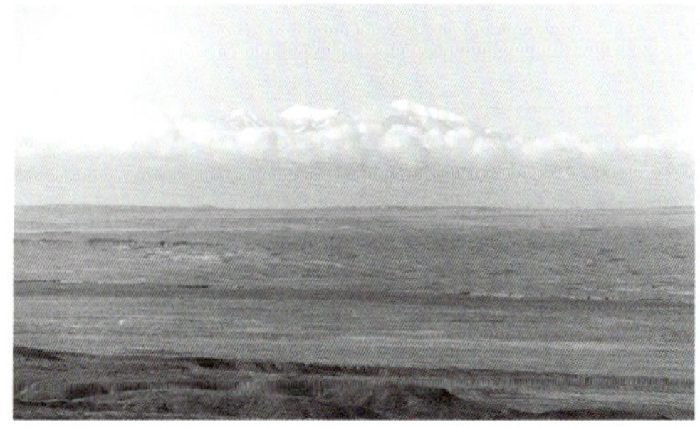

PLATE 89

THE SAN FRANCISCO PEAKS from Second Mesa, Hopi. This is how the Ancients and the present-day Hopi might see the kachinas approaching.

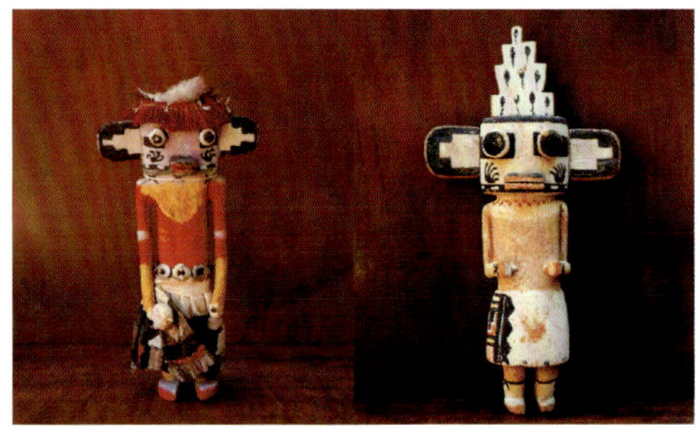

PLATE 90

The Badger Kachina, **Honan Kachina**, an animal from the south, knows a great many medicines, for where he lives underground there are medicinal roots. He is also the spirit partner of the Badger Clan.

Hopi, ca. 1890–1900

Gift of Clay Lockett to MNA in 1967.

The Museum of Northern Arizona, Flagstaff, Arizona
MNA Catalogue no. E3771

PLATE 91

This kachina is called Pavatea because of the pollywogs on its tableta, but its actual name is **Honan**, Badger Kachina. There are a surprising number of variations on the appearance of this kachina, yet they all seem to be *wuye*, or spirit partners, of the Badger Clan.

Hopi, ca. early 1900s

Tony Berlant Collection, Santa Monica, California

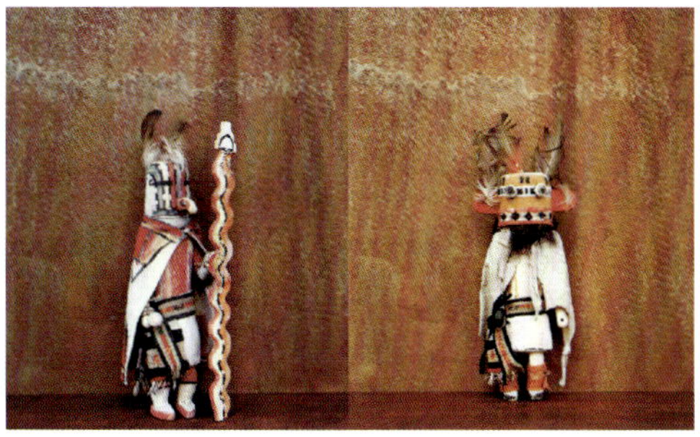

PLATE 92

This is a *wuye* or Tobacco Clan spirit partner. **Tsitoto** represents the tobacco flower, a plant that is needed for ceremonies. When the kachinas dance and the elders pray for rain they smoke the native tobacco called *kinnikinic.*

Hopi, ca. 1880–1900

Gift of Clay Lockett to MNA in 1967.

The Museum of Northern Arizona, Flagstaff, Arizona
MNA Catalogue no. E3767

PLATE 93

Many of the more important kachinas are referred to as Chief Kachinas as they come only during ceremonies. This **Hototo** is the yellow form that comes as a pair during the Powamu performance.

Hopi, ca. 1800–1900

Gift of Clay Lockett to MNA in 1967.

The Museum of Northern Arizona, Flagstaff, Arizona
MNA Catalogue no. E3801

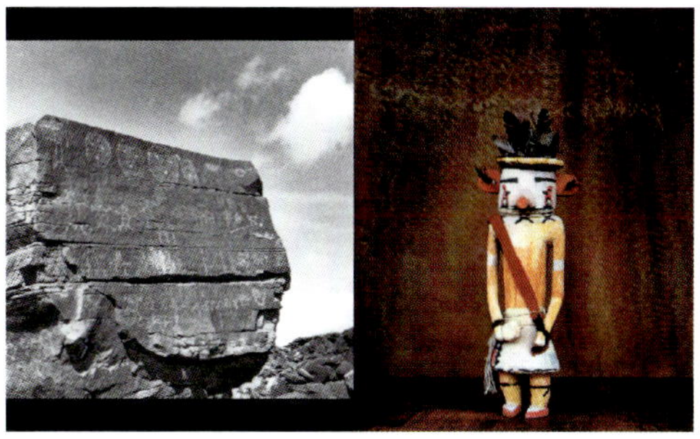

PLATE 94

CLAN ROCKS, NAVAJOLAND. Among the multitudinous symbols is a row of heads representing Masau, the deity who controls the land of the Hopi.

PLATE 95

One of the more important deities of both the Hopi and the Zuni is the Plumed Water Serpent. The kachina **Palolokong** represents this deity in the Mixed Kachina Dance. The deity itself appears in an altar in the kiva.

Hopi, ca. 1890–1900

Gift of Clay Lockett in 1967.

The Museum of Northern Arizona, Flagstaff, Arizona
MNA Catalogue no. E3860

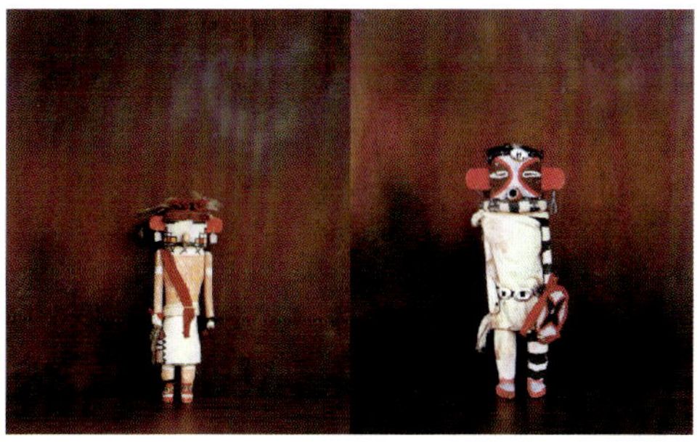

PLATE 96

This is a Corn Kachina. The name **Letcitaka** means things stacked up, in this case corn.

Hopi, ca. 1890–1900

Gift of Clay Lockett in 1967.

The Museum of Northern Arizona, Flagstaff, Arizona
MNA Catalogue no. E3831

PLATE 97

The War Kachina Leader or **Kipok Kachina** is supposed to have been inspired by a personage from the Chemehuevi tribe far to the west. It appears with the clowns at Hopi and warns them to change their ways or disaster will befall them.

Hopi, ca. 1890–1900

Gift of Clay Lockett in 1967.

The Museum of Northern Arizona, Flagstaff, Arizona
MNA Catalogue no. E3769

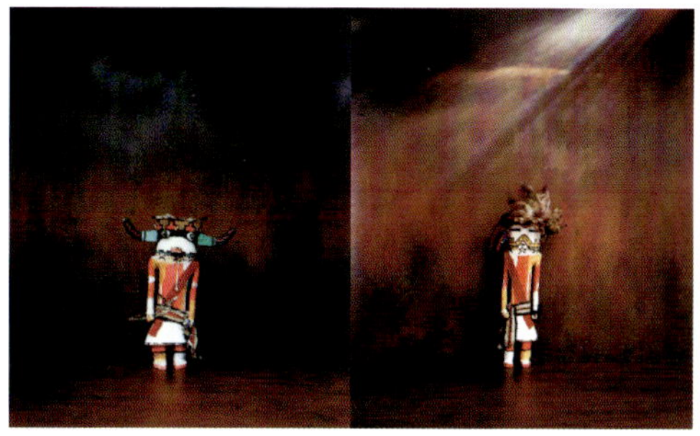

PLATE 98

This is one of the **Hisot Kachinum**, ancient kachinas, whose purpose is unclear, as they have not appeared for a lengthy period of time. His name, Silakaptaka, is derived from the ruff of cornhusks around his neck.

Hopi, ca. 1890–1900

Gift of Clay Lockett in 1967.

The Museum of Northern Arizona, Flagstaff, Arizona
MNA Catalogue no. E3768

PLATE 99

Quoi-a is reputed to be a Hopi kachina that was inspired by a Navajo performance, and he sings in that language. However, no similar figure occurs in Navajo ceremonies. He can come in two forms, one old style and one new.

Hopi, ca. 1890–1900

Gift of Clay Lockett in 1967.

The Museum of Northern Arizona, Flagstaff, Arizona
MNA Catalogue no. E3841

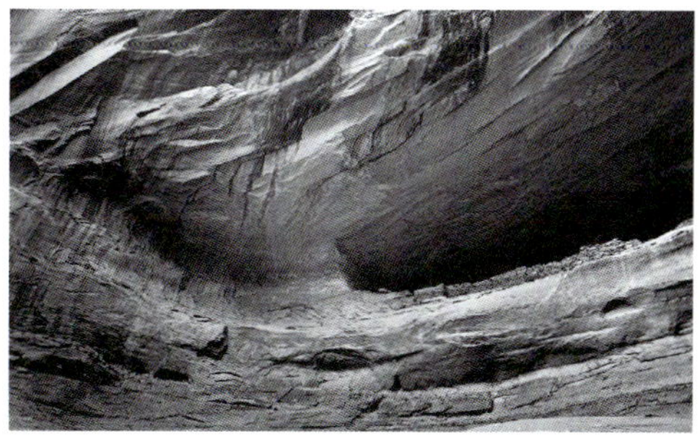

PLATE 100

MYSTERY VALLEY, UTAH. The early people lived in convenient caves. Scholars think that they lived up there so that they didn't take up scarce farming land or as a refuge from enemies.

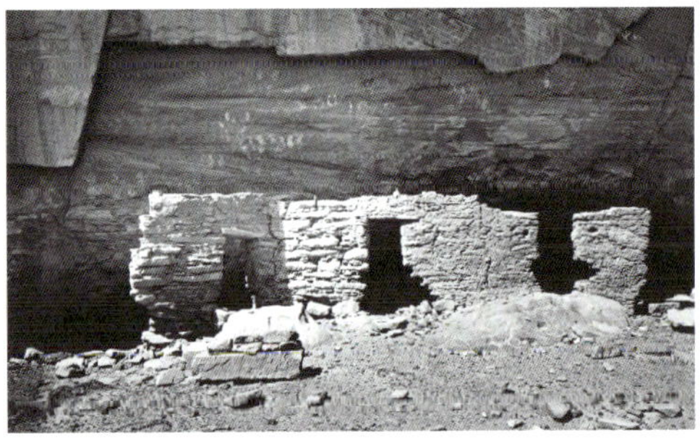

PLATE 101

MYSTERY VALLEY, UTAH. Deep within Mystery Valley is a small ruin that is notable for the line of white handprints on the cave wall behind it.

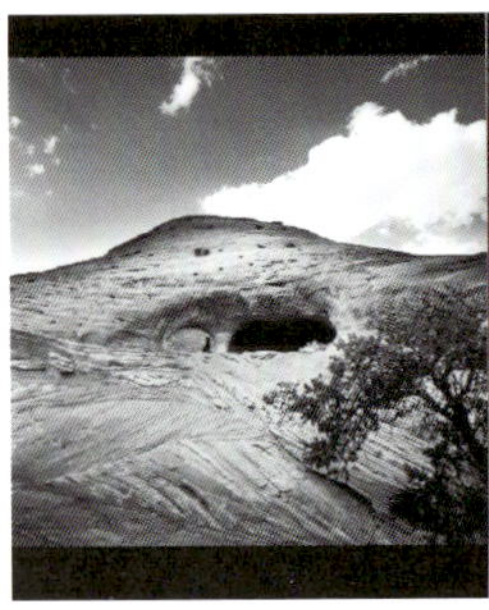

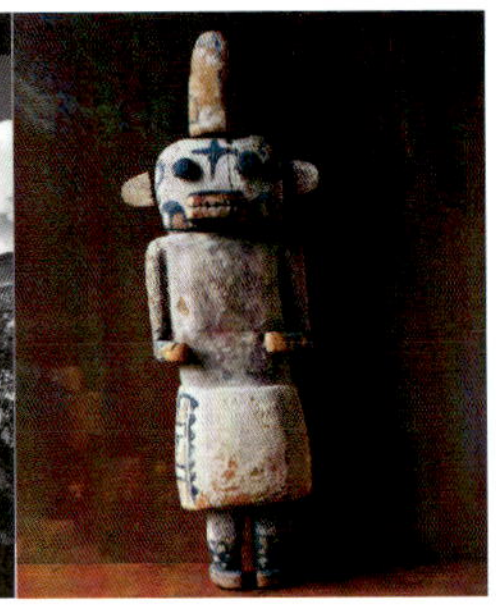

PLATE 102

MYSTERY VALLEY, UTAH. An ancient dwelling tucked up under a hill on a cliff.

PLATE 103

The deity of the sky and all of its attributes is **Sotuknangu**. He is a fearsome personage who can strike people with lightning, scattering them about in pieces. He then puts them back together, but when he does this, they are put together wrong.

Hopi, ca. late 1800s

George Terasaki Collection, New York, New York

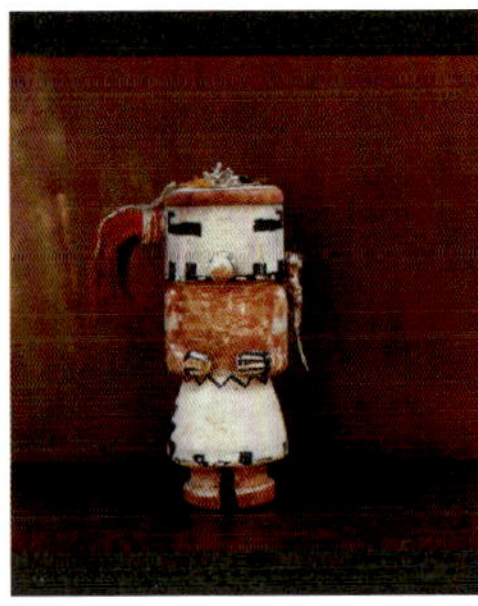

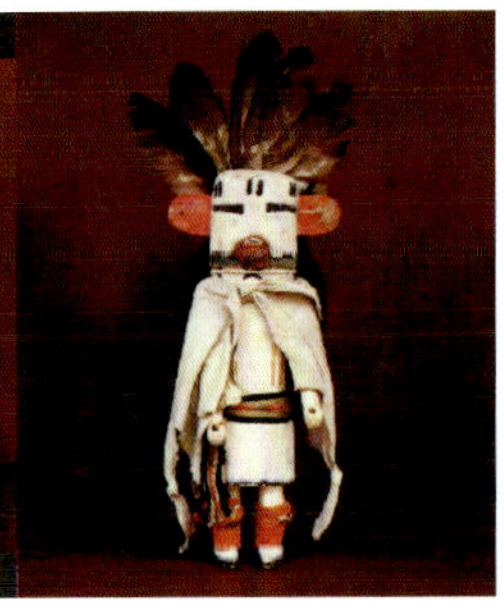

PLATE 104

The **Tasap Kachina** is a visualization by the Hopi of their nearby neighbors, the Navajo. The kachina is a representation both of those people and one of their more important ceremonies, the Yeibichai performance.

Hopi, ca. 1890–1900

Greer Garson Collection, Santa Fe, New Mexico
Buddy Fogelson Collection, Santa Fe, New Mexico
Alan Kessler Collection, Santa Fe, New Mexico
Private Collection

PLATE 105

Si'vunain is the other one of the Hototos. His costume and mask are different from the Yellow Hototo. He is called the Lazy One because he apparently does not gather wood for the kiva as do the other kachinas.

Hopi, ca. 1800–1900

Gift of Clay Lockett to MNA in 1967.

The Museum of Northern Arizona, Flagstaff, Arizona
MNA Catalogue no. E3815

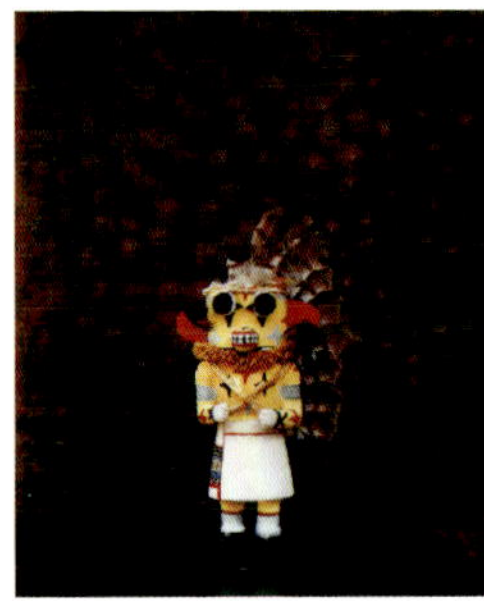

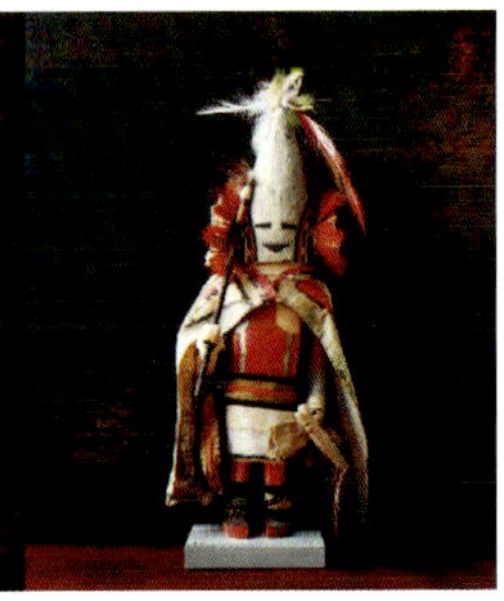

PLATE 106

This kachina has an exact counterpart in Zuni, where it is a personage who punishes all those who transgress traditional mores. The Hopi **Ahoté** does not function in this role although he may punish the clown's behavior.

Hopi, ca. 1920s

Obtained by the Museum from the Stevens Collection in 1930.

The Museum of Northern Arizona, Flagstaff, Arizona
MNA Catalogue no. E674

PLATE 107

The partner of Eototo. A clan ancient of kachinas from the Young Corn Clan. He always comes together with Eototo, never separate, during the Bean Dance or Powamu Ceremony.

Hopi, ca. early 1900s

Purchased for the Museum in 1910 by AMNH ethnologist Dr. Clark Wissler, as part of a large group of mixed artifacts known as the Voth Collection, from the Fred Harvey Indian Store at the Grand Canyon. Mennonite missionary and ethnologist Henry R. Voth, who lived in Hopi from 1893 to 1902, collected the kachinas in this group.

The American Museum of Natural History, New York, New York
AMNH Catalogue no. 50/9523

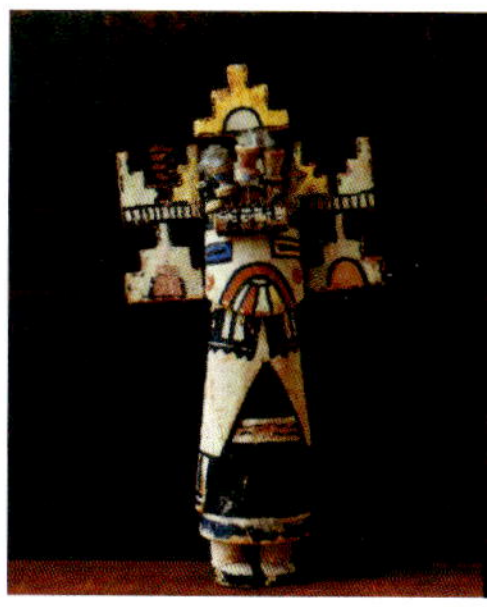
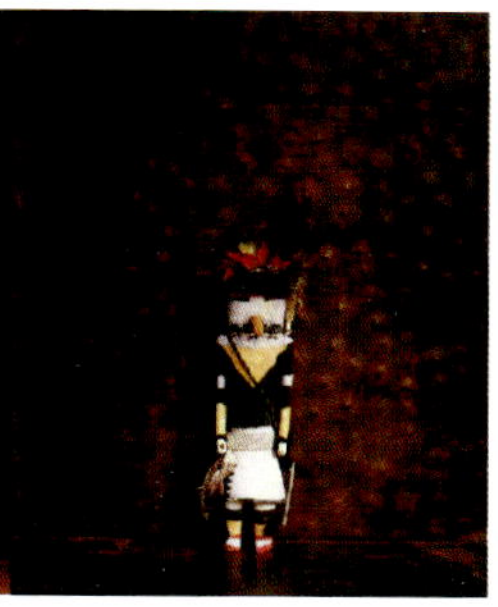

PLATE 108

Although this personage closely resembles the Shalako female, it is considered to be the water-drinking maiden **Palhik' Mana**. It belongs to the Mamzrau, a women's society, and is not considered a kachina.

Hopi, ca. late 1800s

George Terasaki Collection, New York, New York

PLATE 109

Duck Kachina. The duck is an animal associated with water among both the Hopi and the Zuni. Consequently the **Pawik Kachina** is important to ensure an increase in ducks. It is the only animal that can walk, swim, and fly.

Hopi, ca. 1800–1900

Gift of Clay Lockett in 1967.

The Museum of Northern Arizona, Flagstaff, Arizona
MNA Catalogue no. E3726

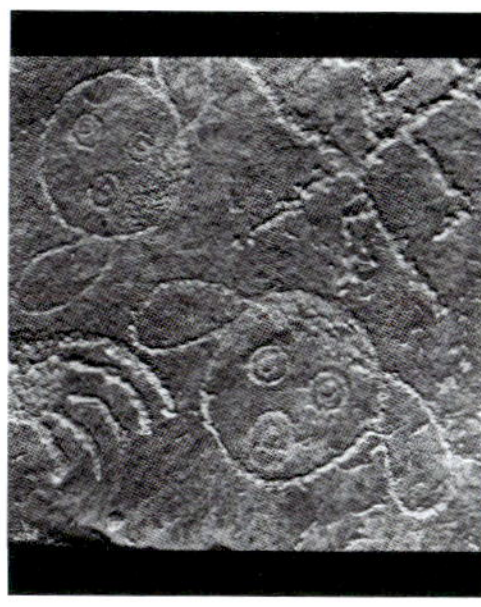
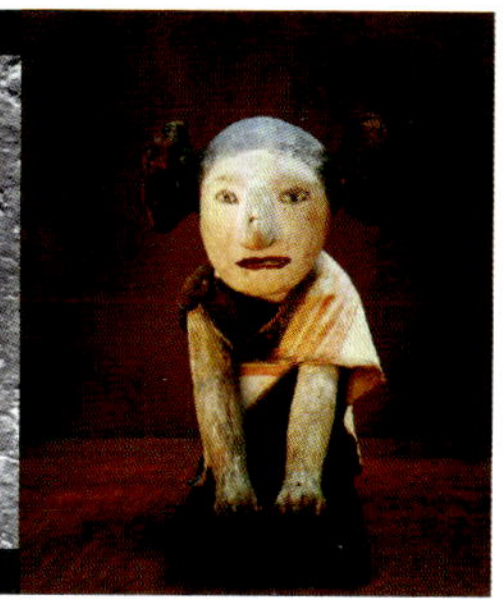

PLATE 110

MAIDEN WHORLS PETROGLYPH. Very old and rare carvings of Hopi maidens.

PLATE 111

This is a carving of a familiar scene at Hopi, that of a maiden grinding corn, a **Nguman Mana**. Her hair dress shows that she is unmarried. She is working a metate, a grindstone, with a mano, a hand stone, to grind corn.

Hopi, ca. 1920–30

Tony Berlant Collection, Santa Monica, California

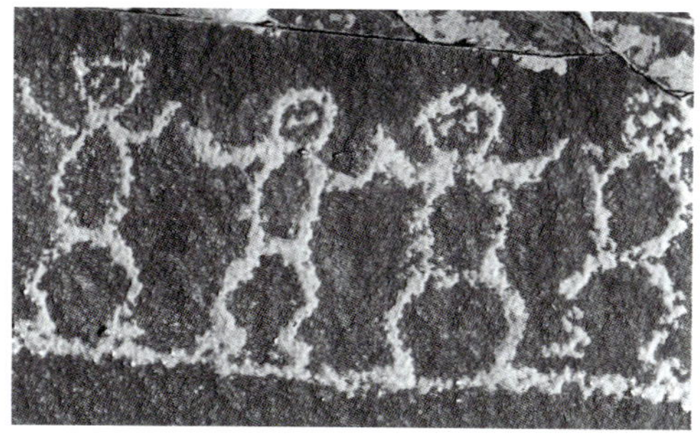

PLATE 112

PETROGLYPH FIGURES. A row of dancing figures parade across the laboriously carved, black-coated rock face. Some petroglyph meanings remain unknown to us, but others are like a prehistoric mural, as in this one in which the figure on the left wears the maiden's hair dress as she accompanies three other individuals in what may have been a kachina ceremony.

PUEBLO CULTURES

BARTON WRIGHT

THE PUEBLO INDIANS OF THE AMERICAN SOUTHWEST are popularly known as the descendants of the cliff dwellers. The attraction of their romantic setting and the ease of reaching the small compact villages to witness dances or pause by a roadside to purchase their interesting arts and crafts have drawn travelers for decades. For more than one hundred years their colorful and distinctive culture has also brought ethnographers who came to study and to produce imposing bibliographies of learned treatises. Despite the length and intensity of this interest by both layman and scientist, it is only in recent years that analysis of Pueblo philosophy and cosmological concepts has been possible. Partially this is a result of the complexity arising from the diverse origins of the Pueblo people themselves, but it is also compounded by over four hundred years of European domination and Christian indoctrination.

Contrary to the popularly held opinion, the Pueblo people are not a single, homogeneous group. Their diverse origins are reflected linguistically. In the west, the Hopi speak Shoshonean, a branch of the Uto-Aztecan family closely related to the Numic languages farther to the west, while their closest Pueblo neighbors to the east, the Zuni, converse in the Zunian language, possibly a Penutian derivative. Along the Rio Grande valley of New Mexico, the unique Keresan family is represented by the pueblos of Santo Domingo, Cochiti, San Felipe, Santa Ana, Zia, and to the west, Acoma and Laguna. The Kiowa-Tanoan family is composed of several subgroups. The Tiwa branch encompasses the pueblos of Taos, Picuris, Isleta, and Sandia. Tewa is spoken by the towns of San Juan, Pojoaque, Nambe, Tesuque, Santa Clara, San Ildefonso, and the village of Hano among the Hopi. Quarai, Abó, and the El Paso community are members of the Piro branch. Jemez is spoken exclusively by that village, while Tano was the language of the extinct town of Pecos (Spicer 1962, 10). In addition to this linguistic ancestry, the land base is shared with non-Pueblo tribes such as the Athapascan Navajo and Apache, the Yuman Hualapai, Havasupai, and Yavapai, as well as the Shoshonean Paiute and Ute.

Geographically, the Pueblo Indians occupy portions of two states, Arizona and New Mexico. This land reaches from the Little Colorado River on the west to the headwaters of the Canadian and Pecos rivers on the east. In the north it borders the high mountains of Colorado and extends southward to the long arc of the Mogollon Rim with associated mountain ranges that bisect both states. The most heavily occupied area lies along the upper Rio Grande valley in New Mexico.

The region is a high desert sporadically surrounded by snow-covered mountains of even greater elevation. It is a land of flat-topped mesas and buttes, deep cliff-lined canyons, and broad sage-covered sandy valleys. Countless ephemeral watercourses debouch into the few permanent rivers whose waters are fed by precipitation in the mountains. Stands of piñon and juniper trees cover the foothills and mesas, merging into extensive pine forests at higher elevations and into desert vegetation in the lower reaches. Within this larger environment the twin factors of elevation and exposure to the sun produce radical changes in small areas. The scant annual moisture of 25–30 cm comes in violent summer thunderstorms or in generalized winter snows when the temperature may plunge to -45° Celsius. This marginal precipitation is seldom adequate for the crops of Pueblo agriculturalists, and in consequence the need for water is a central theme in Pueblo religion.

In response to the yield of their marginal environment, the Pueblo subsistence pattern was twofold (Ford 1972, 1–17). The warm growing season was used to produce their staple crop, maize,

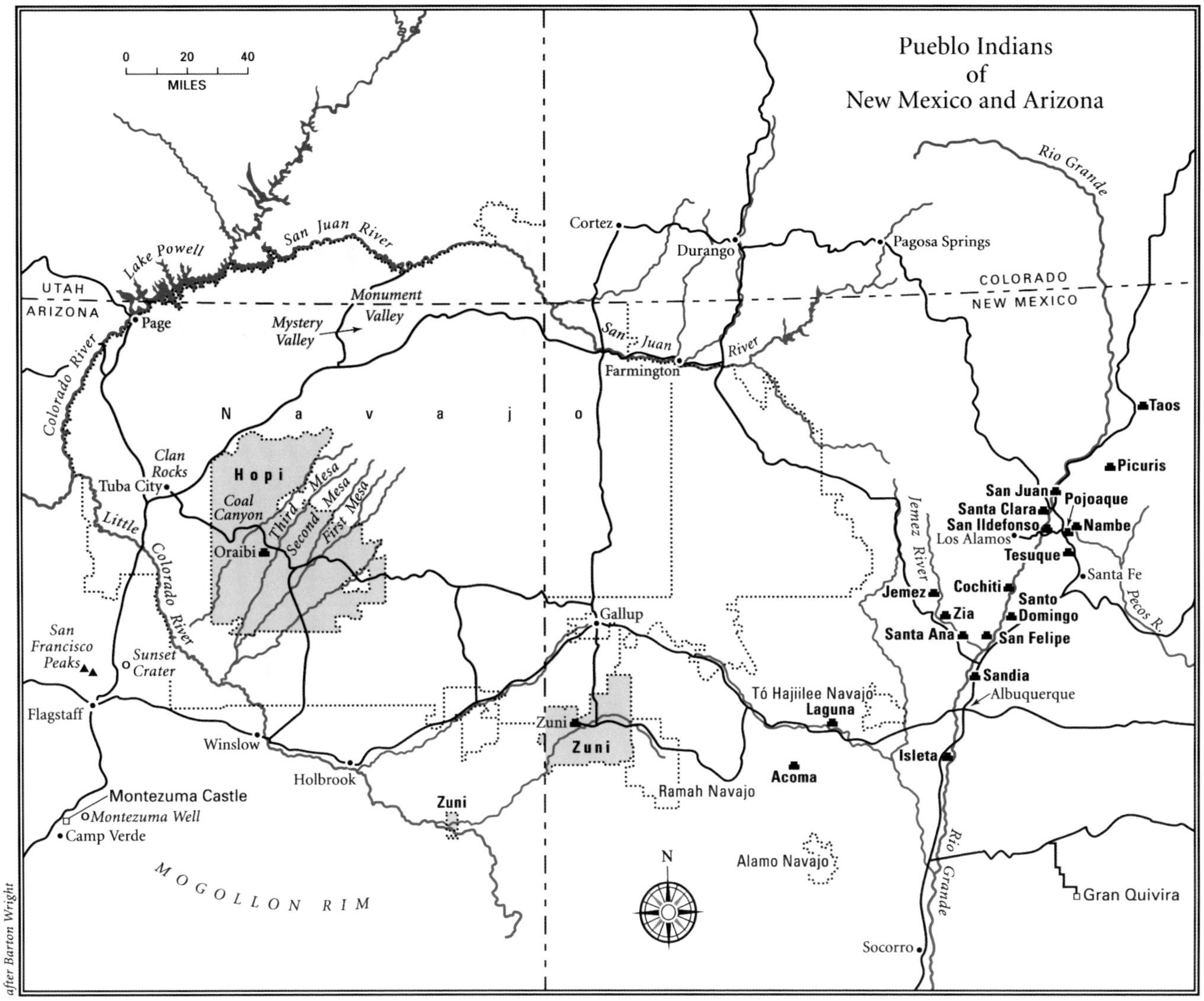

after Barton Wright

through intensive irrigation in the east or dry farming in the west. Secondly, during the cold winter and early spring months a dependence on game and wild foods supplemented the products of the harvest. This response to their environment produced one of the most characteristic elements of the Pueblo culture, a bipartite concept that permeates all interactions and relationships. This dual approach manifests itself in their ceremonial organization, where it forms the common or articulating principle between Pueblo ideological concepts and societal structure. Each pueblo is organized according to a cooperating duality rather than an amalgamation based on linguistic similarities, lines of consanguinity, economic motives, or political drives. No system links the autonomous Pueblo villages, not even those closely related to one another. There are pan-Pueblo similarities in subsistence patterns, social organization, and religious concepts, although there is a considerable difference between eastern and western pueblos, possibly as a result of varying adaptations to water supplies (Dozier 1954, 98). An ongoing problem is how a people so linguistically diverse came to share a common Pueblo ethos.

A heterogeneity of population is apparent from the first evidence of people in the Southwest over 20,000 years ago. Archaeological evidence indicates Paleo-Indian hunters scattered along the flanks of the Rocky Mountains to the east of the Continental Divide. Equally early were the bands of Archaic desert dwellers occupying the arid lower elevations to the south and west. By the third or fourth millennium BC the Paleo-Indian hunters had disappeared and only the Archaic desert people remained and, around the time of Christ, were joined by other Archaic peoples from the Great Basin. A reconstructed picture of this era suggests a far-flung but sparse population with a foraging economy that emphasized plant foods and small game and occupied a region of unusually varied topography and natural resources.

The appearance of maize among these people over 4,000 years ago marked two important occurrences. It was the first of the sporadic but continuous impulses of influence from the higher cultures of Mesoamerica, and it was the beginning of the cultural adaptation that produced the Pueblo Indians of today. Although the demographic changes were imperceptible for centuries after the appearance of maize, adaptations to the new plant led eventually to stable, successful, and essentially permanent agricultural societies with complex social structures.

To insure survival in a marginal land, a hunting and gathering family or band requires an intensive knowledge of the regional ecology. Insufficient information about either food or water resources carries the threat of death; for knowledge is life. For maize to be successfully grown in the variable conditions of the Southwest, knowledge of proper soils, microclimates, available water at specific times, and an awareness of the limitations of elevation and general weather variables were required. In addition to a knowledge of the land, the mobility to follow the cycle of usable plants to higher elevations or more favored locations as their fruits ripened with the progression of the season was a second essential factor. Native plants reproduce in sufficient numbers to insure their survival against predators or natural disasters but introduced plants do not. Maize in particular requires an almost day-to-day protection by human beings against the abiotic factors as well as against an army of animal and insect predators.

The knowledge of the land gained by hunting and gathering techniques is the integral part of the inventory of a foraging band. But mobility must be compromised to offer the amount of protection required by maize. This demand was diametrically opposed to survival, for the crop was undoubtedly insufficient in the beginning to support the band from one growing season to the next, yet it formed a critical supplement to their food supply. The presence of maize in the Southwest for nearly two millennia, without appreciable demographic change, indicates both its value and the difficulty of adaptation. The hunting and gathering subsistence pattern was retained because the variables affecting the growth of maize in this environment precluded the abandonment of foraging and the consequent total adoption of agriculture. However, the presence of maize in most archaeological sites denotes adoption of this cereal. The social and ceremonial structure of the Pueblos indicates that both subsistence patterns of farming and hunting-gathering coexisted with the band divided into a cooperating duality, occupying a semipermanent base, and bonded together by social structures to retain band identity.

The era that began with the introduction of pottery and lasted until contemporary times has been named "Anasazi," a Navajo word meaning the "Ancient Ones." The 2500-year span of the Anasazi era is divided into two horizons. The earlier, ending in the eighth century, is called Basketmaker from the proclivity of the people in this craft. The later horizon, lasting from the termination of the Basketmaker sequence to contemporary times, is named Pueblo. Each horizon is further subdivided into numbered periods marked by the innovation of important changes in cultural inventory. These changes, or markers, are events such as the shift from atl-atls to bows and arrows; the addition to the economy of beans, squash, cotton, or a larger species of maize; but most often by a change in the ceramic style. The prehistory is one of refinement of existing culture traits and continuous additions of new elements, some of which were introduced from outside the region but most of which were developed locally. The abundant artifacts that have survived are grouped into patterns indicative of growing diversity.

By AD 1150, several distinct groups are recognizable either in or immediately adjacent to the region being considered. Present and sharing most of the basic aspects of Pueblo existence were the people of the Mesa Verde phase of southwestern Colorado, southeastern Utah, most of New Mexico, and the northeastern part of Arizona. The Largo phase in the Gallina River area of north central New Mexico, the Tularosa phase in west central New Mexico, the Kayenta culture of northeastern Arizona, and the Sinagua of central Arizona are also recognizable. The differences among these groups were primarily in their ceramics, architectural styles, and the disposal of their dead. Certain concepts of their religion are inferred from the presence of specialized rooms with ceremonial features and associated ritual artifacts. Of great interest during the interval between AD 1050 and 1200 is the presence of articles of Mesoamerican derivation: parrots, cast copper bells, architectural features, a new variety of maize, and other attributes all indicating contact with the more sophisticated cultures of Mexico.

Beginning in the 1100s, the Pueblo culture along the westernmost margin of the Pueblo region in southern Nevada collapsed. In some areas the Pueblo Indians disappeared completely; in others they consolidated until at the end of this period there was a concentration of people along the Rio Grande, the central drainage of New Mexico, at Acoma, and in the Zuni and Hopi country. In the interval between 1450 and the arrival of the Spanish in AD 1540, the nomadic Athapascan tribes of the Apache and Navajo appeared.

When the Spaniards arrived in the sixteenth century they found the Pueblo Indians occupying over ninety villages along the Rio Grande, from Taos to central New Mexico and from Pecos to Jemez. They also lived in the isolated town of Acoma and, farther west, in the six Zuni and seven Hopi villages. In many respects, the Spanish were harsher in their efforts to colonize and Christianize these Pueblo people than they had been with any Indians they had previously encountered to the south (Spicer 1962, 167–69). The result was that their merciless pressure caused the reduction of the population by half in less than eighty years. Dissension from the Indians resulted in the pan-Pueblo Revolt of 1680, which succeeded in driving the Spanish out of the Rio Grande valley for sixteen years. The revolt and fear of Spanish reprisals produced further widespread dislocation and resettlement among the Pueblos. By 1700 the Revolt and pestilence introduced by the Spanish had reduced the number of Rio Grande pueblos to nineteen (Spicer 1962, 169). Disintegrating Spanish political and military power opened the region to raiding by nomadic tribes in the late 1700s. These raids for food and slaves continued and even increased during the Mexican regime from 1821 to 1848 and during the initial occupation of the Anglo-Americans before being brought under control.

In the period between 1840 and 1880 relatively few Anglo-Americans came to the southwestern deserts unless jobs took them there. The region lacked the lure of lusher lands and was inhabited by the feared Apache and Comanche warriors. Subjugation of these tribes, coupled with the coming of the railroad in 1800, effected permanent change as non-Indian towns and settlements sprang up along the railroad right-of-way. The process of acculturation for the Puebloans, which began with bloodshed at the hands of the Spaniards, continued in the political, economic, and social pressures of the Anglo-Americans. The Pueblo people, particularly along the Rio Grande, retreated even further and entrenched themselves as conservative, insular villages that, through passive resistance and secretive practices, succeeded in preserving the essence of their culture into contemporary times.

The countless religious and military documents left by the Spaniards convey mere scraps of information about the lifestyles of the Pueblo people. Even less was added to these tantalizing glimpses during the Mexican regime in the first quarter of the nineteenth century. With the coming of the Anglo-Americans this changed to a certain extent, for their focus in writing was to describe in detail the new country they were entering. Some of the best of these accounts were the well-kept diaries of early explorers or the writings of members of the United States Army who kept accurate accounts of the people and the ceremonies they witnessed. Such descriptions awakened interest among other travelers whose relationships involved the Indians and produced a most complete record extant of Pueblo life.

Following the arrival of the railroad in the 1880s all manner of people visited the Southwest and wrote their impressions of Indian life. Most often these writings were biased for the express purpose of discrediting or disrupting native patterns of existence in order to promote government or ecclesiastical programs. Despite this negative aspect, the new surge of visitors added materially to the documentation of Pueblo life in the period from 1860 to 1900.

The Pueblo people responded to this unwanted attention with increasingly stringent secretiveness about all of their activities, religious or otherwise. In the early years of the twentieth century, programs of acculturation progressively obscured or destroyed even more of the native patterns. Undoubtedly the most unusual aspect of the interaction between Anglo-Americans and the Pueblo Indians is not what the native peoples have lost, but that they have been able to retain as much of their culture as exists today.

PATTERNS OF CULTURE

At present, most of the Pueblo villages are small, compact towns of adjoining houses made of stone masonry or adobe and situated near arable land. If the village is large enough, the houses form several irregular streets or plazas, usually oriented east-west. Formerly, the house structures were at least two or three stories in height, with a few having five or six levels. House entry, in earlier times, was from the second level for protection against enemies. The ladders used for access could be drawn up during an emergency. Nowadays, the houses are seldom more than a single story and are constructed and equipped like those of their Anglo-American neighbors. Family life is usually centered around one large room which may function as a living room, kitchen, and bedroom, with smaller outlying rooms used for storage of food, utility, or auxiliary quarters if the family is large. Personal possessions were formerly stored in bundles or other containers and suspended from the beamed ceilings. Sacred paraphernalia belonging to individual members were hung in the same manner without fear of disturbance. Nowadays, they are kept in locked trunks or overnight bags. Clan relics, ritual gear, and masks are kept in special storage areas or even outside the villages in caves because of their latent power that may cause injury to the young or uninitiated.

Each town is tightly organized under the direction of a priesthood which controls the social, political, and religious systems. These priests and their sodalities perform elaborate ceremonials for the good of the people: to control the weather and the movements of the sun, to promote fertility in all living things, to exorcise, and to cure. These ceremonials insure the well-being of the people by placing them in concordance with their world, organizing the interaction of all parts for the greatest benefit. It is a religion that grew by augmentation, increasing its complexity with the addition of a new ritual for each variation in the environment. This ceremonialism with its complex religious techniques gives every evidence of having been derived from a single root or a common ideology, which in contemporary times varies only in the degree of acculturation that it has undergone during its tenure in this region.

In all probability, this common ideology began with an as yet undetermined group whose answers to the pressures inherent in the practice of agriculture were particularly successful and satisfactory. Other tribes coming in contact with this core group who adopted agriculture took its agricultural practices as well as its ceremonial investment and embellished it in their own styles. The precepts of this ceremonialism were retained only as long as the people remained within the environmental niche we recognize as the core of the Southwest. Beyond these particular circumstances the pattern dissipates.

The normal difficulty of synthesizing the beliefs of twenty disparate groups is compounded among the Pueblos by the extreme secrecy that surrounds even the least ritual act. It is possible that this pervasive secrecy today often masks a loss of religious knowledge rather than concealing a specific belief. The interdiction by the Spanish against the practice of the native religion and the harsh penalties associated with it undoubtedly destroyed entire ceremonies and key personnel in the surviving segments. Despite this havoc, Pueblo religion is still viable. This fragmentation is in part offset by the depth of the cultural continuum and the length of observation. Nevertheless it is only in recent years that a coherent image of Pueblo theology has begun to emerge.

COSMOLOGY

Within this cluster of diverse people there is unity of thought and action that leads to a grouping of them as Pueblo people. It is not their technology and social order alone that unites them. It is their perception of reality, their philosophy, and the mechanics whereby they interact with their particular environment to perpetuate themselves that is the basic unifier. The other aspects of the various tribes are merely symptomatic of this underlying pattern. Because of this, it is often possible, through comparison, to abstract universals that transcend tribal boundaries, variations in social order, and political structure.

Primary among these universals is their perception of reality and the system whereby the Pueblo people interact with their perceived universe. This generalized view is presented most clearly by Ortiz (1969) in his work on the Tewa. From accumulated data he infers the presence of three cosmic levels: the above, the below, and the middle and their interactions. Stated in different terms, these levels represent the sky, the earth's surface, and the Underworld or spiritual realm. It appears more likely, however, that this is in actuality a bipartite division: that the Pueblo universe is organized on only two levels, the visible natural world, or middle, and an invisible partner echoing this world—a cosmic correspondence of the reversed Underworld and the normal middle world. The above, or sky, of the natural world is present in the Underworld but in an alternate state. If it is day above, it is night in the Underworld. A deity who is horrible in the real world is handsome in the nether regions; the winter of the Pueblo world is the summer of the spirit world. The concept of antithesis between the two planes permeates Pueblo thinking, and every attribute, form, principle, or perception reflects this polarity. These polarities do not represent opposition as a competitive position but rather are complementary in a manner similar to the Chinese concept of yin-yang. In addition, both planes are organized by their usefulness to the village, by spatial reference to it, and by the degree of control that can be exercised over each.

Within the natural world there is a basic division into two zones: an agricultural area with the village in the middle and a much larger foraging region that is claimed by use. This same division is apparent in the Underworld but is manifested through the supernaturals, who reflect the Pueblo perception of reality.

A spatial model of a hypothetical Pueblo world is a directionally oriented series of overlapping concentric quadrangles, each marked by shrines and each embodying more specific controls as the use increases. At the center of this ethnocentric conceptualization of space is the village, the "navel of the world" with the *kiva,* a world model, at its heart. The kiva, or ceremonial chamber, is often sunk into the surface of the earth and is considered, as is a grave, a half step into the Underworld. Within the kiva is the "earth navel," or center of centers, the connecting point between the two cosmic planes, the *sipapu.* This small hole in the kiva floor is a direct link with the Underworld. From the original sipapu the inhabitants of the three previous worlds, delineated by myth and legend, emerged to become the villagers. Although there may be two or more kivas in a given village, each will have its own sipapu, a simulacre of the original.

Extending outward from the kiva, the first quadrangle is the space enclosed by the path of the ceremonial circuit through the village that touches the kivas, the clan houses, and the village shrine. It is an emphasis on the identity of the village and its inhabitants. The second quadrate area encloses the outermost limits of the village and is marked by directional shrines that are named for the geographical markers of the most distant region. The third boundary in the sequence, also marked by shrines or other ceremonial locations, lies at the outer margin of the usable agricultural land. The dimensions of this area are dictated by the distance which crops can be carried to the village. Immediately outside of this area are the homes of cannibals, giants, and other monsters. Again, this is a posting of a land division or organization. The ultimate quadrangular zone is the land used by the village as its preserve for foraging. The markers are four sacred peaks or prominences, with associated shrines that lie on the farthest horizons in the cardinal directions.

This structured perception of the land retains the attitudes of the early foragers wherein knowledge, regardless of whether it was acquired by age or frequency of use, meant control of events (Eggan 1972, 297). As men accumulated experience with age and increased ability to cope with crises, so did an understanding of the attributes of the land increase as the village was approached, bringing with it a better chance of survival. It is an inward focus that concentrated the effectiveness of the group where it was most needed yet retained the alternatives of an earlier subsistence pattern.

As space is conceived and echoed in the supernatural, a similar structuring and intensification insofar as it relates to the village is apparent in the interactions that exist between the complementary halves of the Pueblo cosmos. Not only does every object have an intangible replication, but also every action in the normal world affects these alter egos, generating a response that may be positive or negative. The perceived difference in form between the tangible and intangible worlds implies different capabilities, and to secure any potential benefit, avenues of communication must be opened. The initial step is to impart human form to the elemental forces, objects, and other parts of the parallel world, thus making it easier to interact with them. To communicate with these beings, a system of symbols has been developed wherein like represents like. It is an associative language expressed in visual terms and is the basis for the ceremonial art forms of the Pueblos. The establishment of human shape and attributes implies human values as well. Primary among these, for the Puebloans, is the immutable law of reciprocity wherein proper behavior and respect place a heavy obligation to repay upon the recipient. In consequence, correctly performed rituals using the symbolic language to convey desires compels the inhabitants of the Underworld to reciprocate with the desired benefits, usually rain. The relationship between human being and spirit is somewhat analogous to a business partnership in which the full range of assets available to a partner may be unknown to the opposite member, but a courteous relationship will keep the options open for mutual benefit. However, in Pueblo religion the number of "partnerships" is unlimited, and the personnel involved is equally varied. In such an arrangement, the individuals most obviously suited to interact are those most knowledgeable or experienced, namely the older men. The interactive behavior of these individuals with supernaturals has, through time, become the formalized religion of the Pueblo of today.

Although the type of behavior demanded for this interaction is common to all Pueblo groups, the diversity of their origins in consonance with the impact of their immediate environment has produced variations. These variations are the cause of the complexity of ritual in any given group. For when peoples who have been geographically separate are brought into contact with one another, religion is borrowed across political boundaries more rapidly than any linguistic change (Parsons 1939, 769). This borrowing of cultural traits is based on like to like with adaptation to the internal mode of the borrower. No displacement of ritual occurs with this interchange, but rather there is growth by accretion, a steadily increasing complexity as all avenues of interaction are acquired, adapted, and placed in use. This elaboration of ceremonial requires not only an ever-greater number of participants but also an increasing expenditure of time and in consequence a more rigidly structured organization with an intensification of controls.

All of these effects reach their ultimate expression in the kiva, where ceremonies are held that attempt to compel conformity or desired behavior in natural forces, to foretell the future through forced crop growth as an omen for the summer, and to organize the efforts of individuals both living and dead for the common weal of the group. The kiva is the center of centers. It is the prime contact point or interface between both parts of the Pueblo universe (Parsons 1939, 769). There are other places where passage may occur or contact be made between the two planes, such as shrines, caves, springs, lakes, mountain peaks, or graves. In fact, passage may be at any place where the attributes of the two parts are shared in some manner, but it is the kiva where this contact is easiest and most completely controlled.

Centered about the kiva, the perimeters of the shadowy Underworld are delineated by myth and ritual in exactly the same terms as the normal world, fashioning it as a duplicate, a mirror image (Fewkes 1903, 490). Although there is correspondence in form, the two worlds are qualitatively different in substance. One is the epitome of mass: visible, solid, and weighty. The other is the opposite: the insubstantial, ethereal, mist world of the spirits (Voth 1905, 116).

Within this Netherworld there are categories of beings who are organized by their degree of affinity to the village in precisely the same manner that the environment and its inhabitants are arranged in the natural world. This produces four categories or domains of beings. These are not ranked hierarchically within a division but are organized by the degree of familiarity and the amount of control it is possible to exercise over their capabilities for potential benefits. These domains include the dead ancestors who have become like Cloud People, the kachinas, the Cloud People themselves, and the often formless beings or deities whose essence is more that of a philosophical concept than a pseudomorph of humankind.

THE DEAD

The Puebloans believe that there is a constant interaction with the Netherworld with beings passing back and forth. Human life follows a cyclical movement from one plane to the other, returning again and again. The rationale for this belief is recurrent in all the literature, but the method of return from the intangible to the tangible world is very nebulous. The life or soul of human beings may pass from this world to the Underworld for varying periods of time in dreams, unconsciousness, or death. During unconsciousness, an individual may temporarily leave his body and go to this alternate world visiting friends or talking with deceased relatives as a spirit before returning to the normal world. But with death the individual's "breath body" passes into the Underworld to continue an existence that is a repetition or an extension of the real world

(Titiev 1944, 107), with the status, rank, and social relationships of the deceased individual maintained and transferred through symbolic markings.

For the deceased there is a ritual preparation of the body to convert it to its new status of being with the Cloud People. The face is masked with cotton, and cornmeal is rubbed on the face and hands to make the body appear more cloudlike. If the individual held a ceremonial position in the real world this will be symbolized by the same markings and clothing that identified his or her status during life. Prayers and messages are given to the individuals as they are prepared for life in the Underworld regarding behavior, particularly as it applies to those left behind. The journey to the Underworld is believed to require four days, and food and water are provided for this period. During the four days, the deceased person may attempt to return home or bother relatives before continuing on to the other world. Consequently, rites are held and symbols used during this interval to confuse the pathway between the two planes, for not only does the deceased often try to return but also witches may attempt to follow the person with evil intent. The journey to the Underworld is today fraught with moral interpretations that are an inextricable combination of Christian and native beliefs.

Obviously the domain most closely allied to the living is that of the ancestors who through death have shed their corporeal forms to become breath bodies in the intangible world and as such are believed to reappear as clouds (Stephen 1936, 826) or dressed as clouds; they may form clouds with their breath (Bunzel 1933, 193), or be embodied through smoking; as the dead they eat only the essence of food (Voth 1905, 116). The conceptual thread linking these statements is the similarity of form among breath, clouds, and smoke. This imponderable concept links the breath body of the deceased with clouds, mist, or fog and confers on them the potential of rain-bringers, a function shared by other inhabitants of the Underworld. The fundamental belief in the continuity of life after death assures the Pueblo people that the dead will retain a proprietary interest in the welfare of the living and behave in a familiar manner despite their change in form. Nevertheless, their attitudes toward the dead may vary, depending on context, from one of veneration to one of fear (Titiev 1944, 108, n50). Efforts are made to continue to incorporate the deceased in functions they were involved in during life. Consequently, the dead are often invited to functions, included in ceremonies, expected to visit the villages at particular times, and consistently represented on altars (Stephen 1936, 709). Because the dead are merely an altered state of the living, it is not surprising to find formalized prayers from the dead being offered by proxy for the living, as well as prayers being offered by the living to invoke the dead (Parsons 1925, 75, 77). Through incorporation into the ceremonial structure and continuing the assignment of status, the same amount and type of control is extended to the dead that is exercised over the living. The dead, while more potent than the living, having the least power of all the denizens of the Underworld, are capable only of bringing rain by the nature of their form.

THE KACHINAS

In defining their universe, the Pueblo people as supreme animists give life, anthropomorphic form, and personality to the elements of their environment and assign certain attributes to each of these manifestations. The supernatural being who represents the life force or quintessence of an object or thing is called kachina. The sun, stars, and moon as cosmic objects may have a kachina form. The elemental forces of nature—thunderstorms, wind, hail, cold, and others—are also represented. Animals, regarded as people who wear skins, also have one or more embodiments. Plants, insects, other Indian tribes, in fact, all organic and many inorganic objects are given a pseudo-human form. These personages form the pantheon of supernaturals called kachinas.

Kachinas manifest themselves in the tangible world through ordinary events such as corn sprouting, rain falling, or the increase in animals or human beings. They account for all events that transpire in the relationship between people and nature. The forms and functions of the kachinas help to codify or organize the events of the Pueblo world. As a part of the intangible world, the kachinas are similar in form to the dead. Despite this similarity between the kachinas and the dead which has caused many authorities to consider them as one (Titiev 1944, 108 n43), they are a distinctly different category of beings. For the Hopi, Titiev (171) states that it is the acquisition of supernatural power which is caused by their ethereal state that equates the dead with the kachinas or clouds. Whereas more aptly, the dead are equated with kachinas by the nature of their form and have only a modicum of power as supernaturals in bringing rain.

The position of the dead in the Underworld is a direct reflection of their position in the ceremonial and social fabric of their particular Pueblo group during their life in the normal world. Kachinas, on the other hand, have a corresponding but separate status system. It is a ranking of potential power or capabilities, a replication of the structure within a particular pueblo with emphasis on those aspects important to the specific group. As members of the intangible world, kachinas possess powers that human beings, living or dead, do not. They affect not only rainfall but also other processes such as fertility, curing, protection, and growth.

Kachinas are a domain of beings who of and by themselves represent a potential for benevolence, a latent force that can be released by human actions. Kachinas require veneration and respect from human beings, for without these they will not respond with benevolence but avoidance. Their absence removes any benefit and allows misfortune to occur. In consequence, they can cause or cure disease and illness. They can promote fertility in both plants and animals and effect increase in living things or prevent its occurrence. Kachinas can assist in growth and prolong life or, because of improper behavior on the part of human beings, produce the opposite results. Among these collective spirits there are those who represent and exercise control of specific things or environmental forces while others are a more general expression of nature, but all affect something essential to the various Puebloans.

In myth these anthropomorphic beings were said to have mingled with mankind, bringing munificent gifts until misunderstanding and jealousy caused animosity and, at last, fighting whereupon the kachinas withdrew. Hardship and death were the result until a few kachinas took pity upon men and gave them the knowledge of how to conduct ceremonials and how to impersonate the kachinas through mask and costume. If these are properly attended to and the people are happy and festive during the dances, the kachinas come again to the pueblos, bringing gifts with them.

Kachinas are not only given a historic association with the Pueblo people but also a comparable social order as well. They are construed as beings who, like their human counterparts, have uncles and grandfathers, sisters and mothers; as individuals who marry, have offspring, and are subject to other human frailties. It is much easier to interact with beings whose form and social structure are more nearly one's own than with remote deities.

Each kachina, with few exceptions, can be given a visual reality by the men of the village through the use of mask, paint, and costume (Parsons 1939, 173–74). In appearance the impersonated kachina is visualized not as an image of the actuality but rather as an abstraction designed to convey, through its symbolic iconography, the intrinsic nature of its function. It is the consensus of opinion among ethnographers that the mask and the symbols painted on it are the most important part of the visualization of a kachina, with the costume being only a minor addition to the total impersonation. Neither costume, mask, nor paraphernalia, however, can be deleted in any definition of the kachina impersonation without depleting the symbolic content of the personage.

The mask is made of leather, skin, basketry, cloth, or gourd. The material is not important, but the overall effect to be created is. The mask is almost always decorated on the back, top, or sides with feathers in different arrangements. Despite its fabrication as an artifact, the mask is not sacred until painted. It is the paint which imparts this aspect to the newly made or renovated mask. Even then it does not become animate or invested with its full spiritual potential until the eyes have been painted and cut into it. There are two kinds of masks: One that belongs only to a clan and while it may be refurbished it is never changed; the other is an individual mask whose character may be changed at will by the addition or removal of paint and appropriate appurtenances.

The costume, accoutrements, and carried paraphernalia offer additional iconic information about the function of the kachina. The kilt alone serves to indicate that the impersonator is involved in a ceremonial activity. A single bandoleer is worn by those who function as guards, while double bandoleers, adorned with small bags containing parts of the enemy, are used by warriors. Hard items that clank or clash together are worn by kachinas who are associated with winter, cold, and the killing of animals or men. Flutes, flowing hair, jewelry, and beautiful garments are part of the costume of the "soft" kachinas who bring rain, flowers, plant growth, and other similar things and who are the summer people. This division represents once more the Pueblo perception of the duality in their environment.

Kachina appearances are organized in terms of a ceremonial calendar, determined by either solar or lunar observations. This calendar assures that one ceremony will follow another in a prescribed order with rituals adapted to each economic pursuit or need for every season. Because the kachinas are singularly the patrons of agricultural pursuits the oldest and most sacred ones appear in these activities that usually occur in spring and summer. Often these ceremonies, through borrowing and analogous ritual associations, have become clusters, incorporating events that are seemingly unrelated to the outsider. The form of the calendar and those who control it vary from group to group, but always they are priests. The priesthood is composed of all men and boys who have been initiated into the mystery of the kachinas. Additional initiations prepare the men for their roles in the societies, many of which are not associated with the kachinas. Among the Zuni and Keresan peoples, the kachina season lasts the entire year but is divided into three segments. The Hopi kachina season is only half of the year, from winter solstice to summer solstice. But their ceremonial control is divided between the Badger and Kachina clans on a six-month basis between equinoxes. Among the Tewa, the year is also divided in half, but the division is a winter-summer duality with moiety control.

The number of kachinas for a group varies from a few in the eastern pueblos to an enormous number in the west. In this pantheon of Pueblo kachinas there is an order, a web of relationships and obligations that incorporates both cosmic planes and systematizes them. Within this network there are beings who, although not arranged hierarchically, cluster through similar purpose or function. Some of these categories are more clearly defined than others.

Characteristic of this clustering are the kachinas who are "partners" with a particular kinship group. They are not totemic in the strictest sense but are rather tutelary spirits, met during migrations in this world or in mythical journeys through earlier worlds, who have been persuaded to join into a reciprocal relationship with a particular clan or group (Voth 1901, 91–92). These are the clan kachinas, often referred to as "Chief" Kachinas, whose appearances are invariably related to ceremonies rather than to individually sponsored kachina dances. The Chief Kachinas' obligations are for specific duties, which parallel those of the leaders within the village or the clan for which they are the wise ones or the venerated ancients. Thus, a village chief has a supernatural counterpart, as does a war chief or other dignitary.

There is a category of kachinas, usually of fearsome appearance, whose role is that of a guard and whose function is to enforce the social or ceremonial dicta of tribe, society, or kiva in much the same manner as a master-at-arms. These personages often resemble others who are warriors and may actually, though not necessarily, be such. Kachinas associated with war figure strongly in many of the pueblos, for warfare was an important activity for all the pueblos until around 1870.

One of the more distinct kachina categories, particularly among the Hopi and Zuni, is that of the ogres or cannibals. These dread creatures are the impersonations of beings who prey on small children, and folklore abounds with tales of their activities. Their shrines, or "houses," most often lie along the outer perimeter of the land used for agriculture. From these homes on hills or in caves they make occasional forays into the villages in search of misbehaving children or those who wander too far and whom, it is claimed, they use for food. Their function is the incorporation of the children into the organized structure of the village, to insure their survival, to assist in their control, and to promote adult behavior patterns. In essence, these kachinas cure the children of youth (Kealiinohomoku 1980, 59–67).

The largest category of kachinas comprises those associated with the necessities of agriculture. While all kachinas bring rain, there are some who bring the gentle soaking rain needed for crop growth; others, as spirits of the towering and often destructive thunderheads, may bring increased fertility or break a drought. There are cold-bringing kachinas who freeze the ground to hold in the moisture of the winter snows or rescind the promise of the false spring. There are kachinas who represent the plants like corn, beans, and squash and who promote their germination, growth, and increase. Kachinas may evoke impersonations of other Indian tribes, even hostile ones, to capture some essence of their ability to make plants grow or rain to fall. A related kachina category expresses the same desire for increase in animals, and many impersonations address this need by calling up game animals or, since the arrival of the Spanish, domestic species. There are other less-well-defined categories of kachinas whose functions may be to cure, to intensify the farming ability of the men, to race for various reasons, or to emphasize the traditional ways.

Related to the kachinas are clowns of a sacred nature who exhibit special ties with the Underworld because many of their actions are the reverse of acceptable behavior in the normal world. These clowns are viewed not in the European sense of pure amusement but as examples of life as it should not be. Clowns are the foils, the object lessons in immoderate behavior such as gluttony, incontinence, marital squabbles, and political ambitions. They are the irreligious and the untaught. They are also the delight-makers, the interpreters of both the familiar and the unfamiliar in terms of humor or comedy. Mimicry, the visual and verbal pun, the ridiculous and the improbable are all part of their sophisticated repertoire of humor. There are clowns who are kachinas as well as many kachinas who do clowning in their performances but are not considered to be clowns per se. Likewise there are other masked personages who appear to be kachinas and act as clowns, e.g., the Koyemsi, yet are not considered to be kachinas by the Puebloans.

In broad terms, the kachina ceremonial organization is relatively homogeneous among the pueblos; in detail it is unique to each village (Harvey 1972, 203). As in all other Pueblo cults it has a priesthood, a segment of the population devoted to its continuance through a pattern of ritual appearing at specific times during the ceremonial year. It differs in its universality for it is the most pervasive of all cults. The kachina cult rests firmly upon the possession by certain individuals or priests of specific religious knowledge and sacrosanct paraphernalia that they have received through inheritance or sponsorship. These are used to control the actions of both villagers and kachinas. In addition, the priesthood uses a special ceremonial place, the kiva, for its preparations, rehearsals, secret rituals, and the setting up of altars.

Control of the kachinas is through a form of sympathetic magic wherein ritual is automatically effective. Symbols and symbolic actions are compulsive, and the process of their use is the effective element. Proper modes of behavior between spirit and man will establish mutual obligations and bring about specific results. Ritualized dancing, ceremonial behavior and paraphernalia, as well as a "good heart" will compel the kachinas to reciprocate with the desired benefits. However, because all kachinas have varying potentials for good, as well as the ability to withhold it, the nature of the relationship changes with the participants and their desires.

A ceremony begins with a retreat by the leaders of the priesthood to the kiva which will last from one to four days in the east and as many as sixteen days in the west. During this interval the participants' behavior is strictly prescribed and may include either partial or absolute fasting with abstinence always from meat, grease, and salt. Continence is required both before and during the ceremony for fear of misfortune. There are purification rites that include bathing, hair washing, and emetics for internal cleansing. For the major ceremonies, altars are constructed of fetishistic objects such as wood shaped as clouds or corn or kachinas. Panels with symbols are used as backdrops or for hanging devices. Carved wood and stone animals, concretions, and other objects are set before these. Bowls of medicine water or prayer feathers, perfect ears of corn, skin, claws, and teeth of animals are used. Colored sandpaintings of symbolic patterns are executed in front of the altars.

The men spend a large portion of their time making prayer objects such as the prayer stick. These are usually one or two small stems of wood with appropriate paint, specific feathers, and plants bound together that are then offered to particular supernaturals. In addition to preparing these offerings they repair their paraphernalia and repaint their masks. A ceremony begins with ritual smoking and the exchange of relationship terms between the participants. It continues with singing and prayers as the altar is set up and each individual part is properly placed. Often there are ritual races, the securing of special objects for the altar or the plaza where the public performance will be given. Sacrosanct figures may be impersonated that only appear in kivas, and performances acting out clan history may also be presented. The interval of secret rituals culminates in a public performance by the membership.

Members of the kachina cult are usually initiated somewhere between seven and ten years of age. They are sponsored by ceremonial godparents and given a pedagogical monologue by a leader of the priesthood and whipped by one or more of the kachinas. Once initiated, the males are confirmed as kachina dancers, although esoteric learning will continue for years and there may be initiation into non-kachina societies. The role of the women is often limited to the feeding of the kachina dancers and priests, although it is possible for them to hold a full ceremonial position or engage in other ritual activity. Presumably most women and all girls and uninitiated young boys do not know that the kachinas are impersonated by the men and the older boys.

The individual who impersonates a kachina—almost invariably a male—is spoken of as being invested by that spirit and becoming one with it. Among the Hopi, he will refer to both the supernatural and the representative mask by the term "friend," with all the implications inherent in that term. It is a recognition of the relationship of mutual benefit that exists between the man and the kachina spirit. To sever the linkage of the impersonator from that of the supernatural and the potency of the mask, discharming rites are observed at the conclusion of each ceremony. If the mask is an important one, it is then stored in an isolated location, a seldom-used room or a cave where its power will not harm the unwitting or uninitiated.

The public performance by kachina impersonators, which follows the secret portion of each ceremonial, takes the form of a slow procession along a fixed course. The procession may be presented on special occasions without dancing as a ritual enactment of an historic event in the manner of a European medieval religious drama or passion play. But the normal pattern is a line of dancers who perform once in each of the cardinal directions within the kiva or in the village dance plaza. If there is insufficient room, the line bends to fit the shape of the dance area. But the leader, who is always in the center, will be positioned only once in each of the four directions. When the dance starts, movement begins in the center and runs to either end, with the dancers maintaining a line that turns, pauses, and then turns again with the movement "running like a breath of wind through ripening stalks of grain" (Roediger 1941, 38).

The dancers make one complete circuit and then retire for a short interval to rest at a hidden location set aside for the impersonators so they may unmask. During this interval the clowns perform in the plaza. The dance steps appear very simple, with the right foot stamping vigorously, while the heel of the left is lifted only slightly. However the rhythm of pauses and sequenced steps introduced into this simple format makes the dance much more complex. At times one or more dancers will perform at the side of the line, dancing with great vigor by raising both feet alternately, which presents an appearance of the figure not being in contact with the ground. Often the line is interspersed with female kachinas, but these are never women as they are always impersonated by the men.

The music furnished for the dance is primarily by the singing voices of the kachinas themselves. While Zuni priests sing long liturgical songs which never vary, Hopi kachinas' songs are distinctive for each impersonation and new words are composed for every performance. For the Hopi these songs correspond to popular music in that the pleasure of the audience dictates their success. Time is kept by the beat of a large drum. These are usually hollowed cottonwood logs with rawhide stretched over the ends, although occasionally they may be bundles of rawhide or buckskin folded together and laid on the ground and then beaten. Accompanying these are the rhythms of hand-held gourd rattles. Additional rattles and bells may be tied around the waist, knee, and ankle or attached to the hem of the kilt. At the end of the one- or two-day public performances the kachinas are led back to the kivas by the kachina fathers, where they disappear to complete the ceremony.

The kachina dance is an integrating force for the villages in that it offers some form of participation for everyone, either as audience, contributor, or performer. It combines the dramatic presentation of theater with the entertainment of comedy and burlesque, the solemnity of prayer and sacred ritual interspersed with popular song and contemporary humor. It is both theater and church, with the emphasis on the process of the ritual rather than the result. The dancers are the prayer and the audience the contrapuntal support.

The visualization of the kachina spirit as represented in the impersonation is also converted into a distinctive prayer object, the kachina doll. These small wooden figures are, or were, made by nearly all pueblos. Most Pueblo men carve these dolls from cottonwood roots, except the Zuni, who make theirs of pine. In the east the figures are cylindrical in shape with only the painted symbols of the head represented; the body is "clothed" in shell, turquoise, cotton string, and feathers. Among the Zuni and the Hopi the figures are given more realism with most of the dolls being fully carved. An exception is the small flat doll given to the infants by the Hopi. In recent years the Hopi have also begun to clothe their dolls with real cloth or leather in the manner of the Zuni dolls, until the contemporary figurine is an exact replica of the kachina impersonator, down to fingernails, muscles, and even an occasional removable mask. Formerly all adornment was roughly carved and any symbolism was painted on the doll, with hand-held paraphernalia indicated by small feathers put in place of the missing gear. These unique artifacts are presented to infants of either sex but primarily to girls or women of childbearing age. The literature identifies these dolls as an educational device to teach the women the identity of the kachina impersonations. Rather, however, it seems these are prayer objects used to inculcate the women with the benefits of the kachinas, and aid in forming an alliance between them. In all of the pueblos there is an association between this type of doll and fertility and increase.

THE CLOUD PEOPLE

A third category of collective Pueblo spirits are the clouds. Despite the fact that these beings overlap in both form and attributes with the deceased on one hand and the kachinas on the other, they are considered to be a separate group. An indication of this separation from the kachinas is apparent in the terms by which they are called. Occasionally the name is the same or nearly so, as among the Tewa cloud is *'ok* (hook)*uwa* and kachina is *'ok* (hook)*uwa*. The majority, however, use distinctive terms, as among the Zuni, where *uwanami* are the cloud beings and *koko* are the kachinas, or *shiwanna* the storm spirits of the Keresans in contrast with the *k'atsena*, and among the Jemez, the *dyasa* contrast with the *k'ats'ana*.

The difference between the cloud beings and the deceased Pueblo people is a little more difficult to ascertain. These supernaturals are spoken of as "raw people" among the Zuni. They are the *uwanami;* they impersonate clouds with their breath but they are just people. They become clouds also when they put on their beautiful garments (Bunzel 1933, 193). When they die the Zuni become one with the Cloud People, and clouds are spoken of as "our ancestors, the ones who have died," yet the dead are never referred to as *uwanami.* The dead at Cochiti may be spoken of as *shiwanna,* placing them as cloud supernaturals, yet despite this there is a feeling that the *shiwanna* are a group which the deceased may join but that maintain a separate identity. This is supported by the fact that ritualistic actions are different for the dead and the Cloud People, as at Isleta, where food for the dead is held in the left hand and food for the *wenin* or *thlasa* in the right (Parsons 1939, 173 n).

The inference is that the Cloud People are the real inhabitants of the other world, whom the dead may join when they become ephemeral like the clouds. The dissociative beliefs surrounding the dead, such as the cotton mask to resemble a cloud, the prayer feathers placed in the hair to lighten the body, the corn flour applied to whiten the countenance, and the belief that only the essence of food is consumed are all aimed at producing a cloudlike being who can join the true cloud beings. Kachina-like, the Cloud People may come masked by mist and be reached through lakes or springs, yet they are not considered to be kachinas even when their attributes converge.

Four mountains or peaks which lie along the perimeter of the land claimed by a specific pueblo and approximating the primary points of the compass are designated as the homes of the Cloud People. It is almost inevitable that the Pueblo people would locate their cloud beings on these mountaintops, for it is on the most prominent of these that orographic uplift is strongest and where clouds first appear and build to their maximum height. The Zuni alone place the homes of their Cloud People not on the mountaintops but on the shores of an encircling sea.

On the mountaintops at the four corners of the world sit the chiefs of direction, who appear as thunderstorms or storm chiefs. Lightning, the most potent of the rain spirits, is their war chief, and around them are grouped the lesser Cloud People. Occasionally a chief of direction will also be added for the zenith and the nadir. Each of these chiefs is associated with a primary color, most often yellow for the north, blue for the west, red in the south, and white in the east. The zenith is black and the nadir all colors. Surrounding each chief is a cluster of associated objects and beings such as corn, animals, butterflies, and clouds all of the same color.

In the west among the Hopi, where cosmological thought is less shrouded by secrecy, it has been possible to determine not only that the chiefs of direction are considered to be a special class of beings but that they are addressed by societies, such as the Snake/Antelope, which are without kachina connections (Parsons 1939, 173). This same attitude is echoed by Keresan society members, who may on occasion act like *shiwanna.* The ritual actions of these societies are designed to establish analogous situations and, through control of one portion, compel the cloud beings of the other portion into the desired behavior pattern. The planting of prayer sticks in arroyos to hasten rain (more common in the west), the use of turkey and eagle breast feathers as clouds, painting the chin black in imitation of thunderheads, keeping bare feet in contact with the earth, and the use of mud as an imperative for rain are but a few of the elements in this effort at control. Despite the ritual behavior of Keresan and Hopi society members and the Pueblo-wide use of symbolic objects in relation to the Cloud People there is a lack of understanding or depth in the interaction that bespeaks of diminished, partially lost ceremonial. It may represent an earlier belief that is fading, leaving behind only a widespread associative symbolism.

THE DEITIES

Unlike the collective spirits of the dead, the clouds, and the kachinas, there are conspicuously individualized cosmic personages or deities. These beings are not usually given a visual reality in the manner of the kachinas but are nonetheless anthropomorphized in all other attributes. The social imperatives of the Pueblo people are reflected in their divinities, and hence these deities behave more as an interacting group with individual but often equal propensities rather than as a hierarchy of increasing potency with an omnipotent being in control of the system. Among the Pueblo each being maintains a structured relationship with the others yet controls its own sphere without interference, a pattern reflected in human beings as well as deities.

The principal deities in the Pueblo pantheon are a creator of life, a guardian of the lifeways or "roads" of men, a generative force or Earth Mother, a destroyer or divinity of death, a great serpent who controls all water, one who "owns" all game animals, and an embodiment of the staple food, maize. The primary culture heroes are the two juvenile War Gods and their ever-present grandmother, Spider Woman.

These deities represent the elemental forces of nature, and although their potential for benevolence or lack of it is released by interaction with man they are the most remote of all supernaturals and the least predictable. Human adherence to order produces benefit; improper behavior or neglect, a failure to honor obligations or reciprocate with the deities is to invite disaster in the form of famine, drought, or other difficulties. If the cause of these problems is man's failure, then the cure is to locate the causal factor and reinstitute acceptable behavior. Mythically this involved a search for the deities or other supernaturals, which required feats of endurance, great wisdom, and occasionally human sacrifice. The unerring advice of Spider Woman, the ubiquitous grandmother with the unlimited pharmacopoeia of medicines, was sought and secured, for without this assistance success was apparently not possible. Invariable also was the preparation and bestowal of pray feathers or other ritual offerings to those divinities who might help or who had been neglected.

The Pueblo priesthood orchestrates the interaction of the deities with the community through a series of complex ceremonies that occur throughout the year. These may encompass kachina ritual, initiation, observances for the dead, solstice ceremonies, hunting, or other activities. The presence of a priesthood and attendant societies does not, however, preclude individual observances, and anyone may interact with the deities on a one-to-one basis.

The divinities who reflect the interests of the Pueblo people and who control the necessities of life are for the most part clearly conceptualized but, almost without exception, never given visual form. A few may have certain attributes that may be visualized in a kachina form or, even more rarely, as a deity, but in most instances they exist as concepts rather than as concrete images.

The presence of these major deities does not guarantee a similar role in each of the pueblos. The name of a deity and its importance may vary from one village to the next. The function of a deity may be dissipated among several others or simply be reassigned to another divinity as one moves from east to west. Despite this frustrating tendency most villages will have some deity who performs each of the functions listed earlier.

One of the more clearly conceived and individualized deities is the Sun. The Sun is the creator of life; he is the ultimate "holder of the roads of men" who, in essence, controls their fate, for he determines the length and quality of their lives. He is prayed to by casting cornmeal toward him as he rises at dawn. Infants are presented to him twenty days after they are born, with prayers to have a long and good life conferred upon them. He is also the original hunter and warrior. Keresan and Hopi hunters offer prayers to him before any hunting endeavors; he also assists warriors in their activities.

Mythically, for some of the Pueblos, he was placed in the sky by human beings whose first efforts to bring light to the world resulted in the moon. Learning from this mistake they chose brighter objects and succeeded in making the Sun or the Sun shield. In other legends the Sun is a being who scorched the earth when he approached too closely. But in all pueblos he is considered a fallible being who may pause a moment at noon on his journey westward where he enters the house of *Huruing Wuhti,* the goddess of Hard Substances, where he pauses again before continuing on through the Underworld. As he circles the two worlds he wanders from his path and strays too far to the north or the south, where he remains for four days. The Pueblo men persuade him to return through their ceremonies and the offerings of prayer sticks.

Somewhat Jovian in lifestyle, he is the father of one of the two ever-present culture heroes, the Little War Gods or Twin War Gods, one of whom was born of a union between the Sun and a woman. The other was born of rainwater and the same woman yet is considered to be a twin of the first. Another offspring is *Taiowa* or *Paiyetamu*, depending on the group, who is the deity of music, flowers, and amusement and is the patron of the clowning societies. In addition to his sons and *Huruing Wuhti,* the Sun may be associated at daybreak with a collective group of dawn personages such as Dawn Old Man, Dawn Woman, or the Dawn Youths. Sun Kachinas who represent some of his attributes may appear at this moment during the solstice ceremonies.

The moon, which is considered by half of the Pueblos to be male and by the other half to be female, is a relatively unimportant deity and is seldom if ever given visual form.

The imperative of maize is present in the importance of the generative deities with corn-related attributes. Often these deities rival the Sun in importance. In all of the pueblos except among the Hopi, who assign this function to *Muyingwa,* the male Germ God, the generative force of the earth is female, like the Keresan maize mother, *Iyatiku.* From her Underworld house mankind emerged at Shipap, and it is to her they return when dead. Infants are born into this world from her place, and priests who enter springs or retreat into kivas are thought of as returning to visit her and receive her mandates before reappearing. For the Keresans she created the kachinas and the clowns, and she gives entitlement to all societies through a perfect white corn-ear fetish, the ultimate symbol of supernatural support. She is conceived of as the Corn Mother and yet has all the attributes of an Earth Mother as well. It is *Iyatiku,* or *Utset* of Zia, who says her heart is corn (Parsons 1939, 182) just as it is the male *Muyingwa* among the Hopi whose body is covered with corn. But for the Hopi it is *Masau'u* who is not only the owner of all land but also aids in travel and the growth of plants as well as being the deity of ancient foods, fire, darkness, graves, and death. As *Masewi,* son of *Iyatiku,* it is only his warlike aspect that is emphasized. It is apparent that in the east the Earth Mother/Corn Mother is primarily two aspects of a single or double entity, whereas in the west they are two distinct beings.

Among the Zuni it is the Two Little War Gods who are both culture heroes and warriors. Myths and legends abound throughout the Pueblo area and even beyond concerning the deeds of these two war spirits. They are responsible for Zuni curing societies, for ridding the land of monsters, making the mountains, and countless other feats as well as behaving as naughty, disobedient grandsons to their Spider Grandmother. For the Hopi it is *Sotuknangu*, the Heart of the Sky God, who is either the lightning spirit of the thunderstorms or Morning Star, a war spirit of the Tewa. Dark Star or Morning Star, a Pueblo-wide spirit, is prayed to for assistance in either war or hunting, as he is believed to be in charge of all game or domestic animals. This is an attribute shared with *Tihkuyi Wuhti*, the Woman with Protruding Child or Childbirth Water Woman, who is the Hopi Mother of All Game Animals. Each of these deities or culture heroes is present in other Pueblo groups, their "supremacy" or function being a matter of tribal emphasis.

Water is represented throughout the Pueblo area, except for the Tiwa, by the Plumed Water Serpent. This supernatural, undoubtedly derived from Mesoamerica, controls all liquid water regardless of the source. Water in a solid or gaseous state is the purview of other deities, as is rainfall. The appearance of a water serpent is a necessary prerequisite for the presence of water and in consequence ponds and springs dry up when the Water Serpent leaves, is stolen, or destroyed. Similarly, a spring may be planted by filling a vessel with water-associated objects and enticing the Water Serpent to occupy it. The Plumed Water Serpent is either a god of terrestrial waters or a collective spirit of all waters, depending upon context. His function is not only the continuation of water but the promotion of fertility as well. There are separate ceremonies for this deity as well as cult groups, particularly in the west.

Salt is given human attributes among the Zuni in the capricious personage of Salt Old Woman. The Hopi assign *Pookonghoya*, the Elder War God, as a guardian of their salt. The hard substances of turquoise, shell, and coral are the property of *Kohakwa* at Zuni and *Huruing Wuhti* among the Hopi. In addition to the individual deities, whose numbers have been but lightly touched, there is a myriad of lesser deities who merge into folk heroes to take care of all Pueblo needs. There are Squash Girls from several pueblos, Yucca Old Man of the Tewa, Fire Old Woman of Cochiti and Isleta, Clay Woman of the Zuni, Deer Old Woman of Taos, White Shell Woman, Awl Man, Ashes Boy, and countless others.

Underlying the polytheistic system that orders the dual cosmos of the Pueblo people are the philosophical concepts that form its foundation. The abstruse knowledge of how the universe was created, the origin of life, the interrelationships of the elemental forces of nature, and other speculations are the possession of only the oldest and wisest members of the priesthoods. Although all members of a pueblo live an existence governed by the utilization of these physical and metaphysical precepts, they become privy to the inner knowledge of the theocracy only by age-linked increments, in a step-by-step growth (Harvey 1972, 204).

HUMAN POSITION IN THE WORLD

In addition to the dead, kachinas, clouds, and deities, there is the remainder of nature to be considered. Not only are organic and inorganic objects endowed with a life and given a vitality, or "breath," but also elemental forces and actions are similarly endowed, and all are given the possibility of human form. Everything, including mankind, possesses this attribute, for all are merely parts of a universal whole. In a single respect man appears to differ from all else in the universe, for he alone has a permanence of form, broken only by death, where all else has the reality of the object or thing, an anthropomorphic spirit presence and the ability to assume either form of their own volition. Thus animals may be an element of day-to-day life but can go home and hang up their skins to become the animal people living in the manner of mankind. Similarly, there are the stone people, ant people, grass people, and others almost ad infinitum. As systematic animists, the Puebloans have structured their universe with an infinity of modules using themselves as a template. These units are cemented by a single unifying principle, the assumption that the universe is endowed with the same breath, a presence that has always been and will always be, that is both male and female, from whose intentions the very deities coalesced. This concept is most clearly expressed in the abstract nature of *Awonawilona* of the Zuni (Stevenson 1901–2, 22), the ultimate, all-pervasive, male-female presence that permeates the universe.

The anthropomorphic spirits that invest the elements of the environment are not permanently inured within these objects but come and go at will. In consequence, a thing may at one moment have a supernatural ingredient and be empty of it at the next, requiring the human interactor to initiate ritual actions to bring about either the return or removal of the intangible being. While all other objects are imbued with a breath body, those that are more unusual in form, such as concretions and fossils, are assumed to be unique in their attributes and hence are prized as fetishes. As an example, masks are invested by spirits who, when the mask is removed, are asked ritually to depart, presumably leaving the mask an inert object. However, this is not the case, for the mask retains a latent power that can afflict the unwary or impious, an indication that not only are the Pueblo people fetishists and animists but animatists as well (Parsons 1939, 198).

There remains a single principle that must be considered, and that is evil. Although there is inherent potential for harm when reciprocating with the spirits, theirs is an impartial force responding only to the interactive situation and not stemming from malevolence. Evil is not the function of the spirits but rather that of the human witch or, as Parsons (1939, 209) says, "Bad people make good gods." Similarly, there is no evil in normal people who, although they may transgress their bounds and stray from prescribed patterns, are not basically evil. Evil is a deliberate effort to counter good, to thwart the beneficial and bring about all that is undesired or contrary to the common weal, and this is the role of the witch. Evil exists only in the activities of these undesirable people. Witches have been with man since his arrival in the fourth world and are a constant menace with malevolence directed toward entire villages as well as individuals. They are the murderers of the innocent, killers of relative and stranger alike, they cause death and may rob the graves of bodies to serve their purposes. They cause floods, destroy crops with plagues of insects, or stir the wind to chase away the clouds. Witches are the cause of epidemics and most other natural disasters. As perpetrators of evil they are hated, and often any antisocial behavior is believed to be the mark of a person who is either a witch, or a potential one, a belief that insures conformity with idealized behavior. The results of social transgressions often brought on accusations of witchcraft, which were cause for dire punishment, either ostracism or death. Protection from these dreaded people is secured through preventive action, avoidance of their attention or companionship, and exposure of the witch to public scrutiny rather than through the more usual use of prophylactic symbols. Symbolism is more often a method of communicating with the intangible world in sacred rather than secular contexts. As part of the everyday world, only symbols that will confuse or divert their unwanted attention are used, rather than preventive ones.

In summary, the demands of a parsimonious environment and the various strategies that evolved to meet those challenges have left an indelible imprint on all of the Pueblo peoples. These mechanisms, developed individually in answer to common problems, have been borrowed from one another, augmented, reinforced, amalgamated, and inseminated with Mesoamerican elements to produce the present Pueblo culture. These stratagems emphasize the survival of the group rather than the individual (Ortiz 1969, 153) by placing value upon cooperation as opposed to competition. Where competition encourages the development of a strong individual with the attributes for leadership more appropriate to hunting and raiding, Pueblo cooperation reduces this tendency and substitutes instead a group structure of obligations and reciprocal actions largely controlled by a priesthood. Within this social structure relationships are all-important, and position relative to all other beings and elements of the natural world predicate the type of action. The web of relationships extends to the unseen supernaturals of the Pueblo world, emphasizing the same attributes and organizing them into categories or domains where each operates within its own sphere, independent of the others, rather than in a hierarchical system.

Ethnocentrically the Pueblo people assume that all elements of the cosmos have human form that is hidden by donning the perceived reality of the normal world in the same manner as human beings use clothing or masks. This assumption allows the assignment of human values and relationships to the nonhuman parts of the universe and establishes an almost infinite number of potential supernaturals who are conceptualized as needed. The anthropomorphized parts of the cosmos that are most important to the villagers are most clearly delineated in both concept and visualization. Coupled with the connotation of similar motives, methods, and social systems to make interaction a simpler process, the relationship with the supernatural plane has devolved into traditional patterns. Elements of these patterns may be reduced or elaborated and often are passed from one group to another as a need is perceived or contact established.

The Pueblo people organize their religious cosmos in exactly the same terms as the real world. Where the village is surrounded by land less and less known and hence more uncontrollable, the inhabitants of the Underworld are similarly ordered by their familiarity to the living, with the supernaturals being most unanswerable to humans, the most remote and most deified.

A consistent interaction between any two groups or individuals, who are mutually unintelligible, requires the development of a system of communication such as the sign language of the Plains. Among the Pueblo people the communication system between themselves and the supernaturals is one of symbolic art that manifests itself both in the visual and the performing arts to produce an iconography of particular richness. In the visual arts the selection of analogous forms to express desires and needs lays the foundation. Through the process of association the number of these forms has been immensely expanded. From this base, abstraction has removed most of the realistic depictions and converted them to symbolic designs which today, more often than not, have lost their raison d'être. The symbolic action or traditional pattern of behavior for dealing with supernaturals has produced ceremonial drama among the Puebloans of great power and diversity. It possesses elements of grand opera and a passion play coupled with the familiarity of a high school performance where all participants are well known to the audience. It can range from historic reenactment couched in symbolic form to contemporary social problems thinly disguised, or take the form of a majestic religious concept. Incorporated into ceremonial ritual and dance are the full range of iconographic elements, for there is no separation possible of art from religion among the Pueblo people. In consequence, the development of an iconography for communication with the supernaturals has reached a beauty and complexity among the Pueblo peoples unequaled north of Mexico, with the possible exception of the peoples of the Northwest Coast.

What the future holds for the Pueblo people and their religion is hidden, but indications are that it will adapt and continue. The old ceremonies, with their time-intensive demands, are disappearing to be replaced by adaptations of other aspects of their religion that are more consonant with contemporary lifestyles. The basic structure, however, rooted as it is in social as well as religious segments of Pueblo life, appears to be holding firm.

REFERENCES

Bunzel, Ruth L. 1933. *Zuni Texts.* New York: American Ethnological Society Publications, vol. 15.

Dozier, Edward P. 1954. *The Hopi-Tewa of Arizona.* Publications in American Archaeology and Ethnology. Berkeley: University of California Press, vol. 44, no.3.

Eggan, Frederick Russell. 1972. *New Perspectives on the Pueblos.* School of American Research. Albuquerque: University of New Mexico Press.

Fewkes, Jesse W. 1903. *Hopi Kachinas Drawn by Native Artists.* Smithsonian Institution Bureau of American Ethnology Annual Report. Enumclaw, WA: MacRae Publications, 1976.

———1922. *Ancestor Worship of the Hopi Indians.* Washington, DC: Smithsonian Institution Annual Report for year ending June 30, 1921.

Ford, Richard I. 1972. *An Ecological Perspective on the Eastern Pueblos.* School of American Research. Albuquerque: University of New Mexico Press.

Harvey, Byron III. 1972. *An Overview of Pueblo Religion.* School of American Research. Albuquerque: University of New Mexico Press.

Kealiinohomoku, Joann W. 1980. *The Drama of the Hopi Ogres.* School of American Research. Albuquerque: University of New Mexico Press.

Ortiz, Alfonso. 1969. *The Tewa World.* Chicago: University of Chicago Press.

Parsons, Elsie C. 1920. *Notes on Ceremonialism at Laguna.* New York: Anthropological Papers of the American Museum of Natural History, vol. 19, part 4.

———1925. *A Pueblo Indian Journal, 1920–21.* Memoirs of the American Anthropological Assoc., no. 32.

———[*The Social Organization of the Tewa of New Mexico.* American Anthropological Association Memoir, vol. 36, Menasha, 1929.] 1939. *Pueblo Religion.* Chicago: University of Chicago Press.

Roediger, Virginia M. 1941. *Ceremonial Costumes of the Pueblo Indians: Their Evolution, Fabrication, and Significance in the Prayer Drama.* Berkeley: University of California Press.

Spicer, Edward H. 1962. *Cycles of Conquest.* Tucson: University of Arizona Press.

Stephen, Alexander M. 1936. *Hopi Journal.* New York: Columbia University Press.

Stevenson, Matilda C. 1901–2. *The Zuni Indians.* Washington, DC: The 23rd Annual Report of the Bureau of American Ethnology.

Titiev, Mischa. 1944. *Old Oraibi: A Study of the Hopi Indians of Third Mesa.* Cambridge: Peabody Museum of American Archaeology and Ethnology Papers, vol. 22, no. 1, Harvard University.

Voth, Henry R. 1901. *The Oraibi Powamu Ceremony*. Field Museum Publication, Anthropology Series, vol. 3, no. 2. Chicago: Field Museum.

———1905. *The Traditions of the Hopi.* Chicago: Field Columbian Museum Publication 96, Anthropological Series, vol. 8.

BIBLIOGRAPHY

The following were used by Andrea Portago in researching her subjects.

Adams, Ansel. *An Essay on the Land*. New York: Little, Brown, 1976.

Anderson, Duane, ed. *Legacy: Southwest Indian Art at the School of American Research.* Santa Fe, NM: School of American Research Press, 1999.

Antes, Horst. *Kachina-Figuren der Pueblo-Indianer Nordamerikas aus der Studiensammlung.* Lübeck, Germany: Volkerkundesammlung der Hanseastadt, 2000.

———. *Kachina Figuren der Pueblo-Indianer Nordamerikas aus der Studiensammlung.* Karlsruhe, Germany: Badishes Landesmuseum, 1980.

Bolz, Peter, and Hans-Ulrich Sanner. *Native American Art: The Collections of the Ethnological Museum Berlin.* Seattle: University of Washington Press, 1999.

Chase, Katherin L. *Indian Painters of the Southwest: The Deep Remembering.* Santa Fe, NM: School of American Research Press, 2002.

Cushing, Frank Hamilton. *The Mythic World of the Zuni,* illustrated by Barton Wright. Albuquerque: University of New Mexico Press, 1988.

Danto, Arthur, Donna De Salvo, and Frayda Feldman. *Andy Warhol Prints: A Catalogue Raisonné, 1962–1987.* New York: D.A.P./Distributed Art Publishers in association with Ronald Feldman Fine Arts; Andy Warhol Foundation for the Visual Arts, 2003.

Dutton, Bertha P. *American Indians of the Southwest.* Albuquerque: University of New Mexico Press, 1983.

Fane, Diana. *Objects of Myth and Memory: American Indian Art at the Brooklyn Museum.* Brooklyn, NY: Brooklyn Museum in association with the University of Washington Press, 1991.

Feder, Norman. *Two Hundred Years of North American Indian Art.* New York: Praeger Publishers in association with the Whitney Museum of American Art, 1971.

Fergusson, Erna. *Dancing Gods: Indian Ceremonials of New Mexico and Arizona.* Albuquerque: University of New Mexico Press, [1931] 1988.

Fewkes, Jesse Walter. *Hopi Kachinas Drawn by Native Artists*. Smithsonian Institution Bureau of American Ethnology Annual Report 1903. Enumclaw, WA: MacRae Publications, 1976.

Gutiérrez, Ramón A. *When Jesus Came, the Corn Mothers Went Away: Marriage, Sexuality, and Power in New Mexico, 1500–1846.* Stanford, CA: Stanford University Press, 1991.

Hartmann, Horst. *Kachina: Figuren der Hopi-Indianer.* Berlin: Museum Für Völkerkunde Berlin, Staatliche Museen Preussicher Kulturbesitz, 1978.

Hegemann, Elizabeth Compton. *Navaho Trading Days.* Albuquerque: University of New Mexico Press, 1963.

Jones, Courtney Reeder. *Letters from Wupatki.* Tucson: University of Arizona Press, 1995.

Kirk, Malcolm. *Man As Art: New Guinea.* New York: Viking, 1981.

Kopper, Phillip. *The Smithsonian Book of North American Indians: Before the Coming of the Europeans.* Washington, DC: Smithsonian Books, 1986.

Laniel-Le François, Marie-Elisabeth. *Kachina des Indians Hopi.* Saint-Vit, France: Daniele Amez, 1992.

Mora, Joseph Jacinto. *The Year of the Hopi.* New York: Rizzoli, 1982.

Musée d'arts africains, océaniens, amérindiens de Marseille. *Kachina, Poupees Rituelles des Indiens Hopi et Zuni.* Marseille, France: Éditions Musées de Marseille; Paris: Réunion des musées nationaux, 1994.

Ortiz, Alfonso. *The Pueblo.* New York: Chelsea House Publishers, 1994.

———. *The Tewa World: Space, Time, Being, and Becoming in a Pueblo Society.* Chicago: University of Chicago Press, 1969.

Porter, Dean A. *Taos Artists and Their Patrons, 1898–1950.* Notre Dame, IN: Snite Museum of Art; Albuquerque: University of New Mexico Press, 1999.

Riley, Carroll L. *The Kachina and the Cross: Indians and Spaniards in the Early Southwest.* Salt Lake City: University of Utah Press, 1999.

Rubin, William, ed. *"Primitivism" in 20th Century Art: Affinity of the Tribal and the Modern.* Volumes 1 and 2. New York: Museum of Modern Art, 1984.

Schaafsma, Polly. *Kachinas in the Pueblo World.* Albuquerque: University of New Mexico Press, 1994.

———. *Rock Art in New Mexico: Featuring National Sites at Chaco Canyon, Bandelier, Mesa Verde, and the Gila Wilderness.* Santa Fe: Museum of New Mexico Press, 1992.

Star, Gregor, and E. Catherine Rayne. *El Delirio: The Santa Fe World of Elizabeth White.* Santa Fe, NM: School of American Research Press, 1998.

Tuchman, Maurice. *The Spiritual in Art: Abstract Painting 1890–1985.* New York: Abbeville Press, and Los Angeles County Museum of Art, 1986.

Washburn, Dorothy K., ed. *Hopi Kachina, Spirit of Life: Dedicated to the Hopi Tricentennial, 1680–1980.* San Francisco: California Academy of Sciences, 1980.

Webb, William. *Dwellers at the Source: Southwestern Indian Photographs of A. C. Vroman, 1895–1904.* Albuquerque: University of New Mexico Press, 1973.

Wright, Barton. *The Mythic World of the Zuni.* Albuquerque: University of New Mexico Press, 1988.

———. *Kachinas of the Zuni.* Original paintings by Duane Dishta. Flagstaff, AZ: Northland Press, 1985.

———. *Hopi Material Culture: Artifacts Gathered by H. R. Voth in the Fred Harvey Collection.* Flagstaff, AZ: Northland Press, 1979.

———. *The Complete Guide to Collecting Kachinas.* Flagstaff, AZ: Northland Press, 1977.

———. *The Unchanging Hopi: An Artist's Interpretation in Scratchboard Drawings and Text.* Flagstaff, AZ: Northland Press, 1975.

———. *Kachinas: A Hopi Artist's Documentary.* Original paintings by Cliff Bahnimptewa. Flagstaff, AZ: Northland Press, 1973.

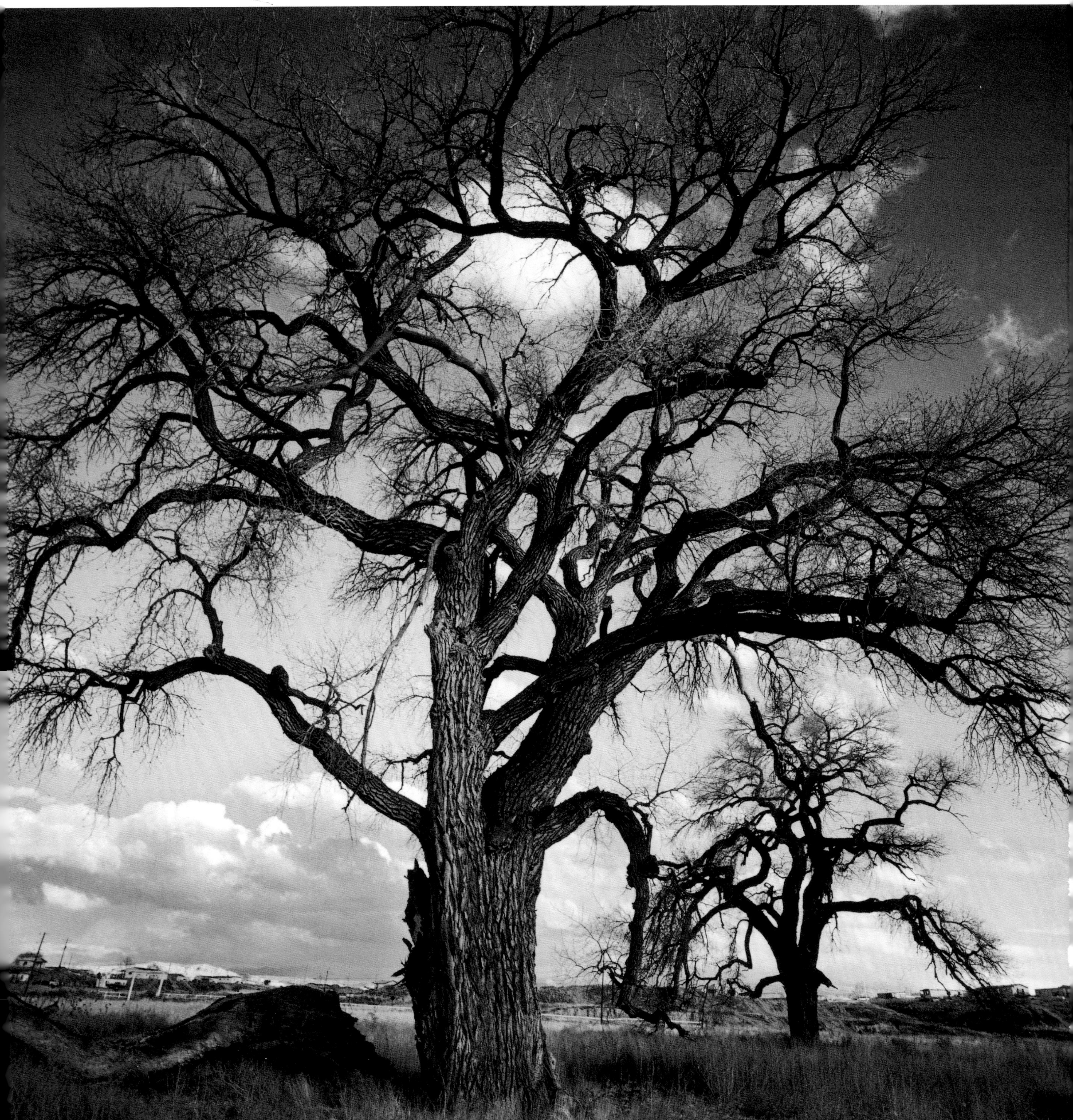